WHO'S ON FIRST CHARLIE BROWN?

CHARLES M. SCHULZ

BALLANTINE BOOKS ★ NEW YORK

A Ballantine Book

Published by The Random House Publishing Group

Copyright © 2004 United Feature Syndicate, Inc.

All rights reserved under International and Pan-American Copyright Conventions. Published in the United States
by The Random House Publishing Group, a division of Random House, Inc., New York, and simultaneously in Canada by Random House
of Canada Limited, Toronto. The comic strips in this book were originally published in newspapers worldwide. The
introduction to this work is adapted from an interview with Cal Ripkin, Jr.

Ballantine and colophon are registered trademarks of Random House, Inc.

www.ballantinebooks.com

www.snoopy.com

Library of Congress Control Number: 2004091997

ISBN 0-345-46412-5

Design by Diane Hobbing of Snap-Haus Graphics

Cover design by United Media

Manufactured in the United States of America

First Edition: May 2004

1   3   5   7   9   10   8   6   4   2

WHO'S ON FIRST, CHARLIE BROWN?

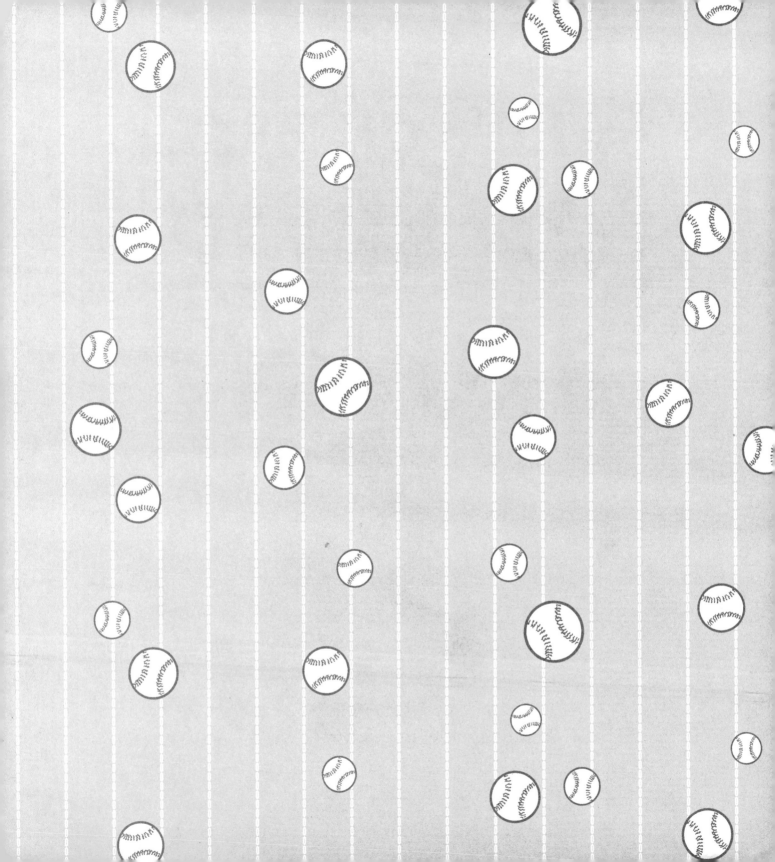

INTRODUCTION

 What would baseball be without peanuts . . . or, in this case, *Peanuts*? When I was asked to write this introduction, I jumped at the chance, because to me, baseball and *Peanuts* go hand in hand, and always have.

Most mornings when I was growing up, my dad would read the paper at the breakfast table. And like most boys who idolize their dads, I wanted to do what he did. So my mom would give me a section of the paper—the comics. That's how I first discovered Charlie Brown, Lucy, Linus, Snoopy, and the rest of the Peanuts Gang. Now, I was nuts about sports when I was a kid. All sports, but baseball especially, because of my dad. And pretty often, *Peanuts* would run a cartoon about baseball, which I thought was cool.

Back then, I liked *Peanuts* because it brought baseball down to a level that I could relate to. When you first start playing baseball, in school or after school or whenever, a lot of strange, funny things happen, and you don't see those things all that often, when you're watching a big league game. Dropping an easy fly ball. Throwing to the wrong base. Getting picked off. When you're just a kid learning how to play, those moments can be pretty embarrassing and painful. It's easy to get discouraged. But when I saw them in a cartoon, when it was Lucy dropping the ball, or Charlie Brown getting picked off, then it was something I could laugh at.

As I got older, I realized that humor is a big part of baseball. Why? Because the game can be so humbling. Even in the pros, there are times when, if you don't laugh, you'll cry. Just ask any Cubs fan. And I had my share of those moments. Every professional does. When a teammate had a bad day, I used to look for a comic strip that poked fun at him, and I'd tape it up on his locker. And it wasn't because I wanted to rub it in. Well, not *only* because of that.

You can't take yourself too seriously in a game like baseball. There are a million things that can go horribly, humiliatingly wrong. And every last one of them happens to Charlie Brown at some point. So when we laugh at Charlie Brown, we're laughing at ourselves, at our own fears. At least, that's how it always seemed to me.

Charlie Brown was no quitter. He persevered. He showed up every single day to play, no matter what . . . and I know a little bit about that myself. That was the hardest part about the streak—to keep on showing up, day after day, even when things weren't going well. My dad used to say that when your back's up against the wall, you've got to come out fighting, and no matter how bad things got for Charlie Brown, he was always back up on that pitcher's mound, hoping for a better result.

It's funny how *Peanuts* crops up in daily life. My brother and I now teach base-ball to kids, through our work with the Cal Ripken Sr. Foundation and the Babe Ruth League. I remember once, when we first started, I had this idea of coaching kids right as they were playing. That way, as soon as they made a mistake, we could explain what they had done wrong, and how to do better. Well, there I was, trying to impart a baseball lesson to a kid who was staring back at me with blank eyes, obviously a million miles away, and suddenly it hit me that I was the teacher in the *Peanuts* TV show. You know, that disembodied voice going *wah-wah-wah*. So now we do things differently!

That just goes to show how much a part of our culture *Peanuts* is. I mean, the line drive back to the pitcher's mound—*Pow!*—that undresses Charlie Brown. . . . In my mind, that's an image of baseball almost as famous, in its way, as any classic photograph you'll see at Cooperstown.

Writing these words, I'm reminded so much of growing up, of reading the comics page there at the breakfast table with my dad. Now that I'm a dad myself, there are so many things I want to pass on to my kids. So many lessons I want to share. When I re-read these great cartoons, I'm struck by how full they are, not just of fun and humor, but of opportunities to teach kids what really matters in baseball . . . and in life.

That's why Charles Schulz will always be a Hall of Famer in my book.

—Cal Ripken Jr.

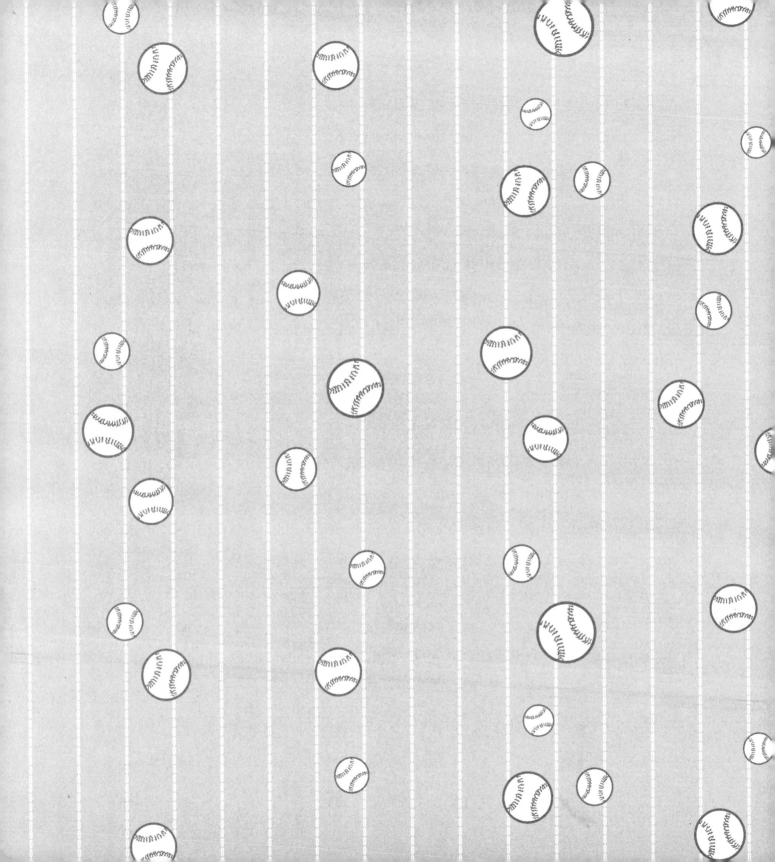

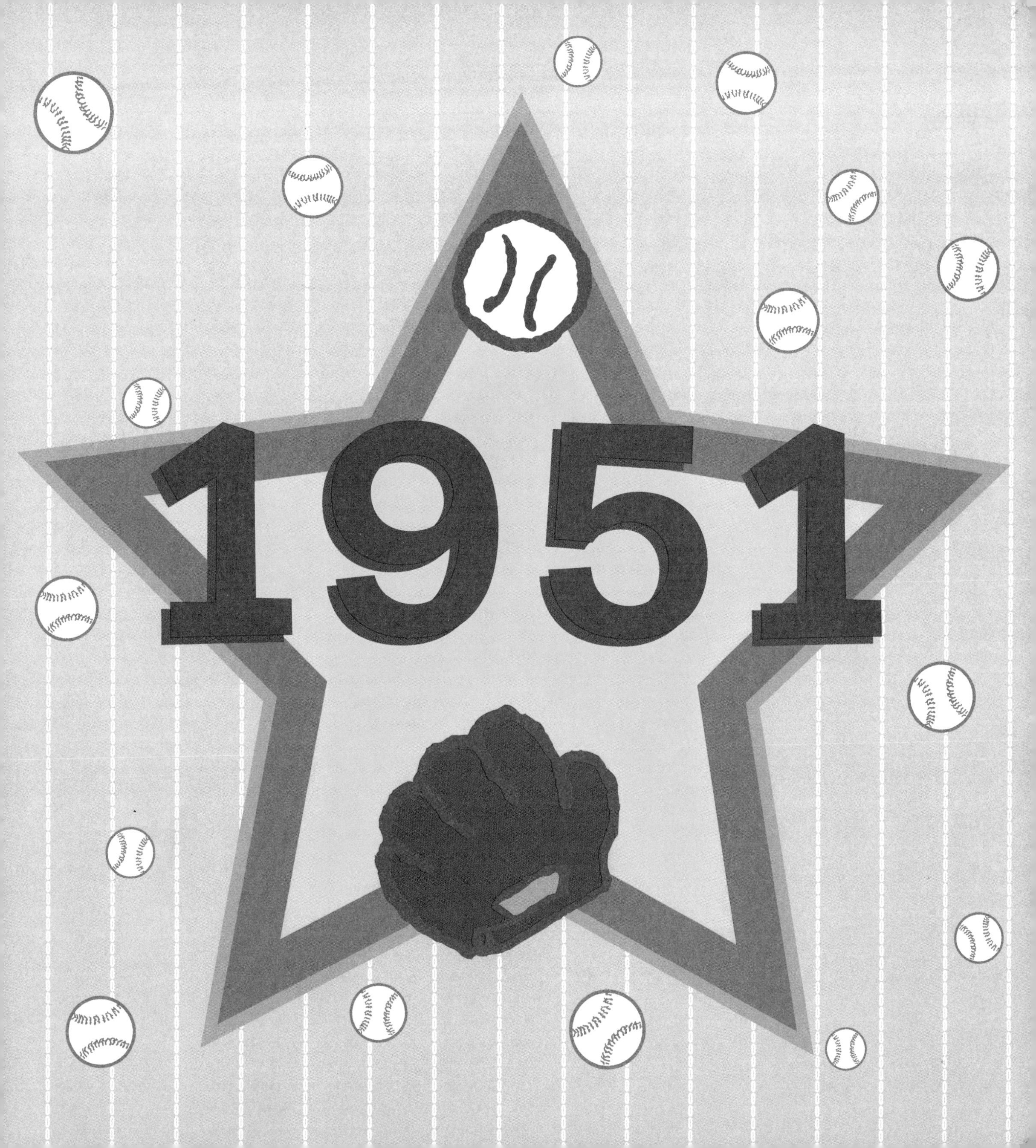
1951

"PEANUTS"
PITCH TO ME, BOY!
THROW IT RIGHT IN HERE! HE CAN'T HIT IT!!
JUST PITCH TO ME, BOY! PITCH TO ME!
O.K., I'M ALL WARMED UP... LET'S START THE GAME!
Copr. 1951 by United Feature Syndicate, Inc.
SCHULZ
3/6

"PEANUTS"
YOU CAN'T BE ON THE TEAM UNTIL YOU GET A SHIRT WITH A SPONSOR'S NAME ON IT
RATS
WHO'D EVER WANT TO SPONSOR ME?!
RATS!
THUD!
UNLESS...
WHY NOT?
Copr. 1951 by United Feature Syndicate, Inc.
O.K., START THE GAME!!
VIOLET'S MUD PIES
4/20
SCHULZ

"PEANUTS"
OUR BASEBALL ROLLED DOWN THE SEWER!
CHARLIE BROWN IS DOWN THERE NOW TRYING TO FIND IT...
DID YOU FIND THE BALL, CHARLIE BROWN?
OR AREN'T YOU CHARLIE BROWN?
6/18
Copr. 1951 by United Feature Syndicate, Inc.
SCHULZ

"PEANUTS"
C'MON! THROW IT RIGHT IN HERE... SHE CAN'T HIT IT!
?
POW
Copr. 1951 by United Feature Syndicate, Inc.
I MISSED YOU WHILE YOU WERE AWAY!
7/10
SCHULZ

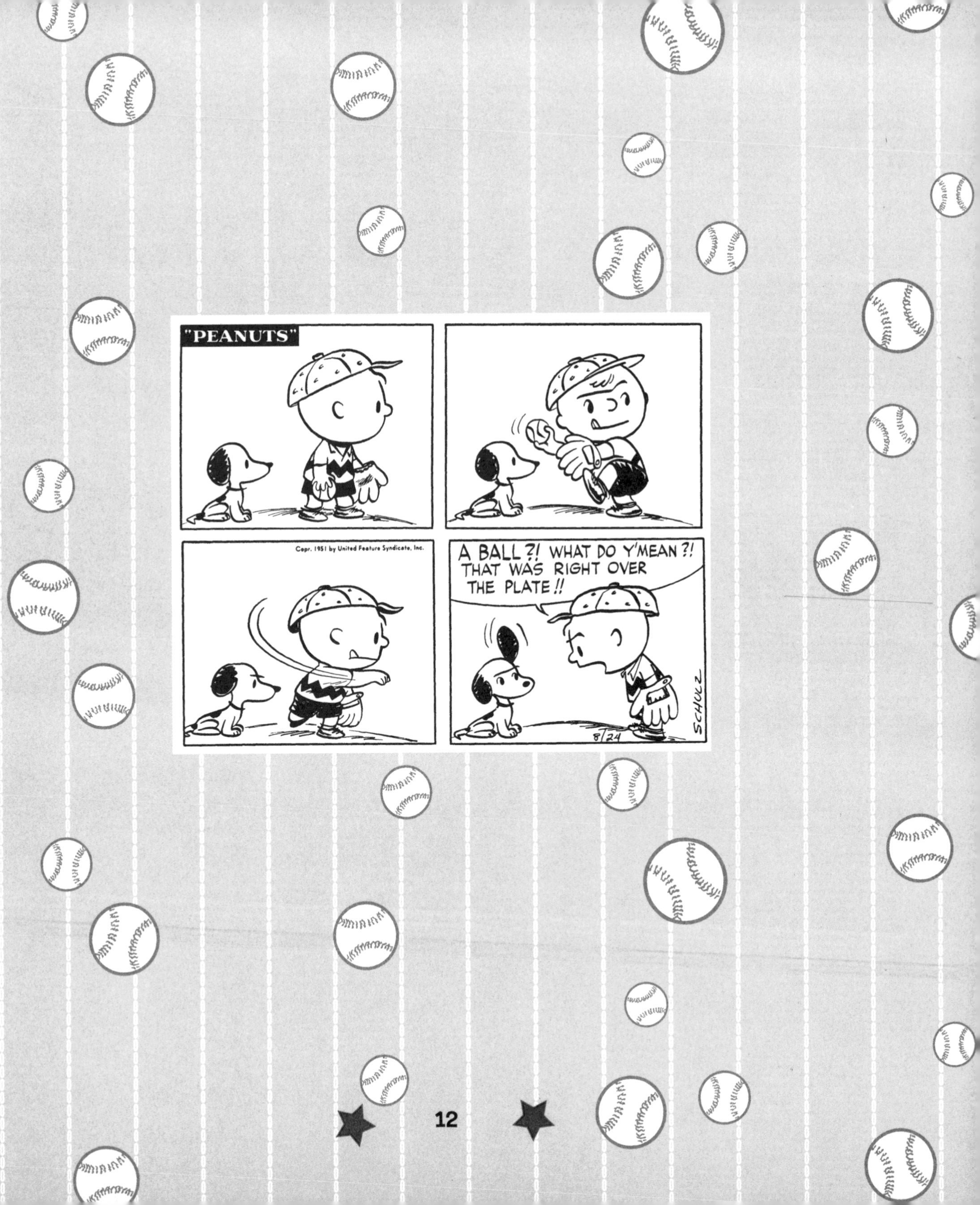
"PEANUTS"
Copr. 1951 by United Feature Syndicate, Inc.
A BALL ?! WHAT DO Y'MEAN ?! THAT WAS RIGHT OVER THE PLATE !!
SCHULZ
8/24

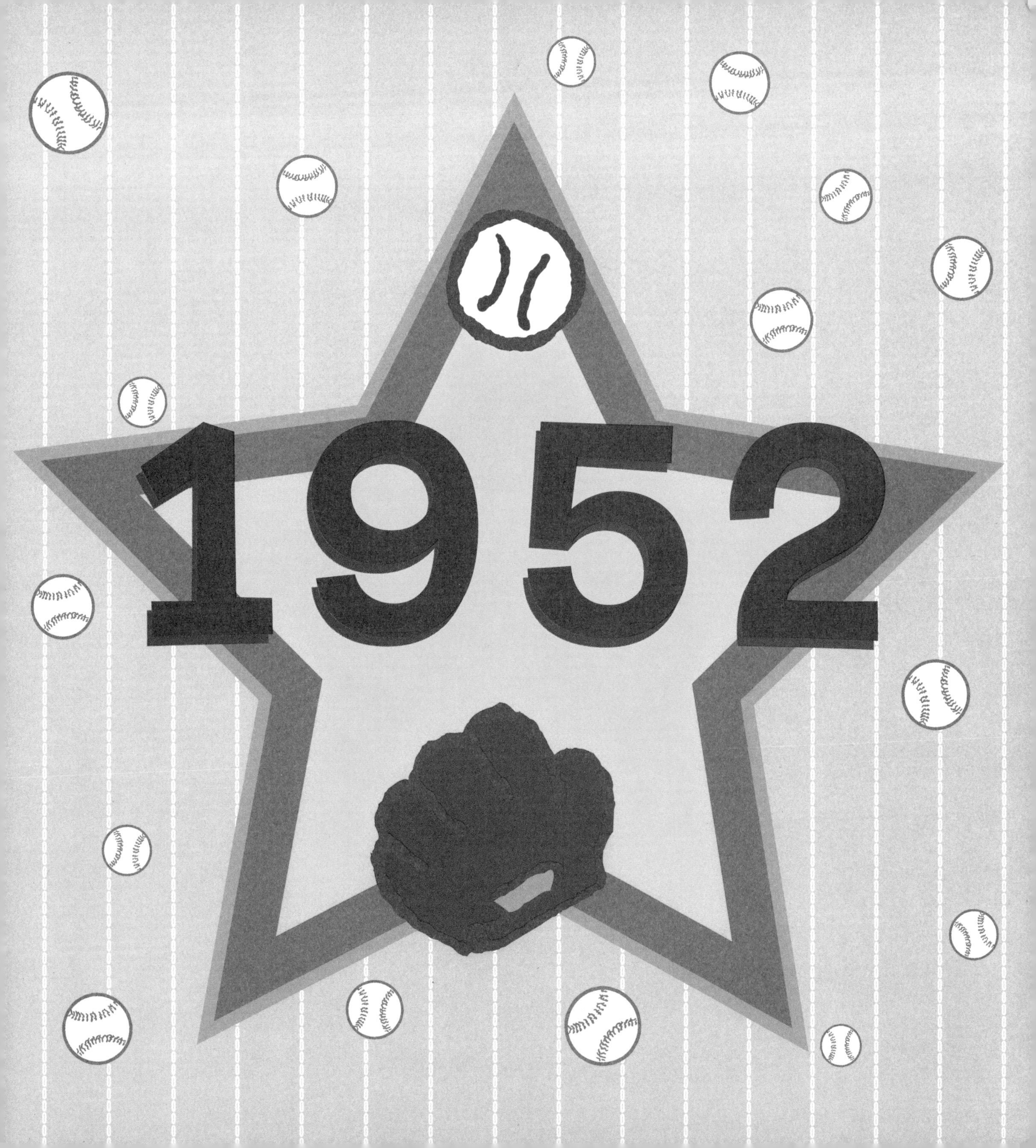
1952

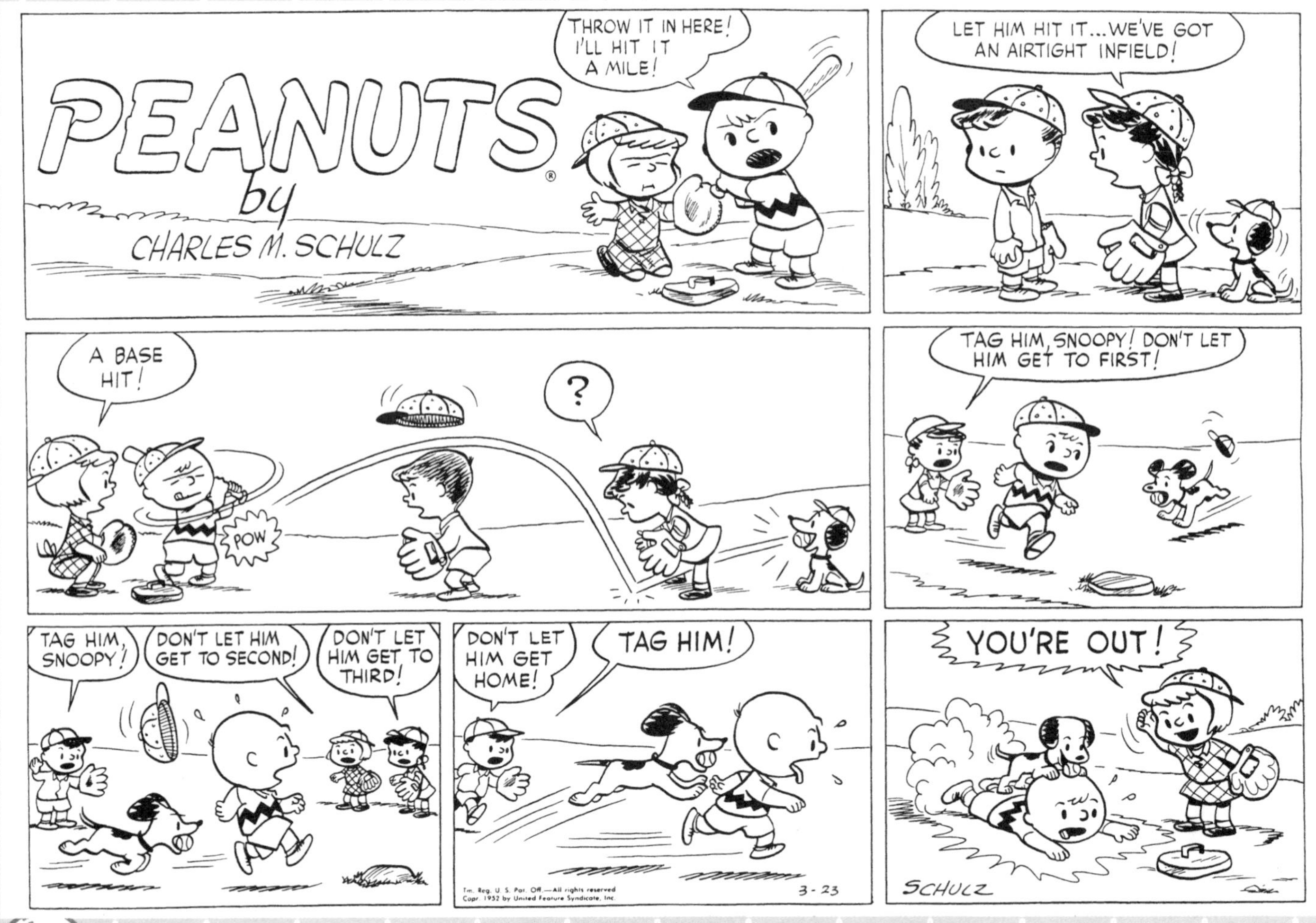
PEANUTS
by
CHARLES M. SCHULZ
THROW IT IN HERE! I'LL HIT IT A MILE!
LET HIM HIT IT...WE'VE GOT AN AIRTIGHT INFIELD!
A BASE HIT!
POW
?
TAG HIM, SNOOPY! DON'T LET HIM GET TO FIRST!
TAG HIM, SNOOPY!
DON'T LET HIM GET TO SECOND!
DON'T LET HIM GET TO THIRD!
DON'T LET HIM GET HOME!
TAG HIM!
Tm. Reg. U. S. Pat. Off.—All rights reserved
Copr. 1952 by United Feature Syndicate, Inc.
3-23
YOU'RE OUT!
SCHULZ

"PEANUTS"
Tm. Reg. U. S. Pat. Off.—All rights reserved
Copr. 1952 by United Feature Syndicate, Inc.
BALL ONE!!
4-12
SCHULZ

"PEANUTS"
YOU REALIZE THAT THE SCORE IS SIXTY TO NOTHING, DON'T YOU?
UH, HUH
WELL, DON'T WORRY ABOUT IT...WE'LL GET 'EM BACK IN THE SECOND INNING!
5/28
SCHULZ

"PEANUTS"
6-3
SCHULZ
Tm. Reg. U. S. Pat. Off.—All rights reserved
Copr. 1952 by United Feature Syndicate, Inc.

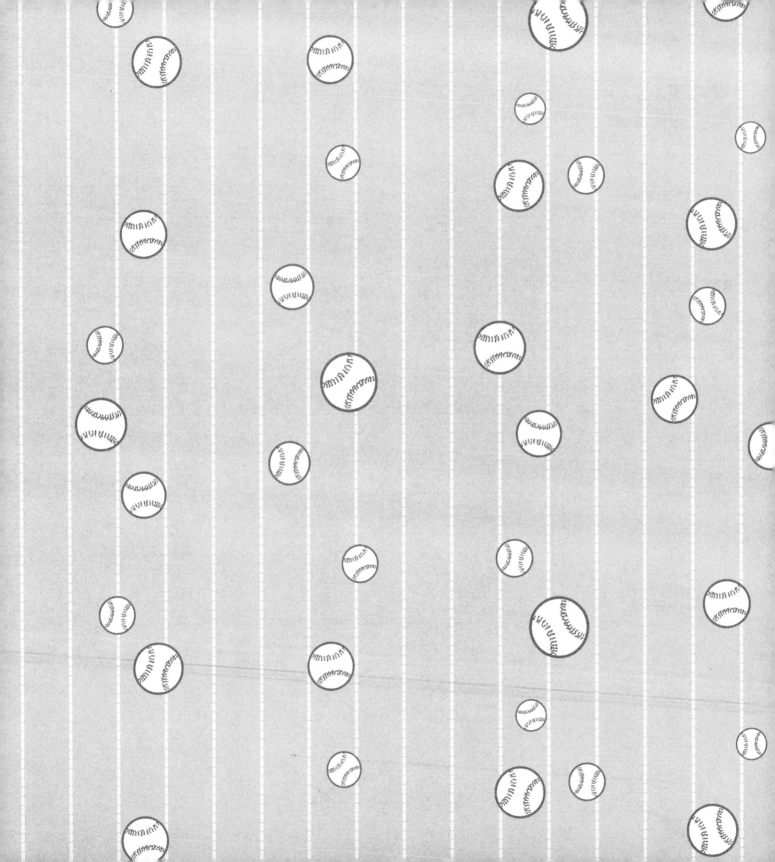

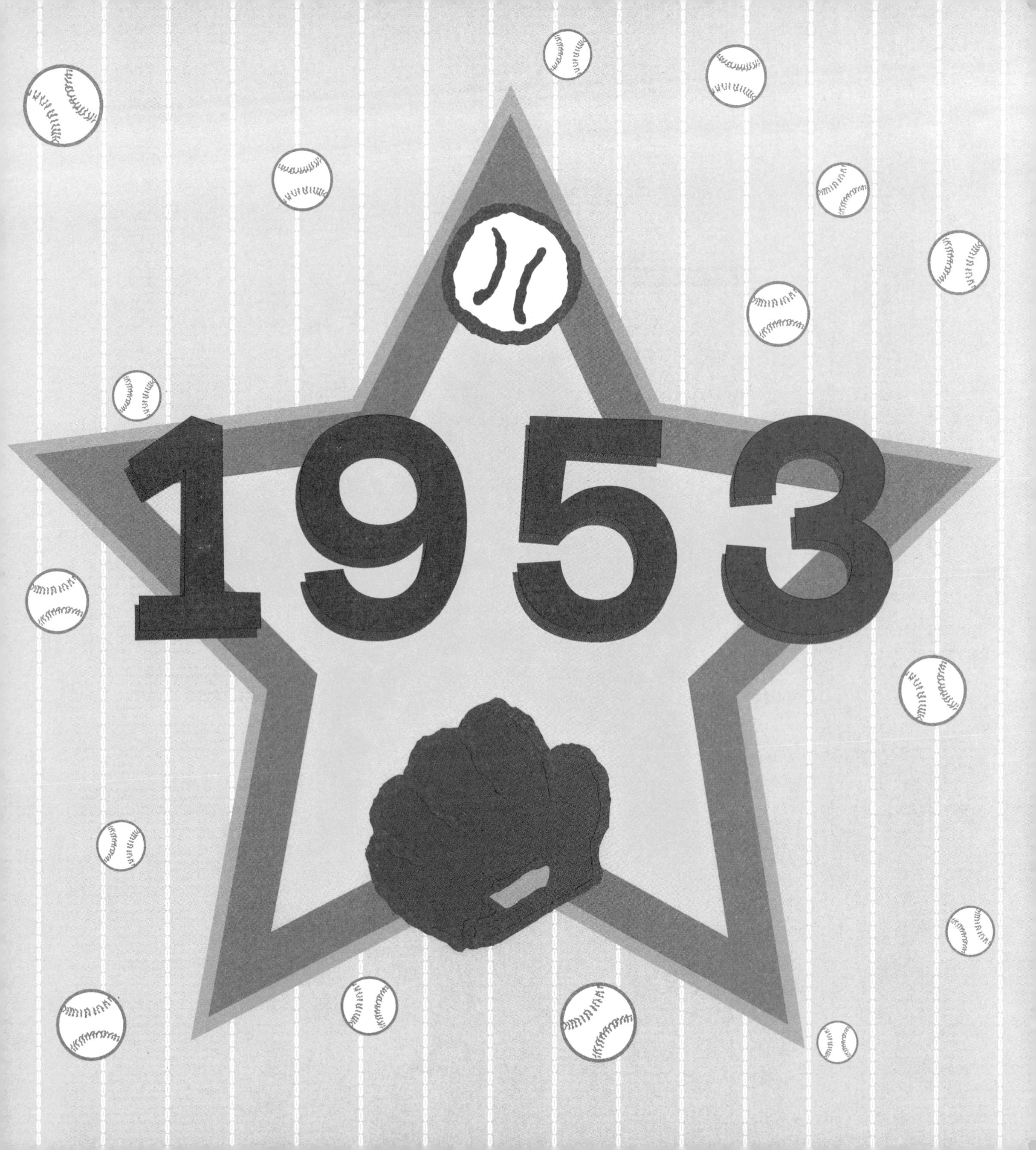
1953

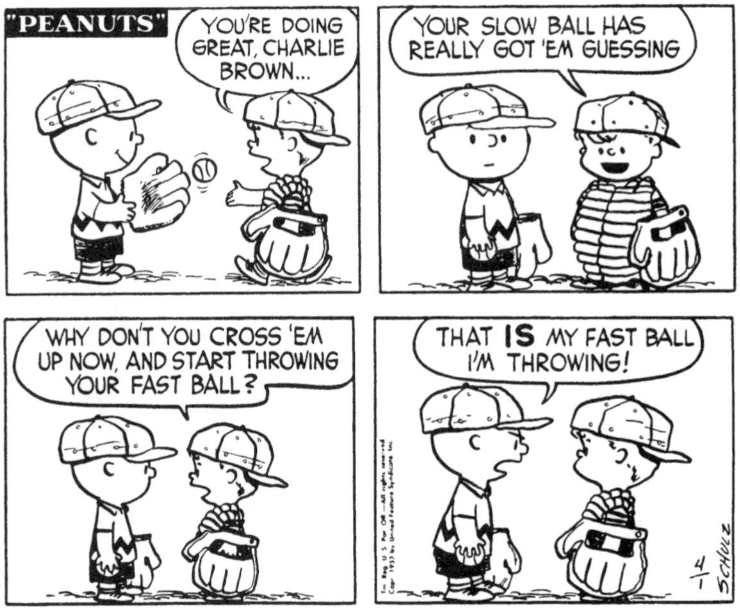
"PEANUTS"
YOU'RE DOING GREAT, CHARLIE BROWN...
YOUR SLOW BALL HAS REALLY GOT 'EM GUESSING
WHY DON'T YOU CROSS 'EM UP NOW, AND START THROWING YOUR FAST BALL?
THAT **IS** MY FAST BALL I'M THROWING!
Tm Reg U S Pat Off —All rights reserved
Copr 1953 by United Feature Syndicate Inc
1-4
SCHULZ

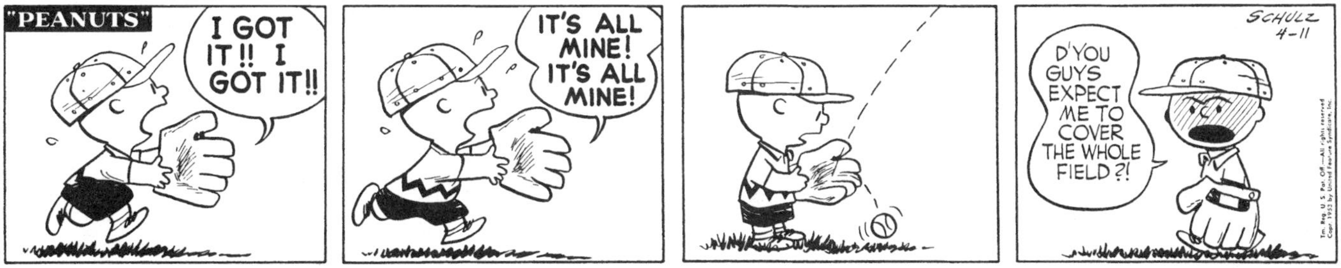
"PEANUTS"
I GOT IT!! I GOT IT!!
IT'S ALL MINE! IT'S ALL MINE!
SCHULZ 4-11
D'YOU GUYS EXPECT ME TO COVER THE WHOLE FIELD?!

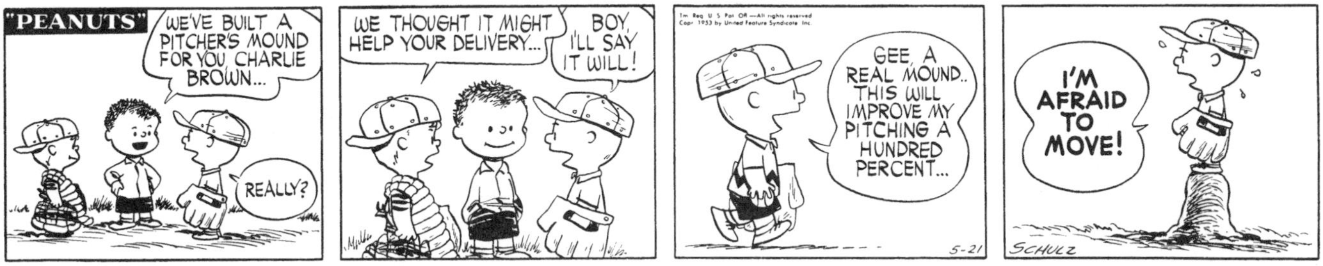
"PEANUTS"
WE'VE BUILT A PITCHER'S MOUND FOR YOU, CHARLIE BROWN...
REALLY?
WE THOUGHT IT MIGHT HELP YOUR DELIVERY...
BOY, I'LL SAY IT WILL!
Tm. Reg. U. S. Pat. Off.—All rights reserved Copr. 1953 by United Feature Syndicate, Inc.
GEE, A REAL MOUND.. THIS WILL IMPROVE MY PITCHING A HUNDRED PERCENT...
5-21
I'M AFRAID TO MOVE!
SCHULZ

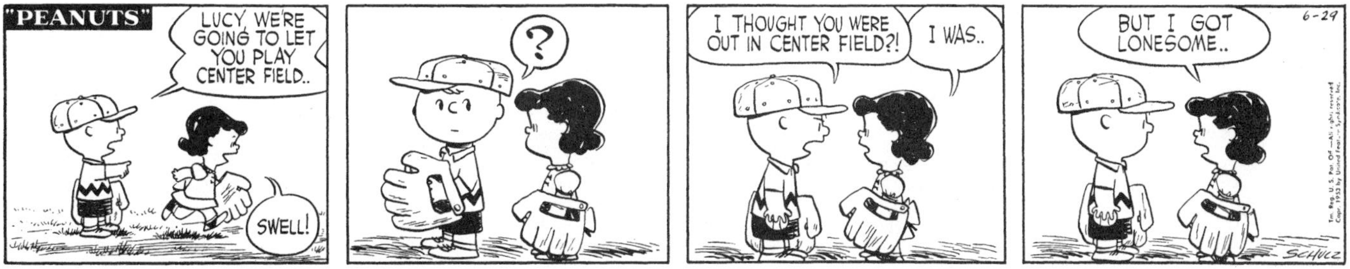
"PEANUTS"
LUCY, WE'RE GOING TO LET YOU PLAY CENTER FIELD..
SWELL!
?
I THOUGHT YOU WERE OUT IN CENTER FIELD?!
I WAS..
6-29
BUT I GOT LONESOME..
SCHULZ

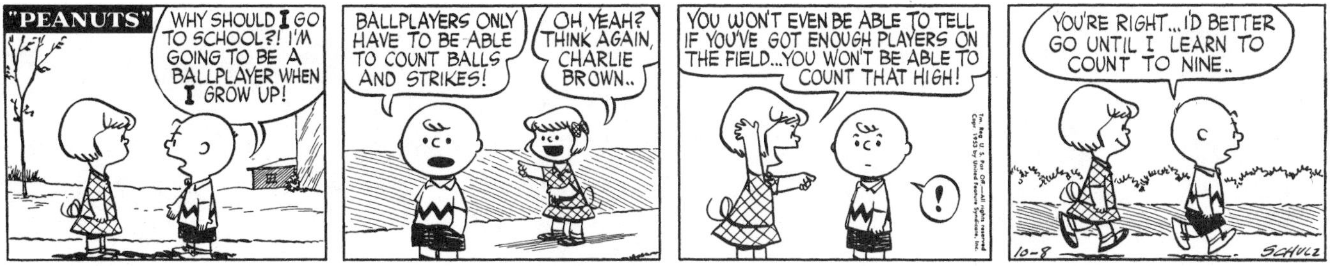
"PEANUTS"
WHY SHOULD I GO TO SCHOOL?! I'M GOING TO BE A BALLPLAYER WHEN I GROW UP!
BALLPLAYERS ONLY HAVE TO BE ABLE TO COUNT BALLS AND STRIKES!
OH, YEAH? THINK AGAIN, CHARLIE BROWN..
YOU WON'T EVEN BE ABLE TO TELL IF YOU'VE GOT ENOUGH PLAYERS ON THE FIELD...YOU WON'T BE ABLE TO COUNT THAT HIGH!
!
10-8
YOU'RE RIGHT... I'D BETTER GO UNTIL I LEARN TO COUNT TO NINE..
SCHULZ

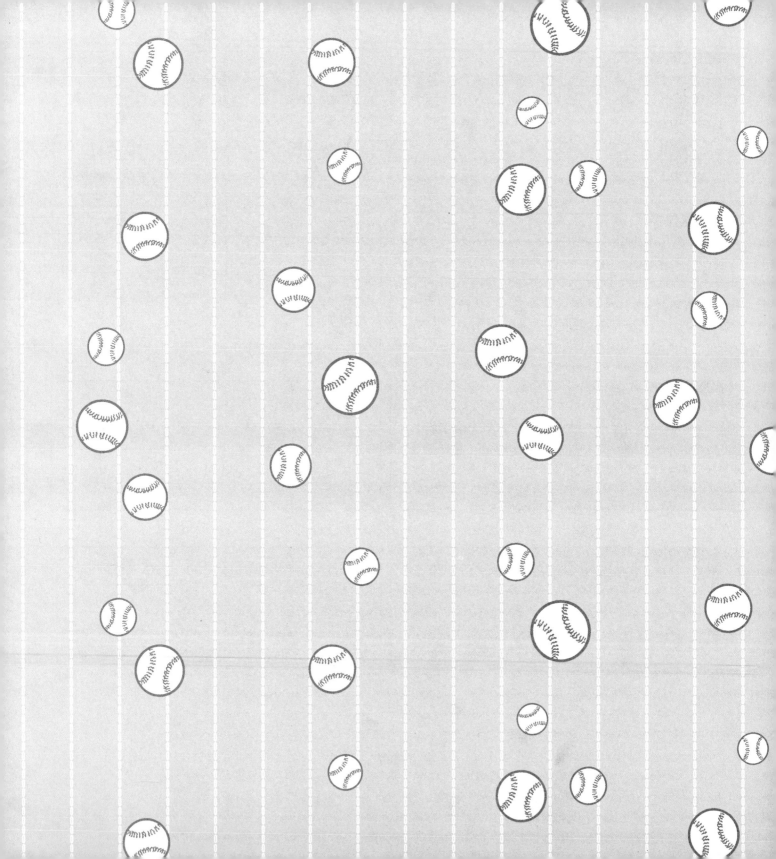

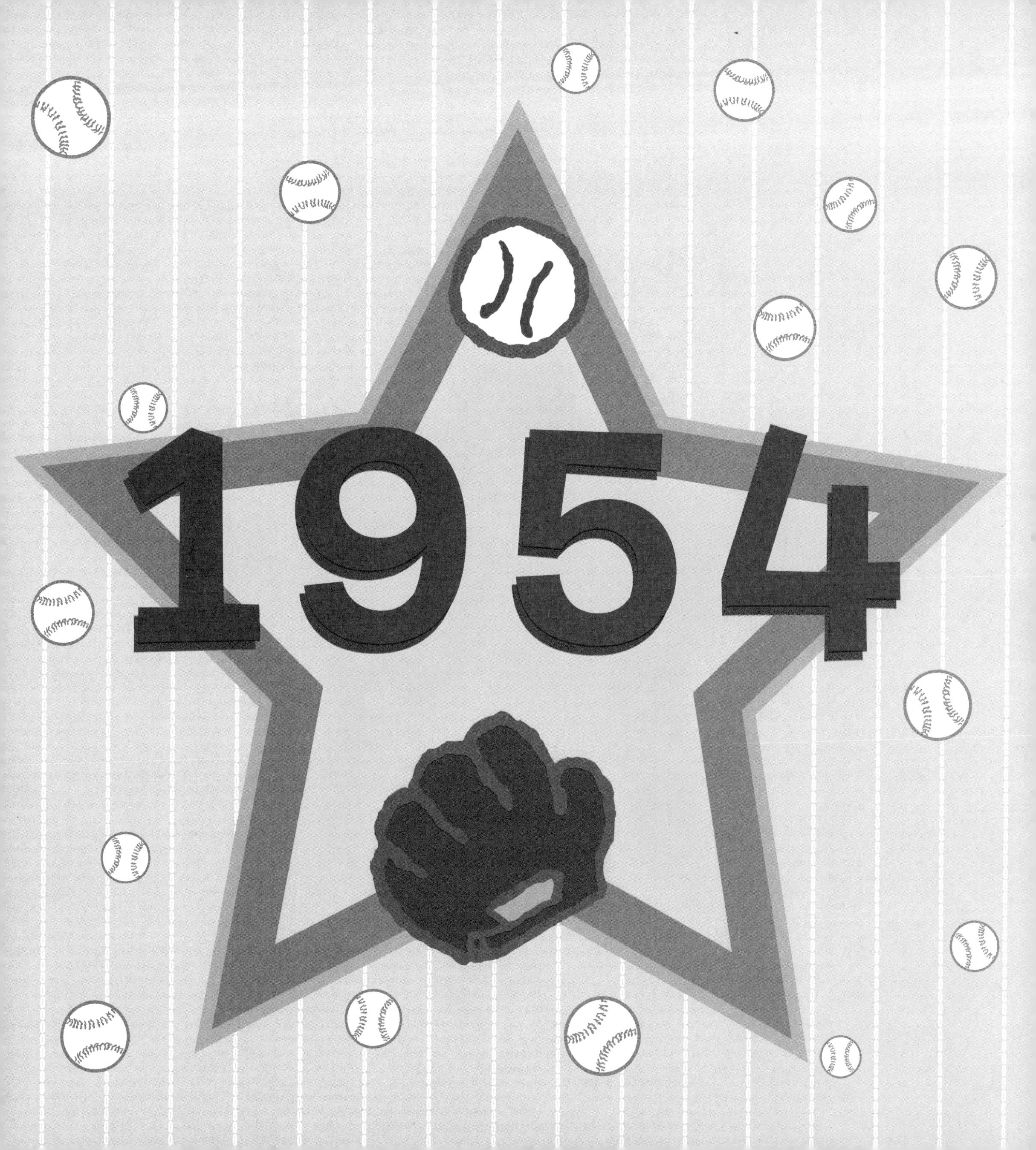
1954

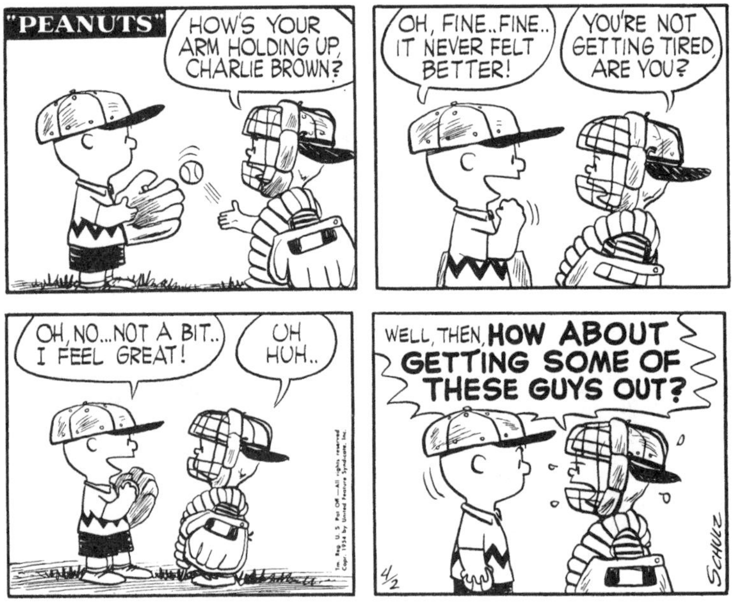
"PEANUTS"
HOW'S YOUR ARM HOLDING UP, CHARLIE BROWN?
OH, FINE..FINE.. IT NEVER FELT BETTER!
YOU'RE NOT GETTING TIRED, ARE YOU?
OH, NO...NOT A BIT.. I FEEL GREAT!
UH HUH..
WELL, THEN, HOW ABOUT GETTING SOME OF THESE GUYS OUT?
4/2
SCHULZ

PEANUTS
by
CHARLES M. SCHULZ
I THINK WE'D BETTER QUIT
I DO TOO
IT'S GOING TO CLEAR UP...
YOU'RE OUT OF YOUR MIND, CHARLIE BROWN!
I THINK IT'S GOING TO CLEAR UP..
WE'RE GOING HOME!
BUT IT'S GOING TO CLEAR UP!
IT'S GOING TO CLEAR UP...
IT'S GOING TO CLEAR UP..
IT'S GOING TO CLEAR UP!
SCHULZ
4-11
IT'S GOING TO CLEAR UP....
Tm. Reg. U. S. Pat. Off.—All rights reserved
Copr. 1954 by United Feature Syndicate, Inc.

"PEANUTS" THIS OLD PIECE OF PAPER CAN BE FIRST BASE

NOW, YOU STAND RIGHT ON TOP OF IT, LUCY... THAT'S THE WAY..

YOU MEAN YOU WANT **ME** TO PLAY FIRST BASE?

NO, YOU JUST STAND THERE, AND KEEP THE PAPER FROM BLOWING AWAY!

"PEANUTS" THROW 'IM THE OL' BEAN-BAG, CHARLIE BROWN!

! C'MON, BOY! THROW 'IM THE GOOD OL' BEAN-BAG!

JUST IN CASE YOU DON'T KNOW IT... THE WORD IS 'BEAN-**BALL**'! OH?

"PEANUTS"

?

WHAT IN THE WORLD DO YOU THINK YOU'RE DOING?

I WAS LISTENING TO THE OCEAN ROAR!

"PEANUTS"
C'MON! HIT ONE OUT HERE! WHAT'S THE MATTER? CAN'T Y'HIT 'EM THIS FAR?!
LOOK, I'M MOVING IN CLOSER! NOW, HIT ONE!!
WHAT'S THE MATTER? ARE YOU WEAK, OR SOMETHING?
5-11
SCHULZ

"PEANUTS"
SAFE!
SCHULZ 6-22

"PEANUTS"
DO YOU HAVE ANY BALLPLAYERS' PICTURES TO TRADE, CHARLIE BROWN?
I'VE GOT THREE EXTRA ONES OF STAN MUSIAL, TED WILLIAMS AND ROY CAMPANELLA...
SCRAP BOOK
THAT'S FINE...WE CAN TRADE EVEN..THREE FOR THREE
SCRAP BOOK
BACH, BEETHOVEN AND BRAHMS!
SCHULZ
6-24

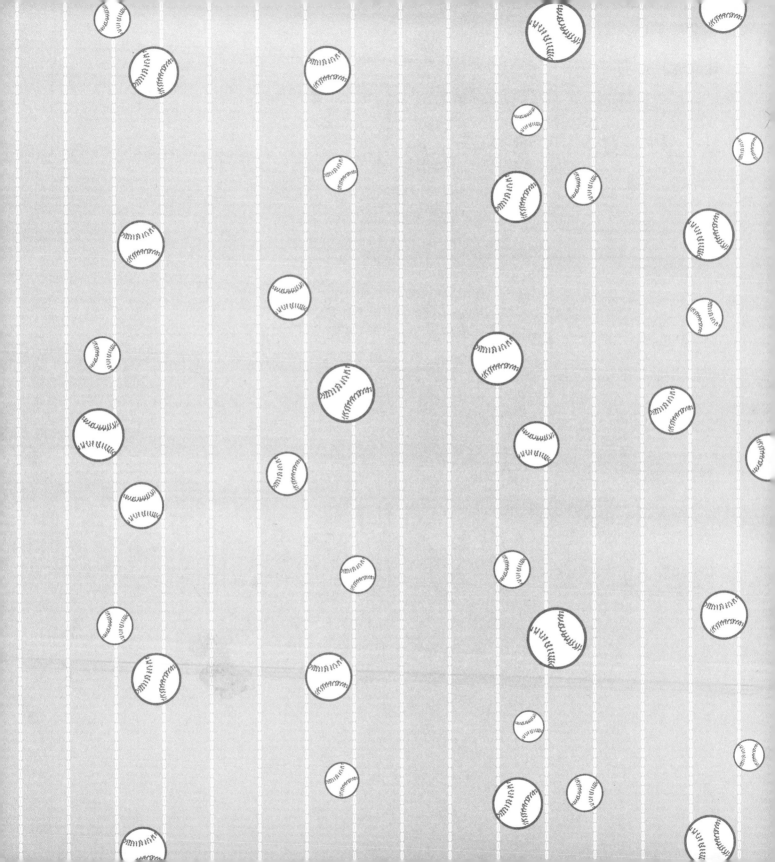

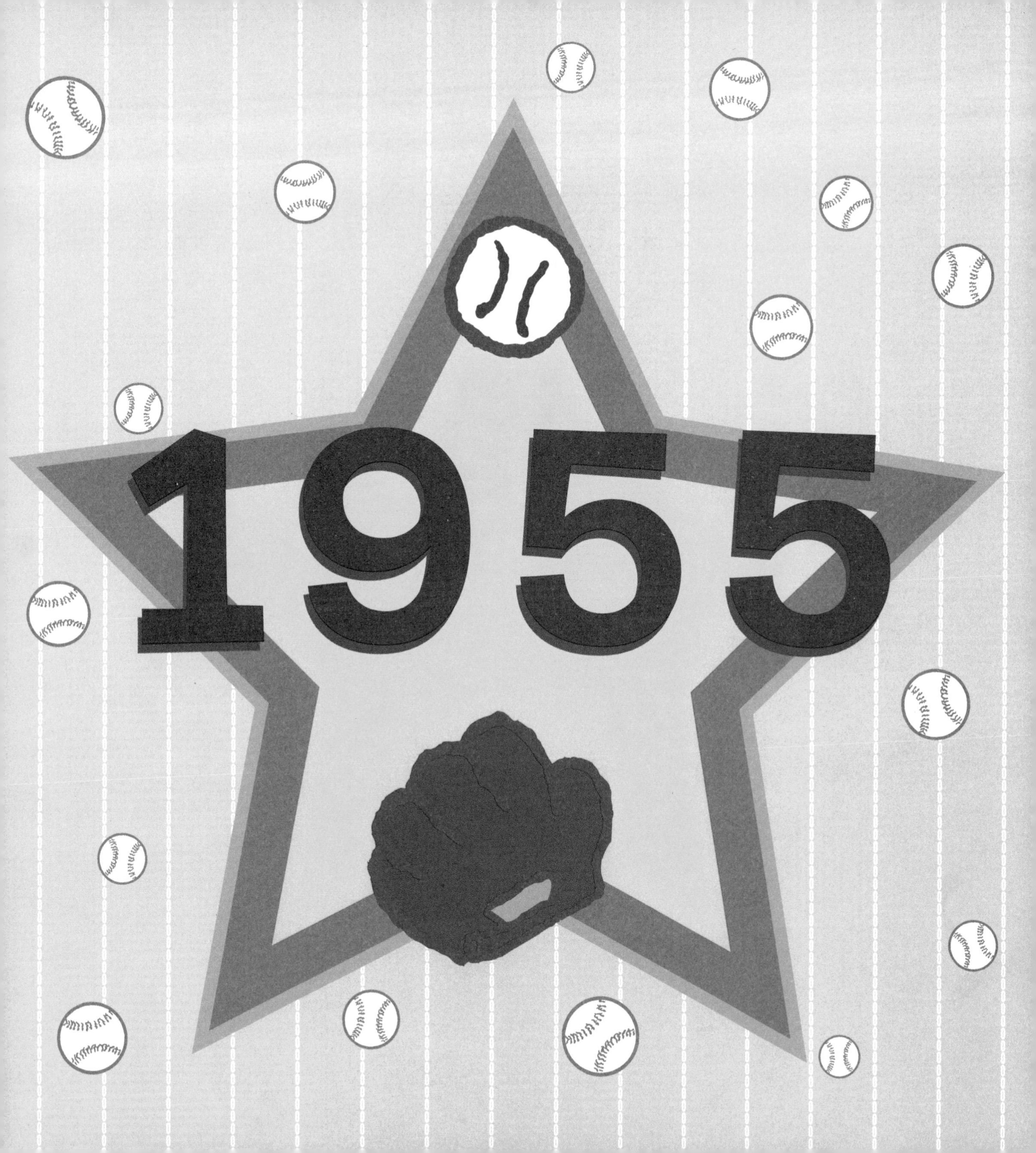
1955

"PEANUTS"
SAY THIS IS A PRETTY GOOD BALL, CHARLIE BROWN...
I'LL HAVE YOU KNOW THIS IS AN 'OFFICIAL' BALL!
'OFFICIAL'! GEE...
YES, SIR..
THIS BALL HAS BEEN TAPED AND RE-TAPED ACCORDING TO OFFICIAL NEIGHBORHOOD-LEAGUE STANDARDS!
4-6
SCHULZ

"PEANUTS"
I GOT IT! I GOT IT! IT'S ALL MINE!
BONK!
WHEW
I COULDN'T DENY IT... IT WAS ALL YOURS..
4-15
SCHULZ

"PEANUTS"
A GOOD CENTERFIELDER IS THE BACKBONE OF A TEAM!
YES, SIR.. CENTERFIELD IS THE MOST IMPORTANT POSITION ON THE WHOLE TEAM..
HEY!
HOW ABOUT LETTING ME PLAY IN THE INFIELD FOR AWHILE?
5-18
SCHULZ

"PEANUTS"
Tm. Reg. U. S. Pat Off.—All rights reserved
Copr. 1955 by United Feature Syndicate, Inc
5-21
SCHULZ

"PEANUTS"
WELL, THERE GOES THE OLD BALL GAME!
MY DADDY SAYS WE NEED RAIN... HE SAYS OUR LAWN IS JUST ABOUT DRIED OUT...
HE SAYS OUR GARDEN NEEDS RAIN, AND OUR NEW HEDGE NEEDS RAIN, AND HE SAYS...
OH, SHUT UP!!
8-5
SCHULZ

"PEANUTS"
STRIKE THREE!
YOU'RE OUT, LINUS! **YOU'RE OUT!**
Tm. Reg. U. S. Pat Off.—All rights reserved
Copr. 1955 by United Feature Syndicate, Inc
SCHULZ
8-9

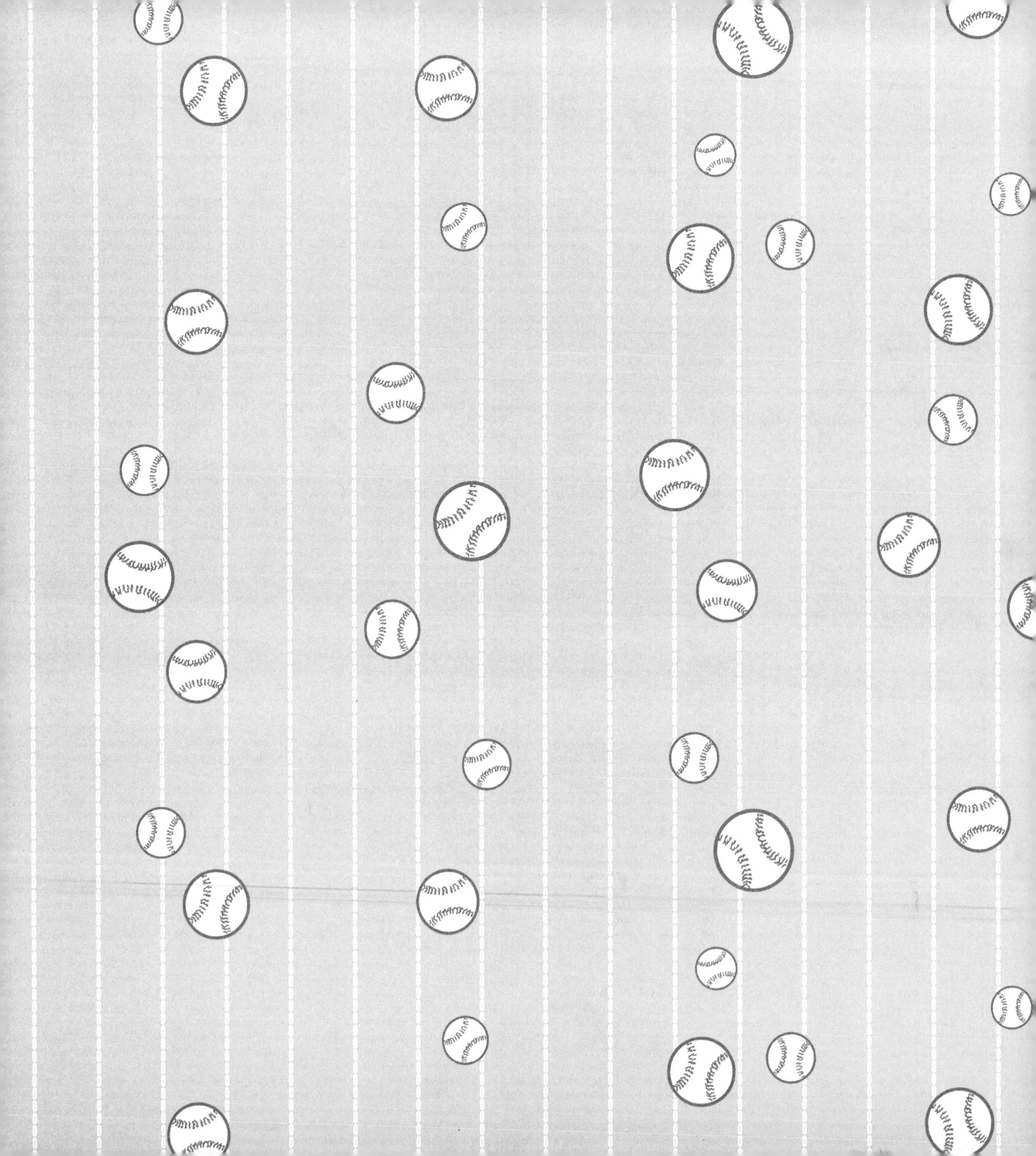

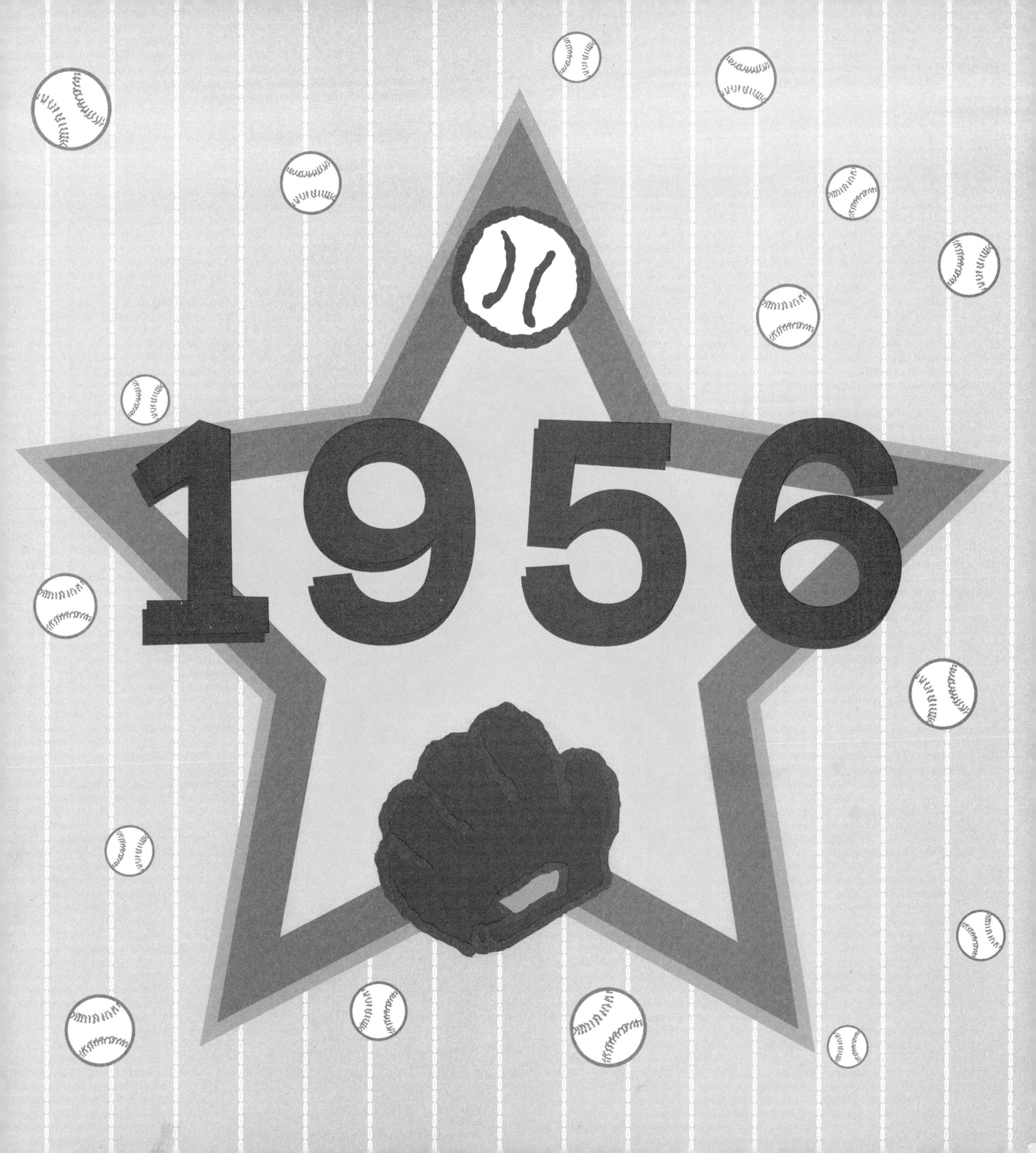
1956

MARCH 1956
SUN MON TUES WED THURS FRI SAT
PEANUTS
JANUARY, FEBRUARY, MARCH...
ONE TWO, THREE, FOUR, **FIVE**!
GOOD GRIEF! SPRING BEGAN **FIVE** DAYS AGO!
I GOTTA CALL SCHROEDER...I'LL BET HE DOESN'T EVEN KNOW IT...
WADDYA MEAN, Y'DON'T CARE WHAT THE CALENDAR SAYS?!
BY GOLLY, **I** SURE CARE WHAT THE CALENDAR SAYS!
C'MON! LET'S PLAY BALL!!
Tm. Reg. U. S. Pat. Off.—All rights reserved Copr. 1956 by United Feature Syndicate, Inc.
3-25
SCHULZ

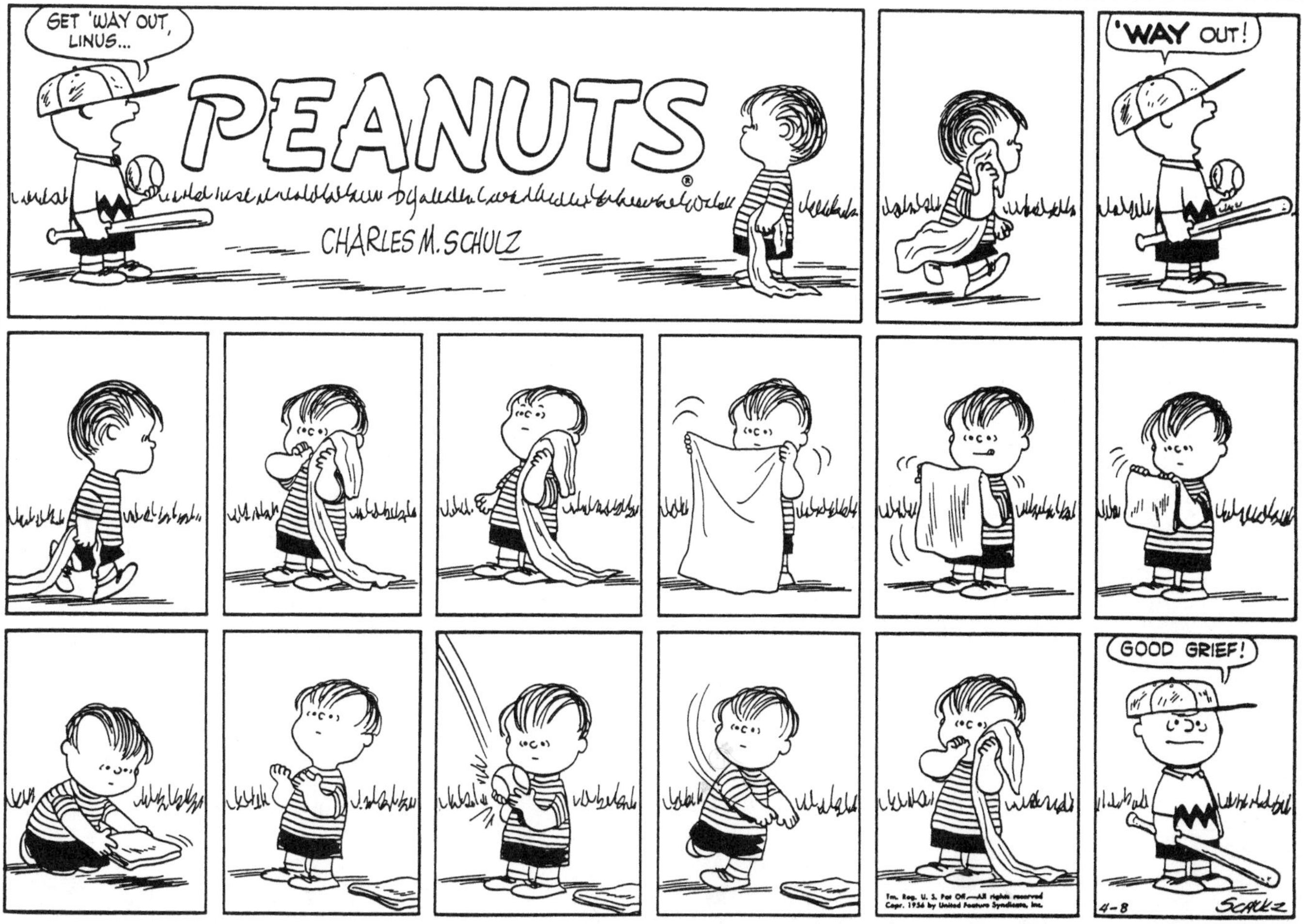
GET 'WAY OUT, LINUS...
PEANUTS
CHARLES M. SCHULZ
'WAY OUT!
GOOD GRIEF!
Tm. Reg. U. S. Pat Off.—All rights reserved
Copr. 1956 by United Feature Syndicate, Inc.
4-8
SCHULZ

PEANUTS
ALL RIGHT, HERE'S A HIGH FLY BALL! ARE YOU READY?!
THIS ONE'S GOING A MILE IN THE AIR!
WHOP!
WELL, Y'GOTTA PRACTICE THOSE GROUNDERS, TOO Y'KNOW!
5-30
SCHULZ

PEANUTS
ARE YOU OUT OF YOUR MIND? YOU'RE SUPPOSED TO BE PLAYING RIGHT FIELD! YOU LET THAT BALL GO RIGHT BY YOU!
OF ALL THE STUPID THINGS! GOOD GRIEF!!
A WISE MANAGER NEVER SHOUTS AT HIS PLAYERS..
SCHULZ
5-31

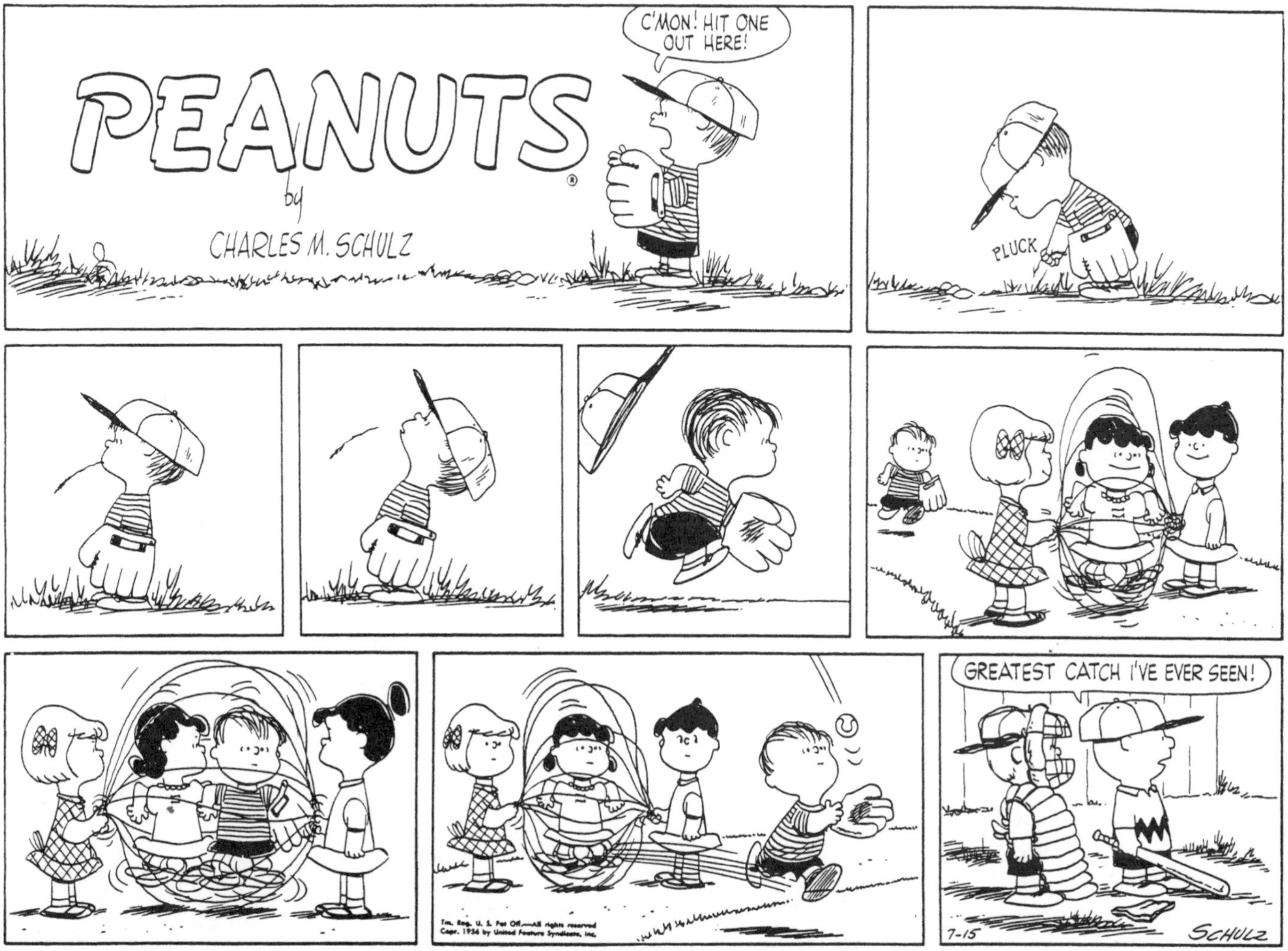
PEANUTS
by
CHARLES M. SCHULZ
C'MON! HIT ONE OUT HERE!
PLUCK
Tm. Reg. U. S. Pat. Off.—All rights reserved
Copr. 1956 by United Feature Syndicate, Inc.
GREATEST CATCH I'VE EVER SEEN!
7-15
SCHULZ

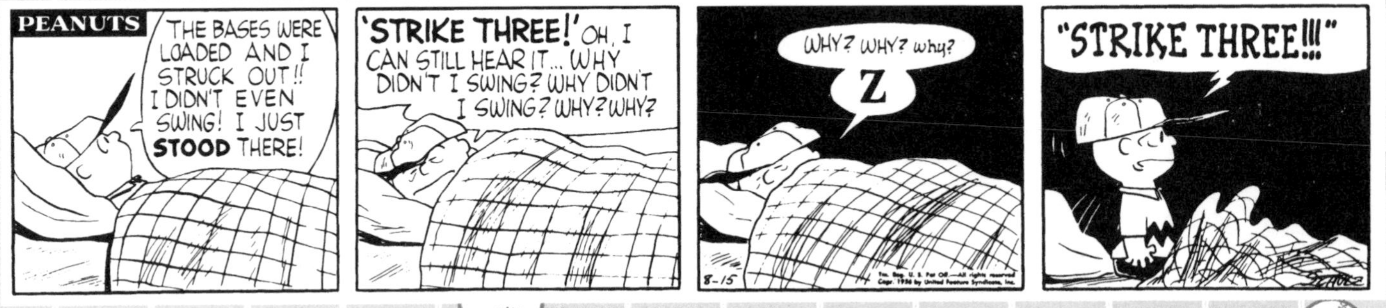
PEANUTS
THE BASES WERE LOADED AND I STRUCK OUT!! I DIDN'T EVEN SWING! I JUST **STOOD** THERE!
'STRIKE THREE!' OH, I CAN STILL HEAR IT... WHY DIDN'T I SWING? WHY DIDN'T I SWING? WHY? WHY?
WHY? WHY? why?
Z
8-15
"STRIKE THREE!!!"
SCHULZ

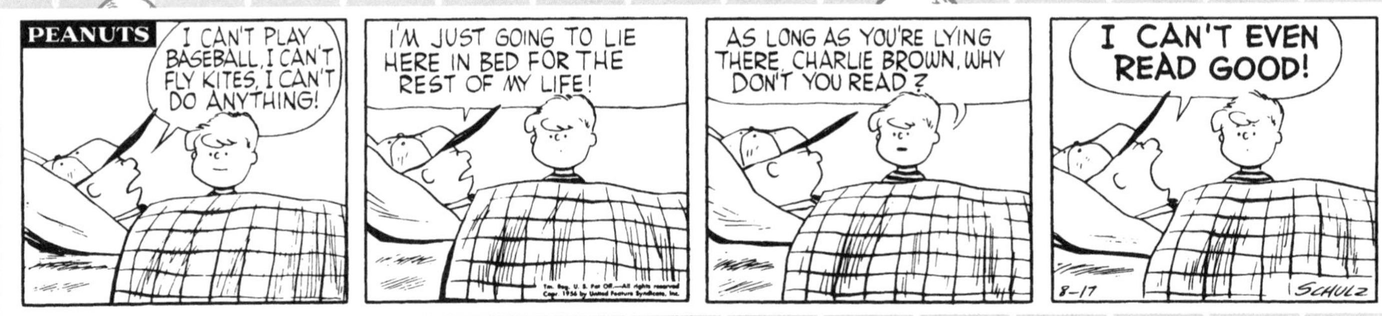
PEANUTS
I CAN'T PLAY BASEBALL, I CAN'T FLY KITES, I CAN'T DO ANYTHING!
I'M JUST GOING TO LIE HERE IN BED FOR THE REST OF MY LIFE!
AS LONG AS YOU'RE LYING THERE, CHARLIE BROWN, WHY DON'T YOU READ?
I CAN'T EVEN READ GOOD!
8-17
SCHULZ

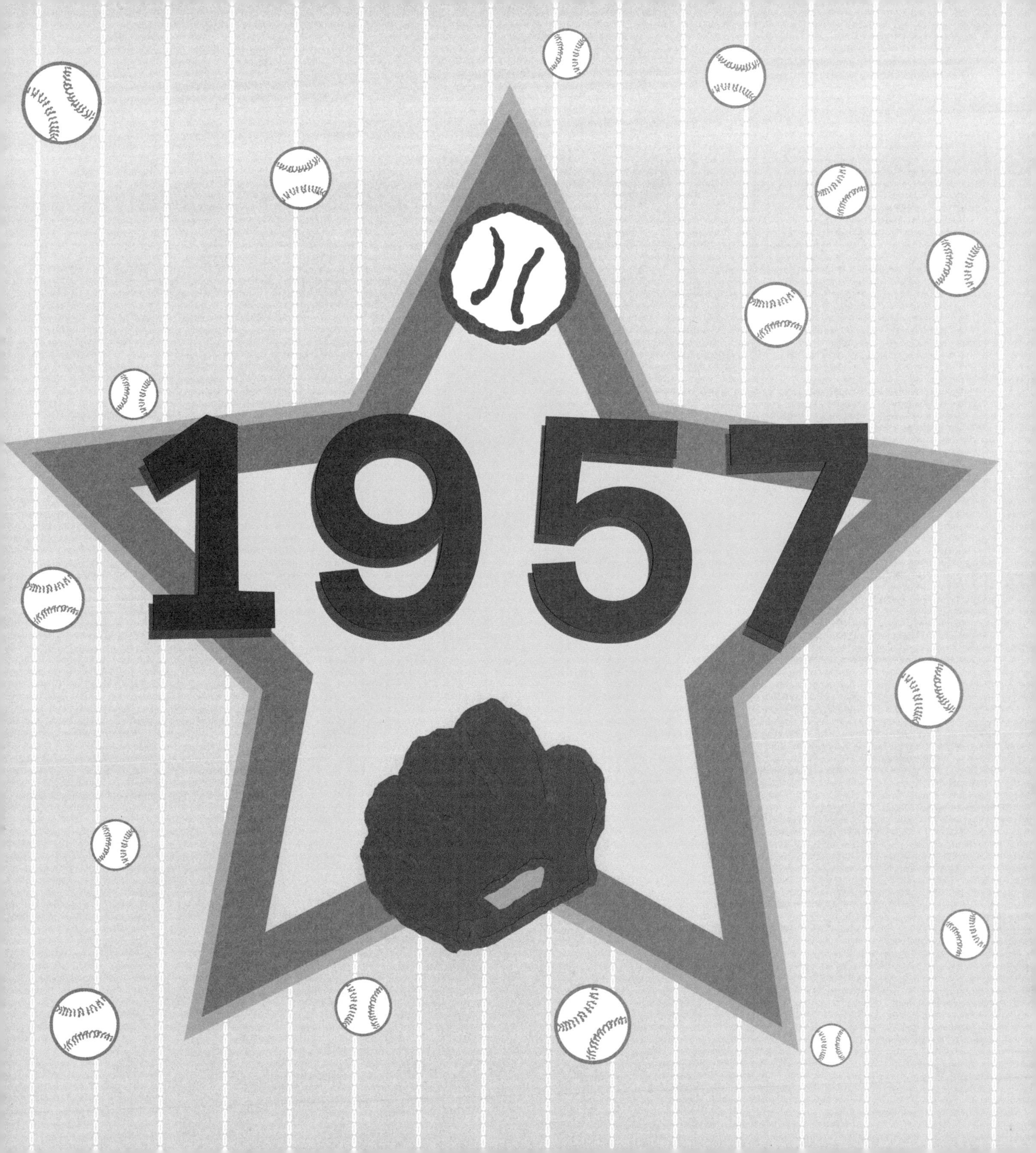
1957

PEANUTS
Tm. Reg. U. S. Pat. Off.—All rights reserved
Copr. 1957 by United Feature Syndicate, Inc.
THIS IS GOING TO BE A LONG SUMMER..
3-19
SCHULZ

PEANUTS
WHAT'S THE MATTER WITH YOU, SCHROEDER?
THAT'S THE THIRD GROUND BALL YOU'VE MISSED TODAY!
I SUPPOSE YOU'RE GONNA SAY IT TOOK A BAD BOUNCE AGAIN, HUH?!
YES, I AM!!
4-11
SCHULZ

PEANUTS

WHAT A TEAM! GOOD GRIEF!!

I'VE GOT A CATCHER WHO CAN'T SEE, A FIRST BASEMAN WHO'S ONLY THREE FEET TALL, AND AN OUTFIELDER WHO CAN'T THROW!

CAN'T **THROW**? I'VE NEVER HEARD OF SUCH A THING...

4-12

WELL, **NOW** YOU HAVE!

SCHULZ

PEANUTS

CHARLIE BROWN, I CAN'T PLAY CENTER FIELD ANY MORE..

WHY NOT?

THE **WEEDS** ARE TOO TALL OUT THERE!

OH, GOOD GRIEF, STOP COMPLAINING, AND GET GOING!

ALL RIGHT..

4-13

BUT SOMEBODY BETTER TELL ME WHEN THE INNING IS OVER!

SCHULZ

PEANUTS
CHARLIE BROWN, I CAN'T GET OUT FAR ENOUGH IN LEFT FIELD..
THAT HOUSE IS RIGHT IN THE WAY!
I KNOW IT IS.. YOU'LL JUST HAVE TO DO THE BEST YOU CAN...
Tm. Reg. U. S. Pat Off.—All rights reserved Copr. 1957 by United Feature Syndicate, Inc.
4-16
SCHULZ

PEANUTS
I NEVER REALIZED THE TROUBLES THAT A BASEBALL MANAGER HAS.. EVERYBODY COMES TO HIM WITH THEIR PROBLEMS...
HEY, MANAGER... TIE MY SHOE!
SURE
Tm. Reg. U. S. Pat Off.—All rights reserved Copr. 1957 by United Feature Syndicate, Inc.
4-17
!
GET OUT OF HERE!!
SCHULZ

PEANUTS
HEY, AREN'T WE SHORT ONE MAN? WHERE'S 'PIG-PEN'?
HE'S RIGHT WHERE YOU PUT HIM...AT SECOND BASE..
OH, YES, SO HE IS..
HE'S HARD TO SEE BECAUSE HE BLENDS IN WITH THE DIRT ON THE INFIELD!
4-18
SCHULZ

PEANUTS
MONDAY IS OUR FIRST GAME, AND I'M SCARED TO DEATH..
WHAT A TEAM I'VE GOT... FIVE BOYS, THREE GIRLS AND A DOG! GOOD GRIEF!!
I DON'T KNOW WHY I EVER TRIED TO BE A MANAGER..I MUST BE OUT OF MY MIND!
I WONDER IF CASEY STENGEL IS ASLEEP?
4-20
SCHULZ

PEANUTS
by
CHARLES M. SCHULZ
5-12
Tm. Reg. U. S. Pat Off.—All rights reserved
Copr. 1957 by United Feature Syndicate, Inc.
SCHULZ

PEANUTS
ALL RIGHT, LET'S CUT OUT THE CLOWNING!
YOU'LL NEVER CATCH A BALL **THAT** WAY..
Tm. Reg. U. S. Pat. Off.—All rights reserved
Copr. 1957 by United Feature Syndicate, Inc.
CLUMP!
6-26
SCHULZ

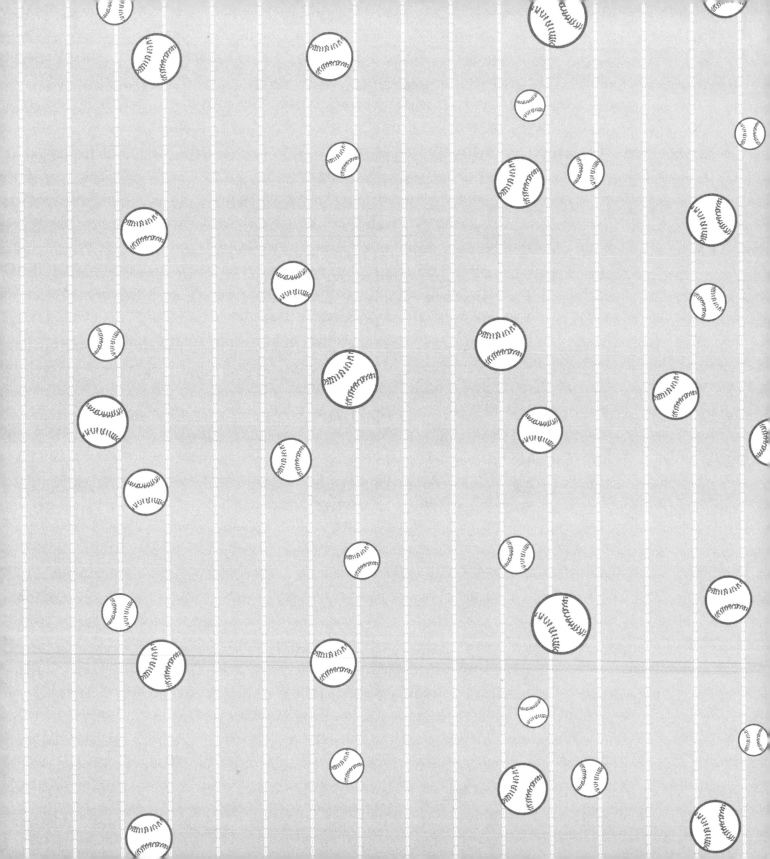

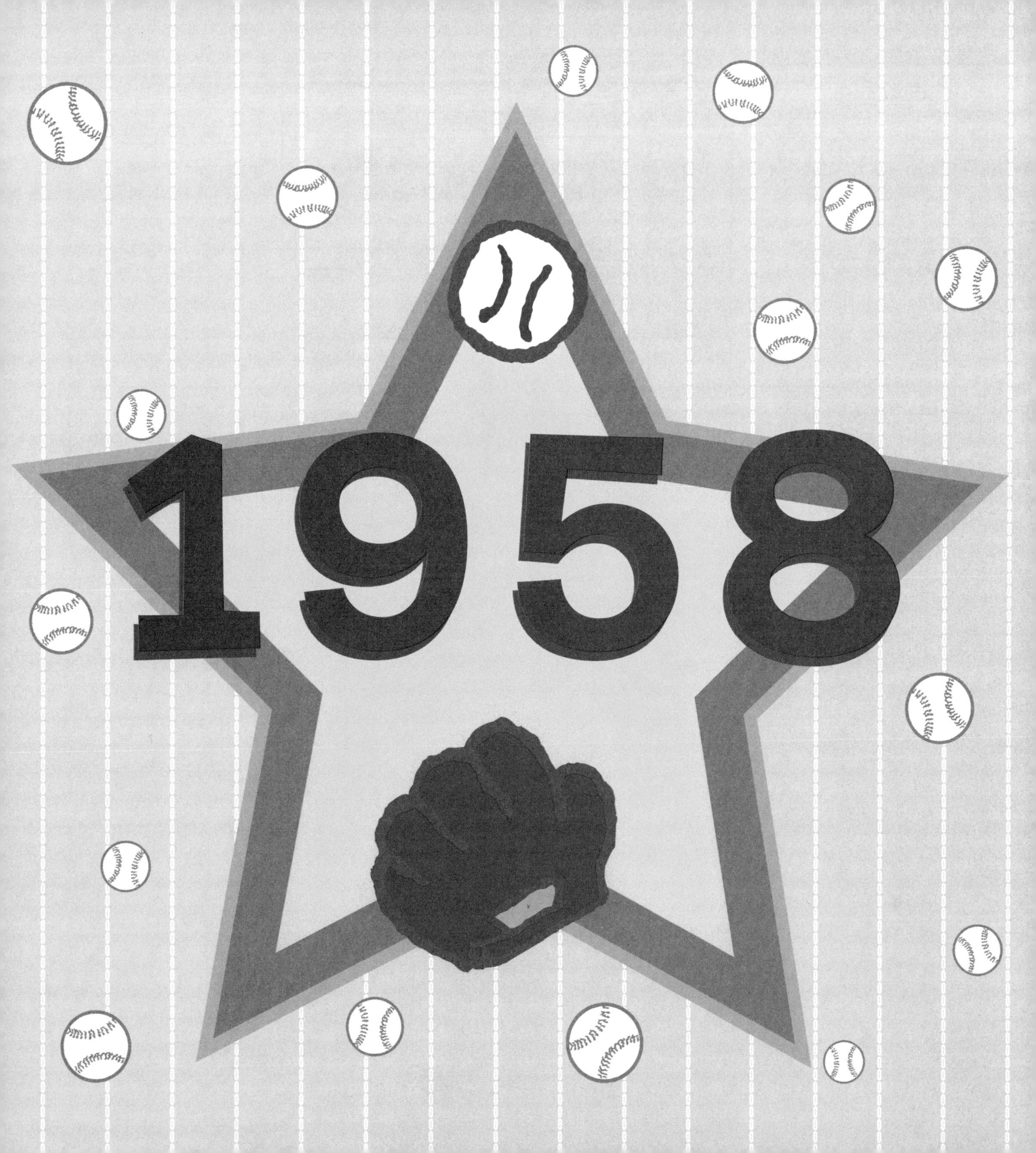
1958

PEANUTS
LUCY, HOW WOULD YOU LIKE TO PLAY SECOND BASE?
NOT ON YOUR LIFE!! I'VE GOT TOO MUCH PRIDE!
WELL, WHAT IN THE WORLD IS WRONG WITH SECOND BASE?
4-15
Tm. Reg. U. S. Pat. Off.—All rights reserved Copr. 1958 by United Feature Syndicate, Inc.
SECOND BASE? OH, PARDON ME...I THOUGHT YOU SAID "SECOND FIDDLE"!
SCHULZ

PEANUTS
Tm. Reg. U. S. Pat. Off.—All rights reserved Copr. 1958 by United Feature Syndicate, Inc.
A PITCHER AND HIS CATCHER NEED A GOOD SET OF SIGNALS...
ONE FINGER WILL MEAN A HIGH BALL...
4-17
TWO FINGERS WILL MEAN A LOW BALL...
AND THREE FINGERS WILL MEAN THE BROAD AREA IN-BETWEEN!
SCHULZ

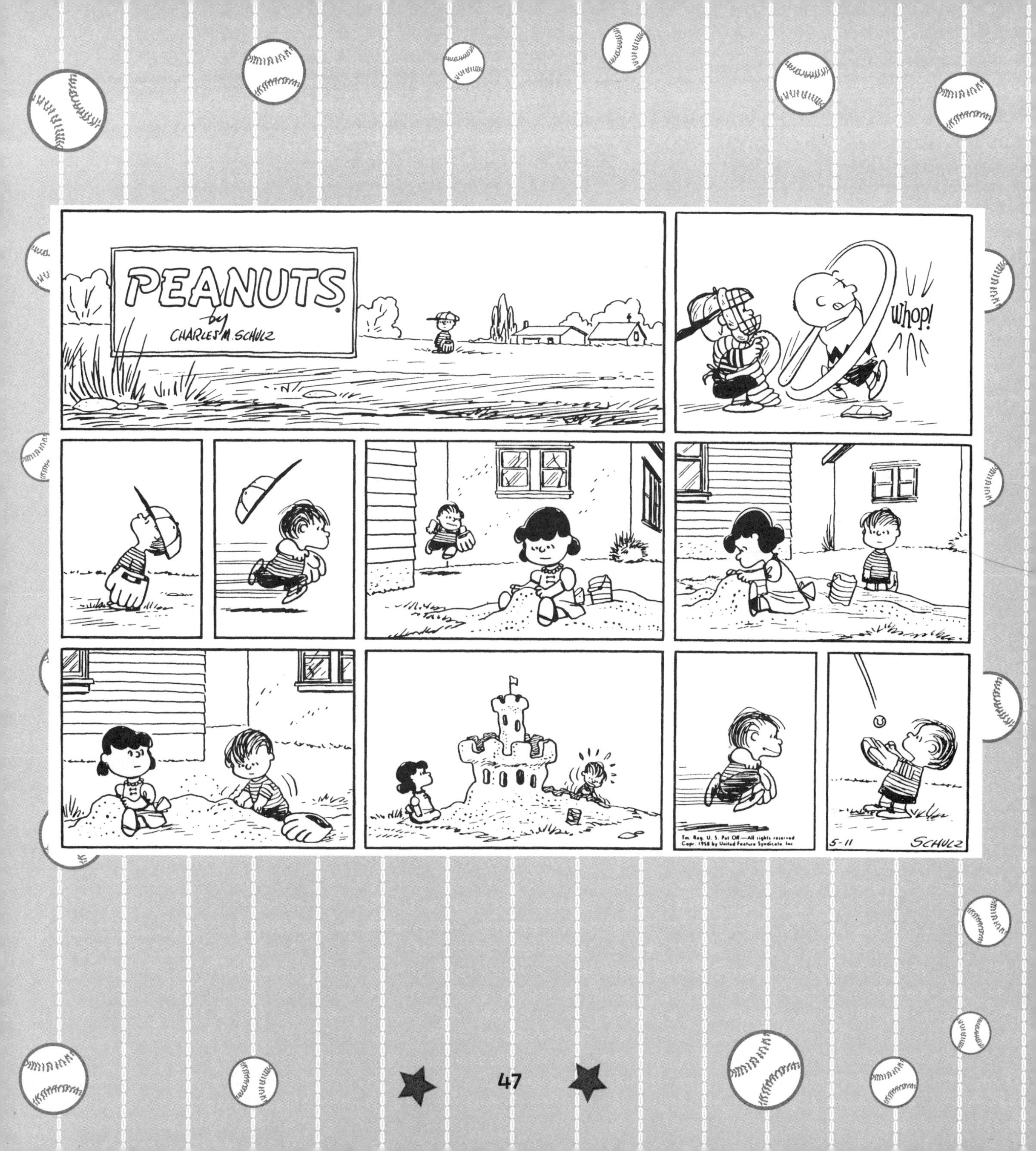
PEANUTS
by
CHARLES M. SCHULZ
whop!
Tm. Reg. U. S. Pat Off.—All rights reserved
Copr. 1958 by United Feature Syndicate, Inc.
5-11
SCHULZ

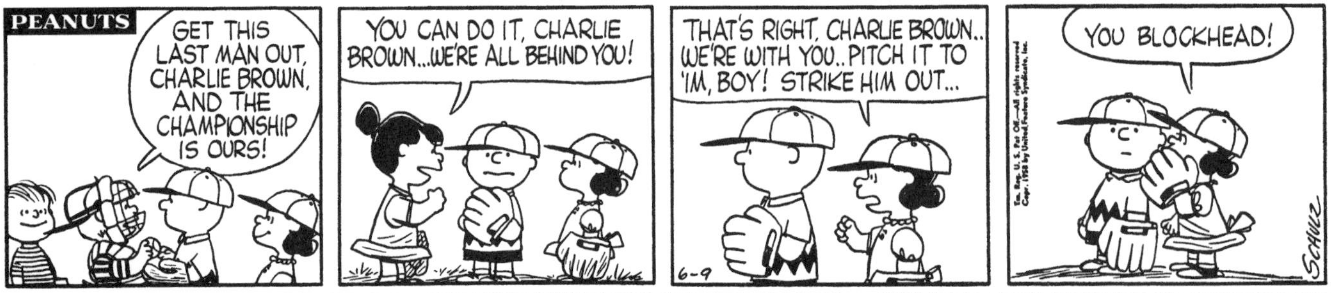
PEANUTS
GET THIS LAST MAN OUT, CHARLIE BROWN, AND THE CHAMPIONSHIP IS OURS!
YOU CAN DO IT, CHARLIE BROWN...WE'RE ALL BEHIND YOU!
THAT'S RIGHT, CHARLIE BROWN.. WE'RE WITH YOU..PITCH IT TO 'IM, BOY! STRIKE HIM OUT...
6-9
YOU BLOCKHEAD!
SCHULZ

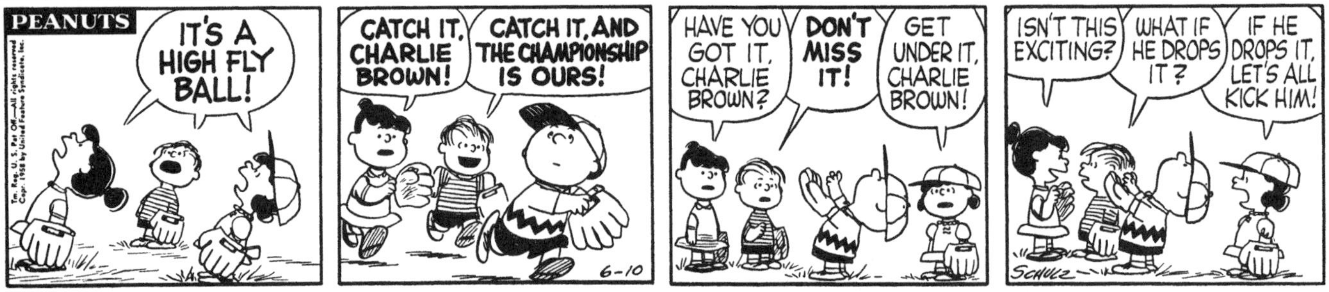
PEANUTS
IT'S A HIGH FLY BALL!
CATCH IT, CHARLIE BROWN!
CATCH IT, AND THE CHAMPIONSHIP IS OURS!
6-10
HAVE YOU GOT IT, CHARLIE BROWN?
DON'T MISS IT!
GET UNDER IT, CHARLIE BROWN!
ISN'T THIS EXCITING?
WHAT IF HE DROPS IT?
IF HE DROPS IT, LET'S ALL KICK HIM!
SCHULZ

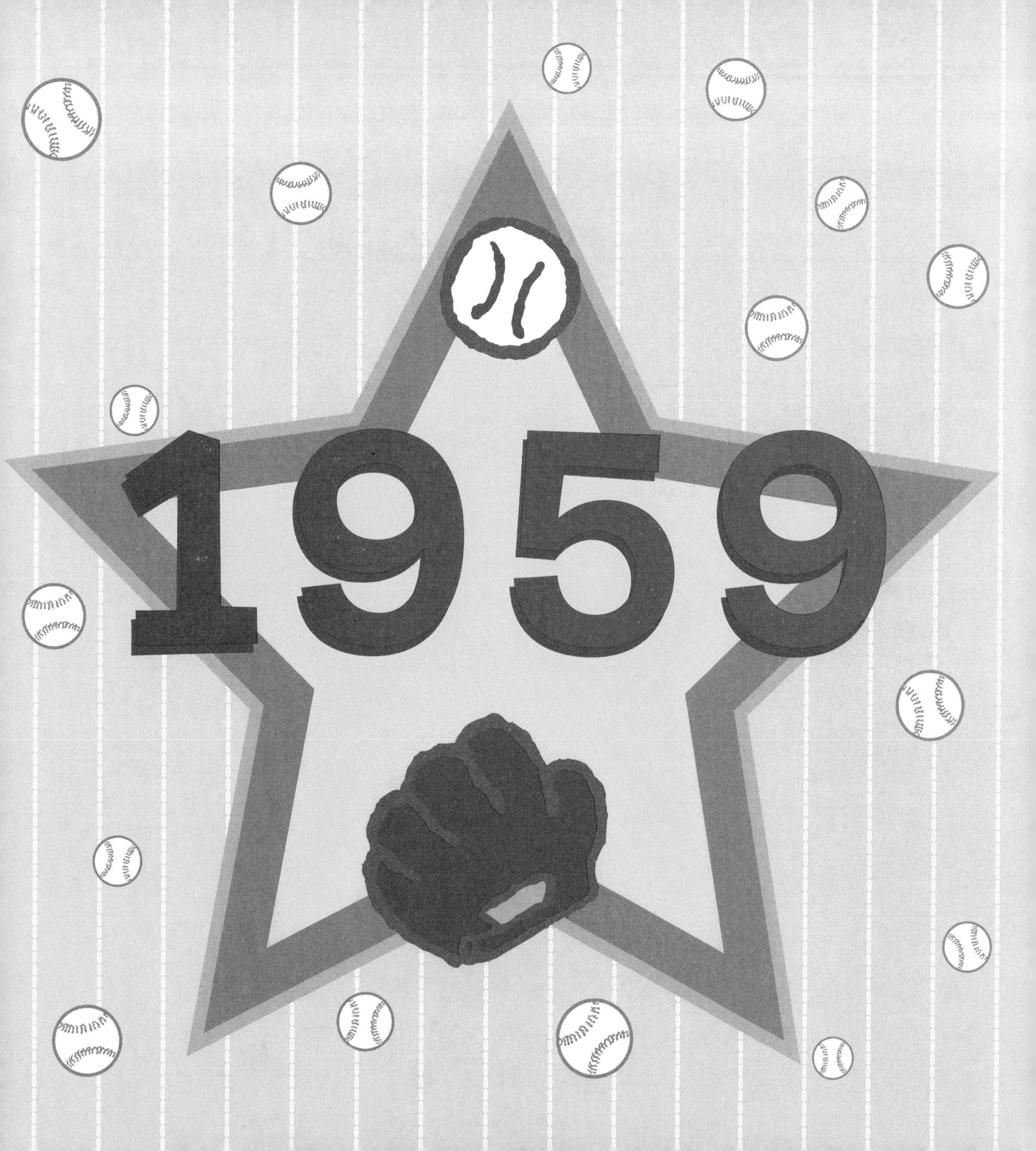
1959

PEANUTS
HI, MANAGER! I'M RARIN' TO GO!! I'M LOOKING FORWARD TO A GREAT SEASON!
YES, SIR...I'VE BEEN THINKING ABOUT NOTHING BUT BASEBALL FOR WEEKS NOW...YES, SIR...
DO YOU THINK MINNEAPOLIS WILL TAKE THE YANKEES THIS YEAR?
4-14
SOME MANAGER! HE ISN'T EVEN INTERESTED IN BASEBALL TALK!
SCHULZ

PEANUTS
WHAT DOES THAT LETTER "M" STAND FOR ON CHARLIE BROWN'S SHIRT?
YOU GOT ME..MAYBE IT STANDS FOR MUSKRAT OR MOLE?
HOW ABOUT MACARONI? OR MACKEREL? OR MAYBE MOUSE? MAGNA CHARTA? MAHLER? MAJOR? MAMMOTH CAVE?
4-18
HI, MANAGER... HOW'S EVERYTHING GOING?
I CAN'T STAND IT.. I JUST CAN'T STAND IT...
SCHULZ

PEANUTS
Tm. Reg. U. S. Pat Off.—All rights reserved Copr. 1959 by United Feature Syndicate, Inc.
ALL RIGHT, NOW THIS IS WHAT WE CALL "SLIDING PRACTICE"!
I WANT EACH OF YOU TO COME INTO THIRD BASE AND DO THE BEST SLIDE YOU CAN!
4-21
EVERY TEAM HAS TO HAVE A CLOWN..
SCHULZ

PEANUTS
WELL, HOW DID PRACTICE GO TODAY LUCY?
FINE...I'VE BEEN CHASING FLY BALLS, AND GETTING IN A LITTLE BATTING PRACTICE..
4-23
OH, INCIDENTALLY, HERE'S MY BILL FOR THREE DOLLARS AND SEVENTY-FIVE CENTS..
Tm. Reg. U. S. Pat. Off.—All rights reserved Copr. 1959 by United Feature Syndicate, Inc.
I DON'T PLAY BASEBALL FOR NOTHING, YOU KNOW!
SCHULZ

PEANUTS
OUR FIRST GAME IS MONDAY, AND I CAN'T SLEEP...I'M A NERVOUS WRECK..
I CAN'T SLEEP... I KEEP THINKING ABOUT ALL THE ERRORS I'M LIABLE TO MAKE.. I'M NO CATCHER.. I'M A PIANO PLAYER!
Tm. Reg. U. S. Pat. Off.—All rights reserved Copr. 1959 by United Feature Syndicate, Inc.
IT'S TWO O'CLOCK, AND I'M STILL AWAKE...I WONDER IF ANY OF THE OTHERS ON THE TEAM ARE HAVING TROUBLE SLEEPING?
4-25
SCHULZ

PEANUTS
Tm. Reg. U. S. Pat. Off.—All rights reserved Copr. 1959 by United Feature Syndicate, Inc.
NO BASEBALL GAME TODAY, CHARLIE BROWN..
IF IT KEEPS ON RAINING, WE MAY NEVER GET TO PLAY..
THAT'S TRUE..
4-28
..AND IF WE NEVER GET TO PLAY, WE WON'T EVER GET BEATEN..
THAT'S TRUE..
C'MON, RAIN!!
SCHULZ

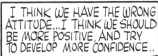

PEANUTS
SOMEHOW IT DOESN'T SEEM RIGHT TO ORGANIZE A BASEBALL TEAM, AND THEN HOPE FOR IT TO RAIN EVERY DAY SO YOU WON'T HAVE TO GO OUT, AND GET BEATEN!
I THINK WE HAVE THE WRONG ATTITUDE...I THINK WE SHOULD BE MORE POSITIVE, AND TRY TO DEVELOP MORE CONFIDENCE..
Tm. Reg. U. S. Pat. Off.—All rights reserved Copr. 1959 by United Feature Syndicate, Inc.
4-29
BOY, I HOPE IT RAINS AGAIN TOMORROW!
SCHULZ

PEANUTS
Tm. Reg. U. S. Pat. Off.—All rights reserved Copr. 1959 by United Feature Syndicate, Inc.
SIX HUNDRED TO NOTHING!!
IT WAS YOUR FAULT WE LOST! YOU'RE THE MANAGER, AND WHEN A TEAM LOSES, IT'S THE MANAGER'S FAULT!
SIX HUNDRED TO NOTHING! GOOD GRIEF!!
5-1
WHY DIDN'T YOU USE SOME STRATEGY?
SCHULZ

PEANUTS
Tm. Reg. U. S. Pat. Off.—All rights reserved Copr. 1959 by United Feature Syndicate, Inc.
"..AND THEN WENT ON TO WIN BY THE OVERWHELMING SCORE OF SIX HUNDRED TO NOTHING."
"WITH SUPERB PITCHING AND POWERFUL HITTING, THEY COMPLETELY DOMINATED THEIR HAPLESS OPPOSITION."
"HAPLESS OPPOSITION"... SIGH THE SPORTS PAGE IS THE CRUELEST PAGE IN THE PAPER..
5-2
SCHULZ

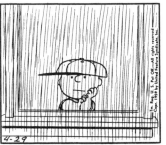

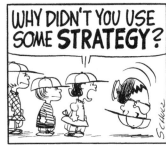

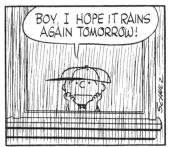

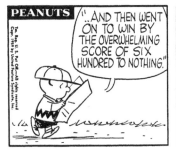

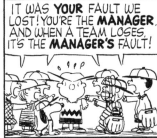

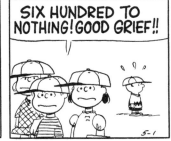

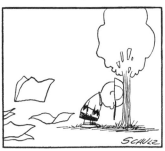

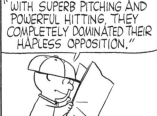

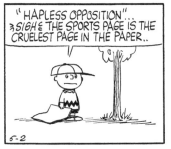

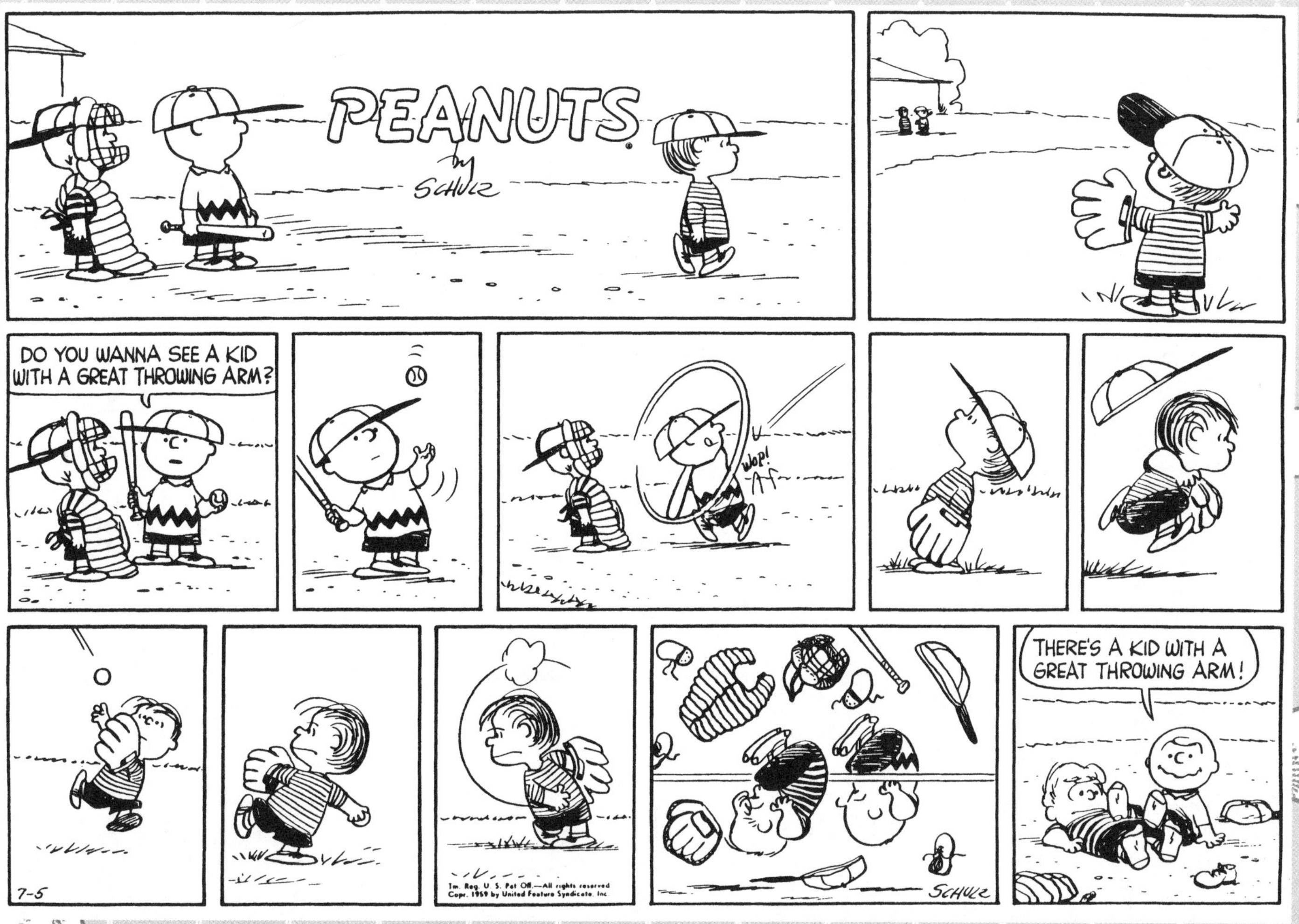
PEANUTS
by SCHULZ
DO YOU WANNA SEE A KID WITH A GREAT THROWING ARM?
WOP!
7-5
Tm. Reg. U. S. Pat. Off.—All rights reserved
Copr. 1959 by United Feature Syndicate, Inc.
SCHULZ
THERE'S A KID WITH A GREAT THROWING ARM!

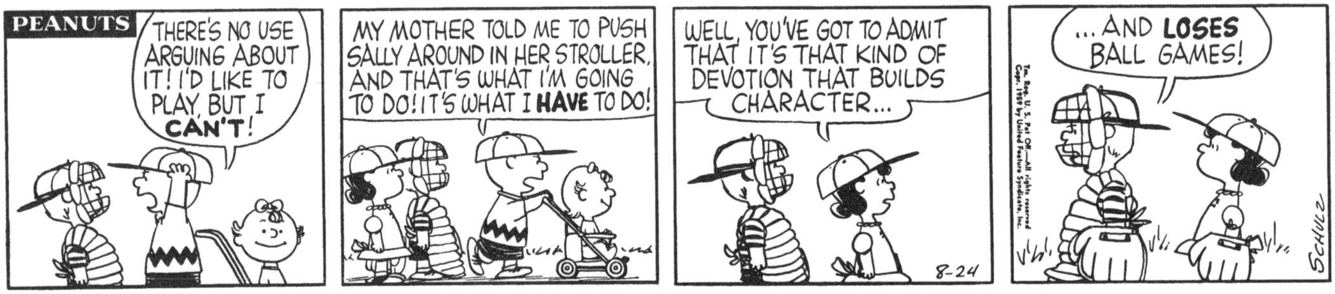
PEANUTS
THERE'S NO USE ARGUING ABOUT IT! I'D LIKE TO PLAY, BUT I CAN'T!
MY MOTHER TOLD ME TO PUSH SALLY AROUND IN HER STROLLER, AND THAT'S WHAT I'M GOING TO DO! IT'S WHAT I HAVE TO DO!
WELL, YOU'VE GOT TO ADMIT THAT IT'S THAT KIND OF DEVOTION THAT BUILDS CHARACTER...
...AND LOSES BALL GAMES!
Tm. Reg. U. S. Pat. Off.—All rights reserved Copr. 1959 by United Feature Syndicate, Inc.
8-24
SCHULZ

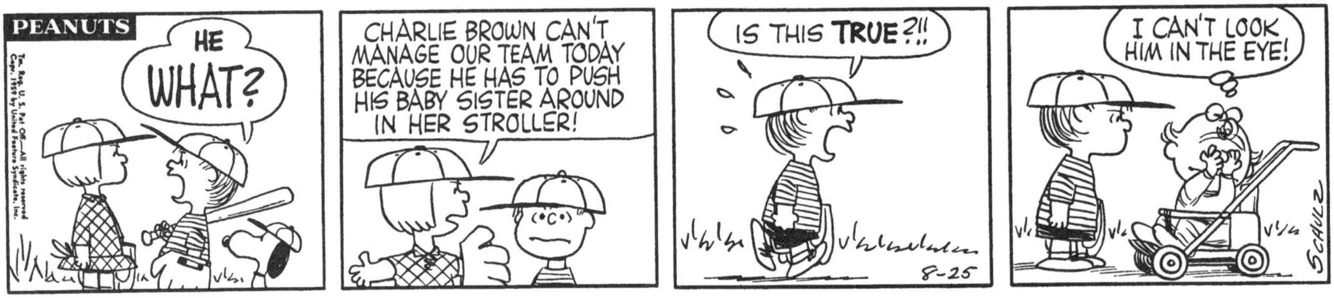
PEANUTS
HE WHAT?
Tm. Reg. U. S. Pat. Off.—All rights reserved Copr. 1959 by United Feature Syndicate, Inc.
CHARLIE BROWN CAN'T MANAGE OUR TEAM TODAY BECAUSE HE HAS TO PUSH HIS BABY SISTER AROUND IN HER STROLLER!
IS THIS TRUE?!!
8-25
I CAN'T LOOK HIM IN THE EYE!
SCHULZ

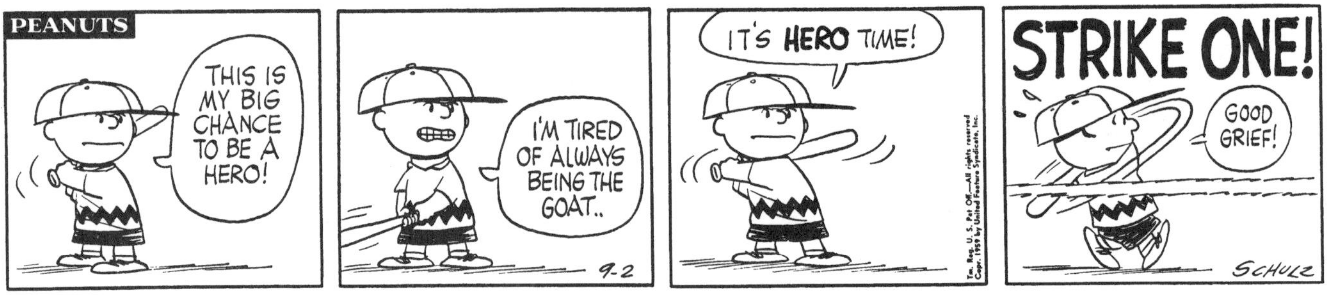
PEANUTS
THIS IS MY BIG CHANCE TO BE A HERO!
I'M TIRED OF ALWAYS BEING THE GOAT..
9-2
IT'S HERO TIME!
Tm. Reg. U. S. Pat. Off.—All rights reserved Copr. 1959 by United Feature Syndicate, Inc.
STRIKE ONE!
GOOD GRIEF!
SCHULZ

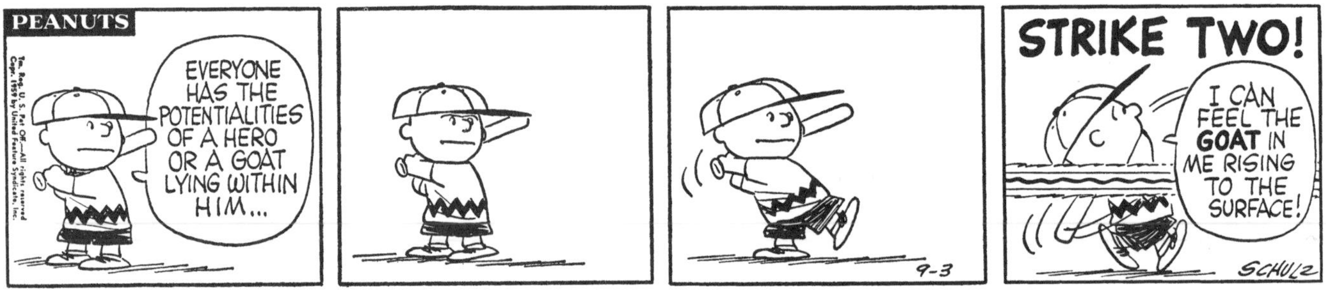
PEANUTS
Tm. Reg. U. S. Pat. Off.—All rights reserved Copr. 1959 by United Feature Syndicate, Inc.
EVERYONE HAS THE POTENTIALITIES OF A HERO OR A GOAT LYING WITHIN HIM...
9-3
STRIKE TWO!
I CAN FEEL THE GOAT IN ME RISING TO THE SURFACE!
SCHULZ

PEANUTS
Tm. Reg. U. S. Pat Off.—All rights reserved
Copr. 1959 by United Feature Syndicate, Inc.
IT ONLY TAKES ONE TO HIT IT.. IT ONLY TAKES ONE TO HIT IT!
THE GAME IS NEVER OVER UNTIL THE LAST MAN IS OUT! I CAN STILL BE A HERO..
9-4
IT ONLY TAKES ONE TO HIT IT...
STRIKE THREE!
THAT WASN'T THE ONE!
SCHULZ

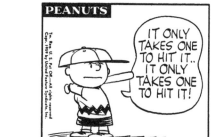

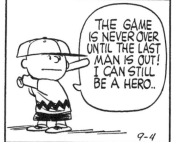

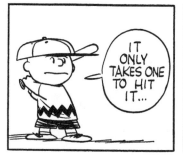

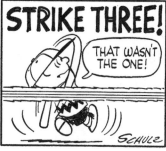

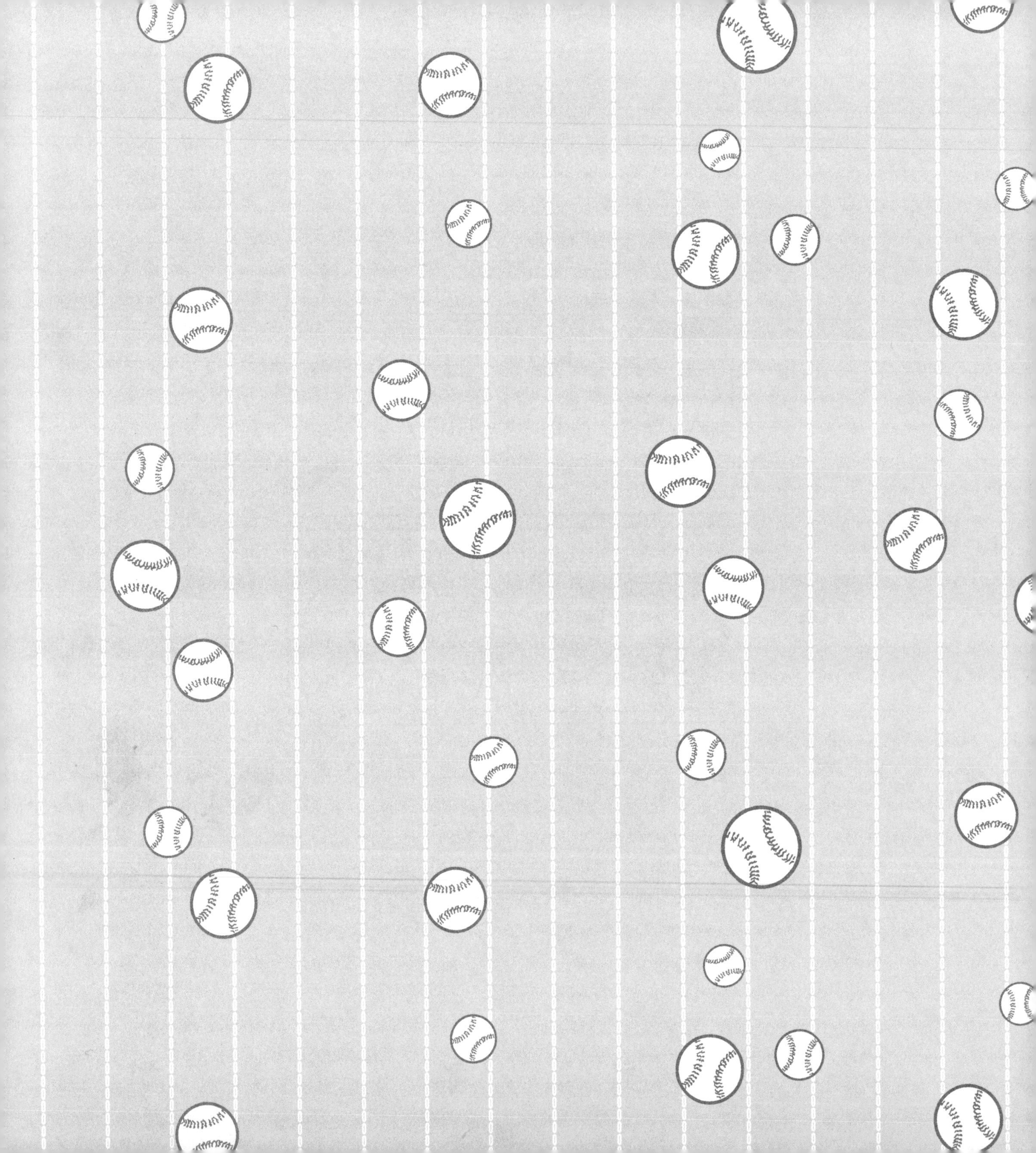

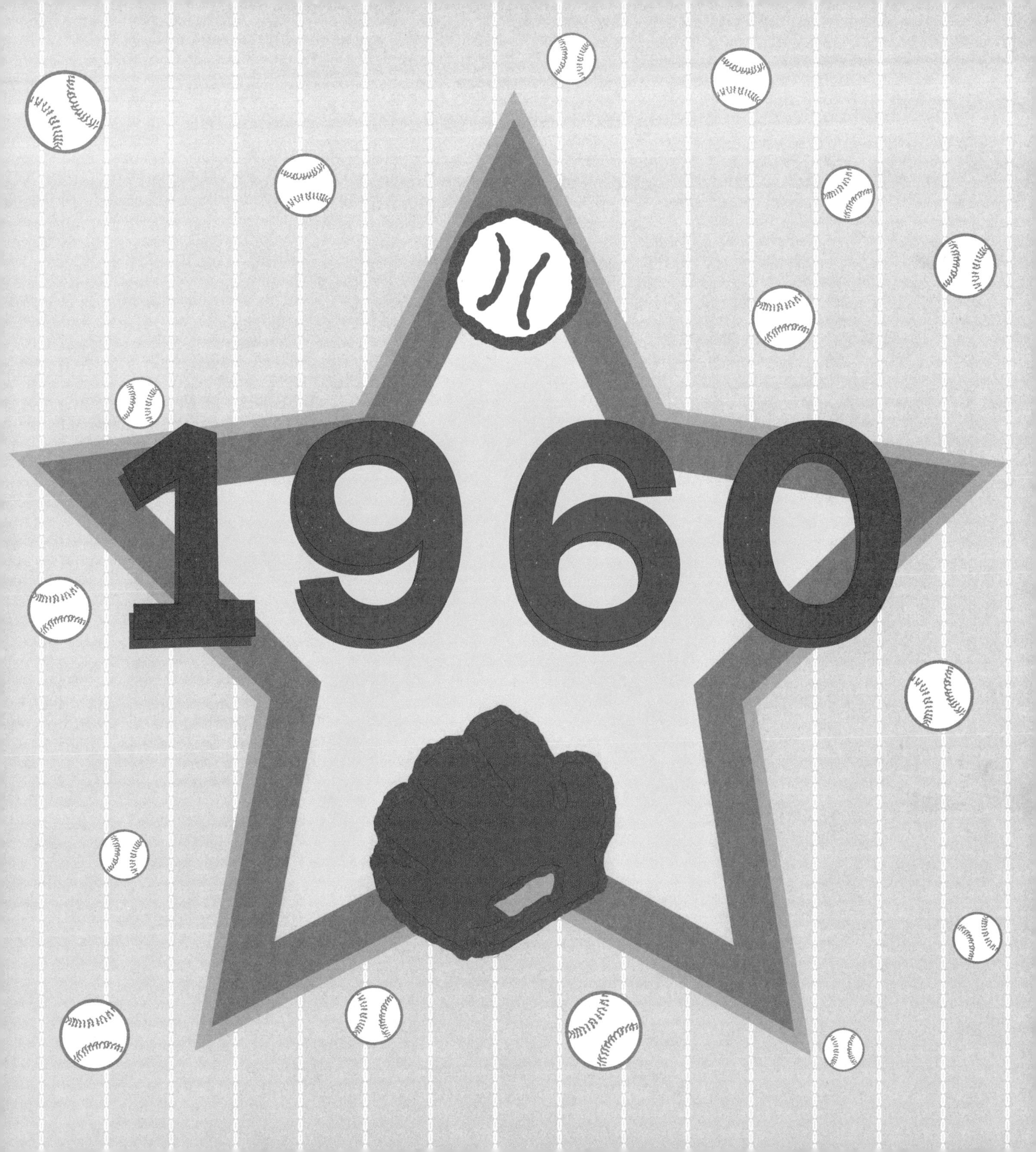
1960

PEANUTS
by SCHULZ

Panel 1: HI, SNOOPY...HI SHERMY...GLAD YOU MADE IT.. HI, PIG-PEN... HI,VIOLET...HOW'S THE WORLD'S PRETTIEST THIRD BASEMAN? HI, LINUS...HI, LUCY... HI, PATTY...HI, SCHROEDER...HOW'S THE OL' THROWIN' ARM?

Panel 2: WELL, IT'S REAL GOOD SEEING YOU ALL HERE READY TO BEGIN THE NEW BASEBALL SEASON...

Panel 3: DUE TO THE RAIN TODAY, WE WILL FOLLOW THE INCLEMENT WEATHER SCHEDULE...THIS MEANS STUDYING OUR SIGNALS..

Panel 4: NOW A GOOD BASEBALL TEAM FUNCTIONS ON THE KNOWLEDGE OF ITS SIGNALS.. THIS YEAR WE WILL TRY TO KEEP THEM SIMPLE...

Panel 5: IF I TOUCH MY CAP LIKE THIS, IT MEANS FOR WHOEVER HAPPENS TO BE ON BASE TO TRY TO STEAL..

Panel 6: IF I CLAP MY HANDS, IT MEANS THE BATTER IS TO HIT STRAIGHT AWAY, BUT IF I PUT THEM ON MY HIPS, THEN HE OR SHE IS TO BUNT...

Panel 7: IF I WALK UP AND DOWN IN THE COACHING BOX, IT MEANS FOR THE BATTER TO WAIT OUT THE PITCHER.. IN OTHER WORDS, TO TRY FOR A WALK....

Panel 8: BUT NOW, AFTER ALL IS SAID AND DONE, IT MUST BE ADMITTED THAT SIGNALS ALONE NEVER WON A BALL GAME...

Panel 9: IT'S THE SPIRIT OF THE TEAM THAT COUNTS! THE **INTEREST** THAT THE PLAYERS SHOW IN THEIR TEAM! AM I RIGHT?

Panel 10: I SAID, AM I RIGHT?

Panel 11: (Charlie Brown alone)

3-27

Tm Reg. U. S. Pat. Off.—All rights reserved
Copr. 1960 by United Feature Syndicate, Inc.

Panel 12: YOU'RE RIGHT... *SIGH*

SCHULZ

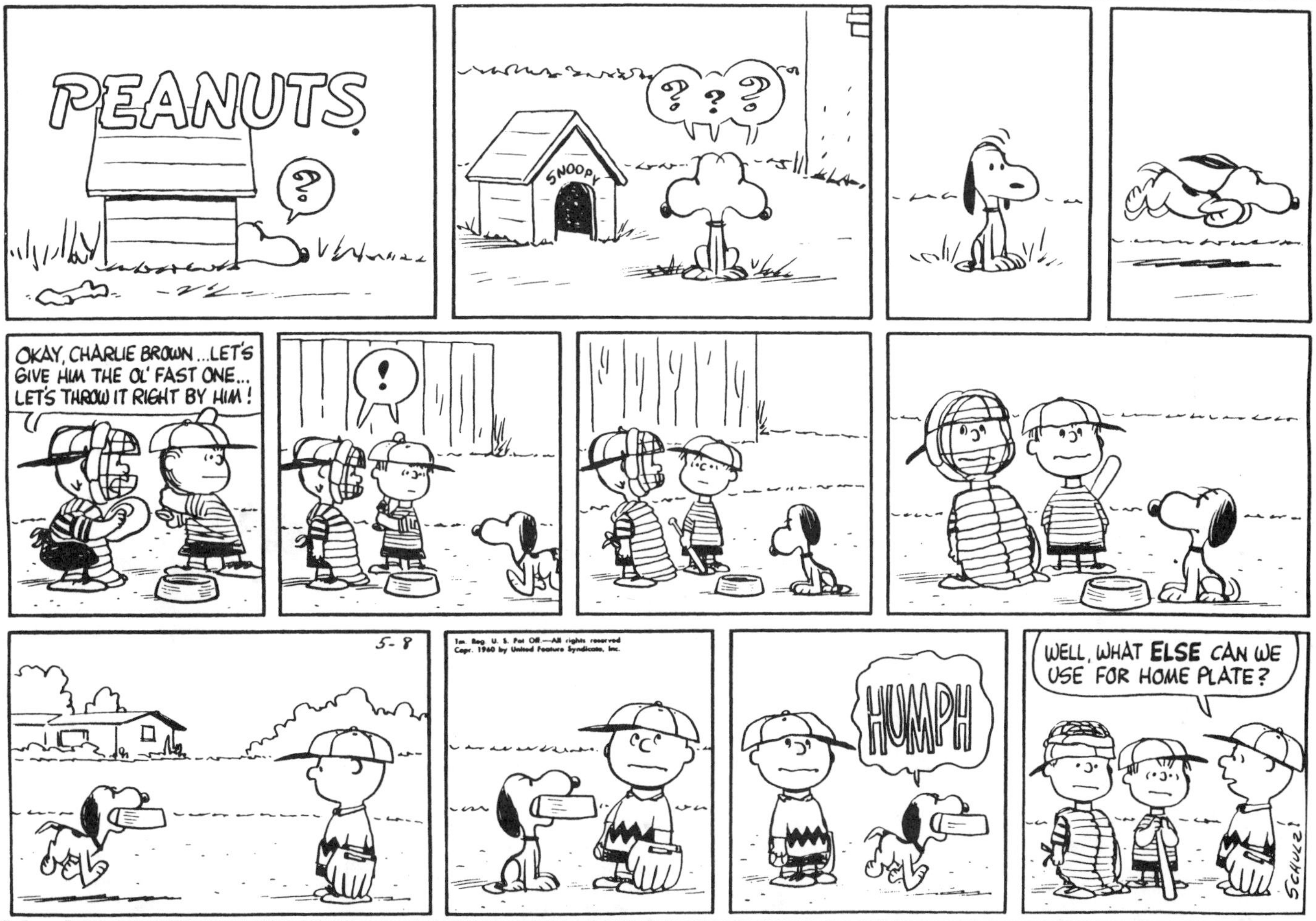
PEANUTS
?
SNOOPY
? ? ?
OKAY, CHARLIE BROWN...LET'S GIVE HIM THE OL' FAST ONE... LET'S THROW IT RIGHT BY HIM!
!
5-8
Tm. Reg. U. S. Pat. Off.—All rights reserved
Copr. 1960 by United Feature Syndicate, Inc.
HUMPH
WELL, WHAT **ELSE** CAN WE USE FOR HOME PLATE?
SCHULZ

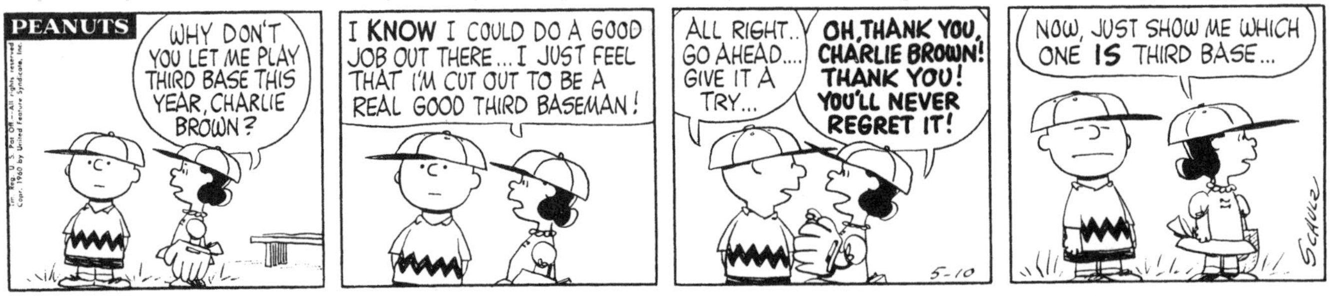
PEANUTS
Tm. Reg. U. S. Pat. Off.—All rights reserved Copr. 1960 by United Feature Syndicate, Inc.
WHY DON'T YOU LET ME PLAY THIRD BASE THIS YEAR, CHARLIE BROWN?
I KNOW I COULD DO A GOOD JOB OUT THERE... I JUST FEEL THAT I'M CUT OUT TO BE A REAL GOOD THIRD BASEMAN!
ALL RIGHT.. GO AHEAD.... GIVE IT A TRY...
OH, THANK YOU, CHARLIE BROWN! THANK YOU! YOU'LL NEVER REGRET IT!
5-10
NOW, JUST SHOW ME WHICH ONE IS THIRD BASE...
SCHULZ

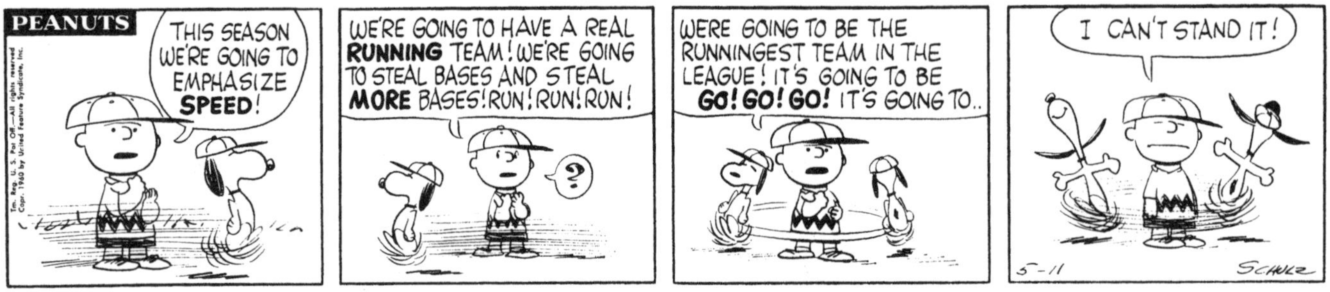
PEANUTS
THIS SEASON WE'RE GOING TO EMPHASIZE SPEED!
WE'RE GOING TO HAVE A REAL RUNNING TEAM! WE'RE GOING TO STEAL BASES AND STEAL MORE BASES! RUN! RUN! RUN!
?
WERE GOING TO BE THE RUNNINGEST TEAM IN THE LEAGUE! IT'S GOING TO BE GO! GO! GO! IT'S GOING TO..
I CAN'T STAND IT!
5-11
SCHULZ

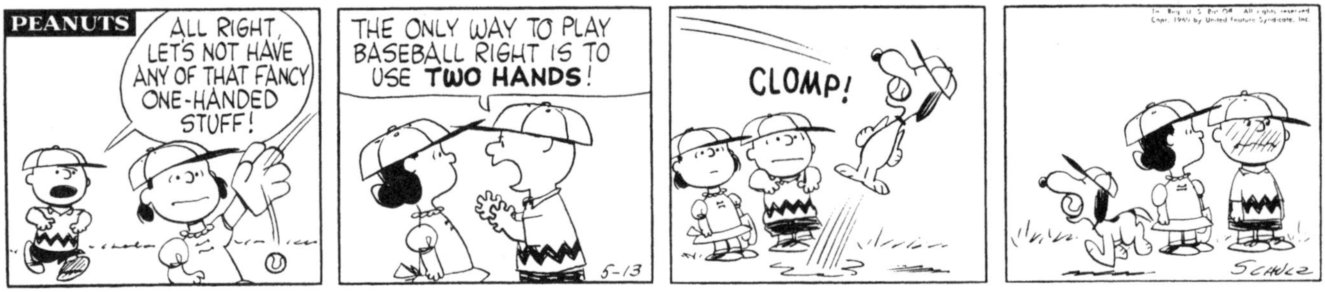
PEANUTS
ALL RIGHT, LET'S NOT HAVE ANY OF THAT FANCY ONE-HANDED STUFF!
THE ONLY WAY TO PLAY BASEBALL RIGHT IS TO USE TWO HANDS!
5-13
CLOMP!
SCHULZ

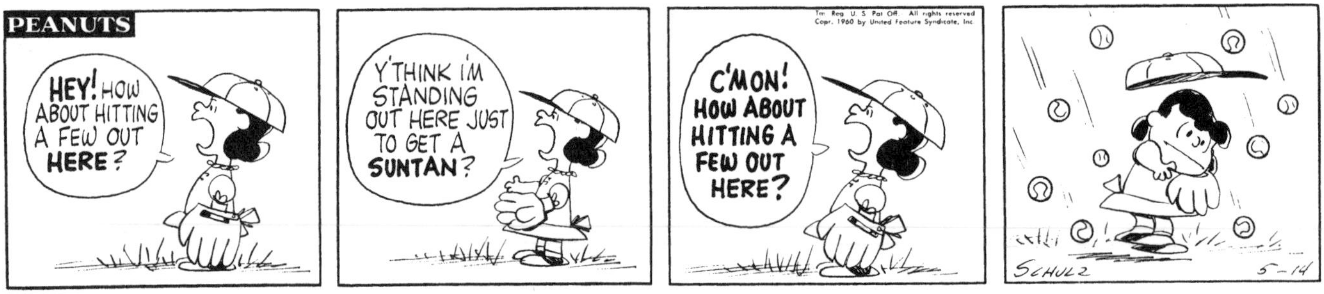
PEANUTS
HEY! HOW ABOUT HITTING A FEW OUT HERE?
Y'THINK I'M STANDING OUT HERE JUST TO GET A SUNTAN?
Tm Reg U S Pat Off All rights reserved Copr. 1960 by United Feature Syndicate, Inc.
C'MON! HOW ABOUT HITTING A FEW OUT HERE?
SCHULZ
5-14

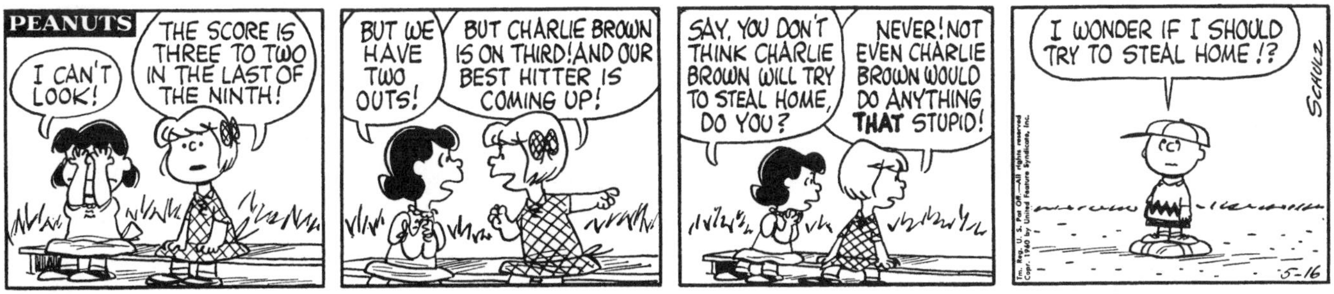
PEANUTS
I CAN'T LOOK!
THE SCORE IS THREE TO TWO IN THE LAST OF THE NINTH!
BUT WE HAVE TWO OUTS!
BUT CHARLIE BROWN IS ON THIRD! AND OUR BEST HITTER IS COMING UP!
SAY, YOU DON'T THINK CHARLIE BROWN WILL TRY TO STEAL HOME, DO YOU?
NEVER! NOT EVEN CHARLIE BROWN WOULD DO ANYTHING THAT STUPID!
I WONDER IF I SHOULD TRY TO STEAL HOME !?
SCHULZ
5-16

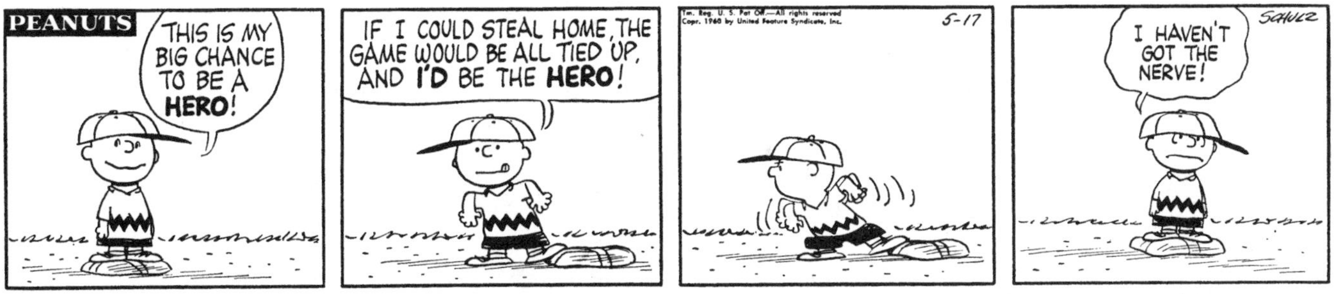
PEANUTS
THIS IS MY BIG CHANCE TO BE A HERO!
IF I COULD STEAL HOME, THE GAME WOULD BE ALL TIED UP, AND I'D BE THE HERO!
Tm. Reg. U. S. Pat Off.—All rights reserved Copr. 1960 by United Feature Syndicate, Inc.
5-17
SCHULZ
I HAVEN'T GOT THE NERVE!

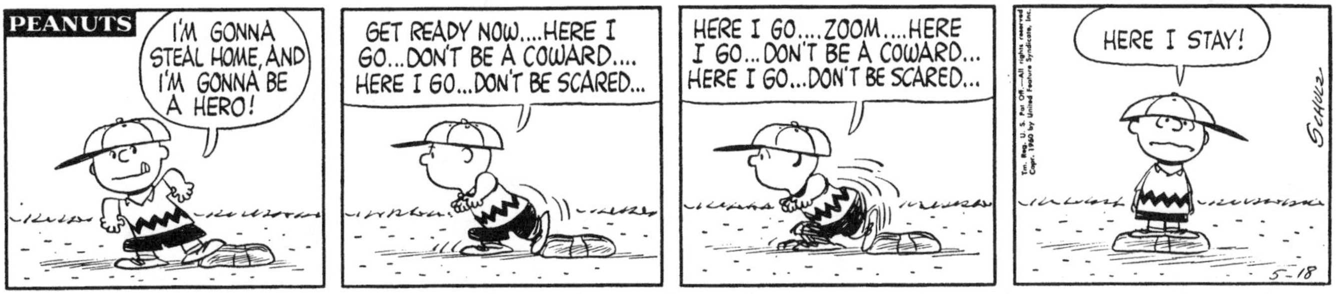
PEANUTS
I'M GONNA STEAL HOME, AND I'M GONNA BE A HERO!
GET READY NOW....HERE I GO...DON'T BE A COWARD.... HERE I GO...DON'T BE SCARED...
HERE I GO....ZOOM....HERE I GO...DON'T BE A COWARD... HERE I GO...DON'T BE SCARED...
HERE I STAY!
SCHULZ
5-18

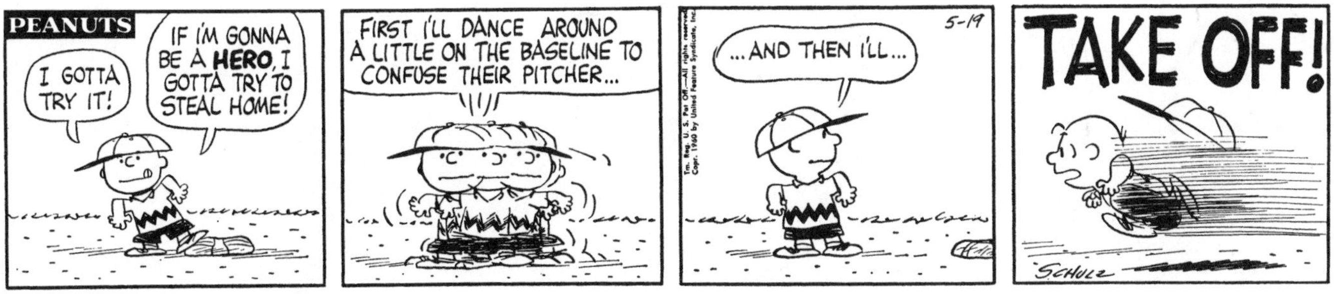
PEANUTS
I GOTTA TRY IT!
IF I'M GONNA BE A HERO, I GOTTA TRY TO STEAL HOME!
FIRST I'LL DANCE AROUND A LITTLE ON THE BASELINE TO CONFUSE THEIR PITCHER...
5-19
...AND THEN I'LL...
TAKE OFF!
SCHULZ

PEANUTS
CHARLIE BROWN IS TRYING TO STEAL HOME!!
SLIDE, CHARLIE BROWN! SLIDE!
Tm. Reg. U. S. Pat Off.—All rights reserved
Copr. 1960 by United Feature Syndicate, Inc.
OH, YOU BLOCKHEAD!
SCHULZ
5-20

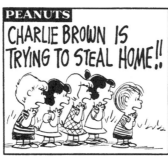

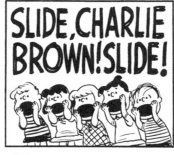

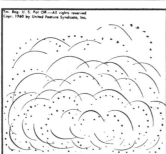

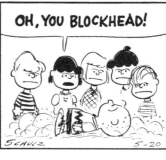

PEANUTS
WHAAAH! WE LOST THE GAME ALL BECAUSE OF CHARLIE BROWN WHHAAAAAHHH!!
WAS I OUT?
OUT?! WHY, YOU BLOCKHEAD, YOU DIDN'T EVEN GET HALF WAY HOME!
Tm. Reg. U. S. Pat Off.---All rights reserved Copr. 1960 by United Feature Syndicate, Inc.
RATS!
SCHULZ
5-21

PEANUTS
WHY DID I HAVE TO GO AND TRY TO STEAL HOME?
WHY? WHY? WHY?
Tm. Reg. U. S. Pat. Off.—All rights reserved
Copr. 1960 by United Feature Syndicate, Inc.
WHY? WHY? WHY? WHY?
I THOUGHT I HEARD A CRY OF ANGUISH..
WHY? WHY? WHY? WHY? WHY?

PEANUTS
WHY DIDN'T I JUST WAIT ON THIRD BASE? WHY DID I HAVE TO TRY TO STEAL HOME?!
WHY? WHY? WHY? WHY?
CHARLIE BROWN?
I HAVE BEEN ASKED TO TELL YOU THAT YOUR CRIES OF ANGUISH ARE KEEPING THE WHOLE NEIGHBORHOOD AWAKE!
WHY? WHY? WHY? WHY?

PEANUTS
I DON'T MIND PLAYING RIGHT FIELD
I DON'T MIND STANDING OUT HERE IN WEEDS OVER MY HEAD...REALLY, I DON'T...
I MEAN, IF THIS IS WHERE I CAN DO THE TEAM THE MOST GOOD, THIS IS WHERE I BELONG
THE ONLY THING THAT BOTHERS ME IS I DON'T KNOW IF I'M FACING THE RIGHT WAY!

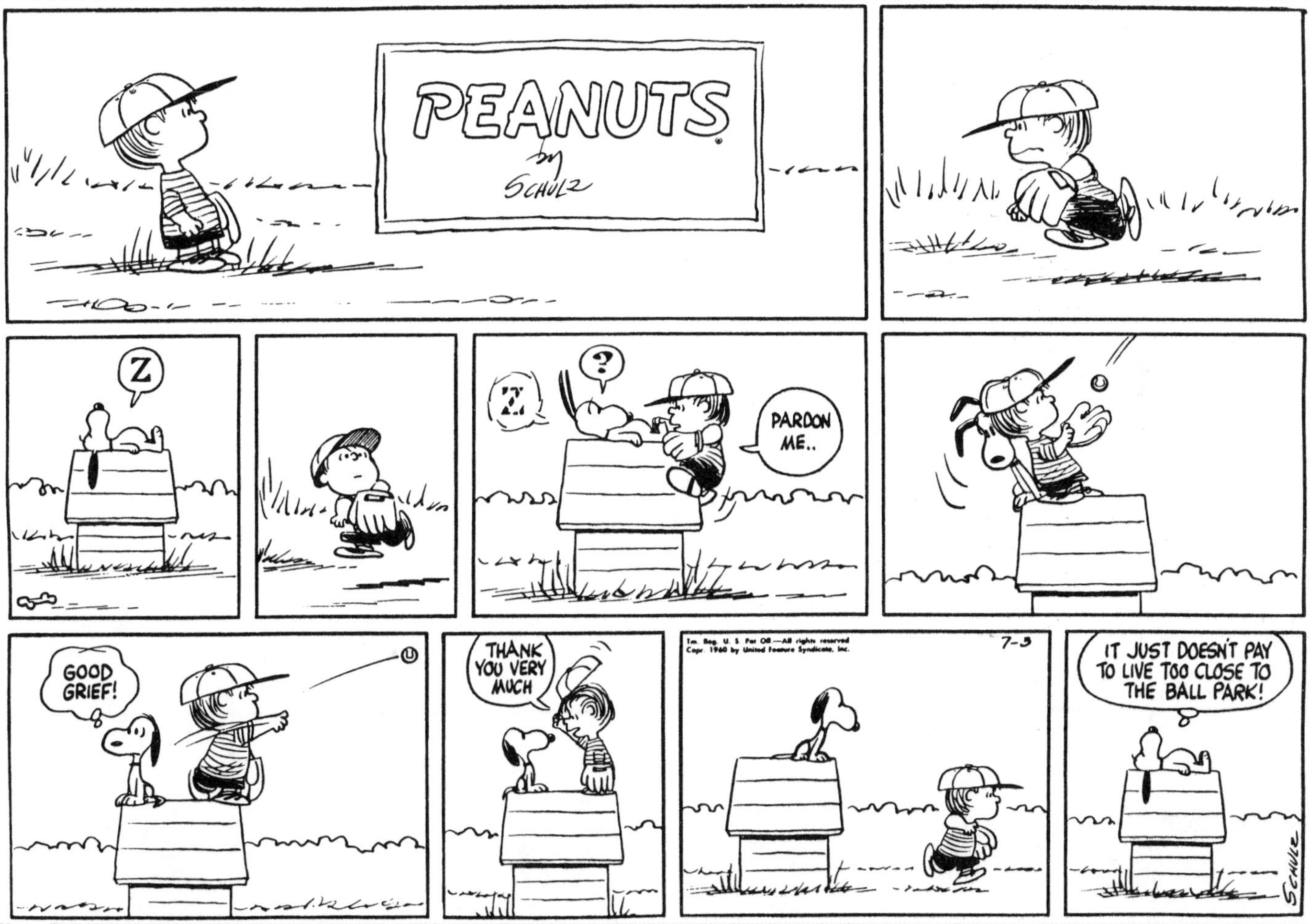
PEANUTS
by SCHULZ
Z
?
Z
PARDON ME..
GOOD GRIEF!
THANK YOU VERY MUCH
Tm. Reg. U. S. Pat. Off.—All rights reserved
Copr. 1960 by United Feature Syndicate, Inc.
7-3
IT JUST DOESN'T PAY TO LIVE TOO CLOSE TO THE BALL PARK!
SCHULZ

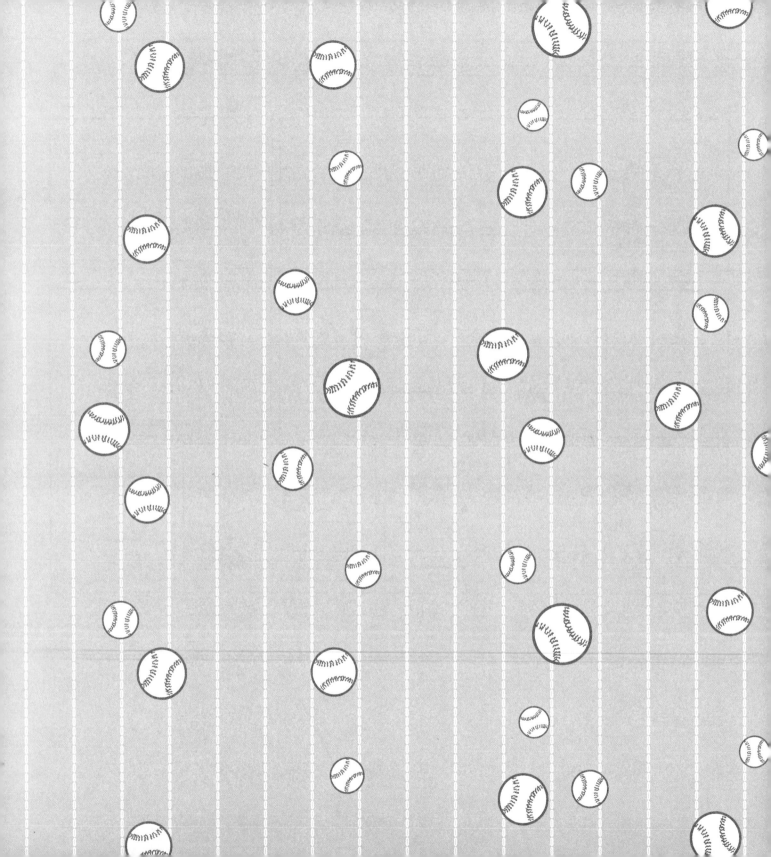

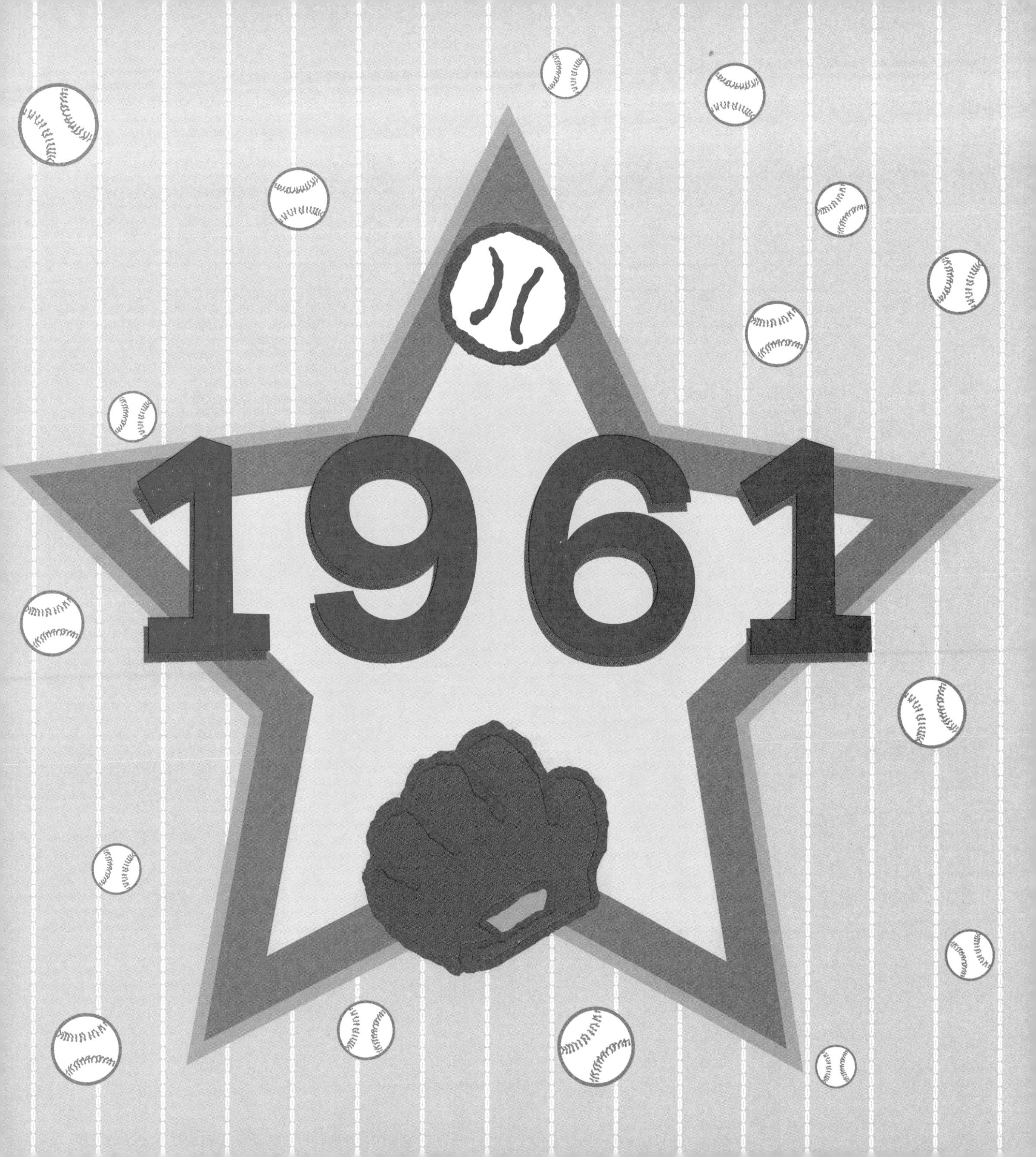
1961

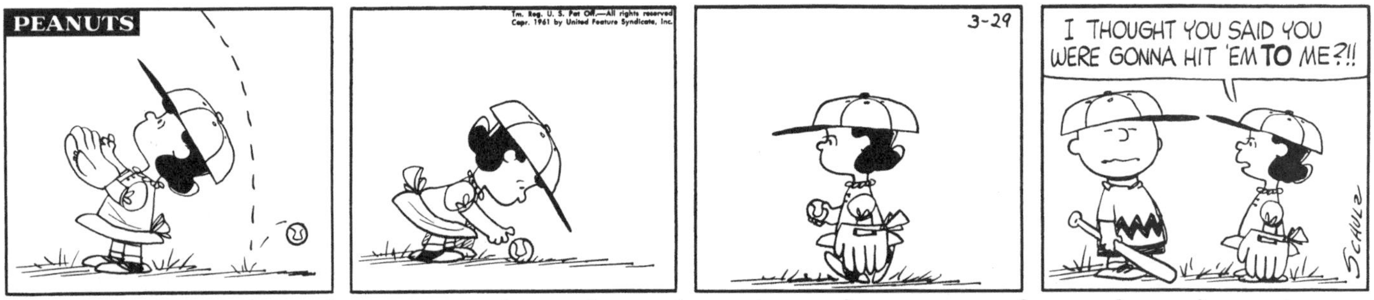
PEANUTS
Tm. Reg. U. S. Pat. Off.—All rights reserved
Copr. 1961 by United Feature Syndicate, Inc.
3-29
I THOUGHT YOU SAID YOU WERE GONNA HIT 'EM **TO** ME?!!
SCHULZ

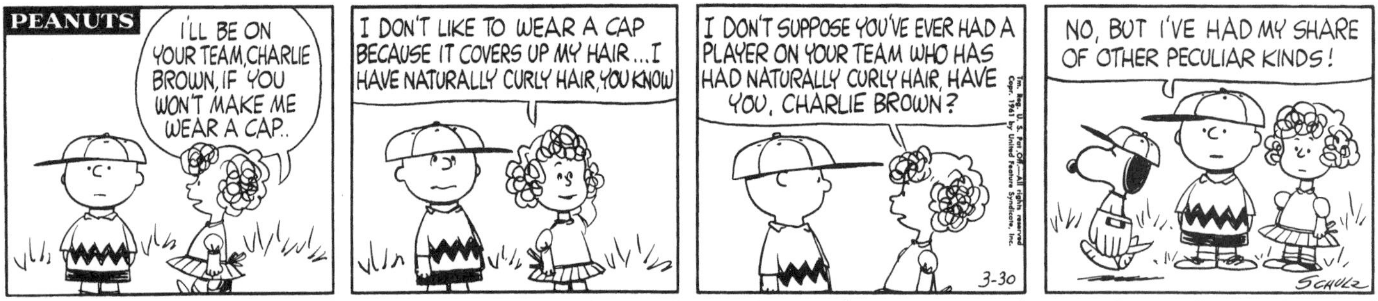
PEANUTS
I'LL BE ON YOUR TEAM, CHARLIE BROWN, IF YOU WON'T MAKE ME WEAR A CAP..
I DON'T LIKE TO WEAR A CAP BECAUSE IT COVERS UP MY HAIR... I HAVE NATURALLY CURLY HAIR, YOU KNOW
I DON'T SUPPOSE YOU'VE EVER HAD A PLAYER ON YOUR TEAM WHO HAS HAD NATURALLY CURLY HAIR, HAVE YOU, CHARLIE BROWN?
Tm. Reg. U. S. Pat. Off.—All rights reserved
Copr. 1961 by United Feature Syndicate, Inc.
3-30
NO, BUT I'VE HAD MY SHARE OF OTHER PECULIAR KINDS!
SCHULZ

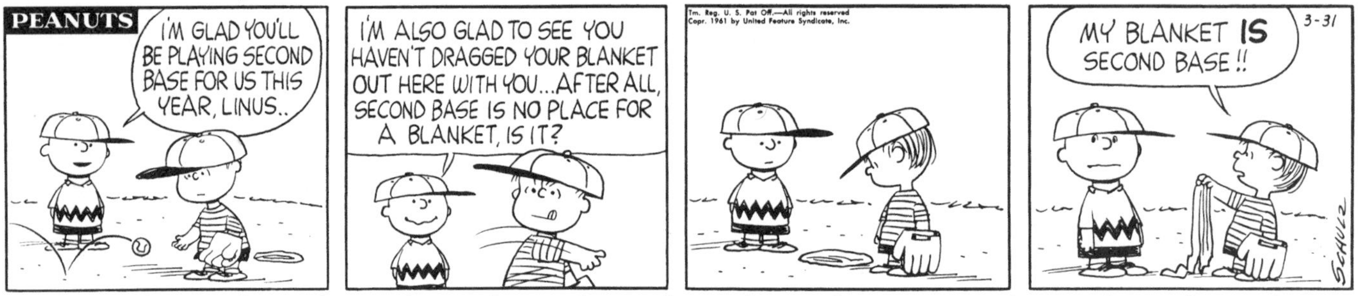
PEANUTS
I'M GLAD YOU'LL BE PLAYING SECOND BASE FOR US THIS YEAR, LINUS..
I'M ALSO GLAD TO SEE YOU HAVEN'T DRAGGED YOUR BLANKET OUT HERE WITH YOU...AFTER ALL, SECOND BASE IS NO PLACE FOR A BLANKET, IS IT?
Tm. Reg. U. S. Pat. Off.—All rights reserved
Copr. 1961 by United Feature Syndicate, Inc.
MY BLANKET **IS** SECOND BASE!!
3-31
SCHULZ

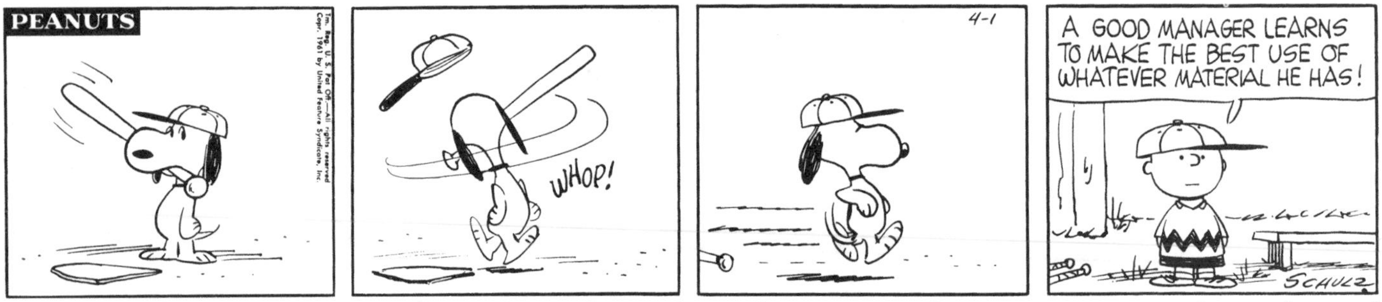
PEANUTS
Tm. Reg. U. S. Pat. Off.—All rights reserved
Copr. 1961 by United Feature Syndicate, Inc.
WHOP!
4-1
A GOOD MANAGER LEARNS TO MAKE THE BEST USE OF WHATEVER MATERIAL HE HAS!
SCHULZ

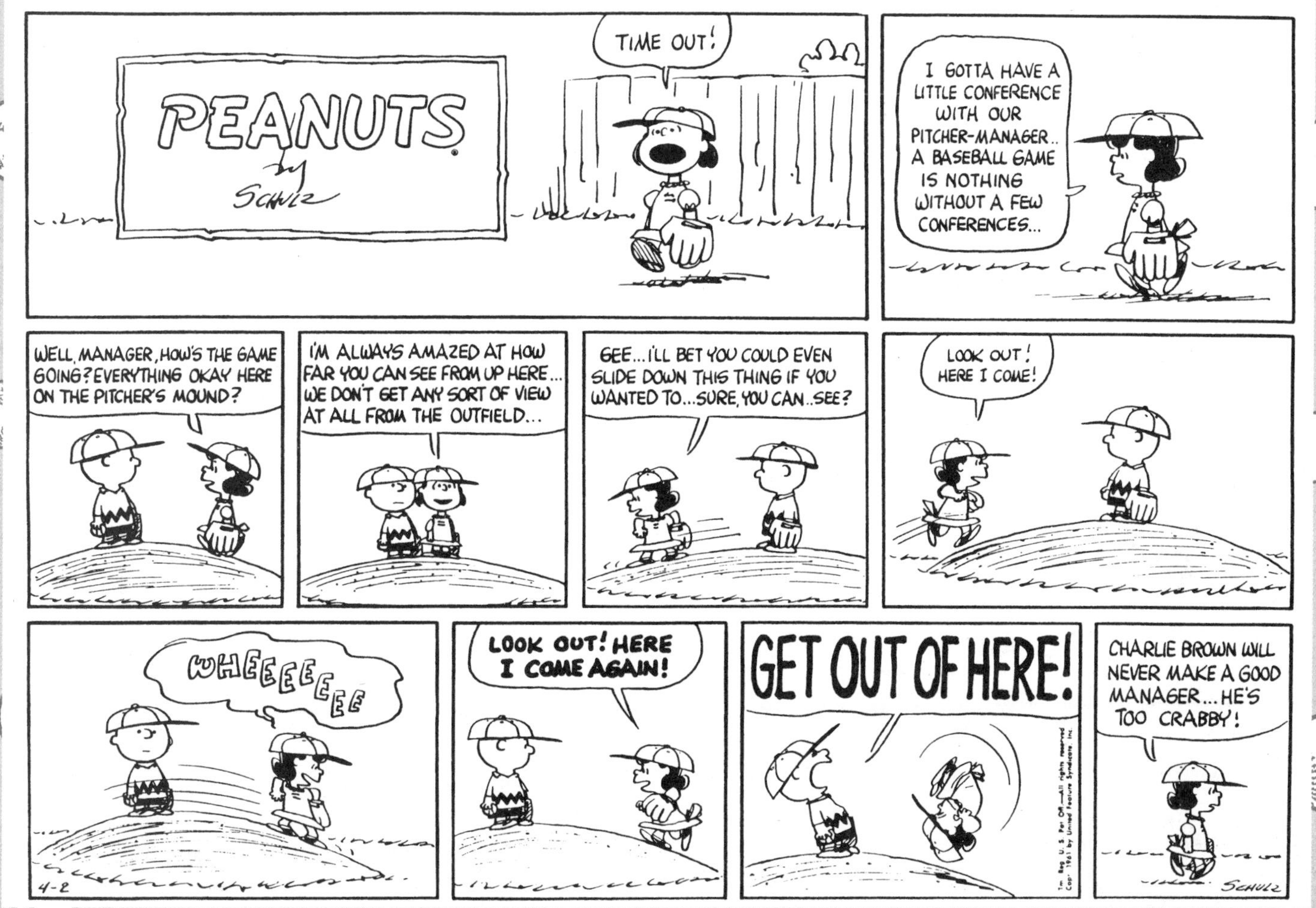
PEANUTS
by SCHULZ
TIME OUT!
I GOTTA HAVE A LITTLE CONFERENCE WITH OUR PITCHER-MANAGER.. A BASEBALL GAME IS NOTHING WITHOUT A FEW CONFERENCES...
WELL, MANAGER, HOW'S THE GAME GOING? EVERYTHING OKAY HERE ON THE PITCHER'S MOUND?
I'M ALWAYS AMAZED AT HOW FAR YOU CAN SEE FROM UP HERE... WE DON'T GET ANY SORT OF VIEW AT ALL FROM THE OUTFIELD...
GEE... I'LL BET YOU COULD EVEN SLIDE DOWN THIS THING IF YOU WANTED TO... SURE, YOU CAN.. SEE?
LOOK OUT! HERE I COME!
WHEEEEEEEE
4-2
LOOK OUT! HERE I COME AGAIN!
GET OUT OF HERE!
Tm Reg. U. S. Pat Off.—All rights reserved
Copr. 1961 by United Feature Syndicate, Inc.
CHARLIE BROWN WILL NEVER MAKE A GOOD MANAGER... HE'S TOO CRABBY!
SCHULZ

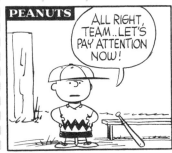

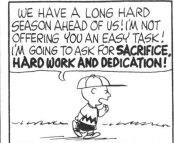

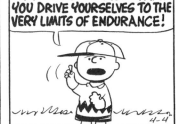

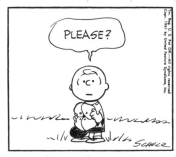

PEANUTS
ALL RIGHT, TEAM..LET'S PAY ATTENTION NOW!
WE HAVE A LONG HARD SEASON AHEAD OF US! I'M NOT OFFERING YOU AN EASY TASK! I'M GOING TO ASK FOR **SACRIFICE, HARD WORK AND DEDICATION!**
I'M GOING TO ASK THAT YOU DRIVE YOURSELVES TO THE VERY LIMITS OF ENDURANCE!
4-4
PLEASE?
Tm. Reg. U. S. Pat. Off.—All rights reserved
Copr. 1961 by United Feature Syndicate, Inc.
SCHULZ

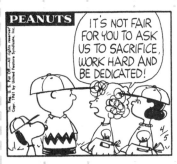

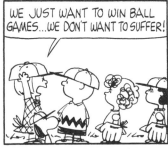

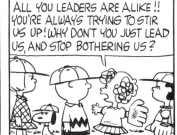

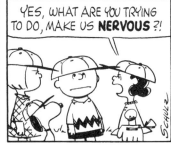

PEANUTS
IT'S NOT FAIR FOR YOU TO ASK US TO SACRIFICE, WORK HARD AND BE DEDICATED!
Tm. Reg. U. S. Pat. Off.—All rights reserved
Copr. 1961 by United Feature Syndicate, Inc.
4/5
WE JUST WANT TO WIN BALL GAMES...WE DON'T WANT TO SUFFER!
ALL YOU LEADERS ARE ALIKE!! YOU'RE ALWAYS TRYING TO STIR US UP! WHY DON'T YOU JUST LEAD US, AND STOP BOTHERING US?
YES, WHAT ARE YOU TRYING TO DO, MAKE US **NERVOUS**?!
SCHULZ

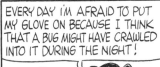

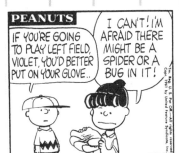

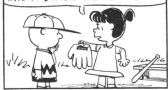

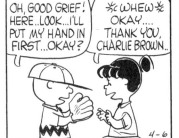

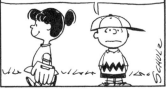

PEANUTS
IF YOU'RE GOING TO PLAY LEFT FIELD, VIOLET, YOU'D BETTER PUT ON YOUR GLOVE..
I CAN'T! I'M AFRAID THERE MIGHT BE A SPIDER OR A BUG IN IT!
Tm. Reg. U. S. Pat. Off.—All rights reserved
Copr. 1961 by United Feature Syndicate, Inc.
EVERY DAY I'M AFRAID TO PUT MY GLOVE ON BECAUSE I THINK THAT A BUG MIGHT HAVE CRAWLED INTO IT DURING THE NIGHT!
OH, GOOD GRIEF! HERE..LOOK...I'LL PUT MY HAND IN FIRST...OKAY?
WHEW OKAY.... THANK YOU, CHARLIE BROWN..
4-6
IN ALL THE HISTORY OF BASEBALL THERE HAS NEVER BEEN A MANAGER WHO HAS HAD TO GO THROUGH WHAT **I** HAVE TO GO THROUGH!
SCHULZ

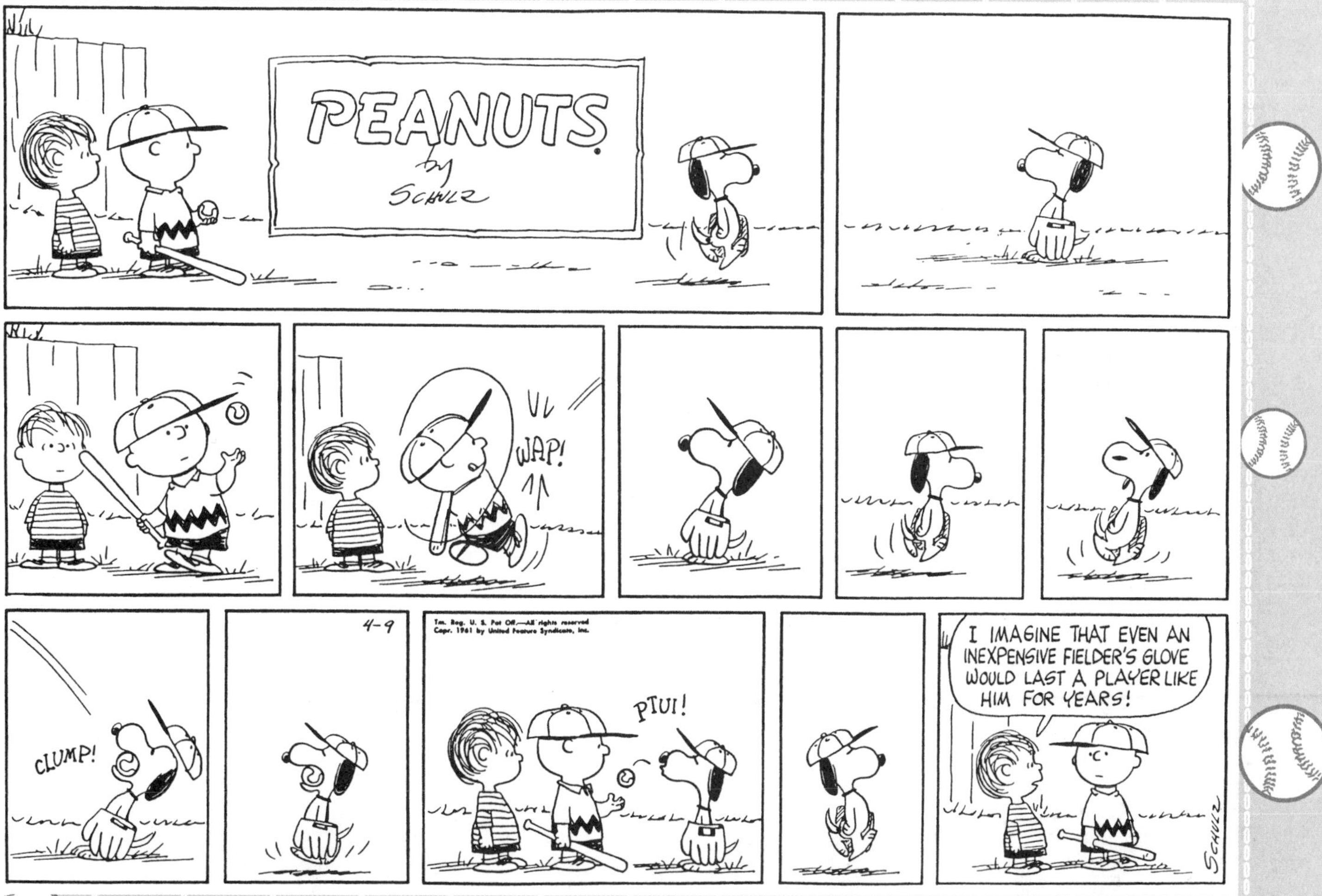
PEANUTS
by
SCHULZ
WAP!
CLUMP!
4-9
Tm. Reg. U. S. Pat Off.—All rights reserved
Copr. 1961 by United Feature Syndicate, Inc.
PTUI!
I IMAGINE THAT EVEN AN INEXPENSIVE FIELDER'S GLOVE WOULD LAST A PLAYER LIKE HIM FOR YEARS!
SCHULZ

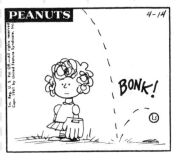

PEANUTS
Tm. Reg. U. S. Pat Off.—All rights reserved
Copr. 1961 by United Feature Syndicate, Inc.
4-14
BONK!
YOU DIDN'T EVEN TRY TO CATCH IT! IT FELL RIGHT NEXT TO YOU!!
THEY SCORED FOUR RUNS!! WHAT'S THE MATTER WITH YOU?!
HOW CAN I PLAY BASEBALL WHEN I'M WORRIED ABOUT FOREIGN POLICY?
SCHULZ

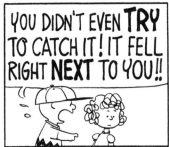

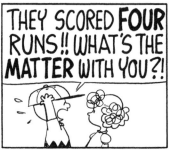

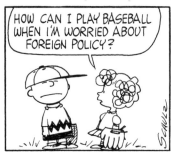

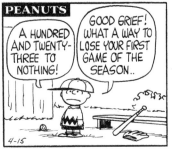

PEANUTS
A HUNDRED AND TWENTY-THREE TO NOTHING!
GOOD GRIEF! WHAT A WAY TO LOSE YOUR FIRST GAME OF THE SEASON..
4-15
WHERE DID EVERYBODY GO?
THEY ALL WENT HOME TO CRY..
SNIF
ALL OF THEM?
ALL OF THEM!
SNIF!
WAAH
SCHULZ
Tm. Reg. U. S. Pat Off.—All rights reserved
Copr. 1961 by United Feature Syndicate, Inc.

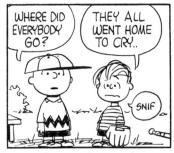

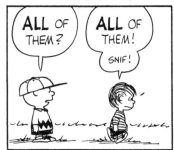

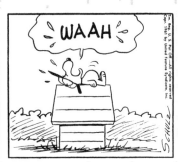

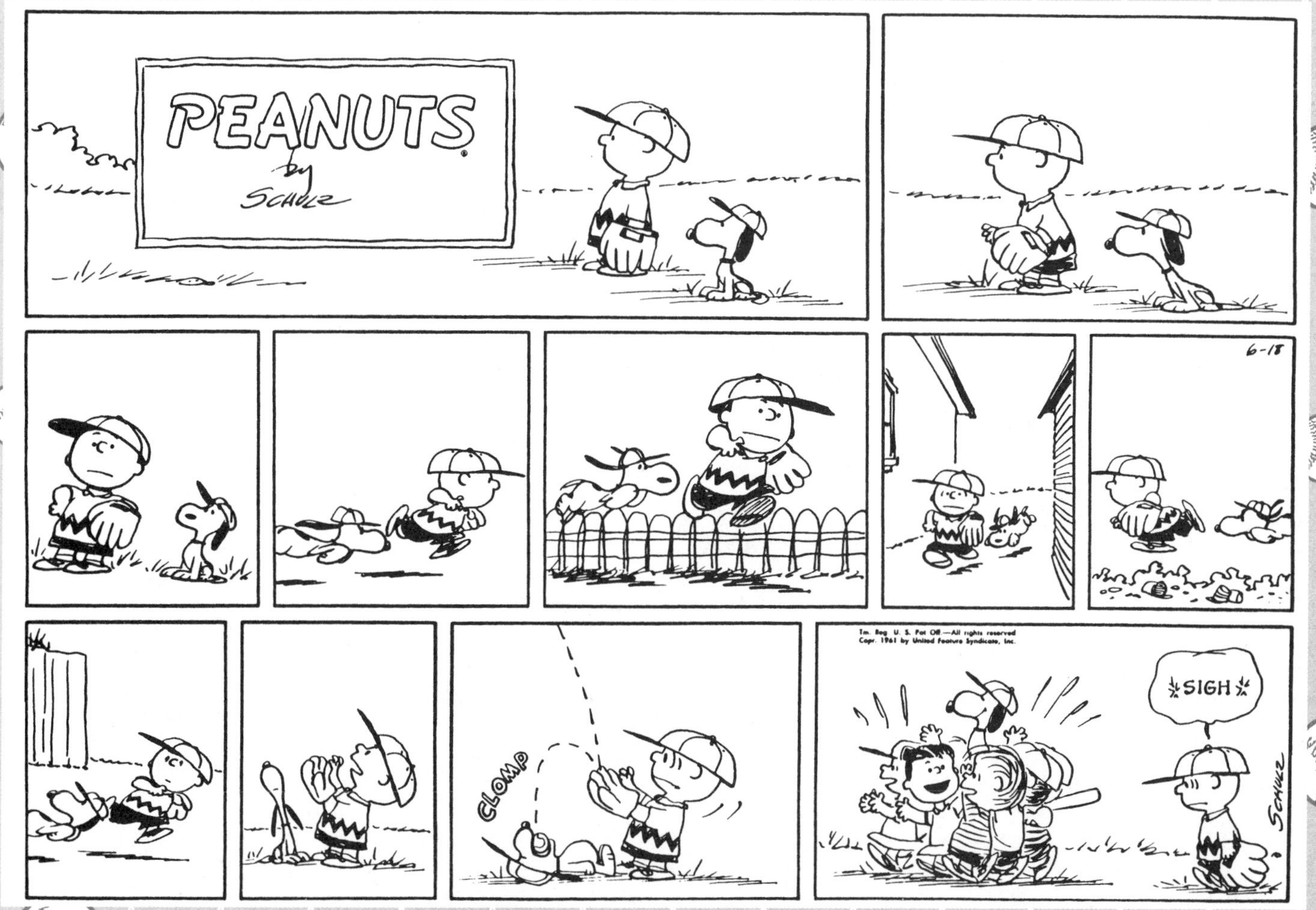
PEANUTS
by
SCHULZ
6-18
Tm. Reg. U. S. Pat. Off.—All rights reserved
Copr. 1961 by United Feature Syndicate, Inc.
CLOMP
SIGH
SCHULZ

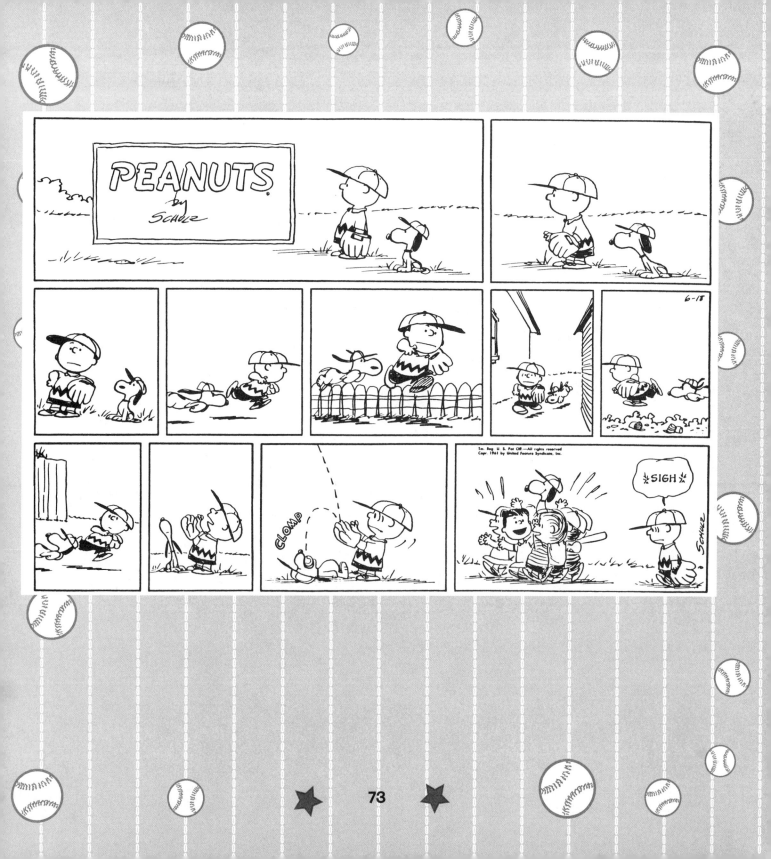

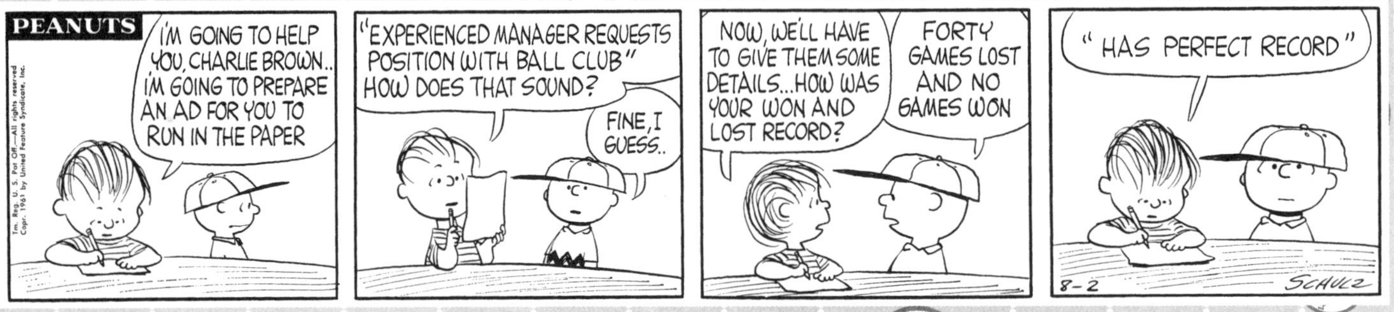
PEANUTS
Tm. Reg. U. S. Pat Off.—All rights reserved
Copr. 1961 by United Feature Syndicate, Inc.
I'M GOING TO HELP YOU, CHARLIE BROWN.. I'M GOING TO PREPARE AN AD FOR YOU TO RUN IN THE PAPER
"EXPERIENCED MANAGER REQUESTS POSITION WITH BALL CLUB" HOW DOES THAT SOUND?
FINE, I GUESS..
NOW, WE'LL HAVE TO GIVE THEM SOME DETAILS...HOW WAS YOUR WON AND LOST RECORD?
FORTY GAMES LOST AND NO GAMES WON
" HAS PERFECT RECORD "
8-2
SCHULZ

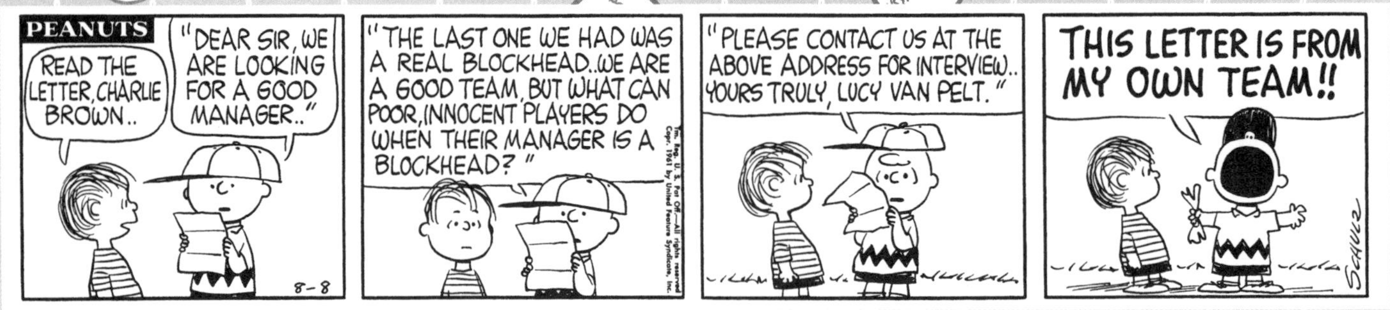
PEANUTS
READ THE LETTER, CHARLIE BROWN..
"DEAR SIR, WE ARE LOOKING FOR A GOOD MANAGER.."
8-8
"THE LAST ONE WE HAD WAS A REAL BLOCKHEAD..WE ARE A GOOD TEAM, BUT WHAT CAN POOR, INNOCENT PLAYERS DO WHEN THEIR MANAGER IS A BLOCKHEAD?"
Tm. Reg. U. S. Pat Off.—All rights reserved
Copr. 1961 by United Feature Syndicate, Inc.
"PLEASE CONTACT US AT THE ABOVE ADDRESS FOR INTERVIEW.. YOURS TRULY, LUCY VAN PELT."
THIS LETTER IS FROM MY OWN TEAM!!
SCHULZ

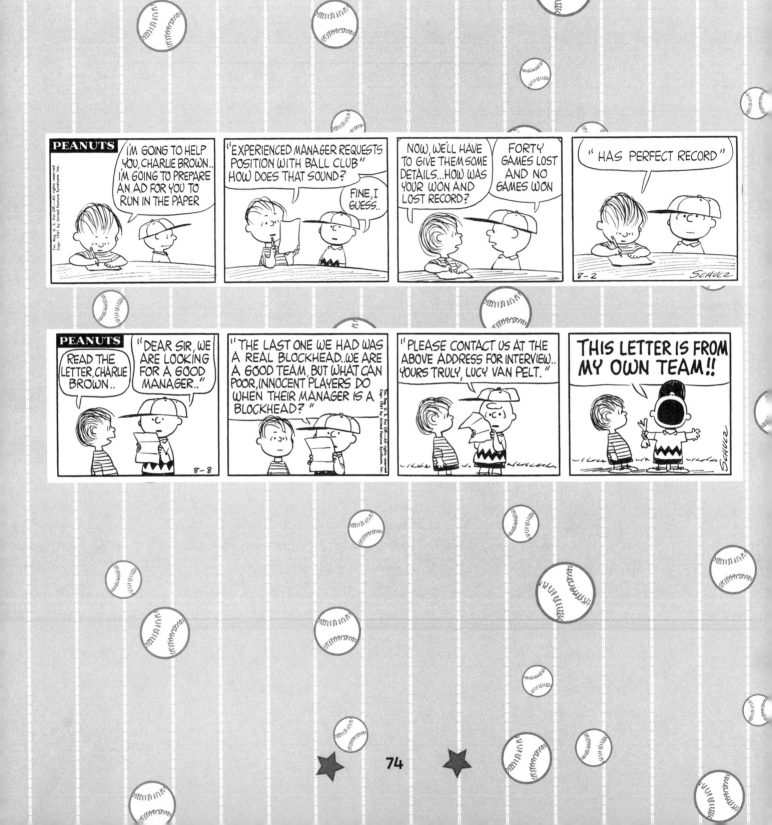

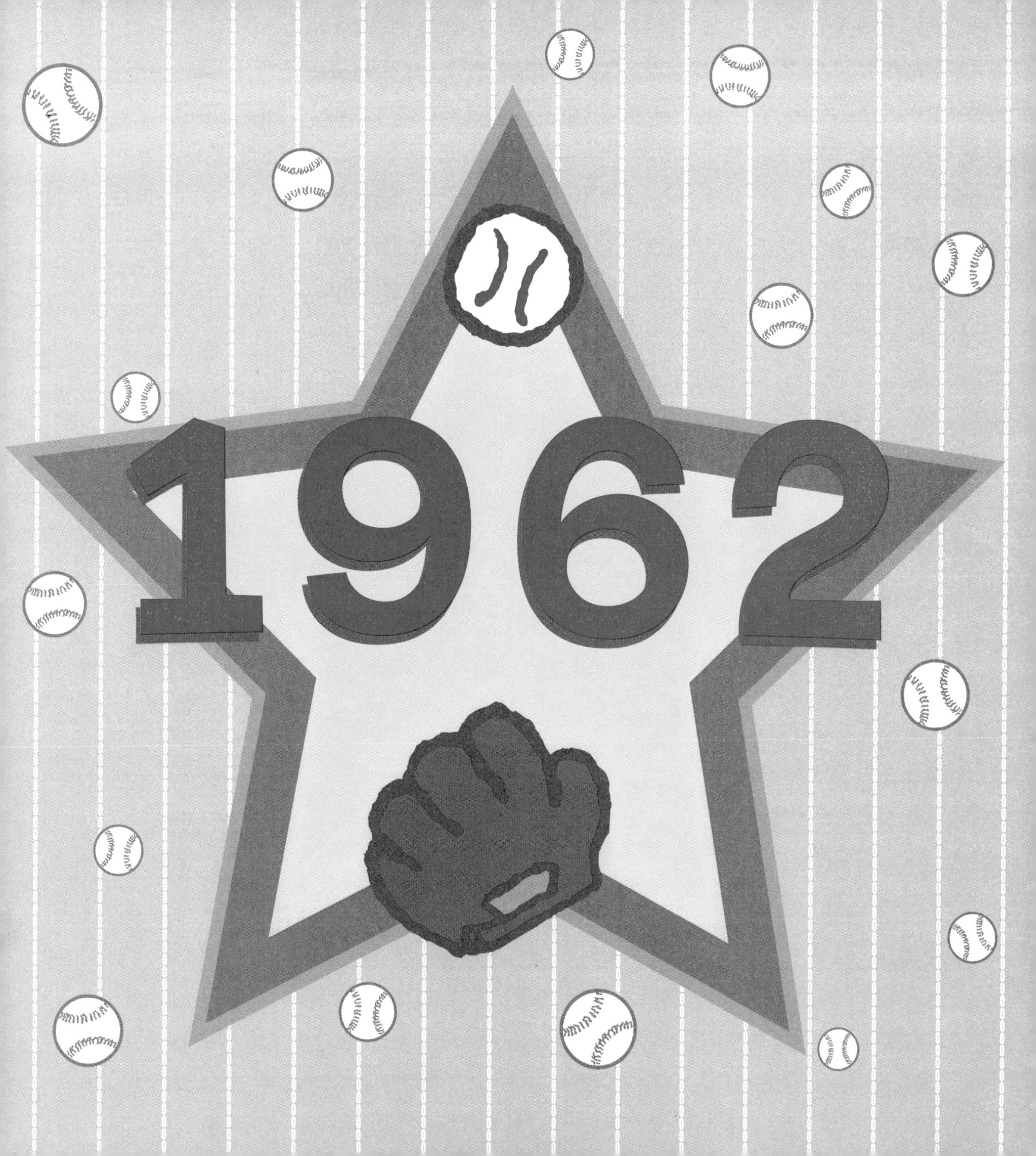
1962

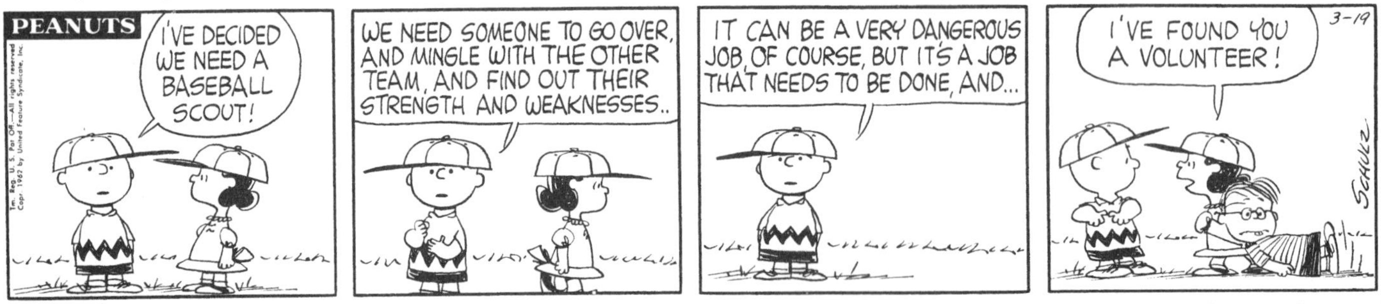
PEANUTS
I'VE DECIDED WE NEED A BASEBALL SCOUT!
WE NEED SOMEONE TO GO OVER, AND MINGLE WITH THE OTHER TEAM, AND FIND OUT THEIR STRENGTH AND WEAKNESSES..
IT CAN BE A VERY DANGEROUS JOB, OF COURSE, BUT IT'S A JOB THAT NEEDS TO BE DONE, AND...
I'VE FOUND YOU A VOLUNTEER!
3-19
SCHULZ

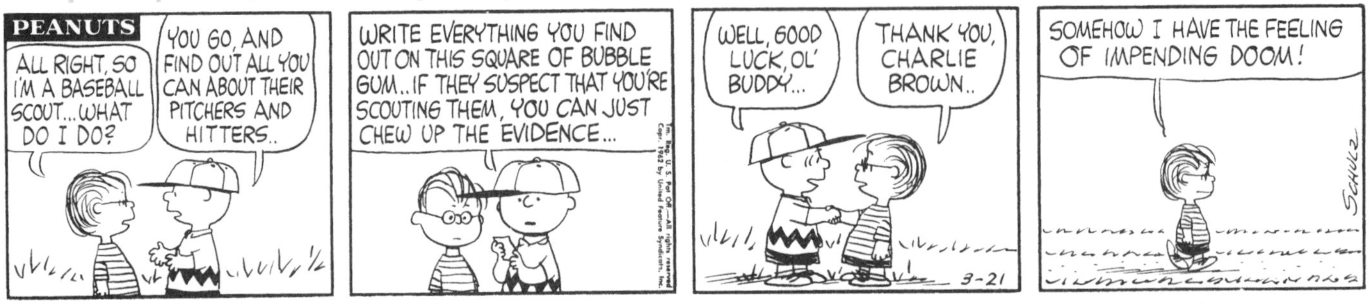
PEANUTS
ALL RIGHT, SO I'M A BASEBALL SCOUT...WHAT DO I DO?
YOU GO, AND FIND OUT ALL YOU CAN ABOUT THEIR PITCHERS AND HITTERS..
WRITE EVERYTHING YOU FIND OUT ON THIS SQUARE OF BUBBLE GUM..IF THEY SUSPECT THAT YOU'RE SCOUTING THEM, YOU CAN JUST CHEW UP THE EVIDENCE...
WELL, GOOD LUCK, OL' BUDDY...
THANK YOU, CHARLIE BROWN..
3-21
SOMEHOW I HAVE THE FEELING OF IMPENDING DOOM!
SCHULZ

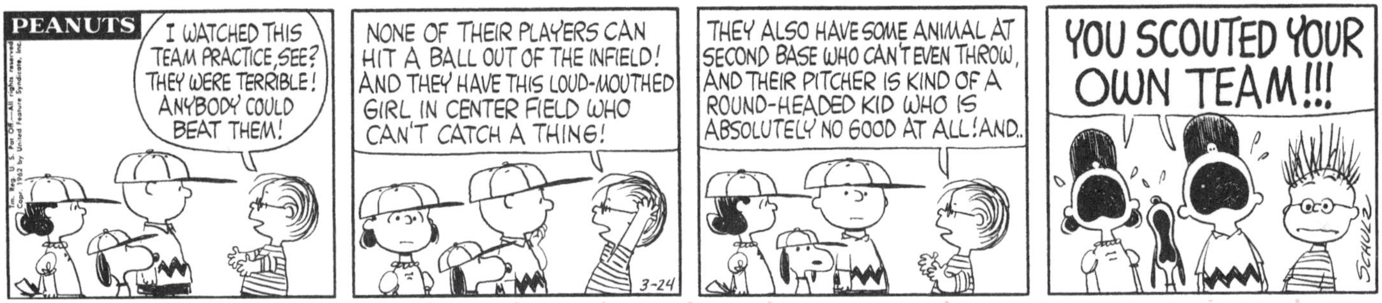
PEANUTS
I WATCHED THIS TEAM PRACTICE, SEE? THEY WERE TERRIBLE! ANYBODY COULD BEAT THEM!
NONE OF THEIR PLAYERS CAN HIT A BALL OUT OF THE INFIELD! AND THEY HAVE THIS LOUD-MOUTHED GIRL IN CENTER FIELD WHO CAN'T CATCH A THING!
3-24
THEY ALSO HAVE SOME ANIMAL AT SECOND BASE WHO CAN'T EVEN THROW, AND THEIR PITCHER IS KIND OF A ROUND-HEADED KID WHO IS ABSOLUTELY NO GOOD AT ALL! AND..
YOU SCOUTED YOUR OWN TEAM!!!
SCHULZ

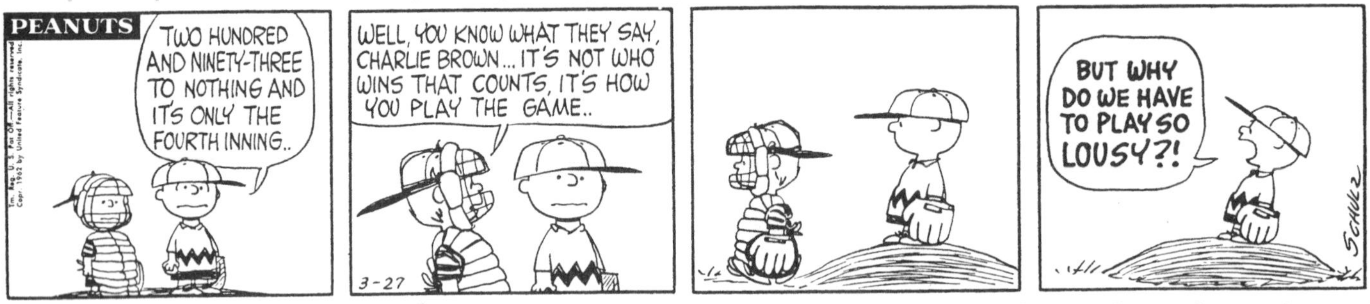
PEANUTS
TWO HUNDRED AND NINETY-THREE TO NOTHING AND IT'S ONLY THE FOURTH INNING..
WELL, YOU KNOW WHAT THEY SAY, CHARLIE BROWN... IT'S NOT WHO WINS THAT COUNTS, IT'S HOW YOU PLAY THE GAME..
3-27
BUT WHY DO WE HAVE TO PLAY SO LOUSY?!
SCHULZ

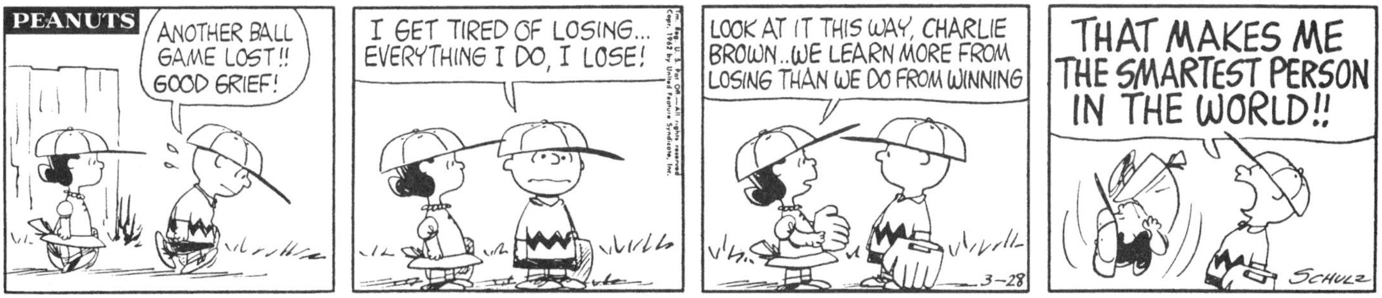
PEANUTS
ANOTHER BALL GAME LOST!! GOOD GRIEF!
I GET TIRED OF LOSING... EVERYTHING I DO, I LOSE!
LOOK AT IT THIS WAY, CHARLIE BROWN..WE LEARN MORE FROM LOSING THAN WE DO FROM WINNING
THAT MAKES ME THE SMARTEST PERSON IN THE WORLD!!
3-28
SCHULZ

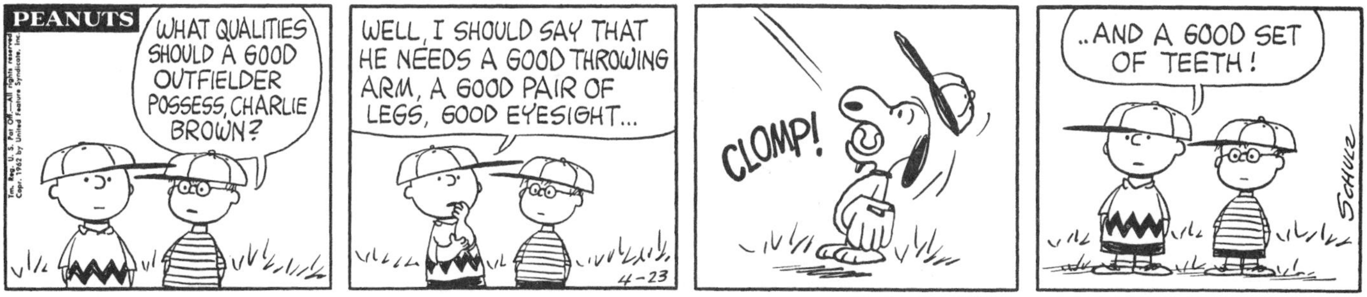
PEANUTS
WHAT QUALITIES SHOULD A GOOD OUTFIELDER POSSESS, CHARLIE BROWN?
WELL, I SHOULD SAY THAT HE NEEDS A GOOD THROWING ARM, A GOOD PAIR OF LEGS, GOOD EYESIGHT...
4-23
CLOMP!
..AND A GOOD SET OF TEETH!
SCHULZ

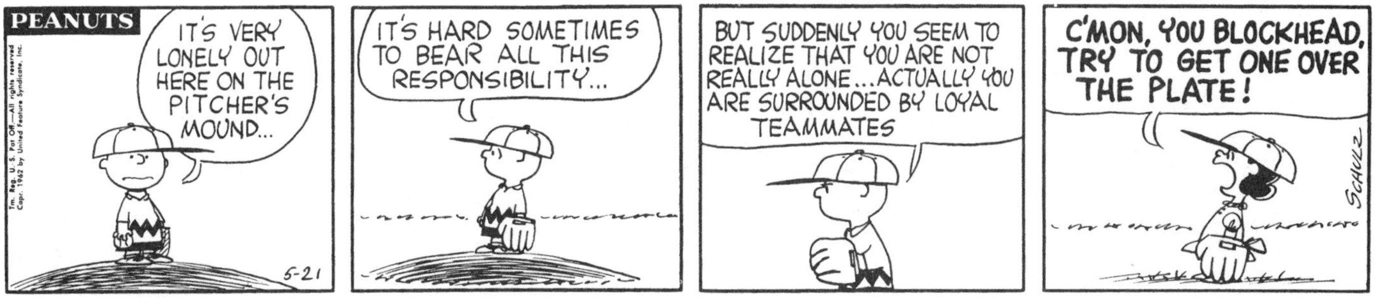
PEANUTS
IT'S VERY LONELY OUT HERE ON THE PITCHER'S MOUND...
5-21
IT'S HARD SOMETIMES TO BEAR ALL THIS RESPONSIBILITY...
BUT SUDDENLY YOU SEEM TO REALIZE THAT YOU ARE NOT REALLY ALONE...ACTUALLY YOU ARE SURROUNDED BY LOYAL TEAMMATES
C'MON, YOU BLOCKHEAD, TRY TO GET ONE OVER THE PLATE!
SCHULZ

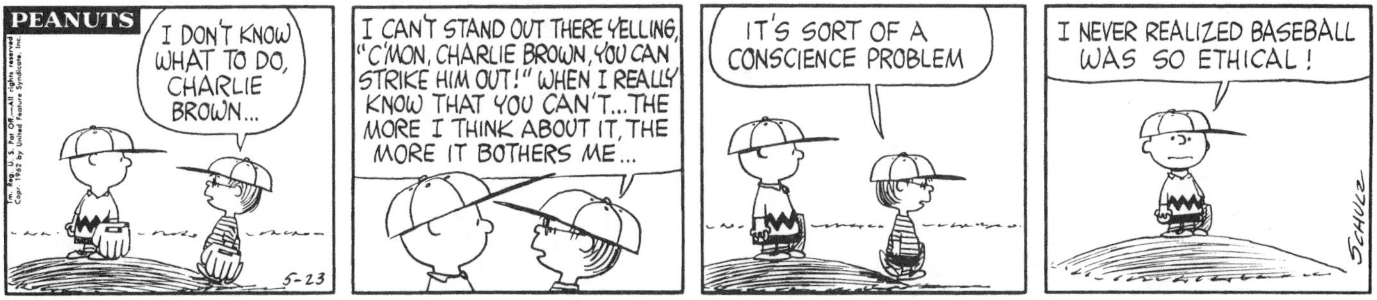
PEANUTS
I DON'T KNOW WHAT TO DO, CHARLIE BROWN...
5-23
I CAN'T STAND OUT THERE YELLING, "C'MON, CHARLIE BROWN, YOU CAN STRIKE HIM OUT!" WHEN I REALLY KNOW THAT YOU CAN'T...THE MORE I THINK ABOUT IT, THE MORE IT BOTHERS ME...
IT'S SORT OF A CONSCIENCE PROBLEM
I NEVER REALIZED BASEBALL WAS SO ETHICAL!
SCHULZ

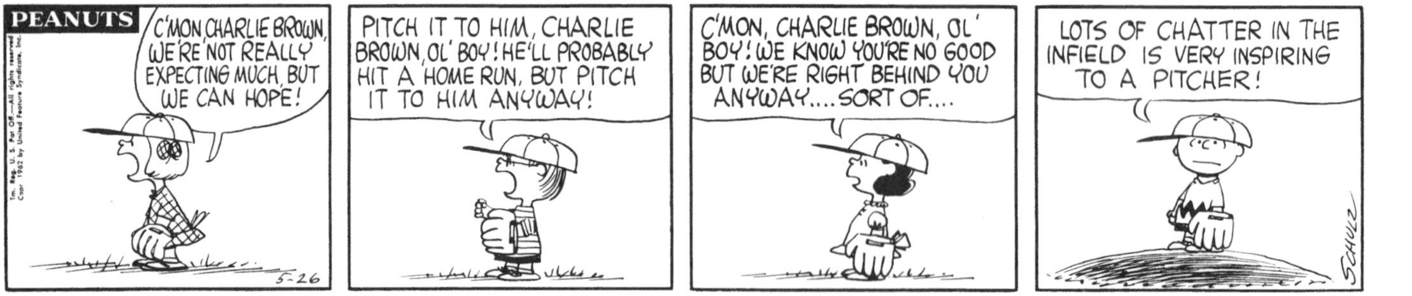
PEANUTS
Tm. Reg. U. S. Pat. Off.—All rights reserved Copr. 1962 by United Feature Syndicate, Inc.
C'MON, CHARLIE BROWN, WE'RE NOT REALLY EXPECTING MUCH, BUT WE CAN HOPE!
5-26
PITCH IT TO HIM, CHARLIE BROWN, OL' BOY! HE'LL PROBABLY HIT A HOME RUN, BUT PITCH IT TO HIM ANYWAY!
C'MON, CHARLIE BROWN, OL' BOY! WE KNOW YOU'RE NO GOOD BUT WE'RE RIGHT BEHIND YOU ANYWAY.... SORT OF....
LOTS OF CHATTER IN THE INFIELD IS VERY INSPIRING TO A PITCHER!
SCHULZ

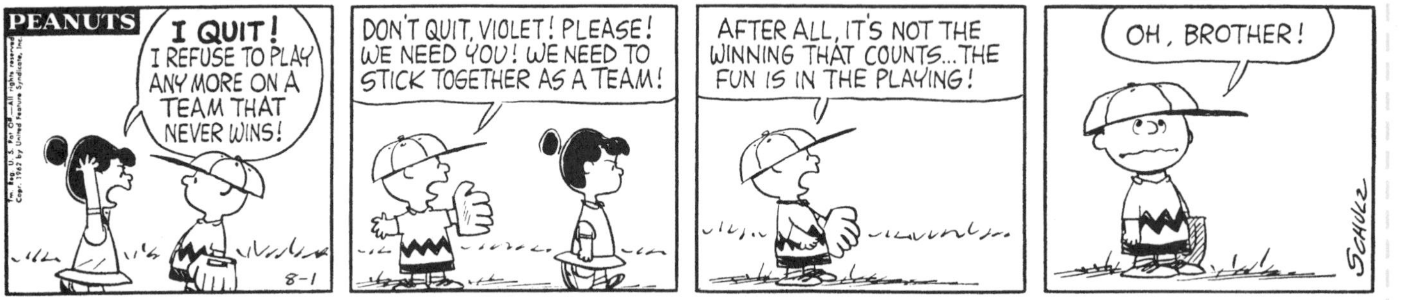
PEANUTS
Tm. Reg. U. S. Pat. Off.—All rights reserved Copr. 1962 by United Feature Syndicate, Inc.
I QUIT! I REFUSE TO PLAY ANY MORE ON A TEAM THAT NEVER WINS!
8-1
DON'T QUIT, VIOLET! PLEASE! WE NEED YOU! WE NEED TO STICK TOGETHER AS A TEAM!
AFTER ALL, IT'S NOT THE WINNING THAT COUNTS...THE FUN IS IN THE PLAYING!
OH, BROTHER!
SCHULZ

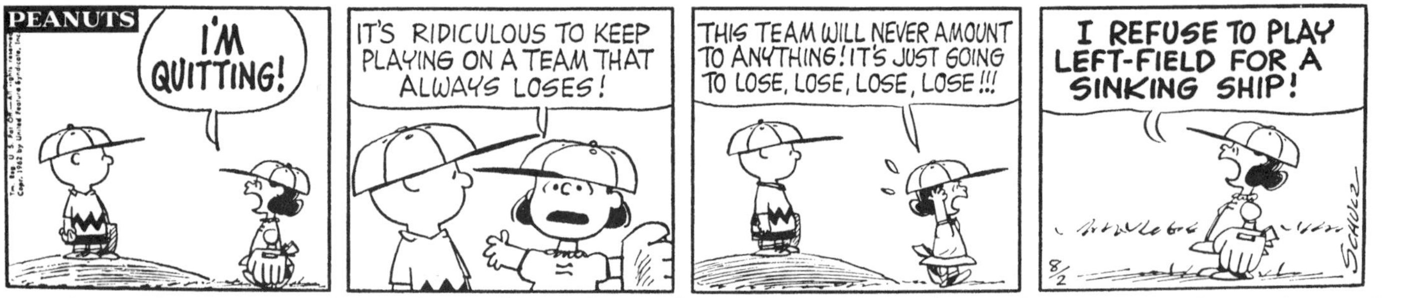
PEANUTS
Tm. Reg. U. S. Pat. Off.—All rights reserved Copr. 1962 by United Feature Syndicate, Inc.
I'M QUITTING!
IT'S RIDICULOUS TO KEEP PLAYING ON A TEAM THAT ALWAYS LOSES!
THIS TEAM WILL NEVER AMOUNT TO ANYTHING! IT'S JUST GOING TO LOSE, LOSE, LOSE, LOSE!!!
I REFUSE TO PLAY LEFT-FIELD FOR A SINKING SHIP!
8/2
SCHULZ

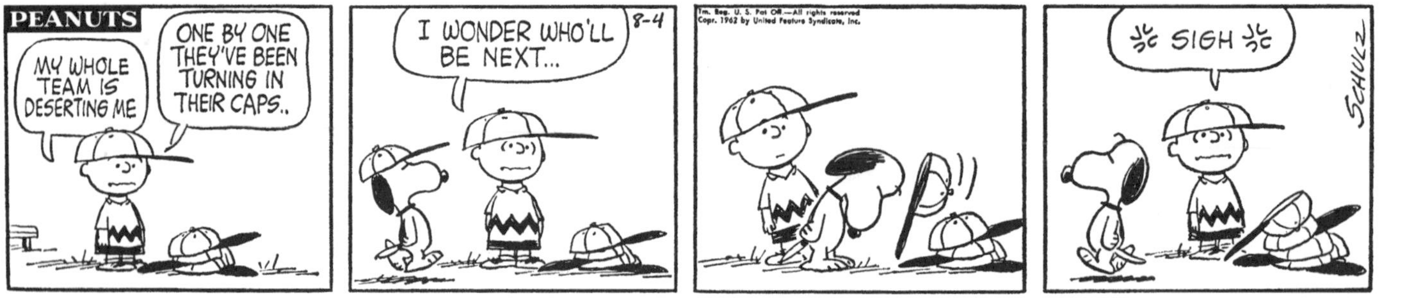
PEANUTS
MY WHOLE TEAM IS DESERTING ME
ONE BY ONE THEY'VE BEEN TURNING IN THEIR CAPS..
8-4
I WONDER WHO'LL BE NEXT...
Tm. Reg. U. S. Pat. Off.—All rights reserved Copr. 1962 by United Feature Syndicate, Inc.
SIGH
SCHULZ

PEANUTS
by
SCHULZ
OKAY, SNOOPY, LET'S TAKE TWO THIS TIME!
WE CAN DO IT, OL' BUDDY!
8-5
CLOMP!
PTUI!
WELL, THAT ENDED THE GAME, SNOOPY! YOU AND I ARE GETTING TO BE A GREAT DOUBLE-PLAY COMBINATION...WE REALLY WORK TOGETHER...
BY THE WAY, WOULD YOU LIKE TO COME OVER TO MY HOUSE? I'VE ASKED CHARLIE BROWN, AND FRIEDA AND VIOLET, AND I THOUGHT WE COULD...
Tm. Reg. U. S. Pat. Off.—All rights reserved
Copr. 1962 by United Feature Syndicate, Inc.
OFF THE FIELD I MAKE MY OWN FRIENDS!
SCHULZ

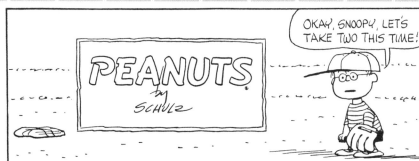

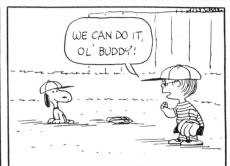

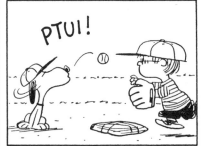

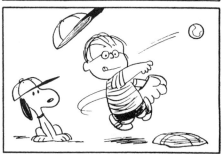

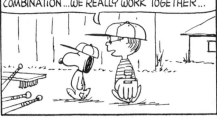

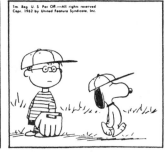

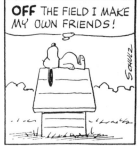

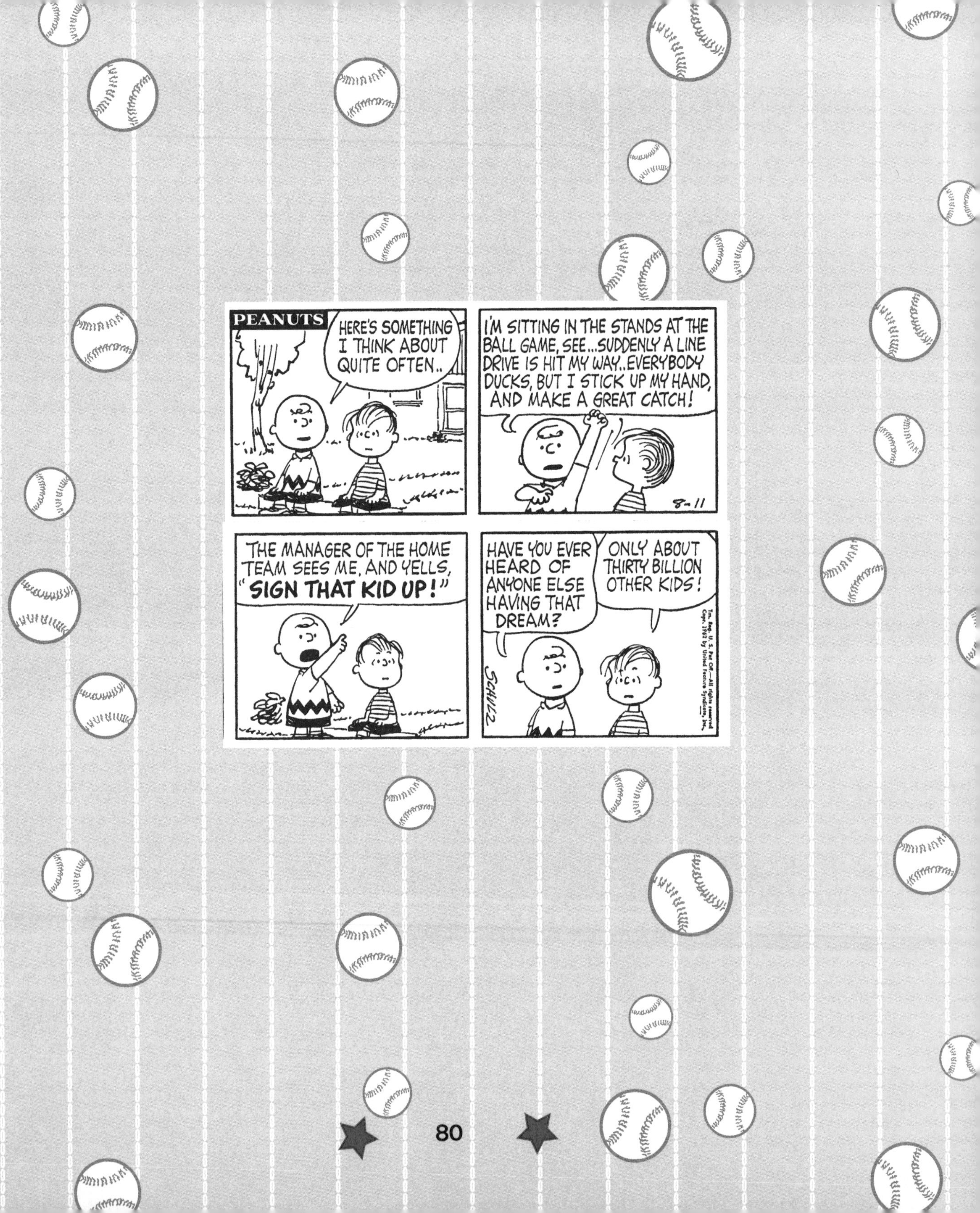
PEANUTS
HERE'S SOMETHING I THINK ABOUT QUITE OFTEN..
I'M SITTING IN THE STANDS AT THE BALL GAME, SEE...SUDDENLY A LINE DRIVE IS HIT MY WAY..EVERYBODY DUCKS, BUT I STICK UP MY HAND, AND MAKE A GREAT CATCH!
8-11
THE MANAGER OF THE HOME TEAM SEES ME, AND YELLS, "**SIGN THAT KID UP!**"
HAVE YOU EVER HEARD OF ANYONE ELSE HAVING THAT DREAM?
ONLY ABOUT THIRTY BILLION OTHER KIDS!
SCHULZ
Tm. Reg. U. S. Pat Off.—All rights reserved
Copr. 1962 by United Feature Syndicate, Inc.

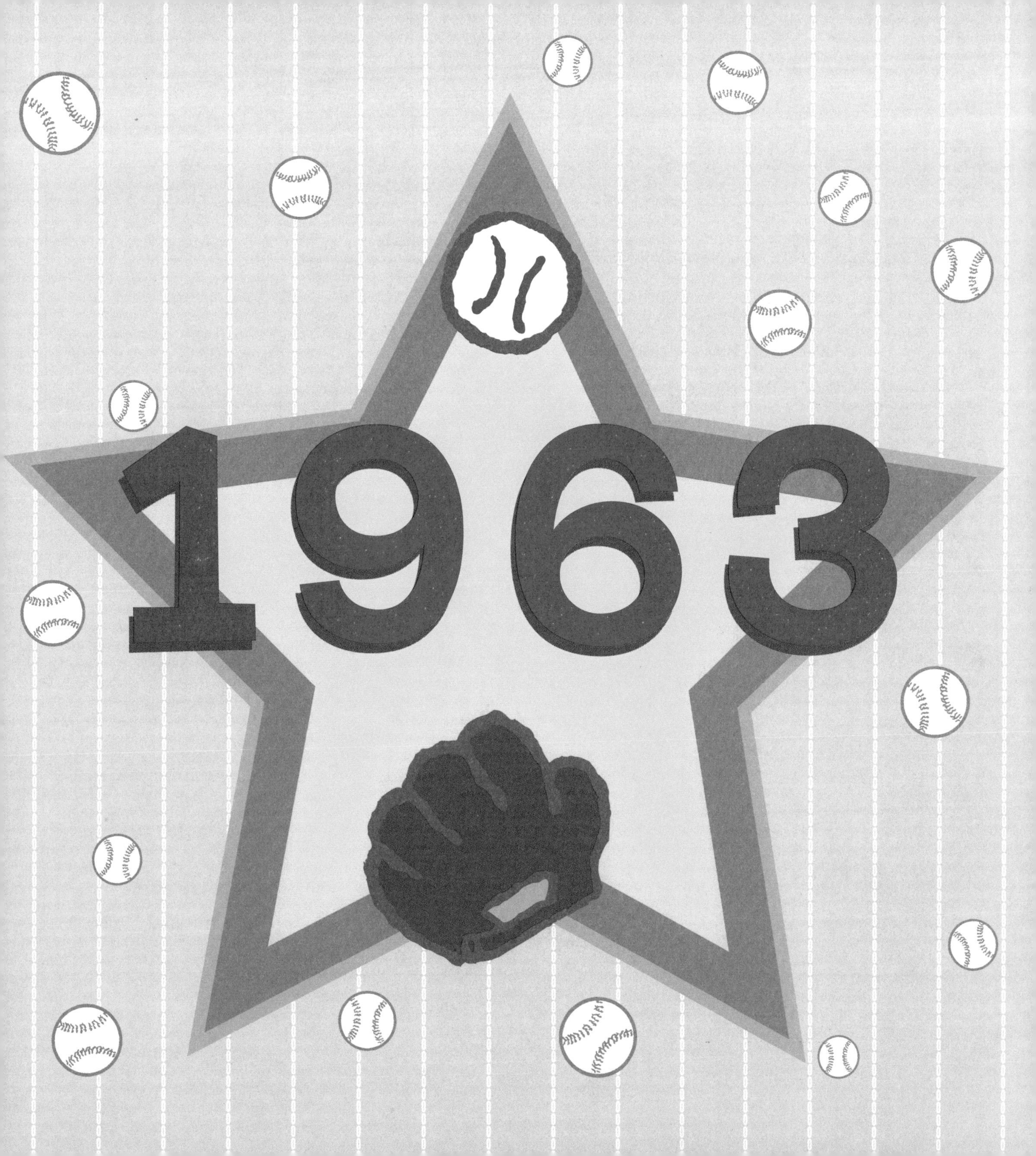
1963

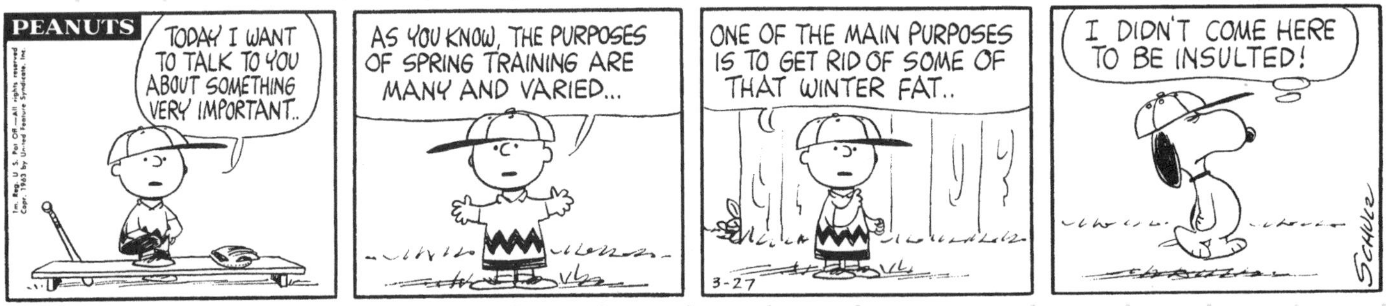
PEANUTS
TODAY I WANT TO TALK TO YOU ABOUT SOMETHING VERY IMPORTANT..
AS YOU KNOW, THE PURPOSES OF SPRING TRAINING ARE MANY AND VARIED...
ONE OF THE MAIN PURPOSES IS TO GET RID OF SOME OF THAT WINTER FAT..
3-27
I DIDN'T COME HERE TO BE INSULTED!
SCHULZ

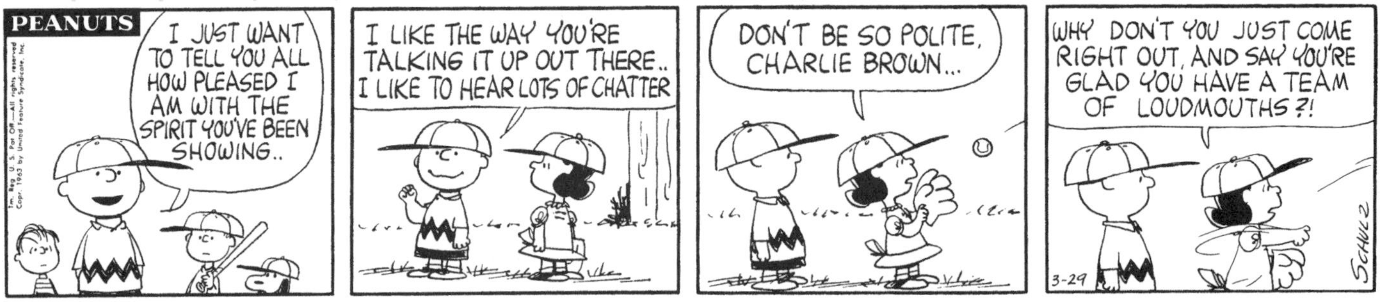
PEANUTS
I JUST WANT TO TELL YOU ALL HOW PLEASED I AM WITH THE SPIRIT YOU'VE BEEN SHOWING..
I LIKE THE WAY YOU'RE TALKING IT UP OUT THERE.. I LIKE TO HEAR LOTS OF CHATTER
DON'T BE SO POLITE, CHARLIE BROWN...
WHY DON'T YOU JUST COME RIGHT OUT, AND SAY YOU'RE GLAD YOU HAVE A TEAM OF LOUDMOUTHS ?!
3-29
SCHULZ

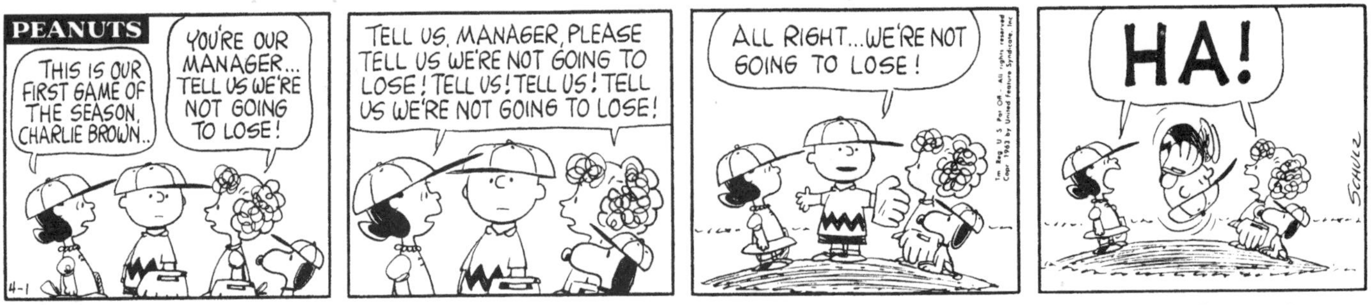
PEANUTS
THIS IS OUR FIRST GAME OF THE SEASON, CHARLIE BROWN..
YOU'RE OUR MANAGER... TELL US WE'RE NOT GOING TO LOSE!
4-1
TELL US, MANAGER, PLEASE TELL US WE'RE NOT GOING TO LOSE! TELL US! TELL US! TELL US WE'RE NOT GOING TO LOSE!
ALL RIGHT...WE'RE NOT GOING TO LOSE!
HA!
SCHULZ

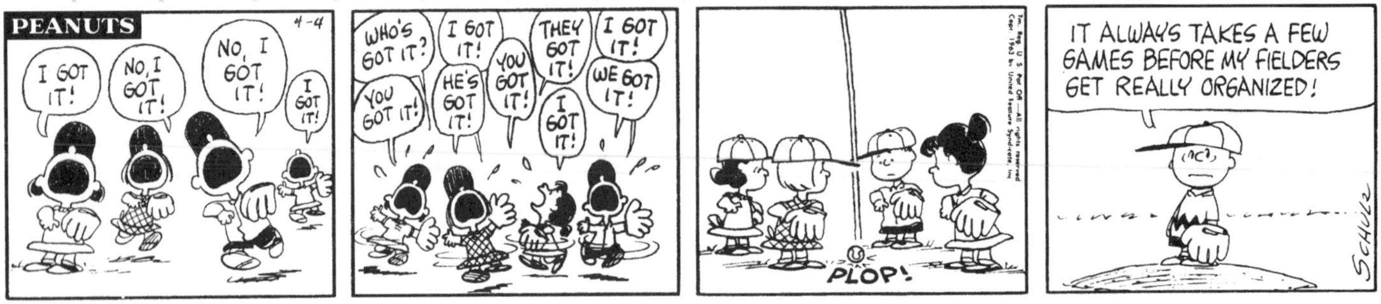
PEANUTS
4-4
I GOT IT!
NO, I GOT IT!
NO, I GOT IT!
I GOT IT!
WHO'S GOT IT?
I GOT IT!
YOU GOT IT!
HE'S GOT IT!
YOU GOT IT!
THEY GOT IT!
I GOT IT!
I GOT IT!
WE GOT IT!
PLOP!
IT ALWAYS TAKES A FEW GAMES BEFORE MY FIELDERS GET REALLY ORGANIZED!
SCHULZ

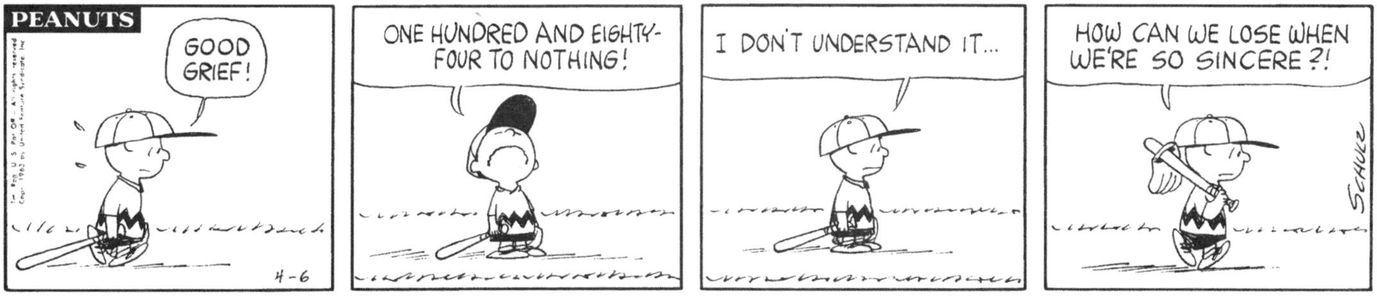
PEANUTS
GOOD GRIEF!
4-6
ONE HUNDRED AND EIGHTY-FOUR TO NOTHING!
I DON'T UNDERSTAND IT...
HOW CAN WE LOSE WHEN WE'RE SO SINCERE?!
SCHULZ

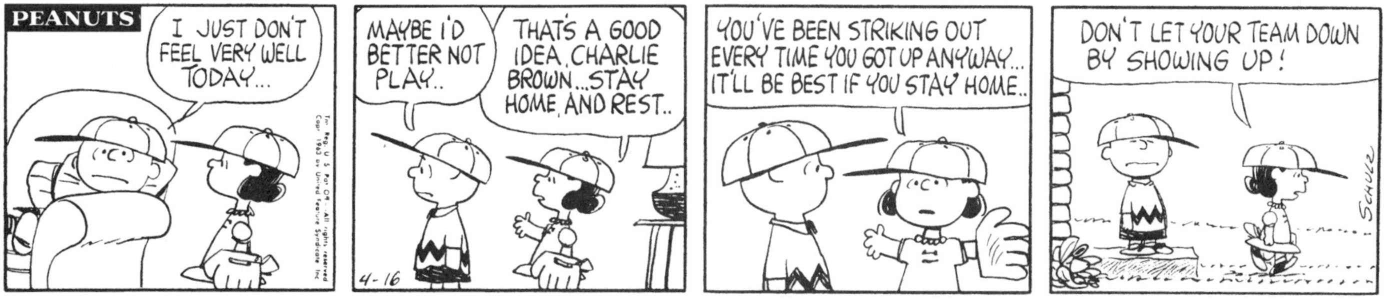
PEANUTS
I JUST DON'T FEEL VERY WELL TODAY...
MAYBE I'D BETTER NOT PLAY..
THAT'S A GOOD IDEA, CHARLIE BROWN...STAY HOME, AND REST..
4-16
YOU'VE BEEN STRIKING OUT EVERY TIME YOU GOT UP ANYWAY... IT'LL BE BEST IF YOU STAY HOME..
DON'T LET YOUR TEAM DOWN BY SHOWING UP!
SCHULZ

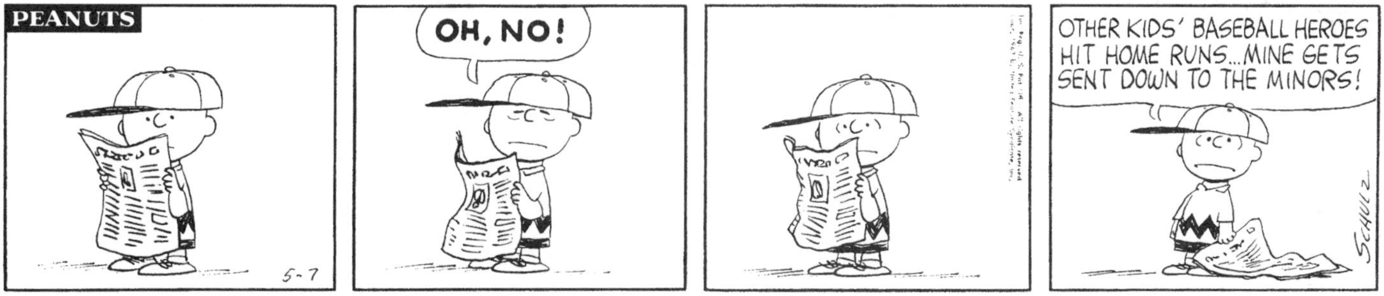
PEANUTS
5-7
OH, NO!
OTHER KIDS' BASEBALL HEROES HIT HOME RUNS...MINE GETS SENT DOWN TO THE MINORS!
SCHULZ

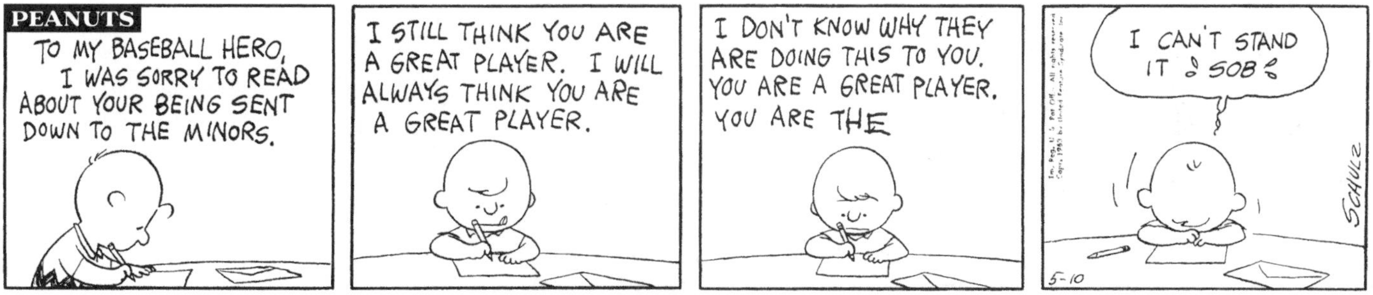
PEANUTS
TO MY BASEBALL HERO, I WAS SORRY TO READ ABOUT YOUR BEING SENT DOWN TO THE MINORS.
I STILL THINK YOU ARE A GREAT PLAYER. I WILL ALWAYS THINK YOU ARE A GREAT PLAYER.
I DON'T KNOW WHY THEY ARE DOING THIS TO YOU. YOU ARE A GREAT PLAYER. YOU ARE THE
I CAN'T STAND IT ¿ SOB ¿
5-10
SCHULZ

PEANUTS
5-13
KLOP!
I WONDER WHY HE WEARS A GLOVE...
WHERE ELSE WOULD I KEEP MY LUNCH?
SCHULZ

PEANUTS
YOU WANT **ME** TO BE CATCHER?
YES, SCHROEDER CAN'T MAKE IT TODAY..
6-6
DO I HAVE TO WEAR ALL **THIS**?
OF COURSE... IT'S FOR YOUR OWN GOOD..
I FEEL LIKE I'M IN A BIRD CAGE...
TWEET TWEET CHIRP CHIRP ♪ ♪ ♪ ♪
ALL RIGHT, WE CAN DO WITHOUT THAT!
SCHULZ

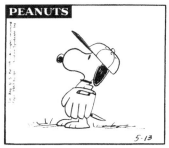

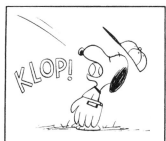

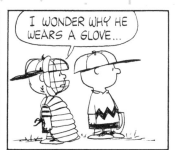

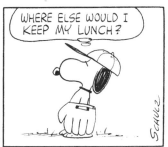

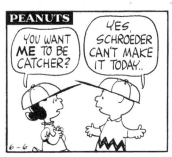

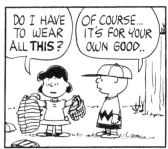

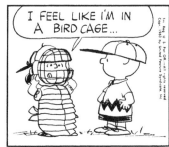

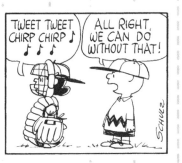

PEANUTS
HERE...TAKE YOUR OL' CATCHER'S OUTFIT! I'M THROUGH!
YOU DIDN'T TELL ME ABOUT FAST BALLS, SWINGING BATS AND FOUL TIPS!
6-7
IT'S **DANGEROUS** BACK THERE!
I REFUSE TO GET HIT BY A FLYING BAT, AND DEPRIVE THE WORLD OF MISS UNIVERSE OF 1975!
SCHULZ

PEANUTS
HEY, MANAGER, WE HAVE A COMPLAINT!
SOME OF THE BOYS ARE THROWING THE BALL TOO HARD
TELL THEM THEY DON'T HAVE TO BURN 'EM IN!
6-17
YES, TELL THEM NOT TO THROW BURNIES
"BURNIES"?!
SCHULZ

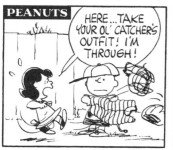

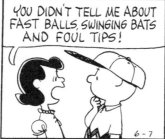

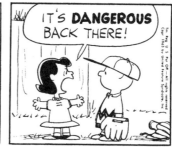

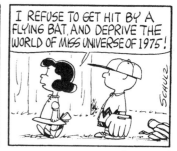

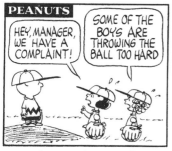

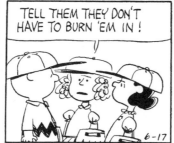

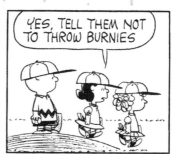

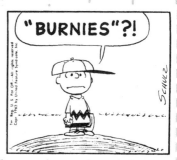

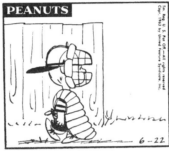

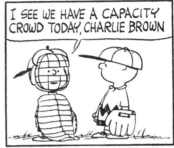

PEANUTS
Tm. Reg. U. S. Pat. Off.—All rights reserved
Copr. 1963 by United Feature Syndicate, Inc.
6-22
I SEE WE HAVE A CAPACITY CROWD TODAY, CHARLIE BROWN
YES, I NOTICED THAT, TOO...
THE SEAT IS JAMMED
SCHULZ

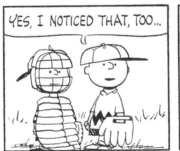

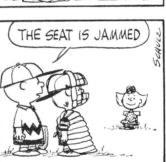

PEANUTS
by SCHULZ
REALLY?
LET'S GO ASK HIM...
HEY, MANAGER! WE HAVE A QUESTION..
WE HEARD THAT SOMEONE SAID, "NICE GUYS DON'T WIN BALL GAMES."...IS THAT TRUE?
IS THAT WHY WE'RE ALWAYS LOSING, CHARLIE BROWN?
ARE WE TOO NICE? IS THAT OUR TROUBLE? IS THAT WHY WE LOSE ALL OUR GAMES?
WELL, I DON'T KNOW....I....
SEE? WHAT DID I TELL YOU?
Tm. Reg. U. S. Pat. Off.—All rights reserved
Copr. 1963 by United Feature Syndicate, Inc.
7-7
I KNEW WE'D NEVER GET A STRAIGHT ANSWER FROM HIM!
WHAT A MANAGER! HE CAN'T EVEN ANSWER OUR QUESTIONS!
HOW CAN I RUN A BASEBALL TEAM, AND SOLVE MORAL ISSUES AT THE SAME TIME?
SCHULZ

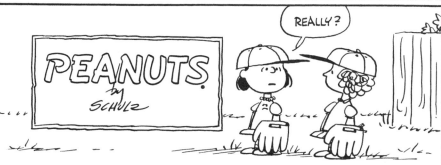

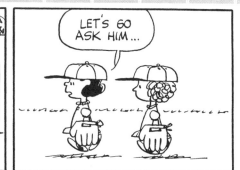

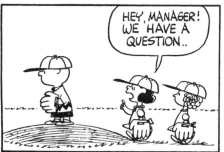

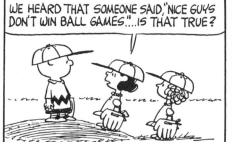

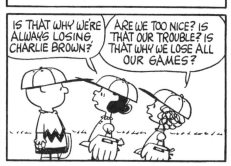

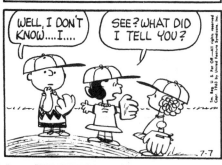

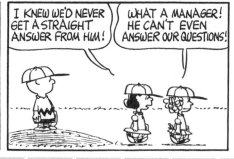

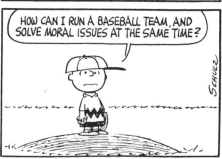

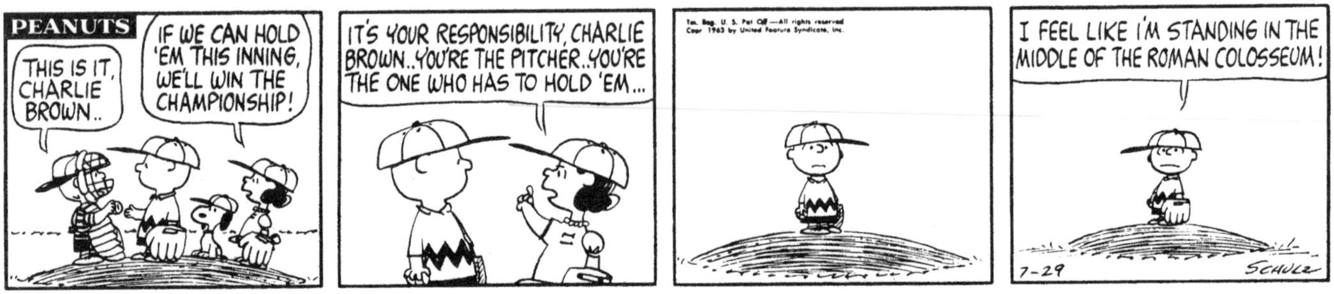
PEANUTS
THIS IS IT, CHARLIE BROWN..
IF WE CAN HOLD 'EM THIS INNING, WE'LL WIN THE CHAMPIONSHIP!
IT'S YOUR RESPONSIBILITY, CHARLIE BROWN..YOU'RE THE PITCHER..YOU'RE THE ONE WHO HAS TO HOLD 'EM...
I FEEL LIKE I'M STANDING IN THE MIDDLE OF THE ROMAN COLOSSEUM!
7-29
SCHULZ

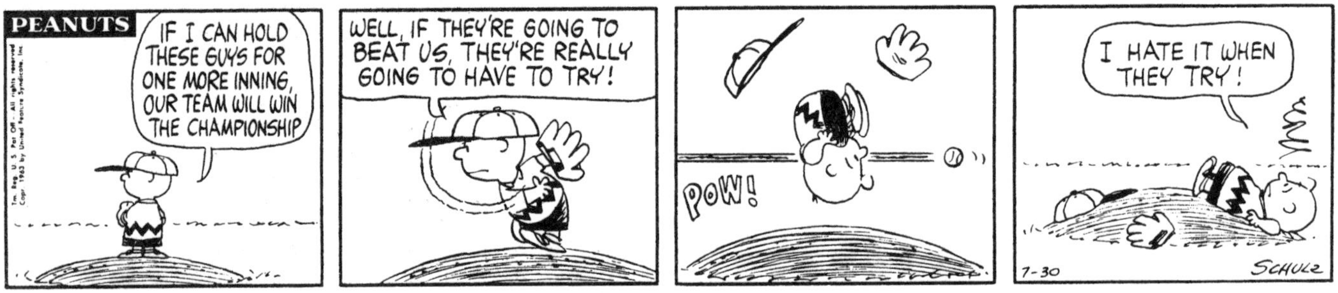
PEANUTS
IF I CAN HOLD THESE GUYS FOR ONE MORE INNING, OUR TEAM WILL WIN THE CHAMPIONSHIP
WELL, IF THEY'RE GOING TO BEAT US, THEY'RE REALLY GOING TO HAVE TO TRY!
POW!
I HATE IT WHEN THEY TRY!
7-30
SCHULZ

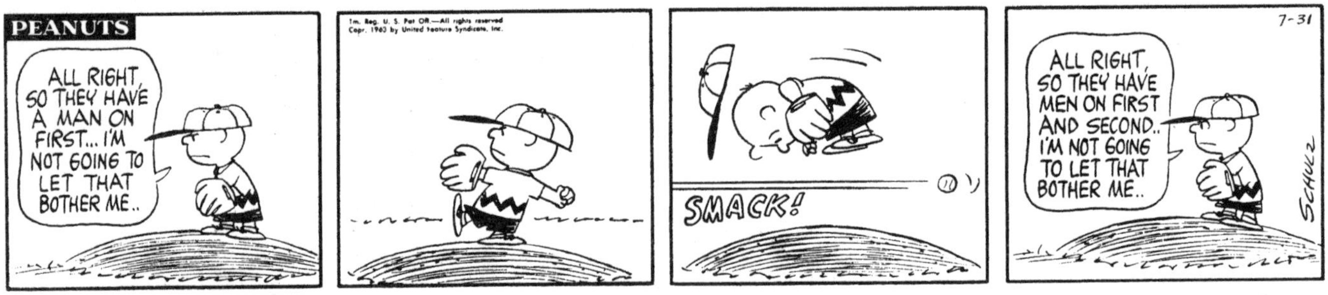
PEANUTS
ALL RIGHT, SO THEY HAVE A MAN ON FIRST... I'M NOT GOING TO LET THAT BOTHER ME..
SMACK!
7-31
ALL RIGHT, SO THEY HAVE MEN ON FIRST AND SECOND.. I'M NOT GOING TO LET THAT BOTHER ME..
SCHULZ

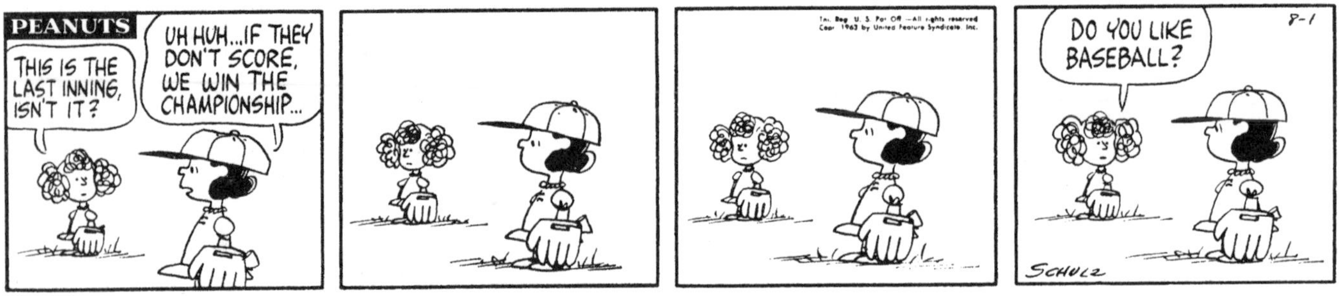
PEANUTS
THIS IS THE LAST INNING, ISN'T IT?
UH HUH...IF THEY DON'T SCORE, WE WIN THE CHAMPIONSHIP...
8-1
DO YOU LIKE BASEBALL?
SCHULZ

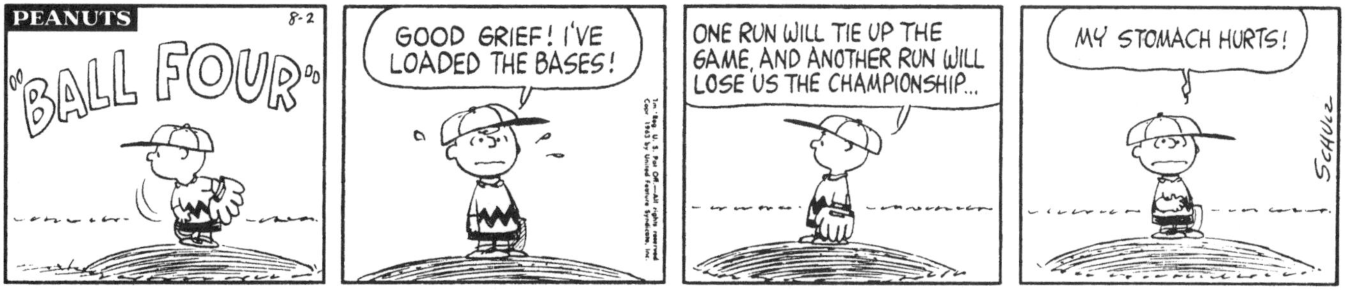
PEANUTS
8-2
"BALL FOUR"
GOOD GRIEF! I'VE LOADED THE BASES!
ONE RUN WILL TIE UP THE GAME, AND ANOTHER RUN WILL LOSE US THE CHAMPIONSHIP...
MY STOMACH HURTS!
SCHULZ

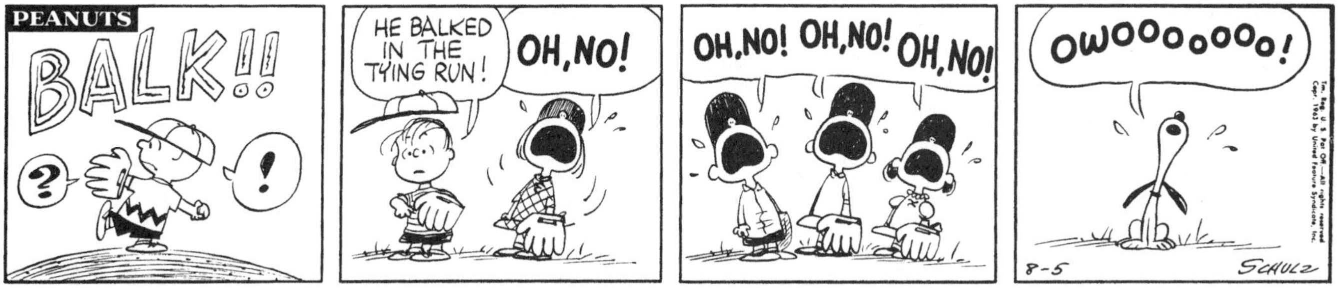
PEANUTS
BALK!!
?
!
HE BALKED IN THE TYING RUN!
OH, NO!
OH, NO! OH, NO! OH, NO!
OWOOOOOOOO!
8-5
SCHULZ

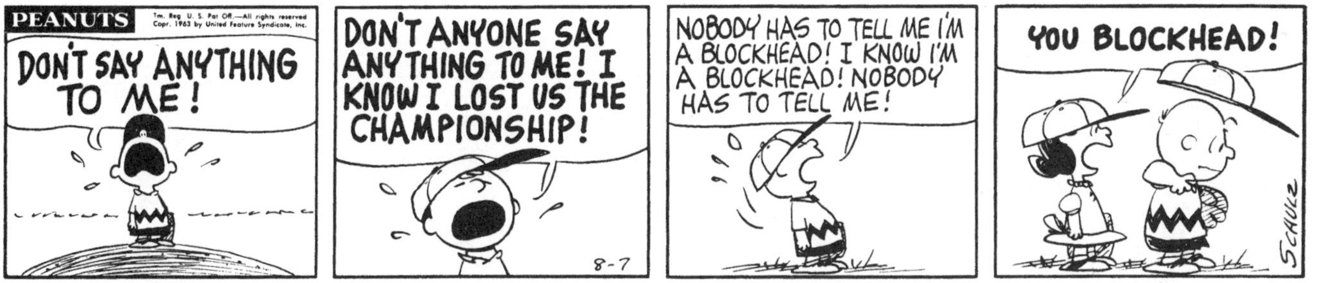
PEANUTS
Tm. Reg. U. S. Pat. Off.—All rights reserved
Copr. 1963 by United Feature Syndicate, Inc.
DON'T SAY ANYTHING TO ME!
DON'T ANYONE SAY ANYTHING TO ME! I KNOW I LOST US THE CHAMPIONSHIP!
8-7
NOBODY HAS TO TELL ME I'M A BLOCKHEAD! I KNOW I'M A BLOCKHEAD! NOBODY HAS TO TELL ME!
YOU BLOCKHEAD!
SCHULZ

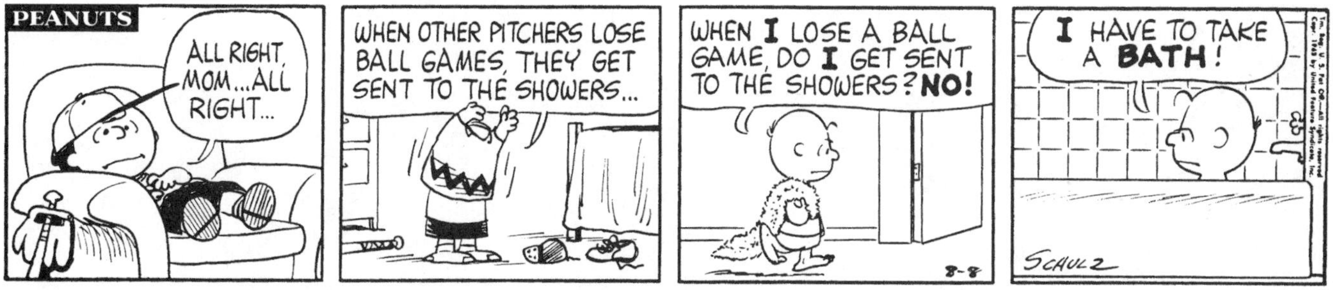
PEANUTS
ALL RIGHT, MOM...ALL RIGHT...
WHEN OTHER PITCHERS LOSE BALL GAMES, THEY GET SENT TO THE SHOWERS...
WHEN I LOSE A BALL GAME, DO I GET SENT TO THE SHOWERS? NO!
8-8
I HAVE TO TAKE A BATH!
SCHULZ

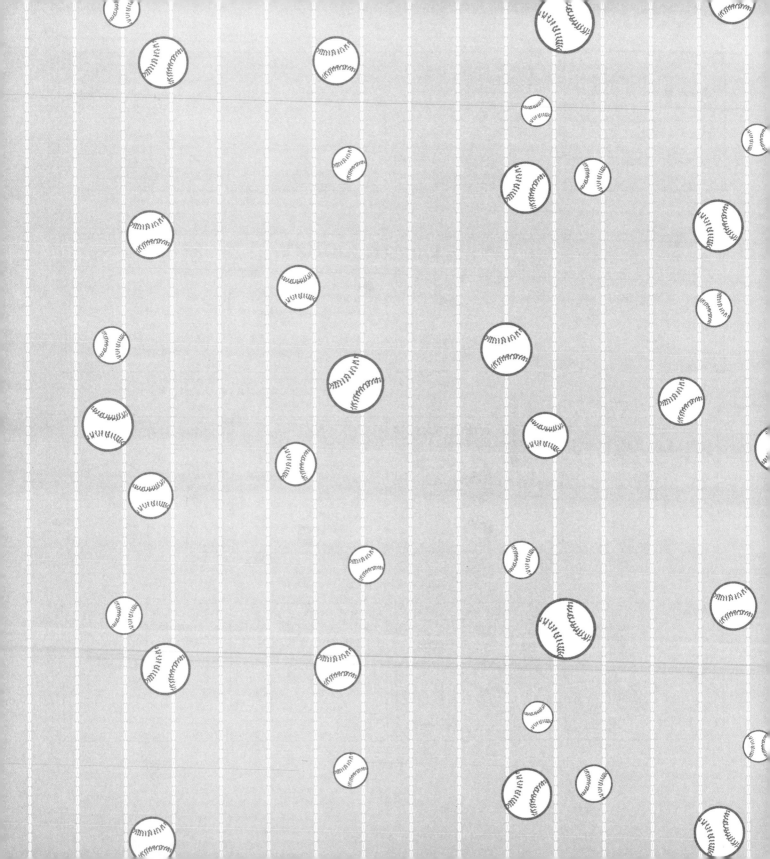

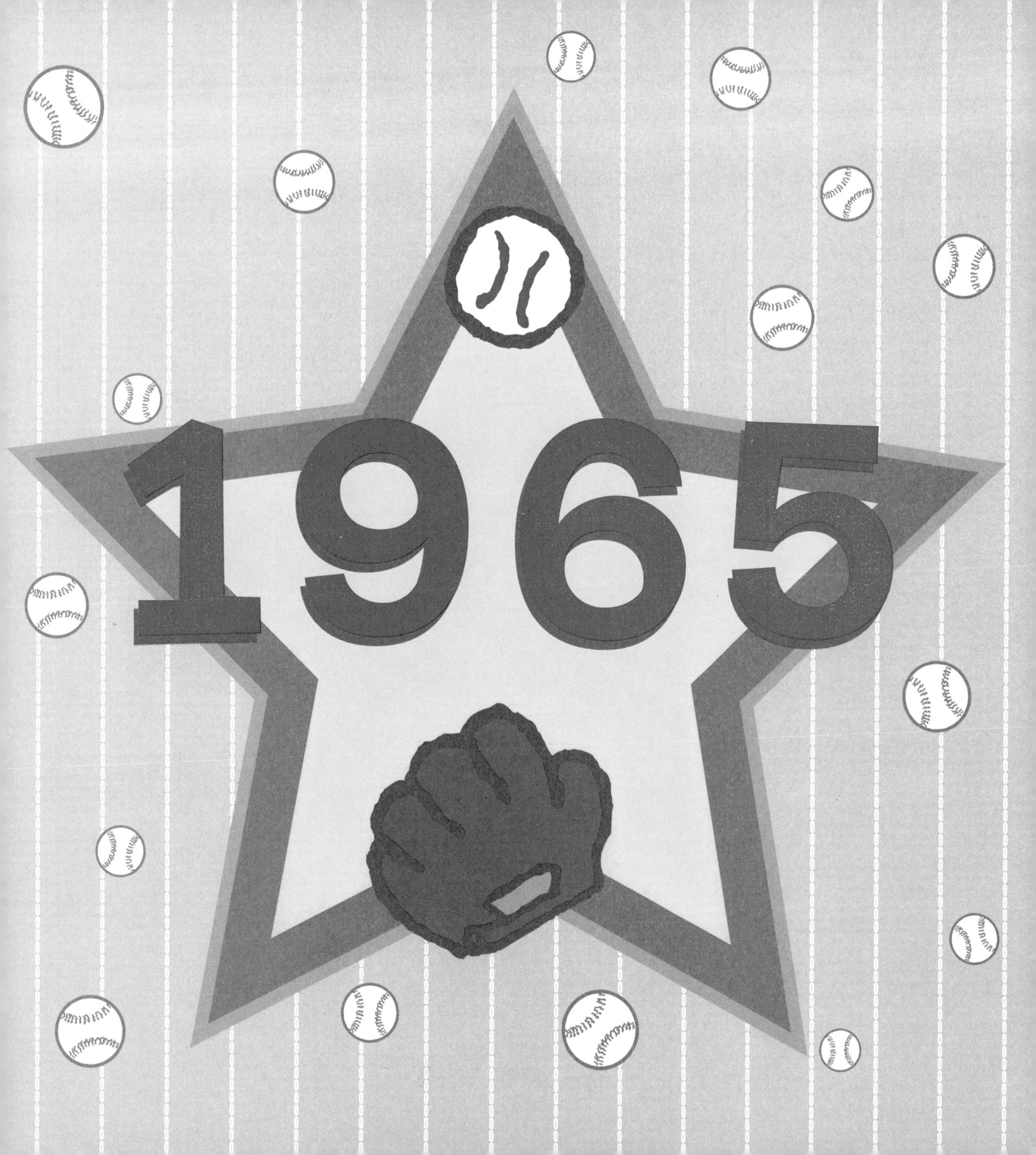
1965

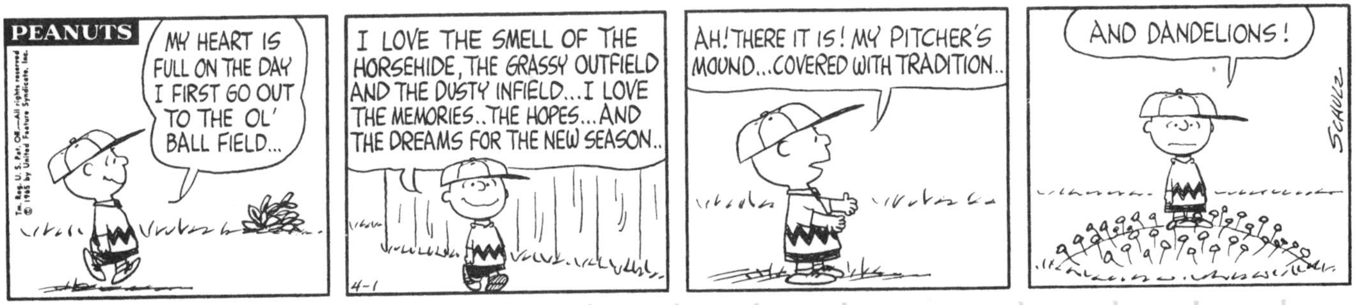
PEANUTS
MY HEART IS FULL ON THE DAY I FIRST GO OUT TO THE OL' BALL FIELD...
I LOVE THE SMELL OF THE HORSEHIDE, THE GRASSY OUTFIELD AND THE DUSTY INFIELD...I LOVE THE MEMORIES..THE HOPES...AND THE DREAMS FOR THE NEW SEASON..
AH! THERE IT IS! MY PITCHER'S MOUND...COVERED WITH TRADITION..
AND DANDELIONS!
SCHULZ

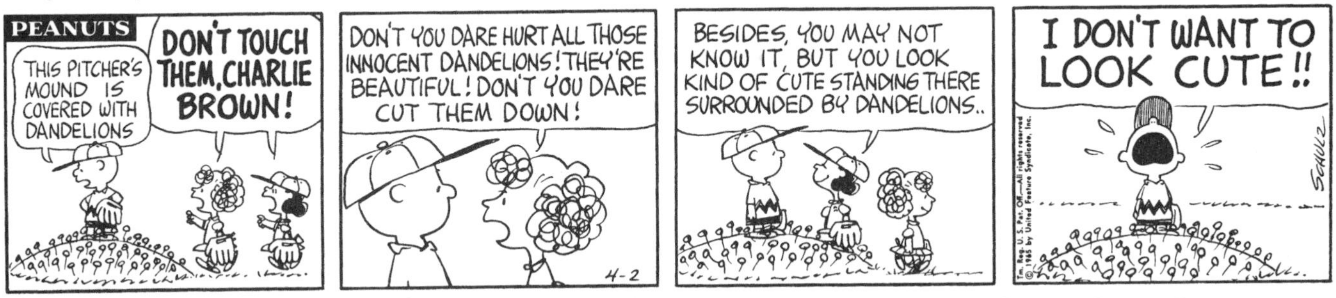
PEANUTS
THIS PITCHER'S MOUND IS COVERED WITH DANDELIONS
DON'T TOUCH THEM, CHARLIE BROWN!
DON'T YOU DARE HURT ALL THOSE INNOCENT DANDELIONS! THEY'RE BEAUTIFUL! DON'T YOU DARE CUT THEM DOWN!
BESIDES, YOU MAY NOT KNOW IT, BUT YOU LOOK KIND OF CUTE STANDING THERE SURROUNDED BY DANDELIONS..
I DON'T WANT TO LOOK CUTE!!
SCHULZ

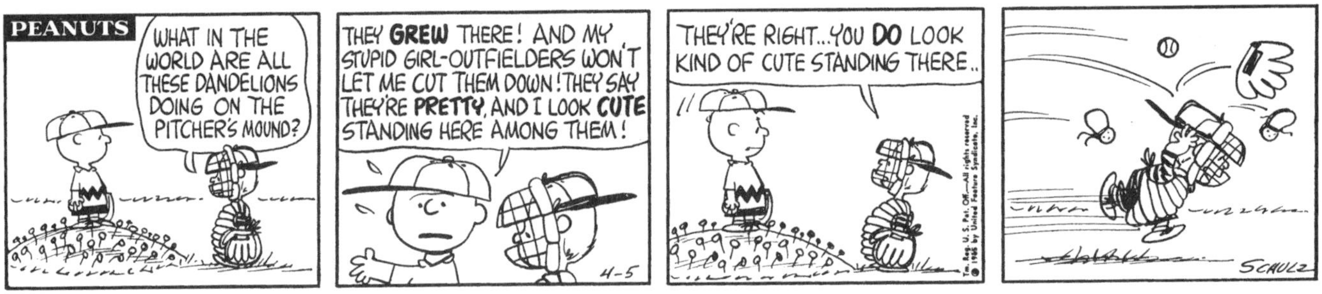
PEANUTS
WHAT IN THE WORLD ARE ALL THESE DANDELIONS DOING ON THE PITCHER'S MOUND?
THEY **GREW** THERE! AND MY STUPID GIRL-OUTFIELDERS WON'T LET ME CUT THEM DOWN! THEY SAY THEY'RE **PRETTY**, AND I LOOK **CUTE** STANDING HERE AMONG THEM!
THEY'RE RIGHT...YOU **DO** LOOK KIND OF CUTE STANDING THERE..
SCHULZ

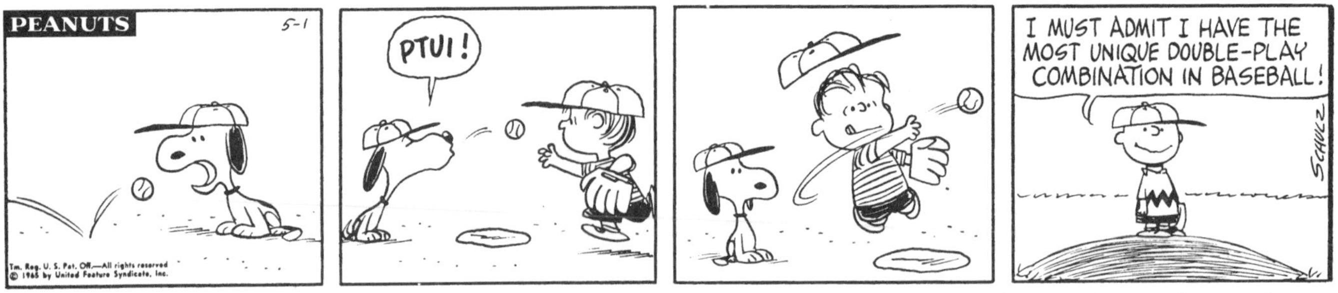
PEANUTS
PTUI!
I MUST ADMIT I HAVE THE MOST UNIQUE DOUBLE-PLAY COMBINATION IN BASEBALL!
SCHULZ
Tm. Reg. U. S. Pat. Off.—All rights reserved © 1965 by United Feature Syndicate, Inc.

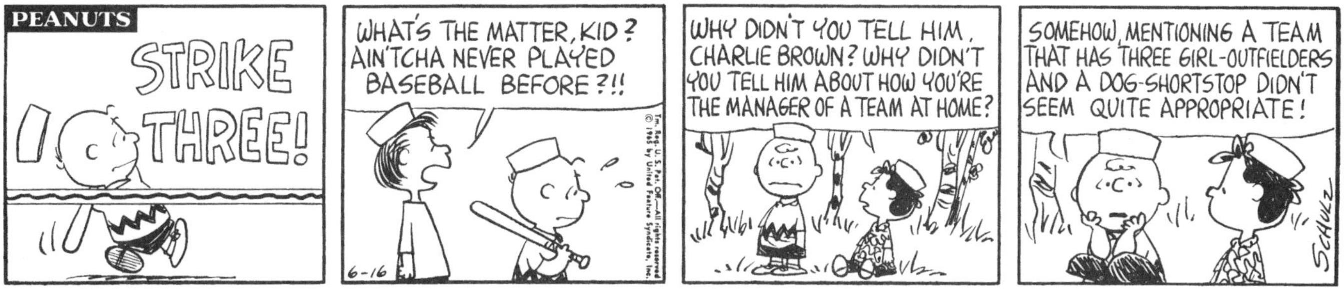
PEANUTS
STRIKE THREE!
WHAT'S THE MATTER, KID? AIN'TCHA NEVER PLAYED BASEBALL BEFORE?!!
6-16
WHY DIDN'T YOU TELL HIM, CHARLIE BROWN? WHY DIDN'T YOU TELL HIM ABOUT HOW YOU'RE THE MANAGER OF A TEAM AT HOME?
SOMEHOW, MENTIONING A TEAM THAT HAS THREE GIRL-OUTFIELDERS AND A DOG-SHORTSTOP DIDN'T SEEM QUITE APPROPRIATE!
SCHULZ

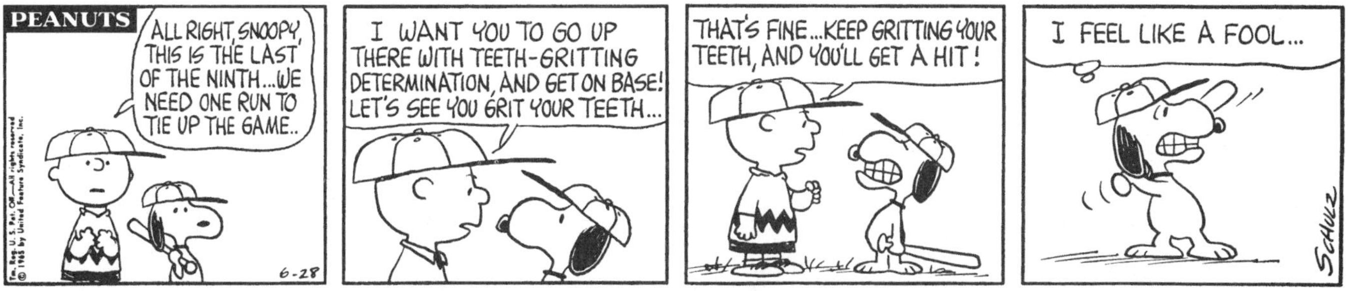
PEANUTS
ALL RIGHT, SNOOPY, THIS IS THE LAST OF THE NINTH...WE NEED ONE RUN TO TIE UP THE GAME..
6-28
I WANT YOU TO GO UP THERE WITH TEETH-GRITTING DETERMINATION, AND GET ON BASE! LET'S SEE YOU GRIT YOUR TEETH...
THAT'S FINE...KEEP GRITTING YOUR TEETH, AND YOU'LL GET A HIT!
I FEEL LIKE A FOOL...
SCHULZ

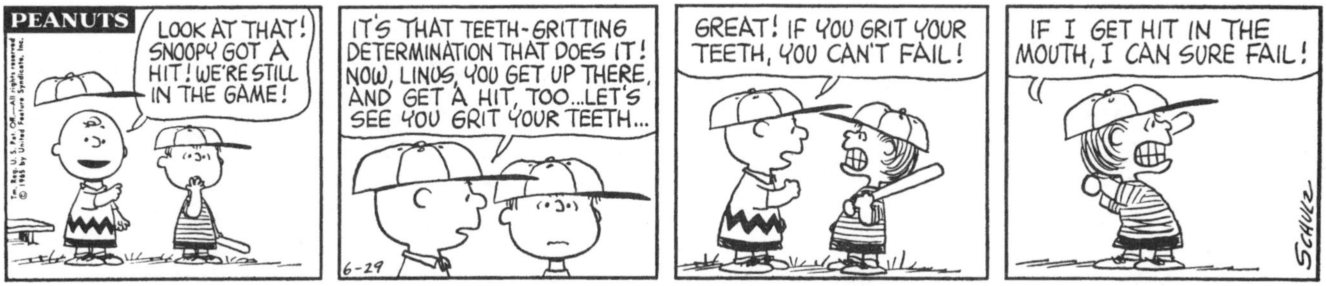
PEANUTS
LOOK AT THAT! SNOOPY GOT A HIT! WE'RE STILL IN THE GAME!
IT'S THAT TEETH-GRITTING DETERMINATION THAT DOES IT! NOW, LINUS, YOU GET UP THERE, AND GET A HIT, TOO...LET'S SEE YOU GRIT YOUR TEETH...
6-29
GREAT! IF YOU GRIT YOUR TEETH, YOU CAN'T FAIL!
IF I GET HIT IN THE MOUTH, I CAN SURE FAIL!
SCHULZ

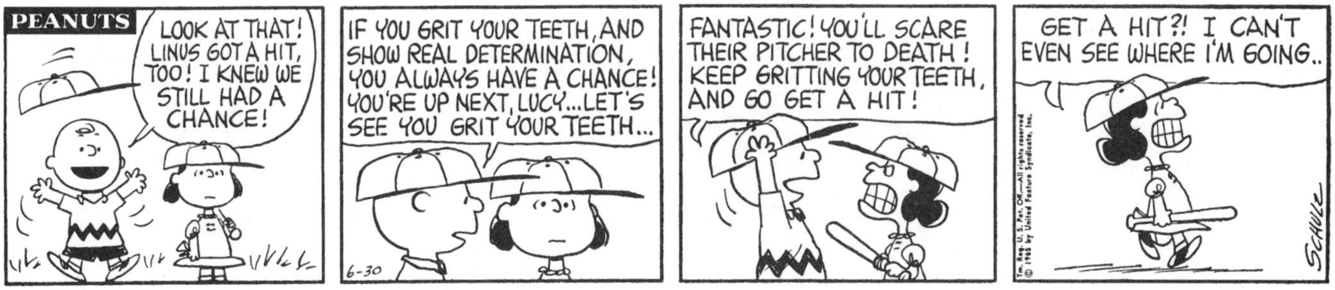
PEANUTS
LOOK AT THAT! LINUS GOT A HIT, TOO! I KNEW WE STILL HAD A CHANCE!
IF YOU GRIT YOUR TEETH, AND SHOW REAL DETERMINATION, YOU ALWAYS HAVE A CHANCE! YOU'RE UP NEXT, LUCY...LET'S SEE YOU GRIT YOUR TEETH...
6-30
FANTASTIC! YOU'LL SCARE THEIR PITCHER TO DEATH! KEEP GRITTING YOUR TEETH, AND GO GET A HIT!
GET A HIT?! I CAN'T EVEN SEE WHERE I'M GOING..
SCHULZ

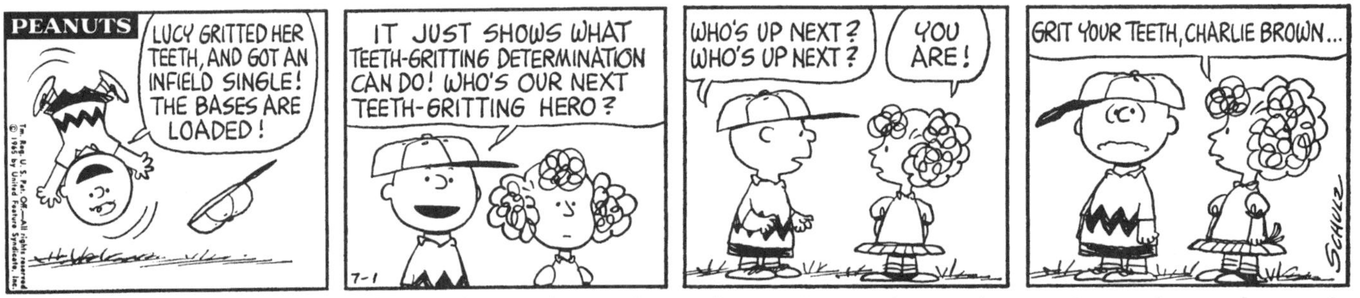
PEANUTS
LUCY GRITTED HER TEETH, AND GOT AN INFIELD SINGLE! THE BASES ARE LOADED!
Tm. Reg. U. S. Pat. Off.—All rights reserved © 1965 by United Feature Syndicate, Inc.
IT JUST SHOWS WHAT TEETH-GRITTING DETERMINATION CAN DO! WHO'S OUR NEXT TEETH-GRITTING HERO?
7-1
WHO'S UP NEXT? WHO'S UP NEXT?
YOU ARE!
GRIT YOUR TEETH, CHARLIE BROWN...
SCHULZ

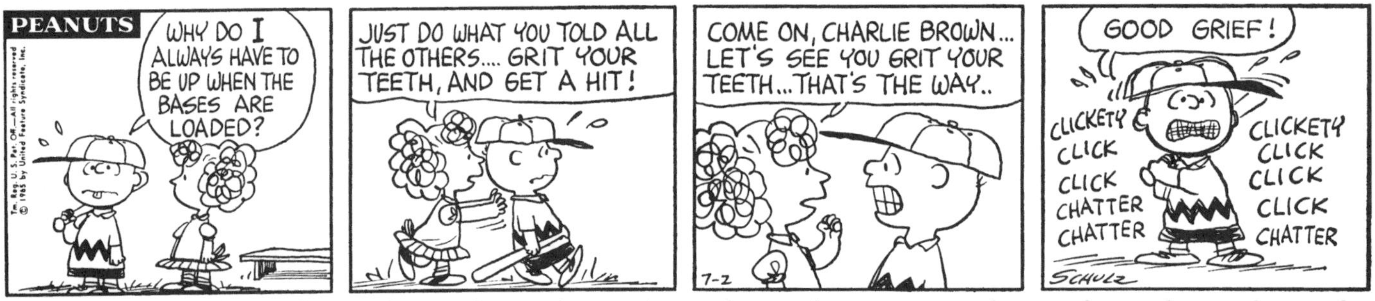
PEANUTS
WHY DO I ALWAYS HAVE TO BE UP WHEN THE BASES ARE LOADED?
Tm. Reg. U. S. Pat. Off.—All rights reserved © 1965 by United Feature Syndicate, Inc.
JUST DO WHAT YOU TOLD ALL THE OTHERS.... GRIT YOUR TEETH, AND GET A HIT!
COME ON, CHARLIE BROWN... LET'S SEE YOU GRIT YOUR TEETH...THAT'S THE WAY..
7-2
GOOD GRIEF!
CLICKETY CLICK CLICK CHATTER CHATTER
CLICKETY CLICK CLICK CLICK CHATTER
SCHULZ

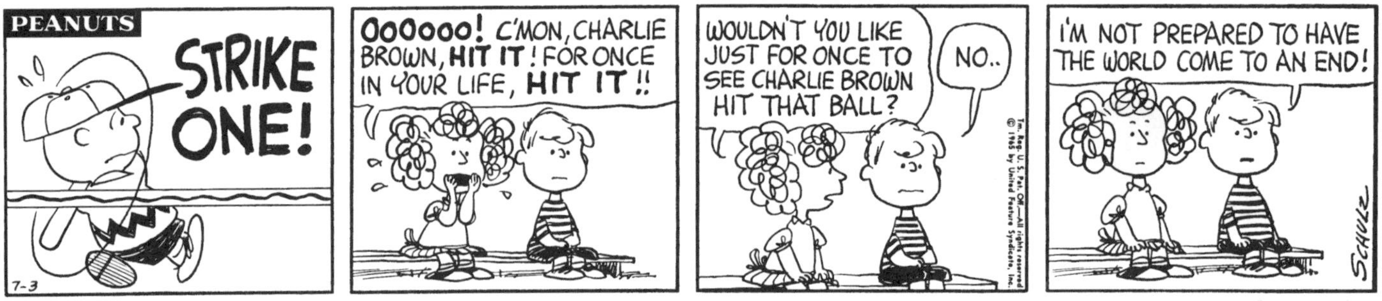
PEANUTS
STRIKE ONE!
7-3
OOOOOO! C'MON, CHARLIE BROWN, HIT IT! FOR ONCE IN YOUR LIFE, HIT IT!!
WOULDN'T YOU LIKE JUST FOR ONCE TO SEE CHARLIE BROWN HIT THAT BALL?
NO..
Tm. Reg. U. S. Pat. Off.—All rights reserved © 1965 by United Feature Syndicate, Inc.
I'M NOT PREPARED TO HAVE THE WORLD COME TO AN END!
SCHULZ

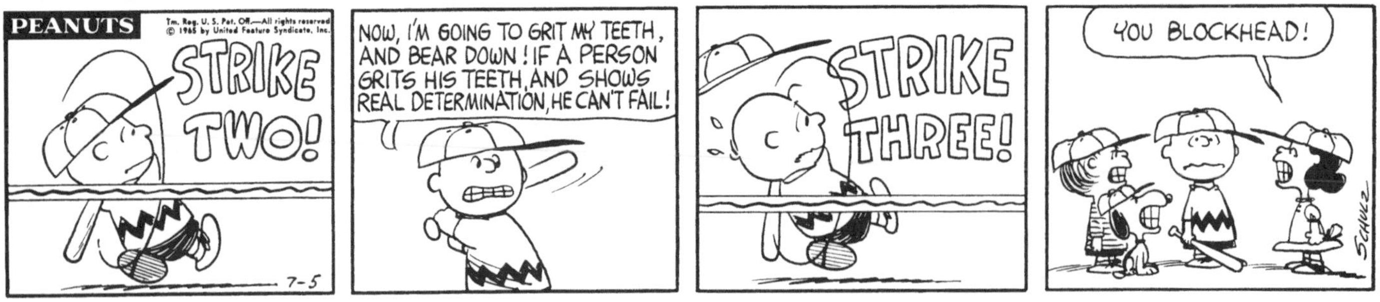
PEANUTS
Tm. Reg. U. S. Pat. Off.—All rights reserved © 1965 by United Feature Syndicate, Inc.
STRIKE TWO!
7-5
NOW, I'M GOING TO GRIT MY TEETH, AND BEAR DOWN! IF A PERSON GRITS HIS TEETH, AND SHOWS REAL DETERMINATION, HE CAN'T FAIL!
STRIKE THREE!
YOU BLOCKHEAD!
SCHULZ

PEANUTS
THERE'S A RUMOR GOING AROUND THAT I WON'T BE PLAYING ANY MORE..
7-9
WELL, I'M NOT QUITTING BASEBALL JUST BECAUSE I GOOFED A FEW TIMES! I'M STILL THE MANAGER OF THIS TEAM, AND WHAT I SAY GOES!
NOW, THERE'S STILL TIME LEFT IN THIS SEASON FOR US TO MAKE A GOOD SHOWING IF WE'LL ALL JUST GRIT OUR TEETH, AND..
Tm. Reg. U. S. Pat. Off.—All rights reserved © 1965 by United Feature Syndicate, Inc.
SCHULZ

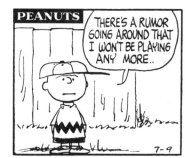

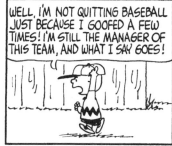

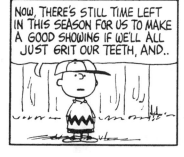

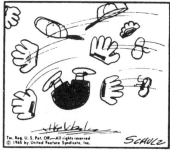

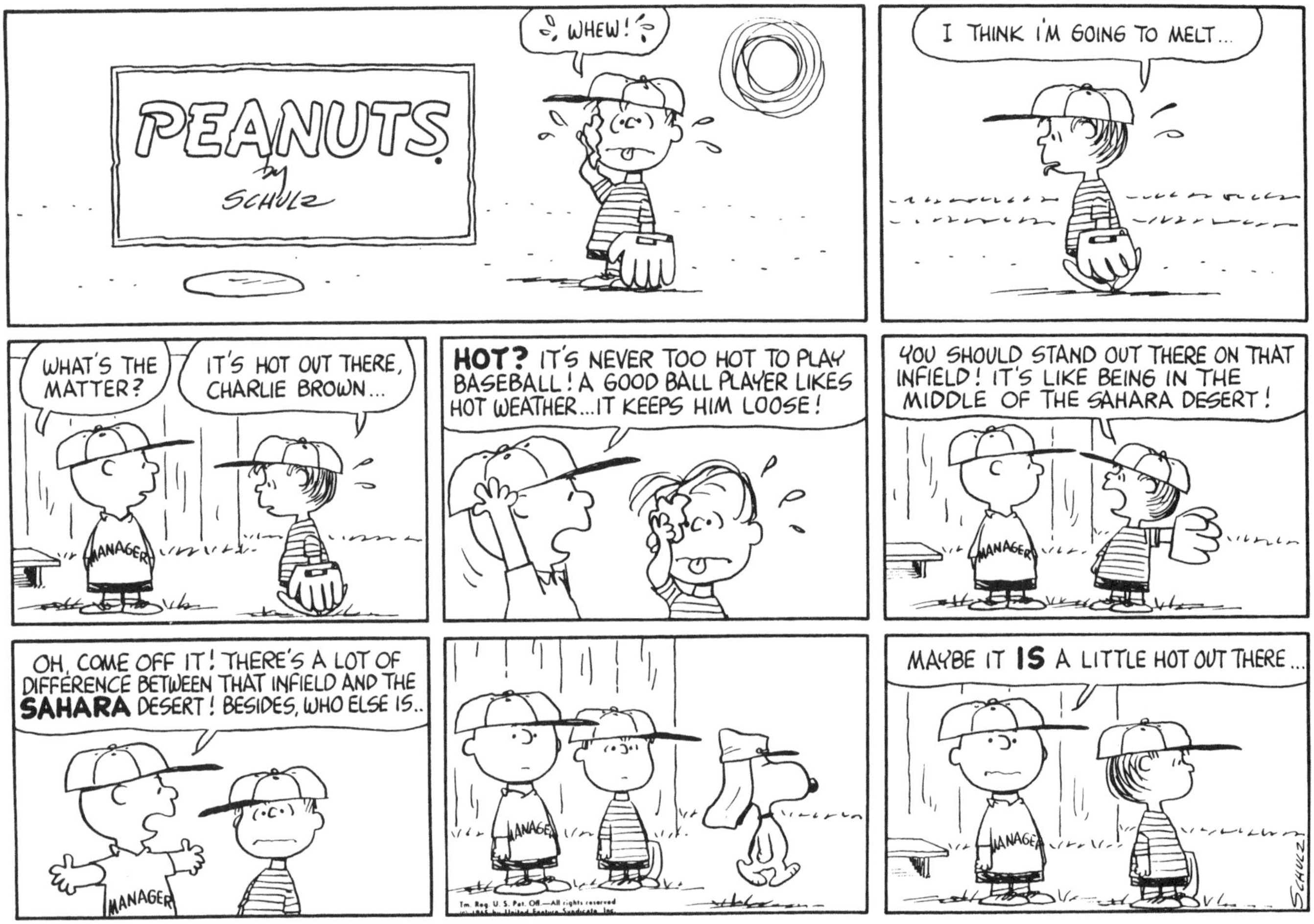
PEANUTS
by SCHULZ
WHEW!
I THINK I'M GOING TO MELT...
WHAT'S THE MATTER?
IT'S HOT OUT THERE, CHARLIE BROWN...
HOT? IT'S NEVER TOO HOT TO PLAY BASEBALL! A GOOD BALL PLAYER LIKES HOT WEATHER...IT KEEPS HIM LOOSE!
YOU SHOULD STAND OUT THERE ON THAT INFIELD! IT'S LIKE BEING IN THE MIDDLE OF THE SAHARA DESERT!
OH, COME OFF IT! THERE'S A LOT OF DIFFERENCE BETWEEN THAT INFIELD AND THE SAHARA DESERT! BESIDES, WHO ELSE IS..
MAYBE IT IS A LITTLE HOT OUT THERE...
SCHULZ

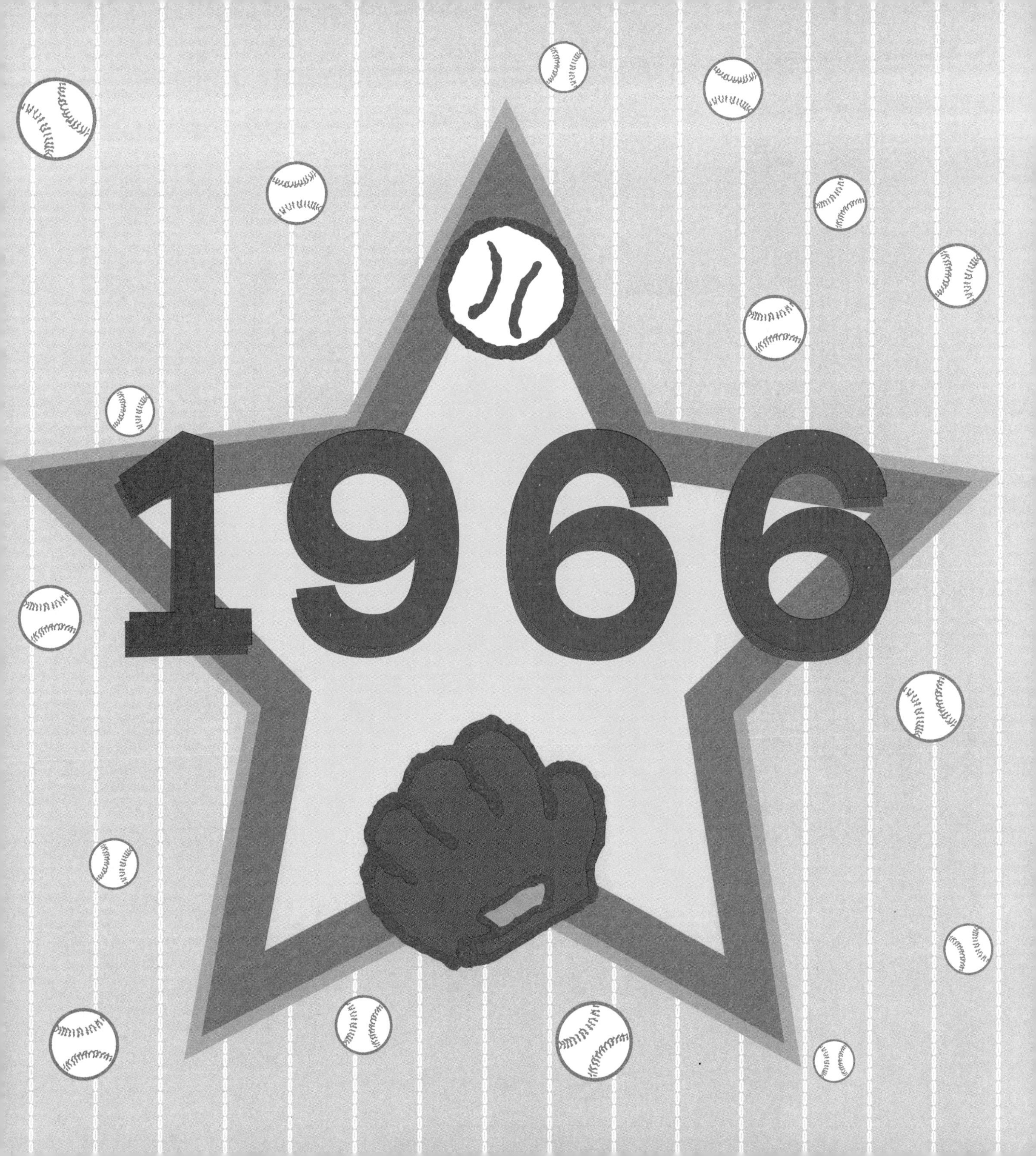
1966

PEANUTS
WHAP
CLOMP
Tm. Reg. U. S. Pat. Off.—All rights reserved
©1966 by United Feature Syndicate, Inc.
3-30
GOOD CATCH, SNOOPY..
THANK YOU..
PTUI!
BLEAH! HORSESHIDE TASTES TERRIBLE IN THE MORNING!
SCHULZ

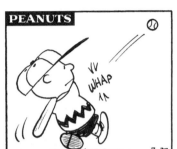

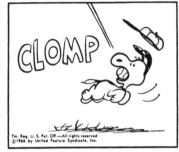

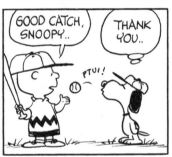

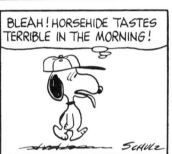

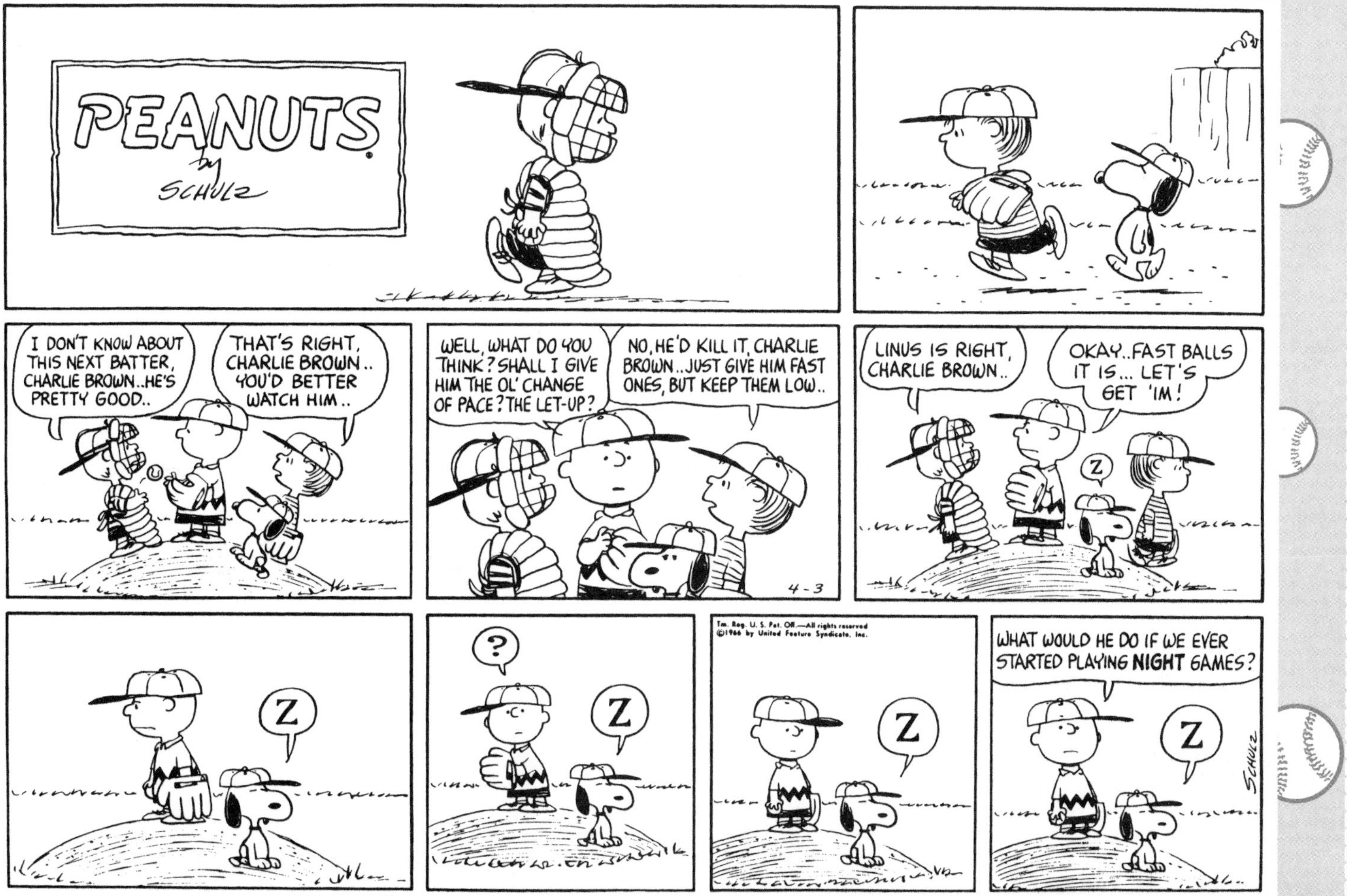
PEANUTS
by SCHULZ
I DON'T KNOW ABOUT THIS NEXT BATTER, CHARLIE BROWN..HE'S PRETTY GOOD..
THAT'S RIGHT, CHARLIE BROWN.. YOU'D BETTER WATCH HIM..
WELL, WHAT DO YOU THINK? SHALL I GIVE HIM THE OL' CHANGE OF PACE? THE LET-UP?
NO, HE'D KILL IT, CHARLIE BROWN..JUST GIVE HIM FAST ONES, BUT KEEP THEM LOW..
4-3
LINUS IS RIGHT, CHARLIE BROWN..
Z
OKAY..FAST BALLS IT IS... LET'S GET 'IM!
Z
?
Z
Tm. Reg. U. S. Pat. Off.—All rights reserved
©1966 by United Feature Syndicate, Inc.
Z
WHAT WOULD HE DO IF WE EVER STARTED PLAYING NIGHT GAMES?
Z
SCHULZ

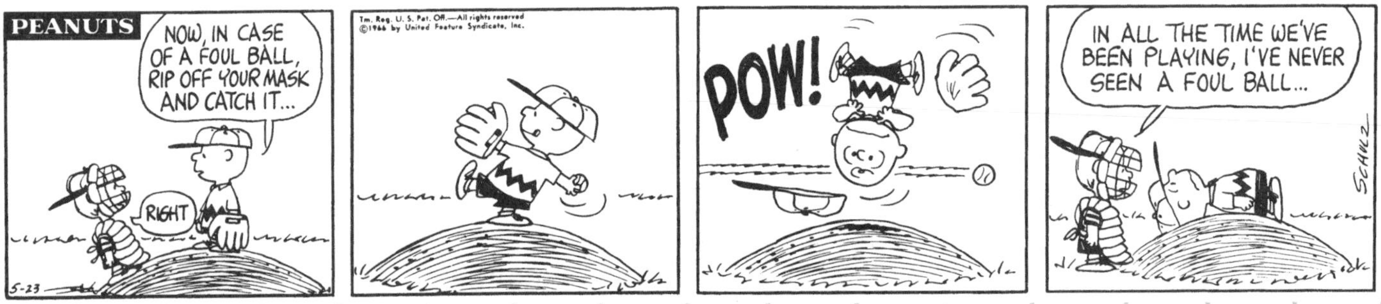
PEANUTS
NOW, IN CASE OF A FOUL BALL, RIP OFF YOUR MASK AND CATCH IT...
RIGHT
5-23
Tm. Reg. U. S. Pat. Off.—All rights reserved ©1966 by United Feature Syndicate, Inc.
POW!
IN ALL THE TIME WE'VE BEEN PLAYING, I'VE NEVER SEEN A FOUL BALL...
SCHULZ

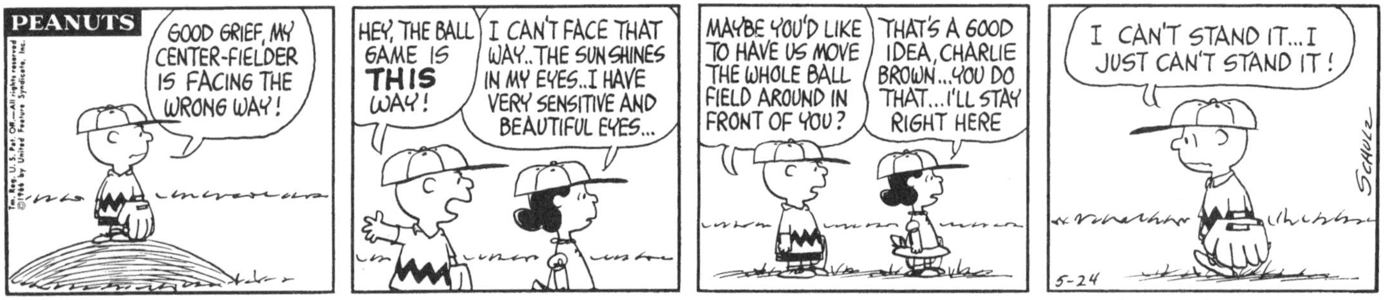
PEANUTS
Tm. Reg. U. S. Pat. Off.—All rights reserved ©1966 by United Feature Syndicate, Inc.
GOOD GRIEF, MY CENTER-FIELDER IS FACING THE WRONG WAY!
HEY, THE BALL GAME IS **THIS** WAY!
I CAN'T FACE THAT WAY.. THE SUN SHINES IN MY EYES..I HAVE VERY SENSITIVE AND BEAUTIFUL EYES...
MAYBE YOU'D LIKE TO HAVE US MOVE THE WHOLE BALL FIELD AROUND IN FRONT OF YOU?
THAT'S A GOOD IDEA, CHARLIE BROWN...YOU DO THAT...I'LL STAY RIGHT HERE
I CAN'T STAND IT...I JUST CAN'T STAND IT!
SCHULZ
5-24

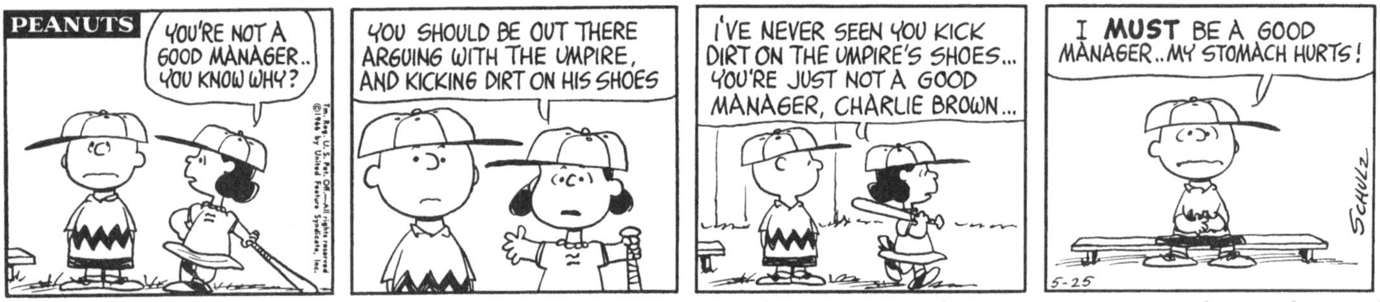
PEANUTS
YOU'RE NOT A GOOD MANAGER.. YOU KNOW WHY?
Tm. Reg. U. S. Pat. Off.—All rights reserved ©1966 by United Feature Syndicate, Inc.
YOU SHOULD BE OUT THERE ARGUING WITH THE UMPIRE, AND KICKING DIRT ON HIS SHOES
I'VE NEVER SEEN YOU KICK DIRT ON THE UMPIRE'S SHOES... YOU'RE JUST NOT A GOOD MANAGER, CHARLIE BROWN...
I **MUST** BE A GOOD MANAGER..MY STOMACH HURTS!
SCHULZ
5-25

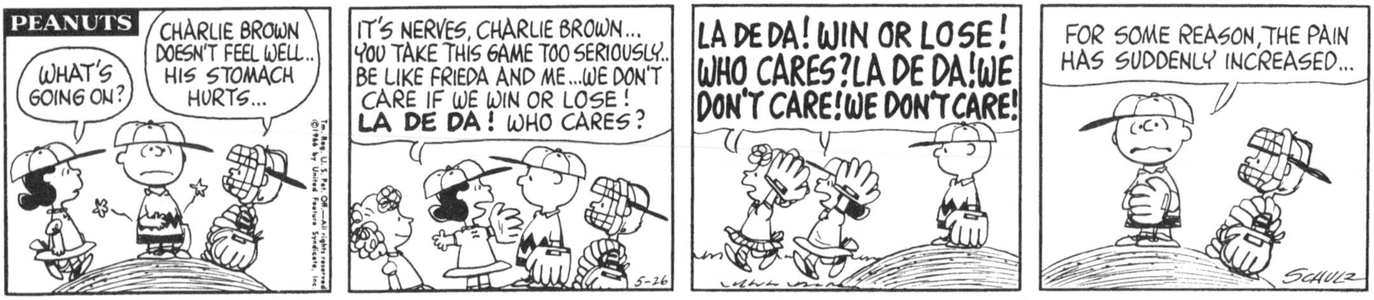
PEANUTS
WHAT'S GOING ON?
CHARLIE BROWN DOESN'T FEEL WELL.. HIS STOMACH HURTS...
Tm. Reg. U. S. Pat. Off.—All rights reserved ©1966 by United Feature Syndicate, Inc.
IT'S NERVES, CHARLIE BROWN... YOU TAKE THIS GAME TOO SERIOUSLY.. BE LIKE FRIEDA AND ME...WE DON'T CARE IF WE WIN OR LOSE! **LA DE DA!** WHO CARES?
5-26
LA DE DA! WIN OR LOSE! WHO CARES? LA DE DA! WE DON'T CARE! WE DON'T CARE!
FOR SOME REASON, THE PAIN HAS SUDDENLY INCREASED...
SCHULZ

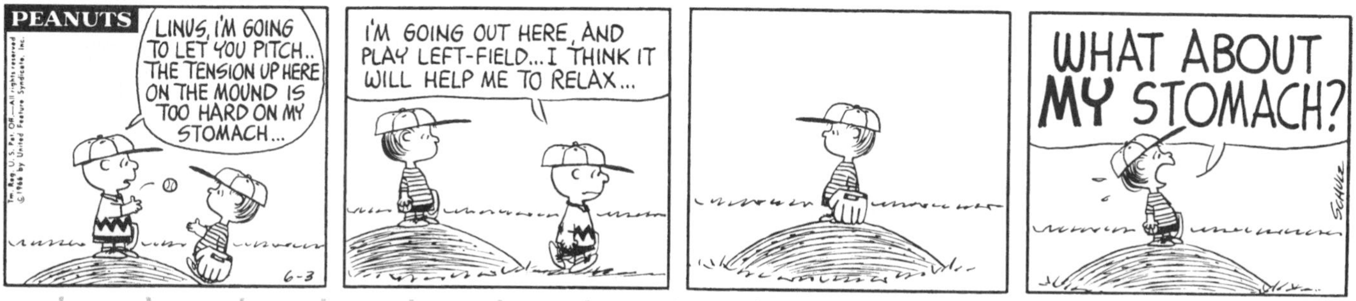
PEANUTS
LINUS, I'M GOING TO LET YOU PITCH.. THE TENSION UP HERE ON THE MOUND IS TOO HARD ON MY STOMACH...
I'M GOING OUT HERE, AND PLAY LEFT-FIELD... I THINK IT WILL HELP ME TO RELAX...
WHAT ABOUT MY STOMACH?
6-3
SCHULZ

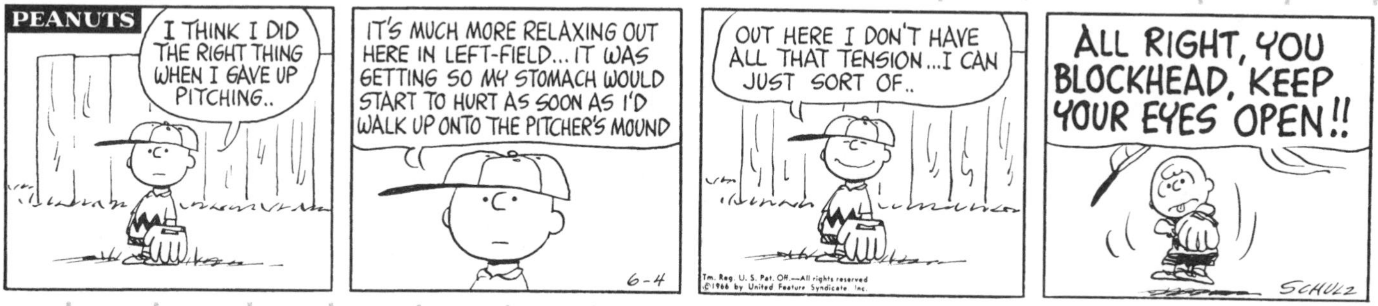
PEANUTS
I THINK I DID THE RIGHT THING WHEN I GAVE UP PITCHING..
IT'S MUCH MORE RELAXING OUT HERE IN LEFT-FIELD... IT WAS GETTING SO MY STOMACH WOULD START TO HURT AS SOON AS I'D WALK UP ONTO THE PITCHER'S MOUND
6-4
OUT HERE I DON'T HAVE ALL THAT TENSION... I CAN JUST SORT OF..
Tm. Reg. U. S. Pat. Off.—All rights reserved ©1966 by United Feature Syndicate, Inc.
ALL RIGHT, YOU BLOCKHEAD, KEEP YOUR EYES OPEN!!
SCHULZ

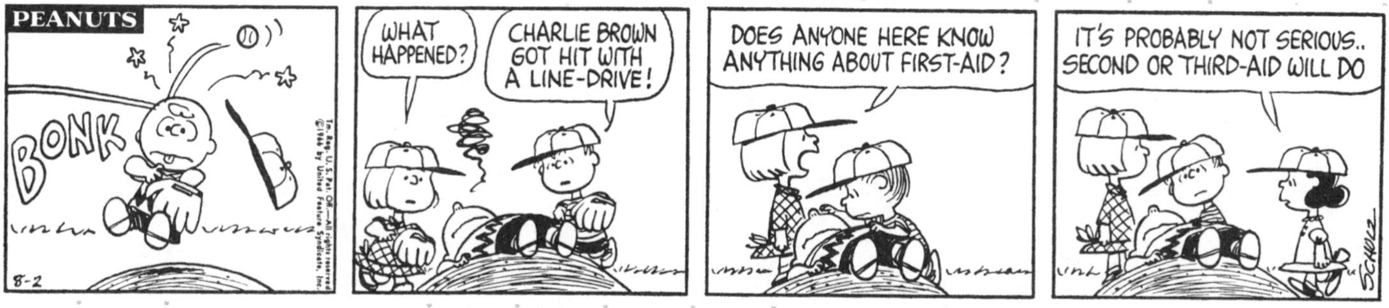
PEANUTS
BONK
8-2
WHAT HAPPENED?
CHARLIE BROWN GOT HIT WITH A LINE-DRIVE!
DOES ANYONE HERE KNOW ANYTHING ABOUT FIRST-AID?
IT'S PROBABLY NOT SERIOUS.. SECOND OR THIRD-AID WILL DO
SCHULZ

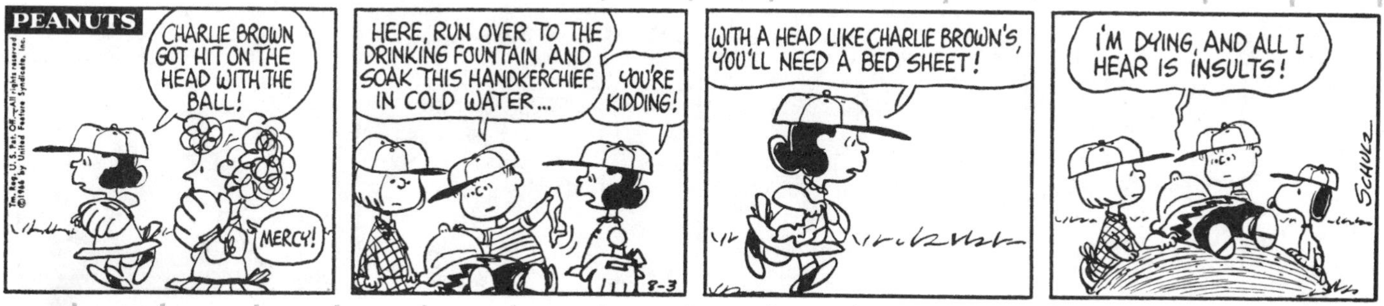
PEANUTS
CHARLIE BROWN GOT HIT ON THE HEAD WITH THE BALL!
MERCY!
HERE, RUN OVER TO THE DRINKING FOUNTAIN, AND SOAK THIS HANDKERCHIEF IN COLD WATER...
YOU'RE KIDDING!
8-3
WITH A HEAD LIKE CHARLIE BROWN'S, YOU'LL NEED A BED SHEET!
I'M DYING, AND ALL I HEAR IS INSULTS!
SCHULZ

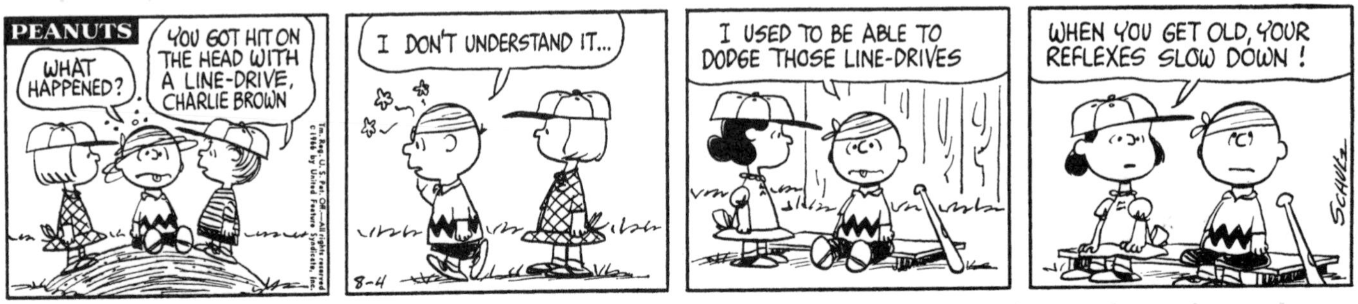
PEANUTS
WHAT HAPPENED?
YOU GOT HIT ON THE HEAD WITH A LINE-DRIVE, CHARLIE BROWN
Tm. Reg. U.S. Pat. Off.—All rights reserved ©1966 by United Feature Syndicate, Inc.
I DON'T UNDERSTAND IT...
8-4
I USED TO BE ABLE TO DODGE THOSE LINE-DRIVES
WHEN YOU GET OLD, YOUR REFLEXES SLOW DOWN !
SCHULZ

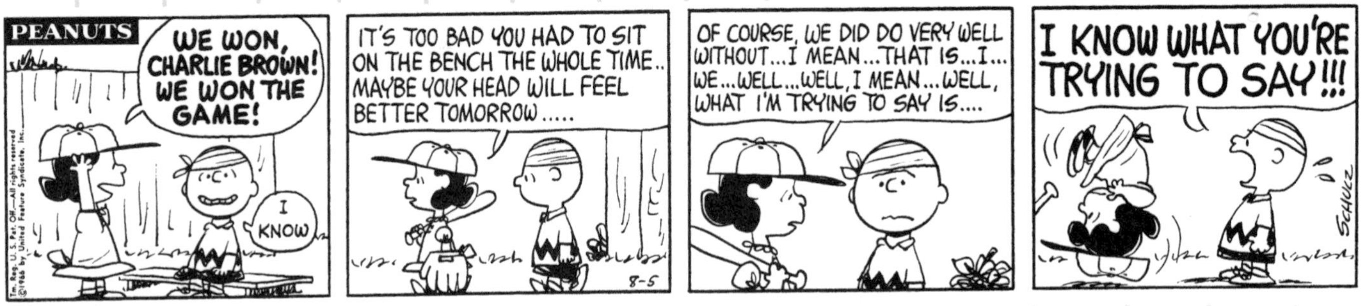
PEANUTS
WE WON, CHARLIE BROWN! WE WON THE GAME!
I KNOW
Tm. Reg. U.S. Pat. Off.—All rights reserved ©1966 by United Feature Syndicate, Inc.
IT'S TOO BAD YOU HAD TO SIT ON THE BENCH THE WHOLE TIME.. MAYBE YOUR HEAD WILL FEEL BETTER TOMORROW.....
8-5
OF COURSE, WE DID DO VERY WELL WITHOUT...I MEAN...THAT IS...I... WE...WELL...WELL, I MEAN...WELL, WHAT I'M TRYING TO SAY IS....
I KNOW WHAT YOU'RE TRYING TO SAY!!!
SCHULZ

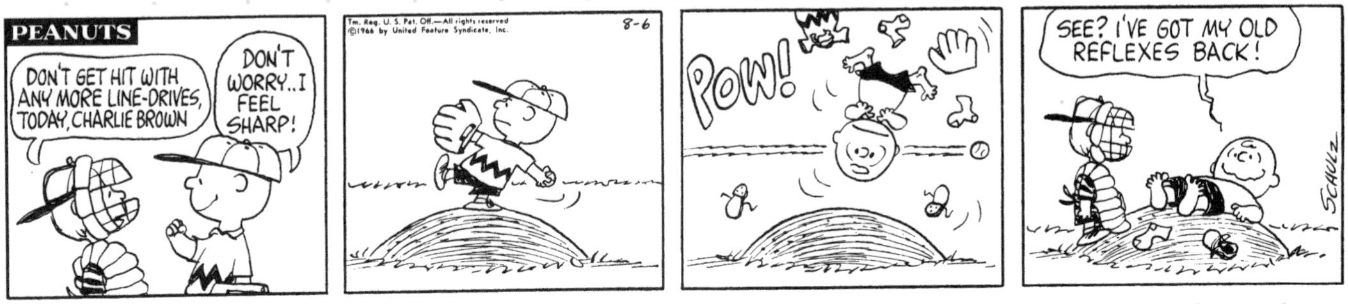
PEANUTS
DON'T GET HIT WITH ANY MORE LINE-DRIVES, TODAY, CHARLIE BROWN
DON'T WORRY..I FEEL SHARP!
Tm. Reg. U.S. Pat. Off.—All rights reserved ©1966 by United Feature Syndicate, Inc.
8-6
POW!
SEE? I'VE GOT MY OLD REFLEXES BACK!
SCHULZ

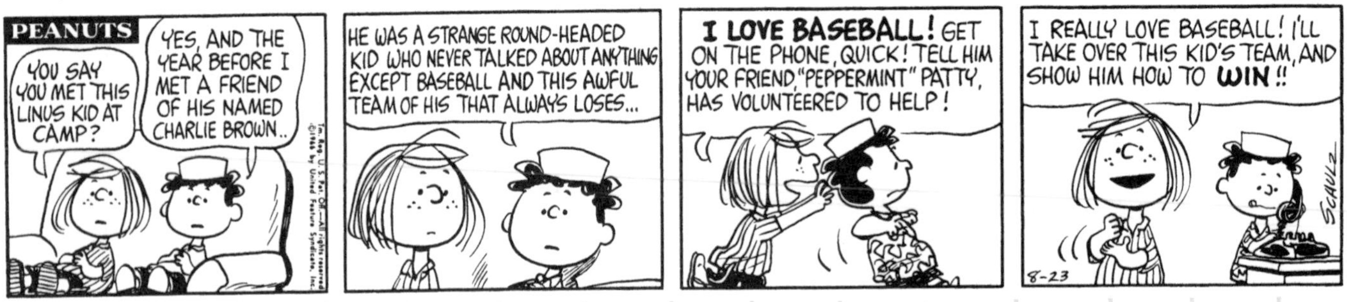
PEANUTS
YOU SAY YOU MET THIS LINUS KID AT CAMP?
YES, AND THE YEAR BEFORE I MET A FRIEND OF HIS NAMED CHARLIE BROWN..
Tm. Reg. U.S. Pat. Off.—All rights reserved ©1966 by United Feature Syndicate, Inc.
HE WAS A STRANGE ROUND-HEADED KID WHO NEVER TALKED ABOUT ANYTHING EXCEPT BASEBALL AND THIS AWFUL TEAM OF HIS THAT ALWAYS LOSES...
I LOVE BASEBALL! GET ON THE PHONE, QUICK! TELL HIM YOUR FRIEND, "PEPPERMINT" PATTY, HAS VOLUNTEERED TO HELP!
I REALLY LOVE BASEBALL! I'LL TAKE OVER THIS KID'S TEAM, AND SHOW HIM HOW TO WIN!!
8-23
SCHULZ

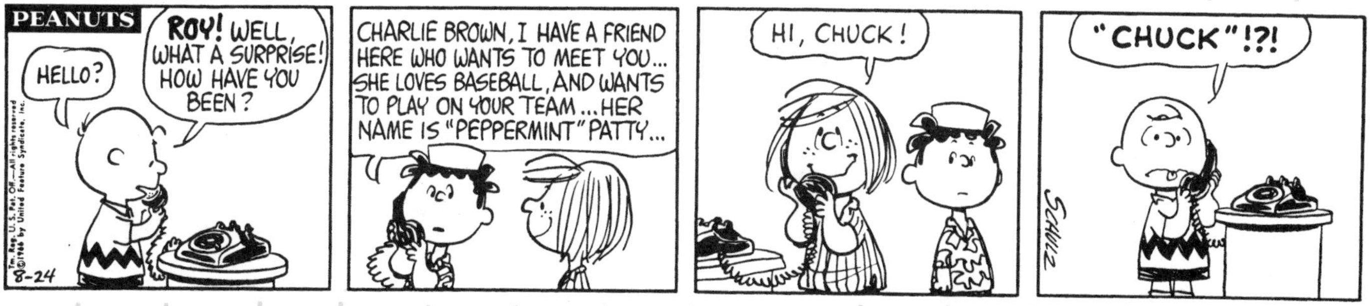
PEANUTS
HELLO?
ROY! WELL, WHAT A SURPRISE! HOW HAVE YOU BEEN?
8-24
CHARLIE BROWN, I HAVE A FRIEND HERE WHO WANTS TO MEET YOU... SHE LOVES BASEBALL, AND WANTS TO PLAY ON YOUR TEAM ... HER NAME IS "PEPPERMINT" PATTY...
HI, CHUCK!
"CHUCK"!?!
SCHULZ

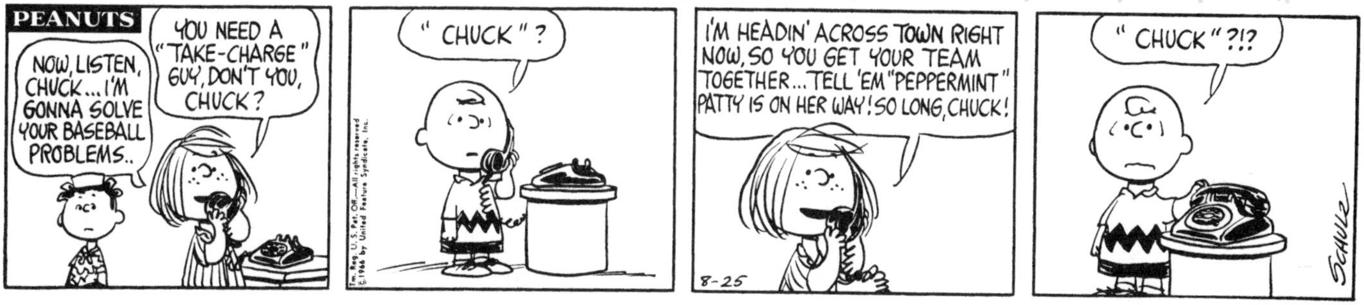
PEANUTS
NOW, LISTEN, CHUCK... I'M GONNA SOLVE YOUR BASEBALL PROBLEMS..
YOU NEED A "TAKE-CHARGE" GUY, DON'T YOU, CHUCK?
"CHUCK"?
I'M HEADIN' ACROSS TOWN RIGHT NOW, SO YOU GET YOUR TEAM TOGETHER... TELL 'EM "PEPPERMINT" PATTY IS ON HER WAY! SO LONG, CHUCK!
8-25
"CHUCK"?!?
SCHULZ

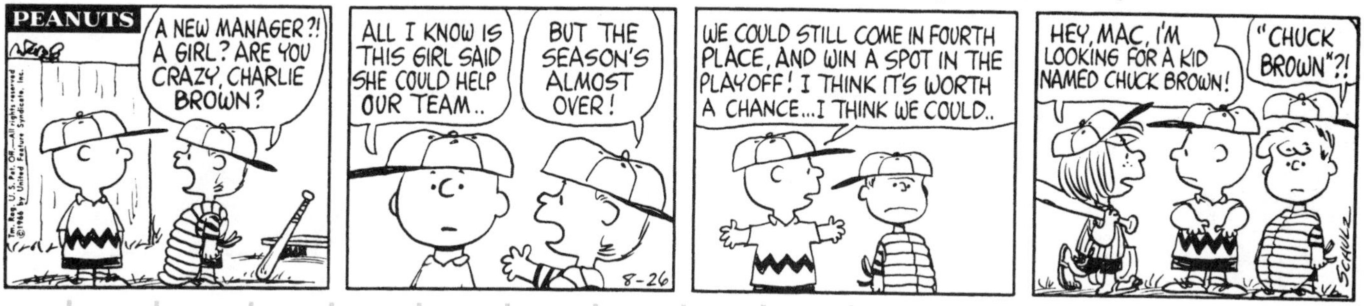
PEANUTS
A NEW MANAGER?! A GIRL? ARE YOU CRAZY, CHARLIE BROWN?
ALL I KNOW IS THIS GIRL SAID SHE COULD HELP OUR TEAM..
BUT THE SEASON'S ALMOST OVER!
8-26
WE COULD STILL COME IN FOURTH PLACE, AND WIN A SPOT IN THE PLAYOFF! I THINK IT'S WORTH A CHANCE... I THINK WE COULD..
HEY, MAC, I'M LOOKING FOR A KID NAMED CHUCK BROWN!
"CHUCK BROWN"?!
SCHULZ

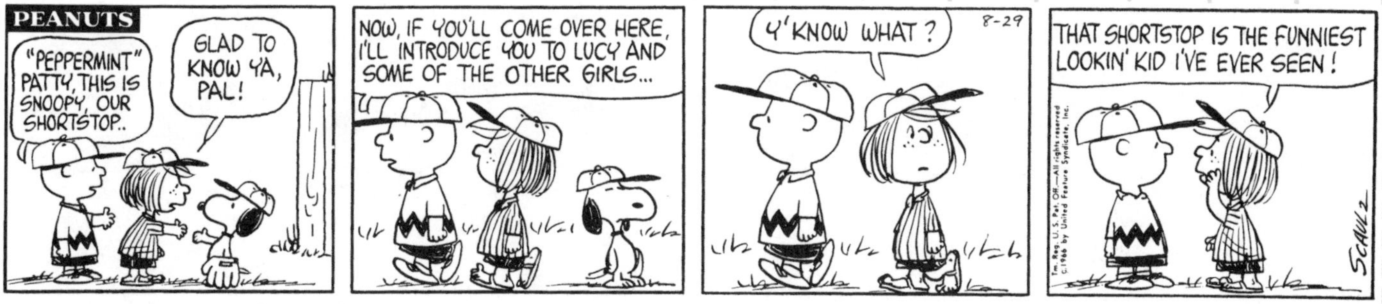
PEANUTS
"PEPPERMINT" PATTY, THIS IS SNOOPY, OUR SHORTSTOP..
GLAD TO KNOW YA, PAL!
NOW, IF YOU'LL COME OVER HERE, I'LL INTRODUCE YOU TO LUCY AND SOME OF THE OTHER GIRLS...
Y'KNOW WHAT?
8-29
THAT SHORTSTOP IS THE FUNNIEST LOOKIN' KID I'VE EVER SEEN!
SCHULZ

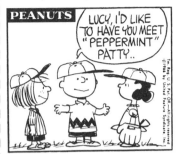

PEANUTS
LUCY, I'D LIKE TO HAVE YOU MEET "PEPPERMINT" PATTY..
Tm. Reg. U.S. Pat. Off.—All rights reserved ©1966 by United Feature Syndicate, Inc.
SHE'S COME CLEAR ACROSS TOWN TO HELP US WIN A FEW BALL GAMES
GLAD TO KNOW YA, LUCILLE, OL' GIRL!
8-30
WE'LL SHOW CHUCK HERE HOW THIS GAME IS REALLY PLAYED, WON'T WE?
"LUCILLE"?! "CHUCK"?!?
SCHULZ

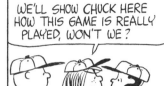

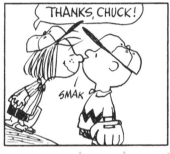

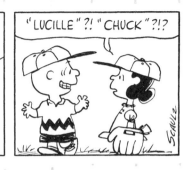

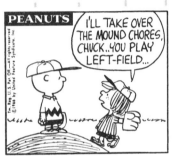

PEANUTS
I'LL TAKE OVER THE MOUND CHORES, CHUCK..YOU PLAY LEFT-FIELD...
Tm. Reg. U.S. Pat. Off.—All rights reserved ©1966 by United Feature Syndicate, Inc.
PSST! HEY, CHUCK! BEFORE THE GAME STARTS, HOW ABOUT A LITTLE KISS ON THE NOSE FOR GOOD LUCK?
8-31
THANKS, CHUCK!
SMAK
I'M SURPRISED AT MYSELF...I NEVER REALIZED HOW FAR I'D GO TO WIN A BALL GAME....
SCHULZ

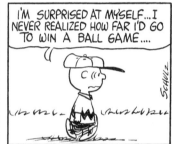

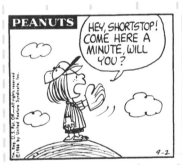

PEANUTS
HEY, SHORTSTOP! COME HERE A MINUTE, WILL YOU?
Tm. Reg. U.S. Pat. Off.—All rights reserved ©1966 by United Feature Syndicate, Inc.
9-2
HOW ABOUT PLAYING JUST A LITTLE MORE TO YOUR RIGHT? OKAY, BABY? THAT'S THE BOY!
THAT'S THE STRANGEST LITTLE KID I'VE EVER SEEN... HE NEVER SAYS ANYTHING!
SCHULZ

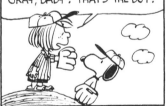

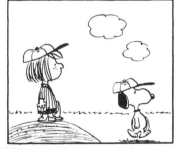

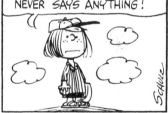

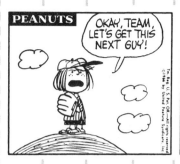

PEANUTS
OKAY, TEAM, LET'S GET THIS NEXT GUY!
Tm. Reg. U.S. Pat. Off.—All rights reserved © 1966 by United Feature Syndicate, Inc.
WE CAN DO IT! WE CAN GET HIM EASY! HE'S NO HITTER! HE'S NO HITTER AT ALL!
C'MON, TEAM, LET'S BEAR DOWN OUT THERE! LET'S REALLY GET THIS GUY!
THAT'S THE ONLY PITCHER I'VE EVER KNOWN WHO SUPPLIED HER OWN INFIELD CHATTER!
9-3
SCHULZ

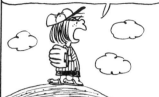

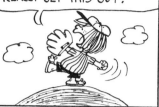

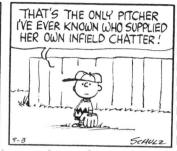

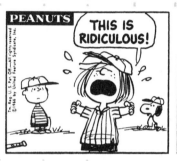

PEANUTS
Tm. Reg. U.S. Pat. Off.—All rights reserved © 1966 by United Feature Syndicate, Inc.
THIS IS RIDICULOUS!
I'VE HIT FIVE HOME RUNS AND PITCHED A NO-HIT GAME, AND WE'RE BEHIND THIRTY-SEVEN TO FIVE! WHOEVER HEARD OF THIRTY-SEVEN UNEARNED RUNS? THIS IS RIDICULOUS!
9-5
I THOUGHT I COULD HELP YOUR TEAM, CHUCK, BUT IT'S HOPELESS! I'M GOING BACK WHERE I CAME FROM!
THAT MUST BE A NICE THING TO BE ABLE TO DO...
SCHULZ

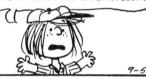

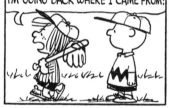

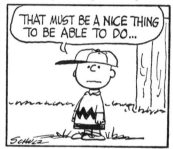

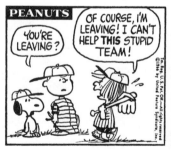

PEANUTS
YOU'RE LEAVING?
OF COURSE, I'M LEAVING! I CAN'T HELP THIS STUPID TEAM!
Tm. Reg. U.S. Pat. Off.—All rights reserved © 1966 by United Feature Syndicate, Inc.
SO LONG, MAC! YOU'RE THE ONLY DECENT PLAYER THEY'VE GOT!
HE'S A GOOD PLAYER, BUT I STILL THINK HE'S THE FUNNIEST LOOKING KID I'VE EVER SEEN!
9-6
SCHULZ

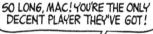

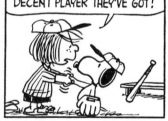

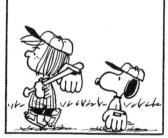

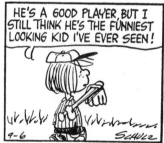

PEANUTS
WHAT ARE YOU DOING, CHARLIE BROWN?
I'M TRYING TO FIGURE OUT MY PITCHING RECORD FOR THIS YEAR..
YOU TAKE THE NUMBER OF EARNED RUNS, AND MULTIPLY BY NINE AND THEN DIVIDE BY THE NUMBER OF INNINGS PITCHED
WHAT DID YOU GET ?
A FIGURE MUCH TOO EMBARRASSING TO MENTION !
10-15
SCHULZ

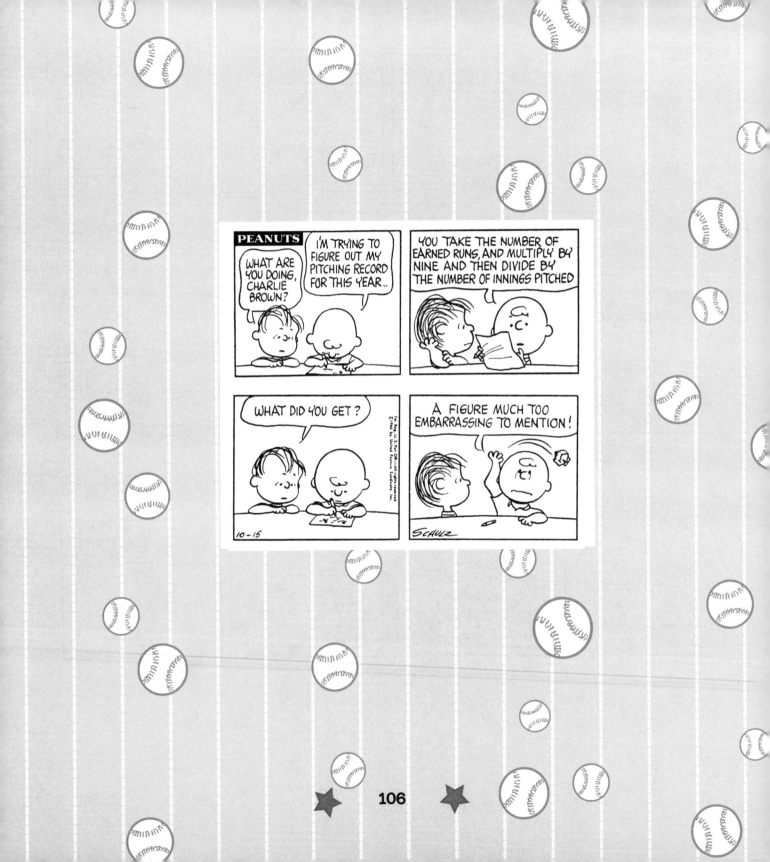

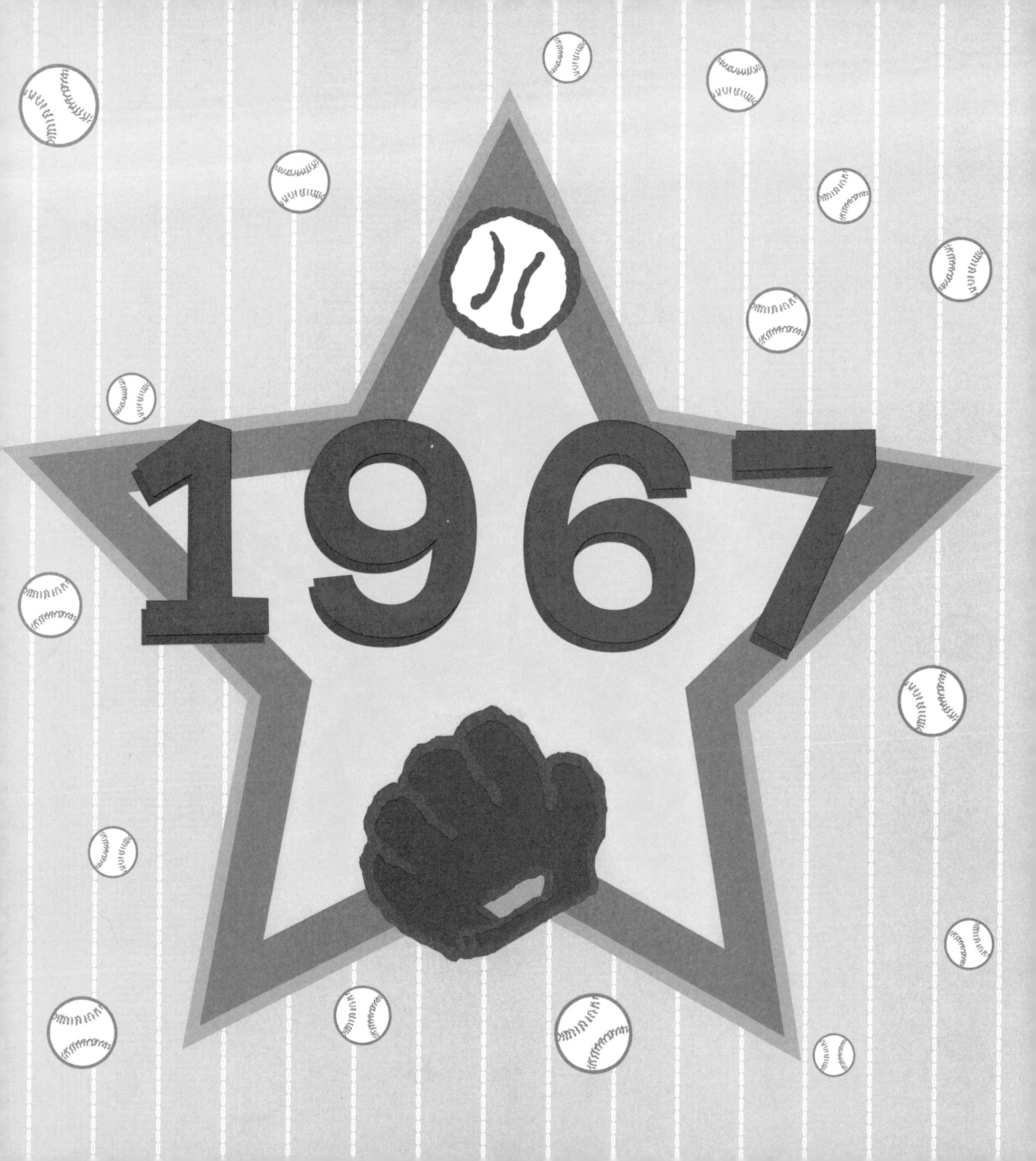
1967

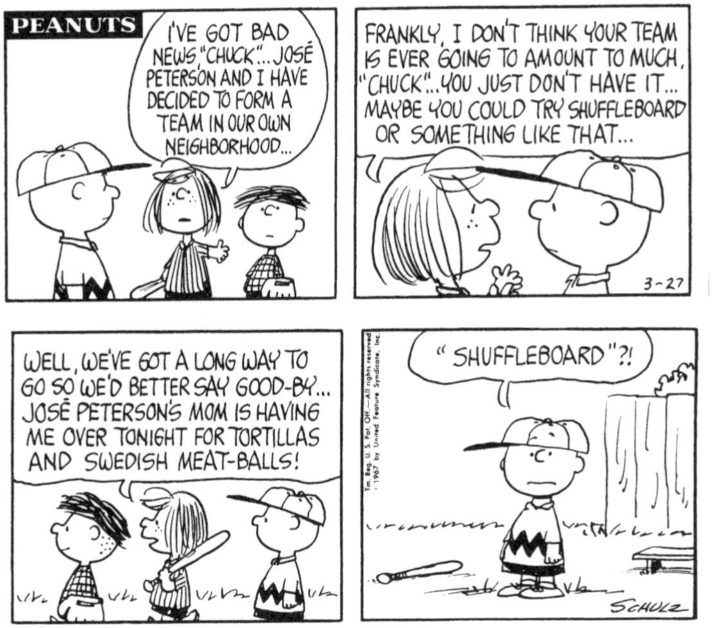
PEANUTS
I'VE GOT BAD NEWS, "CHUCK"... JOSÉ PETERSON AND I HAVE DECIDED TO FORM A TEAM IN OUR OWN NEIGHBORHOOD...
FRANKLY, I DON'T THINK YOUR TEAM IS EVER GOING TO AMOUNT TO MUCH, "CHUCK"... YOU JUST DON'T HAVE IT... MAYBE YOU COULD TRY SHUFFLEBOARD OR SOMETHING LIKE THAT...
3-27
WELL, WE'VE GOT A LONG WAY TO GO SO WE'D BETTER SAY GOOD-BY... JOSÉ PETERSON'S MOM IS HAVING ME OVER TONIGHT FOR TORTILLAS AND SWEDISH MEAT-BALLS!
Tm. Reg. U. S. Pat. Off.—All rights reserved © 1967 by United Feature Syndicate, Inc.
"SHUFFLEBOARD"?!
SCHULZ

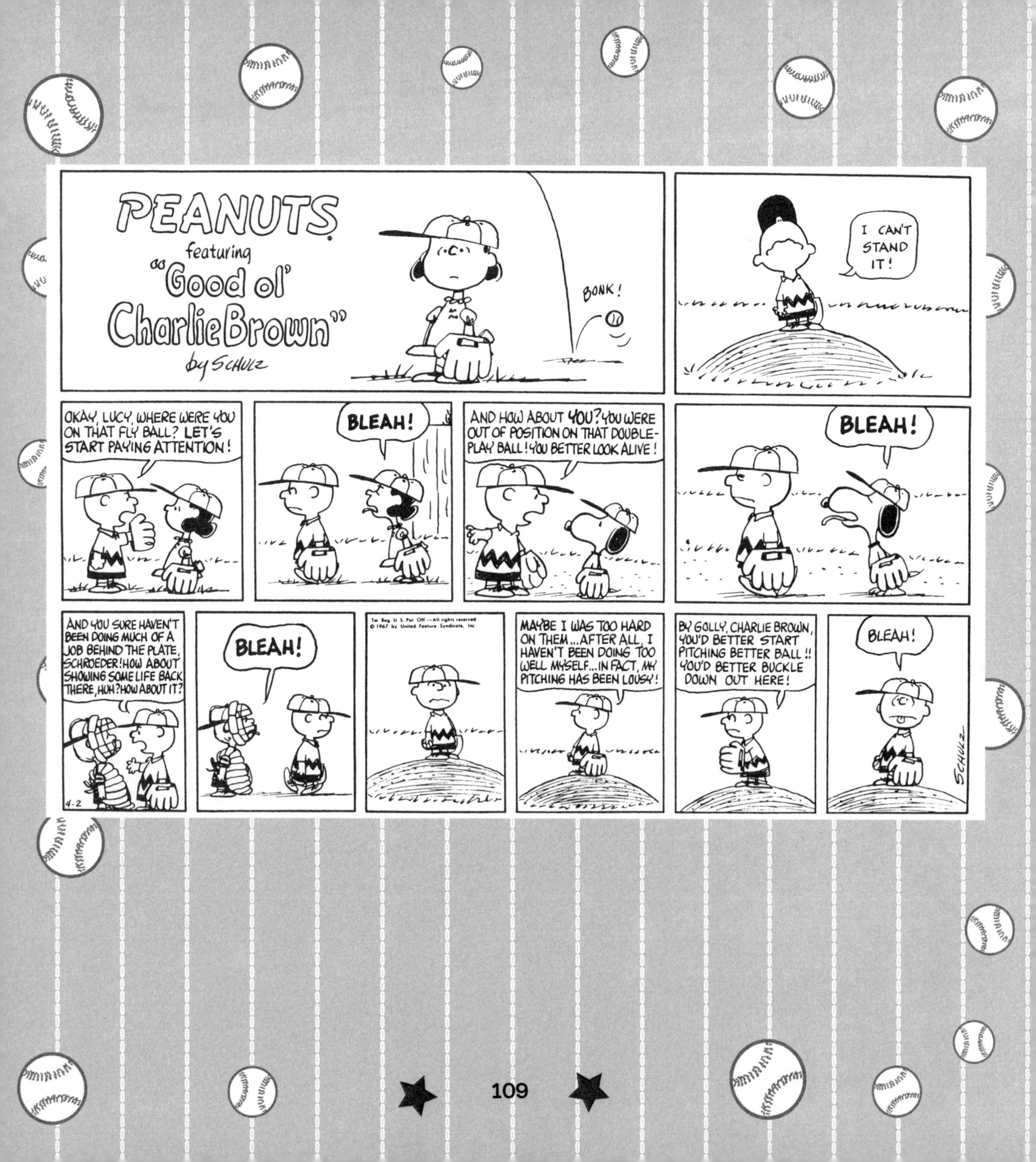
PEANUTS
featuring "Good ol' CharlieBrown"
by SCHULZ
BONK!
I CAN'T STAND IT!
OKAY, LUCY, WHERE WERE YOU ON THAT FLY BALL? LET'S START PAYING ATTENTION!
BLEAH!
AND HOW ABOUT YOU? YOU WERE OUT OF POSITION ON THAT DOUBLE-PLAY BALL! YOU BETTER LOOK ALIVE!
BLEAH!
AND YOU SURE HAVEN'T BEEN DOING MUCH OF A JOB BEHIND THE PLATE, SCHROEDER! HOW ABOUT SHOWING SOME LIFE BACK THERE, HUH? HOW ABOUT IT?
4-2
BLEAH!
Tm Reg. U.S. Pat. Off.—All rights reserved
© 1967 by United Feature Syndicate, Inc.
MAYBE I WAS TOO HARD ON THEM...AFTER ALL, I HAVEN'T BEEN DOING TOO WELL MYSELF...IN FACT, MY PITCHING HAS BEEN LOUSY!
BY GOLLY, CHARLIE BROWN, YOU'D BETTER START PITCHING BETTER BALL!! YOU'D BETTER BUCKLE DOWN OUT HERE!
BLEAH!
SCHULZ

PEANUTS®
featuring "Good ol' Charlie Brown"
by SCHULZ
4-16
AHEM!
!
RIGHT IN THE MIDDLE OF A BALL GAME?
ARE YOU OUT OF YOUR MIND?!
I'M TRYING TO PITCH, CAN'T YOU SEE THAT?!! I'VE GOT TO CONCENTRATE ON WHAT I'M DOING!
OH, NOW YOU'RE GOING TO BE HURT, AREN'T YOU? OH, GOOD GRIEF, ALL RIGHT... COME HERE...
SKRITCH SKRITCH SKRITCH SKRITCH SKRITCH
SIGH!
NO WONDER SANDY KOUFAX RETIRED!
SCHULZ

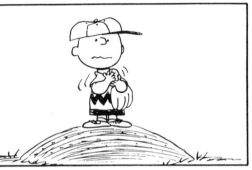

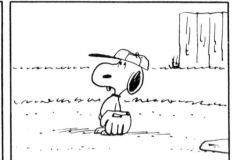

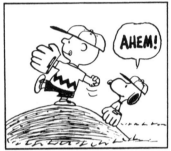

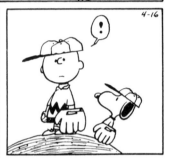

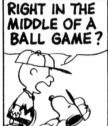

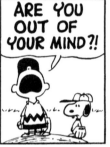

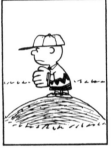

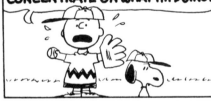

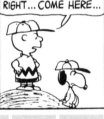

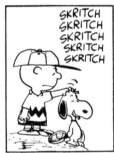

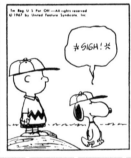

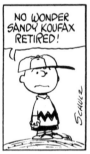

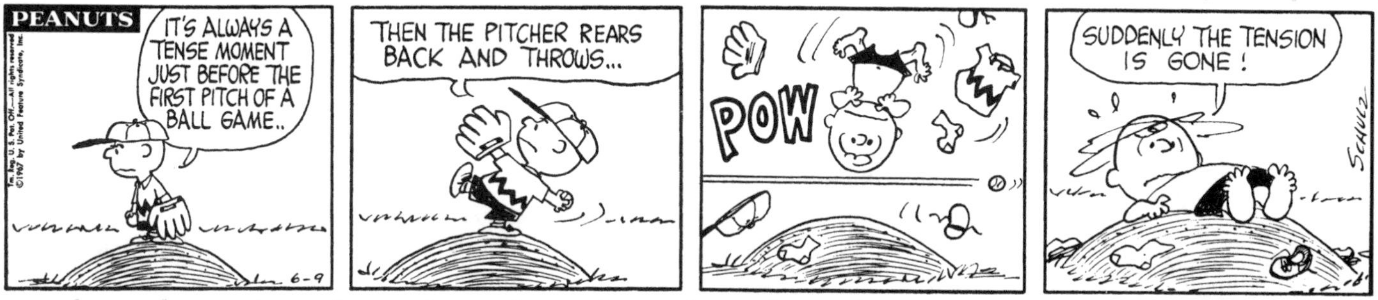
PEANUTS
Tm. Reg. U.S. Pat. Off.—All rights reserved ©1967 by United Feature Syndicate, Inc.
IT'S ALWAYS A TENSE MOMENT JUST BEFORE THE FIRST PITCH OF A BALL GAME..
6-9
THEN THE PITCHER REARS BACK AND THROWS...
POW
SUDDENLY THE TENSION IS GONE!
SCHULZ

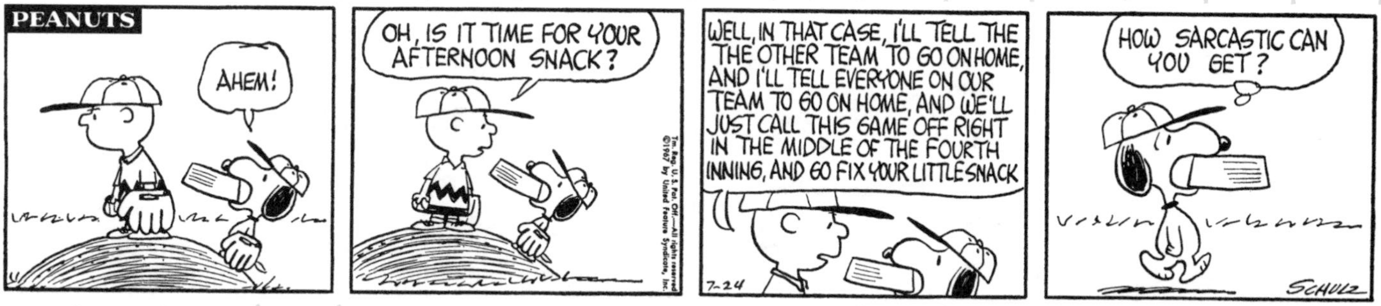
PEANUTS
AHEM!
OH, IS IT TIME FOR YOUR AFTERNOON SNACK?
Tm. Reg. U.S. Pat. Off.—All rights reserved ©1967 by United Feature Syndicate, Inc.
WELL, IN THAT CASE, I'LL TELL THE THE OTHER TEAM TO GO ON HOME, AND I'LL TELL EVERYONE ON OUR TEAM TO GO ON HOME, AND WE'LL JUST CALL THIS GAME OFF RIGHT IN THE MIDDLE OF THE FOURTH INNING, AND GO FIX YOUR LITTLE SNACK
7-24
HOW SARCASTIC CAN YOU GET?
SCHULZ

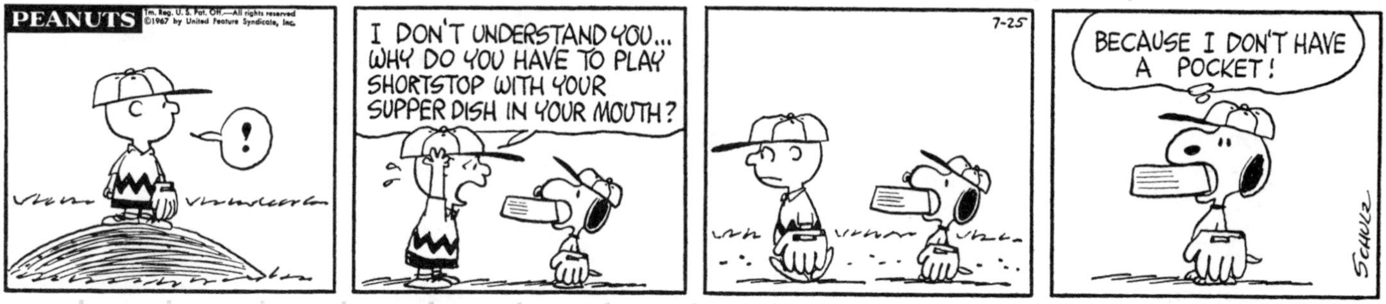
PEANUTS
Tm. Reg. U.S. Pat. Off.—All rights reserved ©1967 by United Feature Syndicate, Inc.
!
I DON'T UNDERSTAND YOU... WHY DO YOU HAVE TO PLAY SHORTSTOP WITH YOUR SUPPER DISH IN YOUR MOUTH?
7-25
BECAUSE I DON'T HAVE A POCKET!
SCHULZ

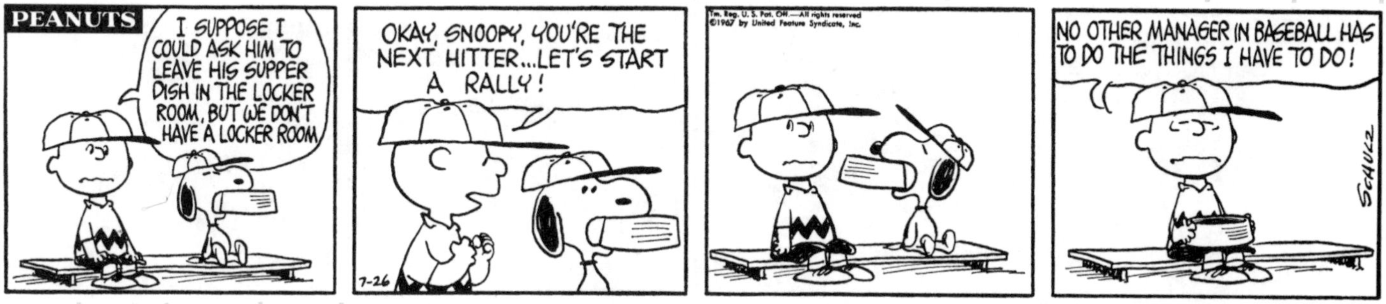
PEANUTS
I SUPPOSE I COULD ASK HIM TO LEAVE HIS SUPPER DISH IN THE LOCKER ROOM, BUT WE DON'T HAVE A LOCKER ROOM
OKAY, SNOOPY, YOU'RE THE NEXT HITTER...LET'S START A RALLY!
7-26
Tm. Reg. U.S. Pat. Off.—All rights reserved ©1967 by United Feature Syndicate, Inc.
NO OTHER MANAGER IN BASEBALL HAS TO DO THE THINGS I HAVE TO DO!
SCHULZ

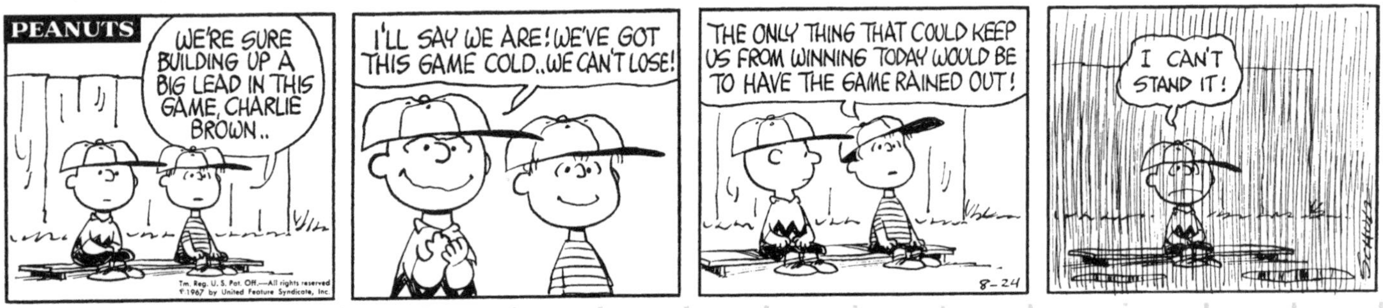
PEANUTS
WE'RE SURE BUILDING UP A BIG LEAD IN THIS GAME, CHARLIE BROWN..
Tm. Reg. U. S. Pat. Off.—All rights reserved ©1967 by United Feature Syndicate, Inc.
I'LL SAY WE ARE! WE'VE GOT THIS GAME COLD..WE CAN'T LOSE!
THE ONLY THING THAT COULD KEEP US FROM WINNING TODAY WOULD BE TO HAVE THE GAME RAINED OUT!
8-24
I CAN'T STAND IT!
SCHULZ

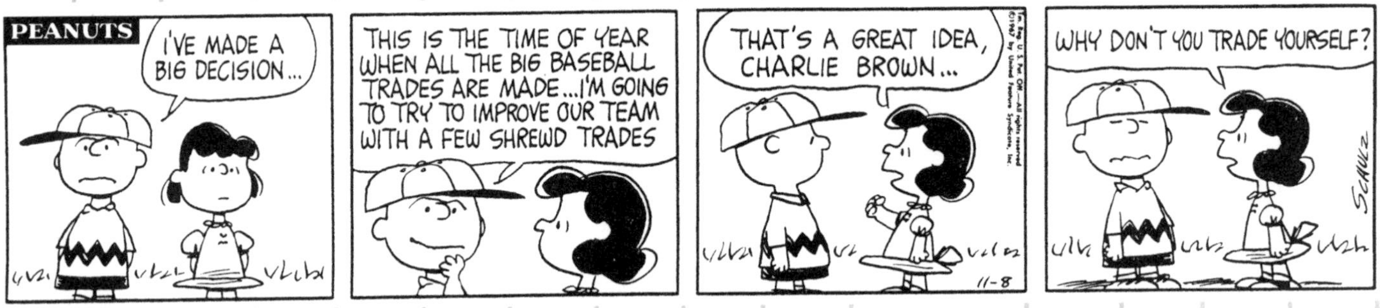
PEANUTS
I'VE MADE A BIG DECISION...
THIS IS THE TIME OF YEAR WHEN ALL THE BIG BASEBALL TRADES ARE MADE...I'M GOING TO TRY TO IMPROVE OUR TEAM WITH A FEW SHREWD TRADES
THAT'S A GREAT IDEA, CHARLIE BROWN...
11-8
WHY DON'T YOU TRADE YOURSELF?
SCHULZ

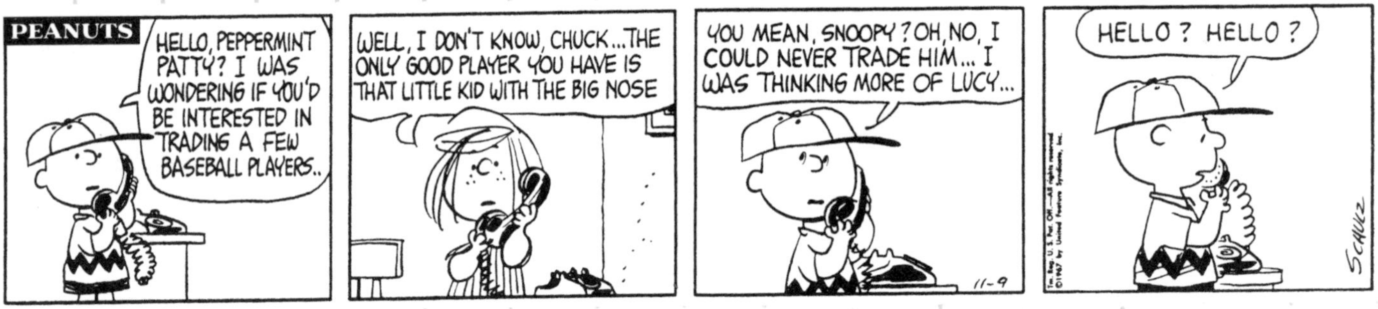
PEANUTS
HELLO, PEPPERMINT PATTY? I WAS WONDERING IF YOU'D BE INTERESTED IN TRADING A FEW BASEBALL PLAYERS..
WELL, I DON'T KNOW, CHUCK...THE ONLY GOOD PLAYER YOU HAVE IS THAT LITTLE KID WITH THE BIG NOSE
YOU MEAN, SNOOPY? OH, NO, I COULD NEVER TRADE HIM... I WAS THINKING MORE OF LUCY...
11-9
HELLO? HELLO?
SCHULZ

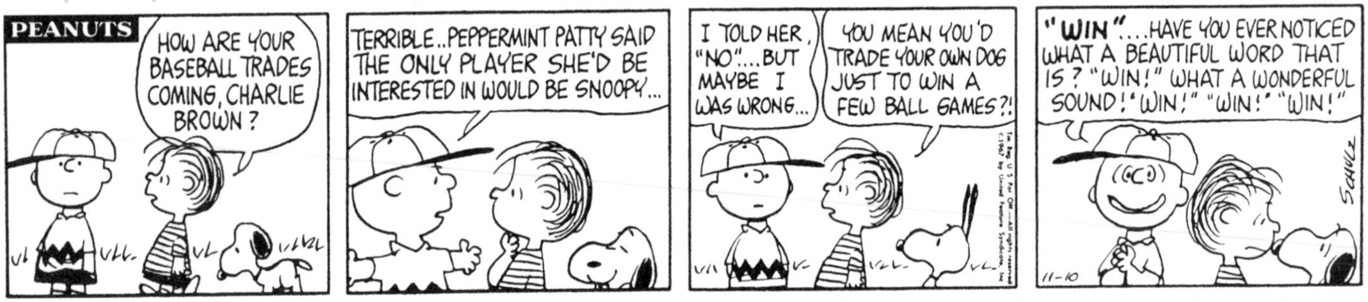
PEANUTS
HOW ARE YOUR BASEBALL TRADES COMING, CHARLIE BROWN?
TERRIBLE..PEPPERMINT PATTY SAID THE ONLY PLAYER SHE'D BE INTERESTED IN WOULD BE SNOOPY...
I TOLD HER, "NO"...BUT MAYBE I WAS WRONG...
YOU MEAN YOU'D TRADE YOUR OWN DOG JUST TO WIN A FEW BALL GAMES?!
"WIN"...HAVE YOU EVER NOTICED WHAT A BEAUTIFUL WORD THAT IS? "WIN!" WHAT A WONDERFUL SOUND! "WIN!" "WIN!" "WIN!"
11-10
SCHULZ

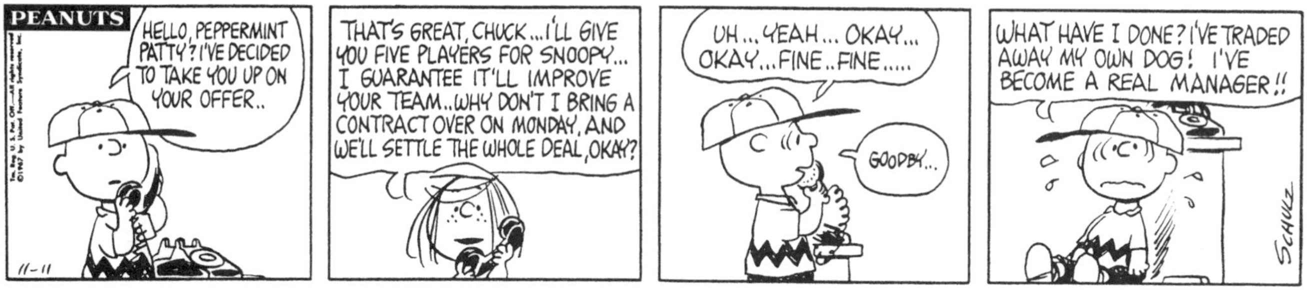
PEANUTS
Tm. Reg. U.S. Pat. Off.—All rights reserved ©1967 by United Feature Syndicate, Inc.
HELLO, PEPPERMINT PATTY? I'VE DECIDED TO TAKE YOU UP ON YOUR OFFER..
11-11
THAT'S GREAT, CHUCK...I'LL GIVE YOU FIVE PLAYERS FOR SNOOPY... I GUARANTEE IT'LL IMPROVE YOUR TEAM..WHY DON'T I BRING A CONTRACT OVER ON MONDAY, AND WE'LL SETTLE THE WHOLE DEAL, OKAY?
UH... YEAH... OKAY... OKAY...FINE..FINE.....
GOODBY...
WHAT HAVE I DONE? I'VE TRADED AWAY MY OWN DOG! I'VE BECOME A REAL MANAGER!!
SCHULZ

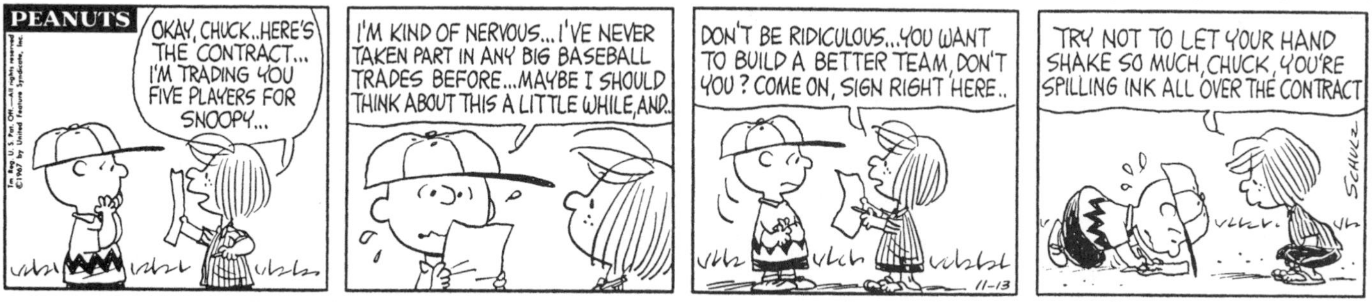
PEANUTS
Tm. Reg. U.S. Pat. Off.—All rights reserved ©1967 by United Feature Syndicate, Inc.
OKAY, CHUCK..HERE'S THE CONTRACT... I'M TRADING YOU FIVE PLAYERS FOR SNOOPY...
I'M KIND OF NERVOUS...I'VE NEVER TAKEN PART IN ANY BIG BASEBALL TRADES BEFORE...MAYBE I SHOULD THINK ABOUT THIS A LITTLE WHILE, AND..
DON'T BE RIDICULOUS...YOU WANT TO BUILD A BETTER TEAM, DON'T YOU? COME ON, SIGN RIGHT HERE..
11-13
TRY NOT TO LET YOUR HAND SHAKE SO MUCH, CHUCK, YOU'RE SPILLING INK ALL OVER THE CONTRACT
SCHULZ

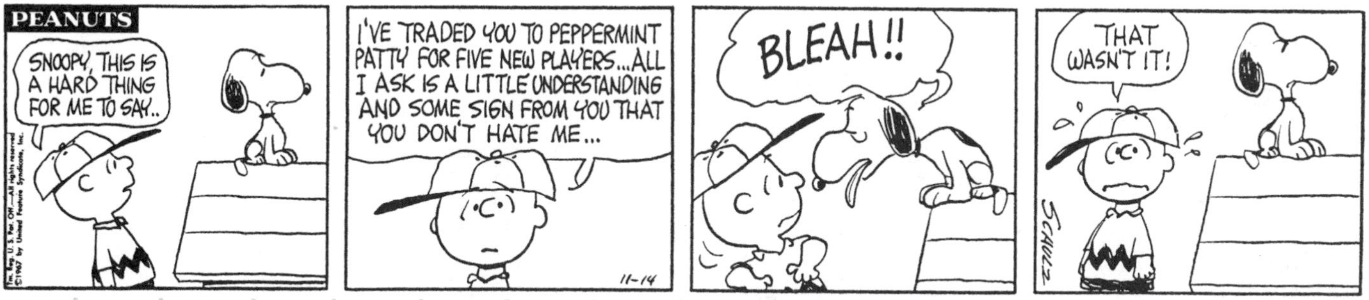
PEANUTS
Tm. Reg. U.S. Pat. Off.—All rights reserved ©1967 by United Feature Syndicate, Inc.
SNOOPY, THIS IS A HARD THING FOR ME TO SAY..
I'VE TRADED YOU TO PEPPERMINT PATTY FOR FIVE NEW PLAYERS...ALL I ASK IS A LITTLE UNDERSTANDING AND SOME SIGN FROM YOU THAT YOU DON'T HATE ME...
11-14
BLEAH!!
SCHULZ
THAT WASN'T IT!

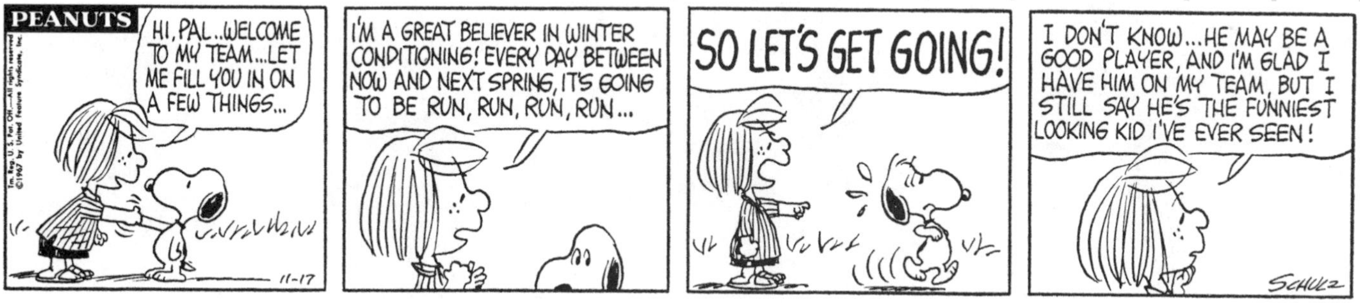
PEANUTS
Tm. Reg. U.S. Pat. Off.—All rights reserved ©1967 by United Feature Syndicate, Inc.
HI, PAL...WELCOME TO MY TEAM...LET ME FILL YOU IN ON A FEW THINGS...
11-17
I'M A GREAT BELIEVER IN WINTER CONDITIONING! EVERY DAY BETWEEN NOW AND NEXT SPRING, IT'S GOING TO BE RUN, RUN, RUN, RUN...
SO LET'S GET GOING!
I DON'T KNOW...HE MAY BE A GOOD PLAYER, AND I'M GLAD I HAVE HIM ON MY TEAM, BUT I STILL SAY HE'S THE FUNNIEST LOOKING KID I'VE EVER SEEN!
SCHULZ

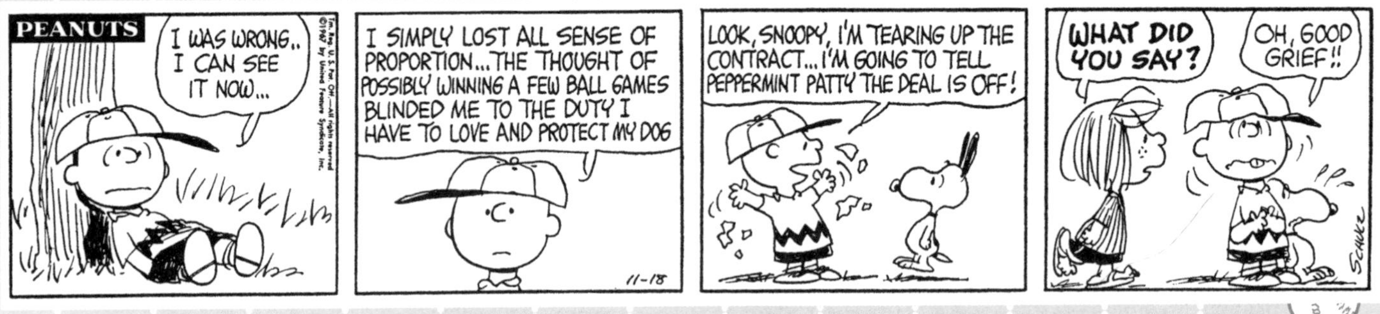
PEANUTS
I WAS WRONG.. I CAN SEE IT NOW...
Tm. Reg. U.S. Pat. Off.—All rights reserved ©1967 by United Feature Syndicate, Inc.
I SIMPLY LOST ALL SENSE OF PROPORTION...THE THOUGHT OF POSSIBLY WINNING A FEW BALL GAMES BLINDED ME TO THE DUTY I HAVE TO LOVE AND PROTECT MY DOG
11-18
LOOK, SNOOPY, I'M TEARING UP THE CONTRACT... I'M GOING TO TELL PEPPERMINT PATTY THE DEAL IS OFF!
WHAT DID YOU SAY?
OH, GOOD GRIEF!!
SCHULZ

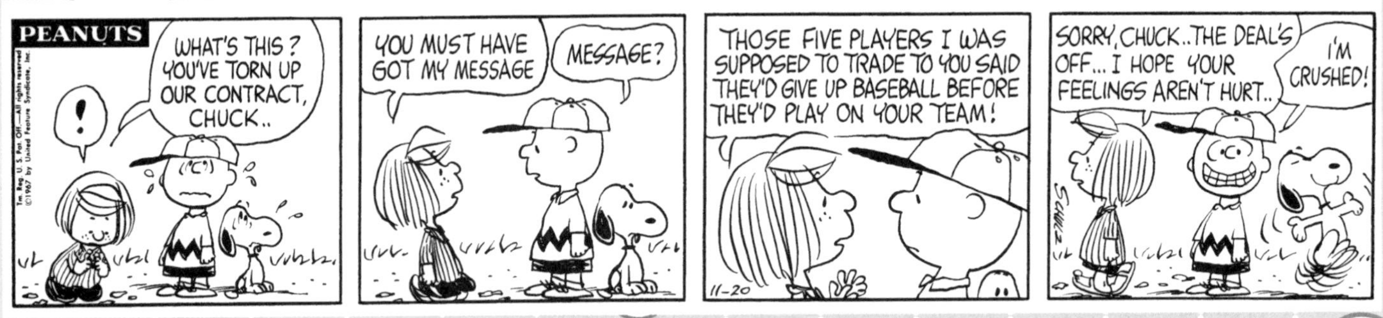
PEANUTS
Tm. Reg. U.S. Pat. Off.—All rights reserved ©1967 by United Feature Syndicate, Inc.
!
WHAT'S THIS? YOU'VE TORN UP OUR CONTRACT, CHUCK..
YOU MUST HAVE GOT MY MESSAGE
MESSAGE?
THOSE FIVE PLAYERS I WAS SUPPOSED TO TRADE TO YOU SAID THEY'D GIVE UP BASEBALL BEFORE THEY'D PLAY ON YOUR TEAM!
11-20
SORRY, CHUCK..THE DEAL'S OFF... I HOPE YOUR FEELINGS AREN'T HURT..
I'M CRUSHED!
SCHULZ

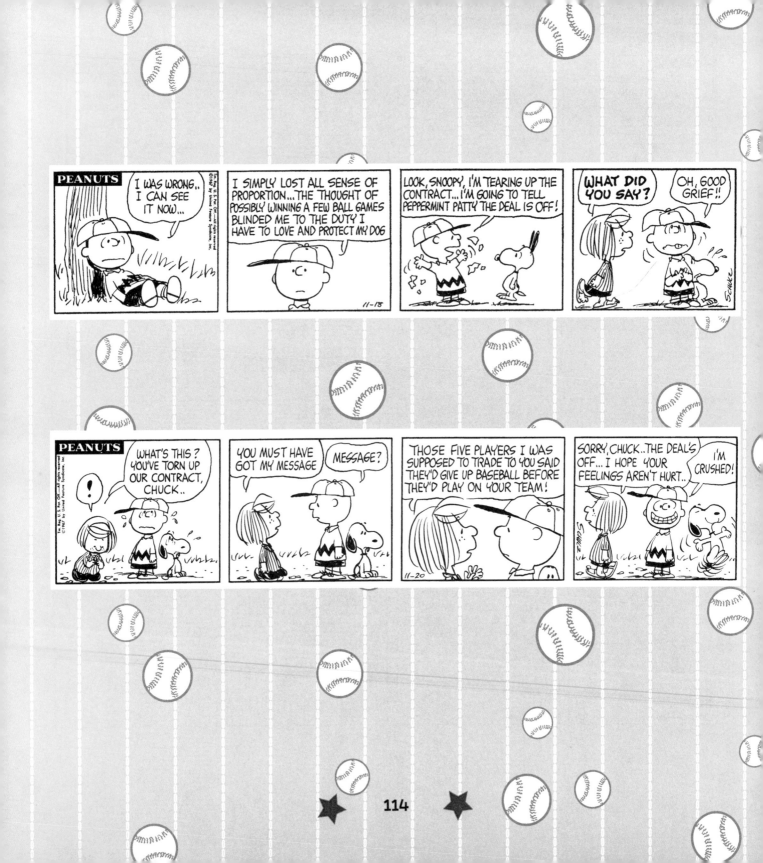

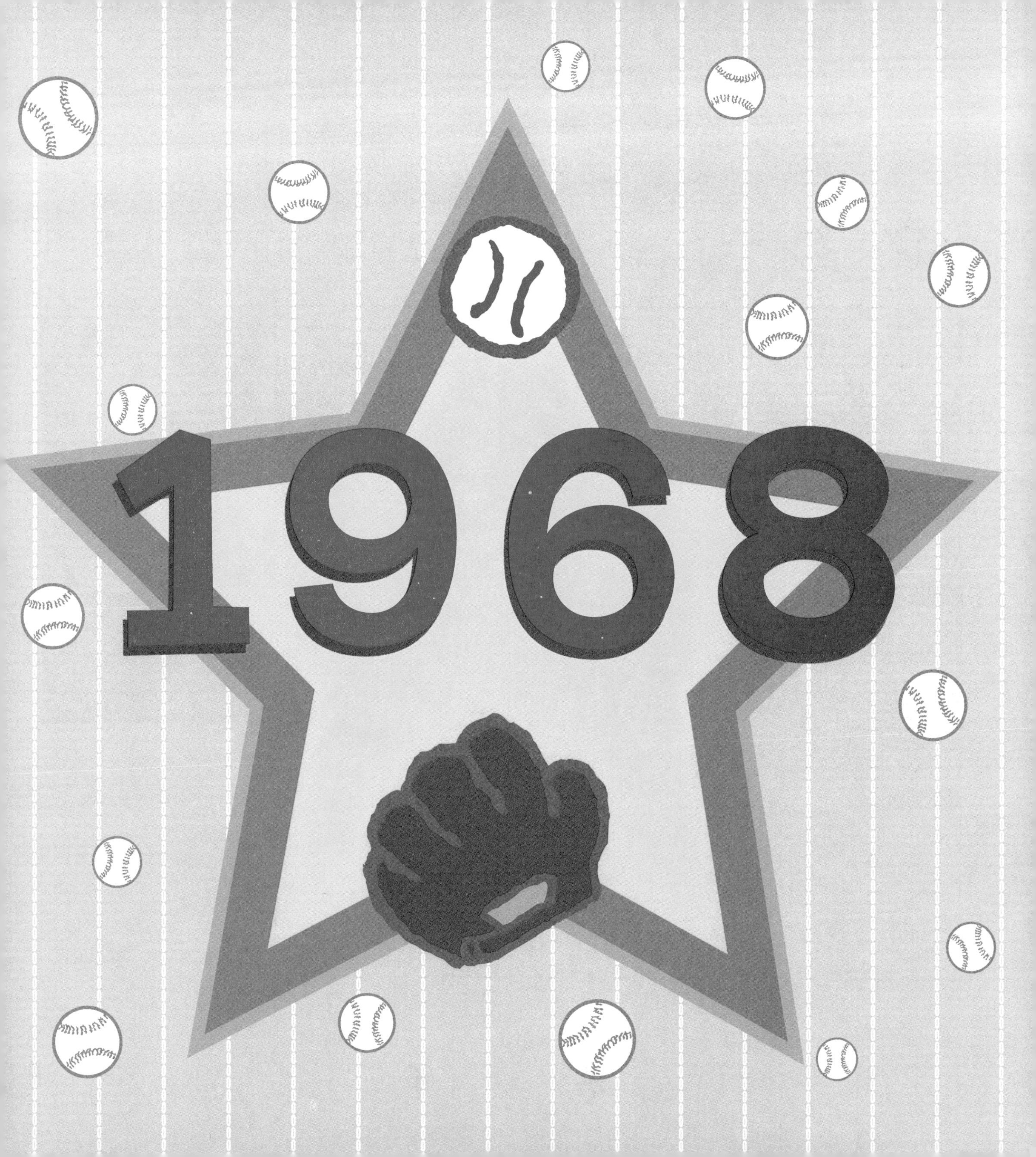
1968

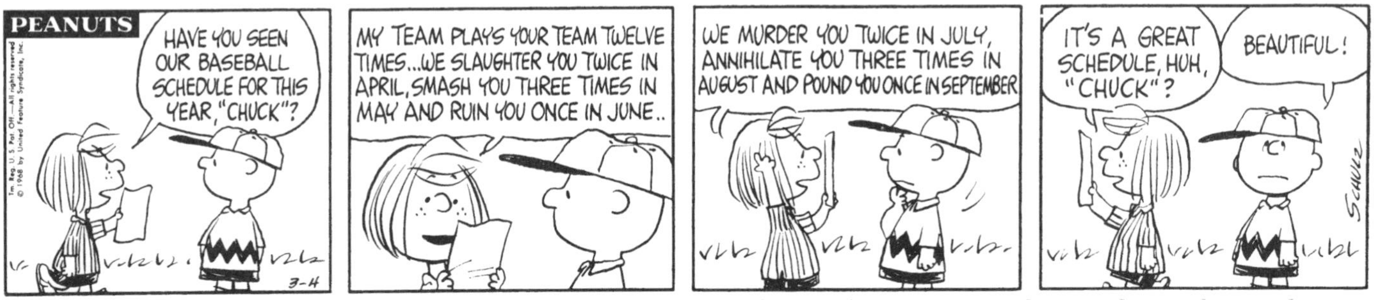
PEANUTS
Tm. Reg. U.S. Pat. Off.—All rights reserved © 1968 by United Feature Syndicate, Inc.
HAVE YOU SEEN OUR BASEBALL SCHEDULE FOR THIS YEAR, "CHUCK"?
3-4
MY TEAM PLAYS YOUR TEAM TWELVE TIMES...WE SLAUGHTER YOU TWICE IN APRIL, SMASH YOU THREE TIMES IN MAY AND RUIN YOU ONCE IN JUNE..
WE MURDER YOU TWICE IN JULY, ANNIHILATE YOU THREE TIMES IN AUGUST AND POUND YOU ONCE IN SEPTEMBER
IT'S A GREAT SCHEDULE, HUH, "CHUCK"?
BEAUTIFUL!
SCHULZ

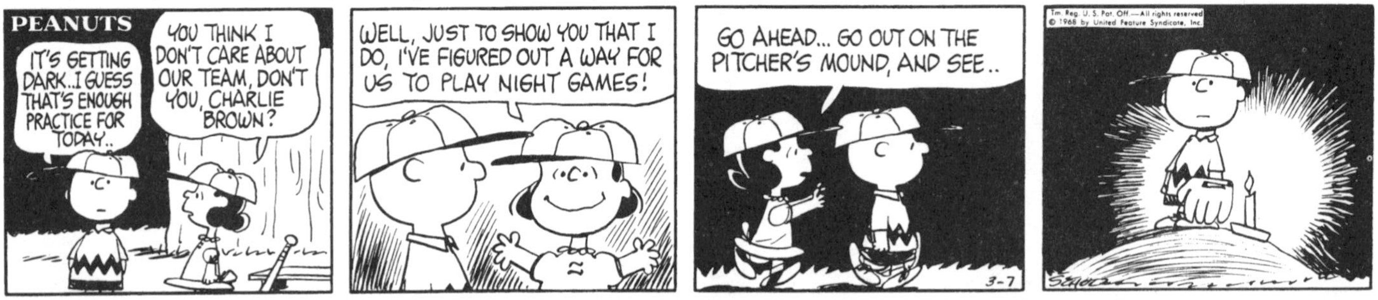
PEANUTS
IT'S GETTING DARK..I GUESS THAT'S ENOUGH PRACTICE FOR TODAY..
YOU THINK I DON'T CARE ABOUT OUR TEAM, DON'T YOU, CHARLIE BROWN?
WELL, JUST TO SHOW YOU THAT I DO, I'VE FIGURED OUT A WAY FOR US TO PLAY NIGHT GAMES!
GO AHEAD... GO OUT ON THE PITCHER'S MOUND, AND SEE..
3-7
Tm. Reg. U.S. Pat. Off.—All rights reserved © 1968 by United Feature Syndicate, Inc.
SCHULZ

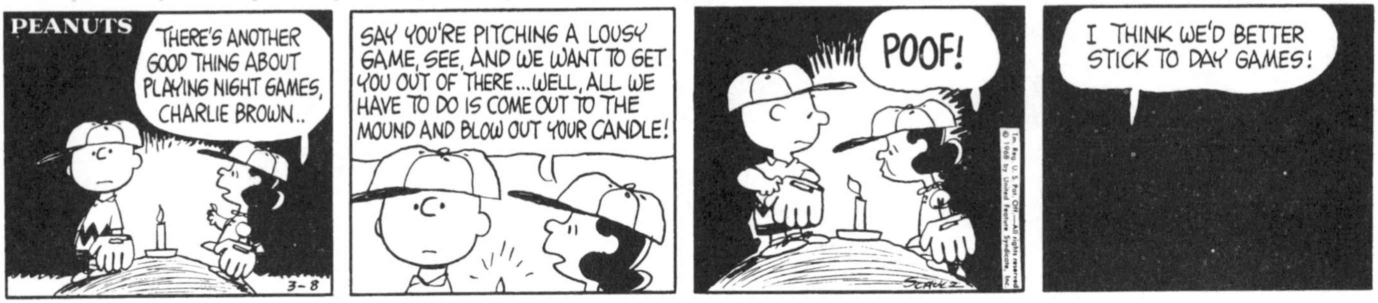
PEANUTS
THERE'S ANOTHER GOOD THING ABOUT PLAYING NIGHT GAMES, CHARLIE BROWN..
3-8
SAY YOU'RE PITCHING A LOUSY GAME, SEE, AND WE WANT TO GET YOU OUT OF THERE...WELL, ALL WE HAVE TO DO IS COME OUT TO THE MOUND AND BLOW OUT YOUR CANDLE!
POOF!
Tm. Reg. U.S. Pat. Off.—All rights reserved © 1968 by United Feature Syndicate, Inc.
SCHULZ
I THINK WE'D BETTER STICK TO DAY GAMES!

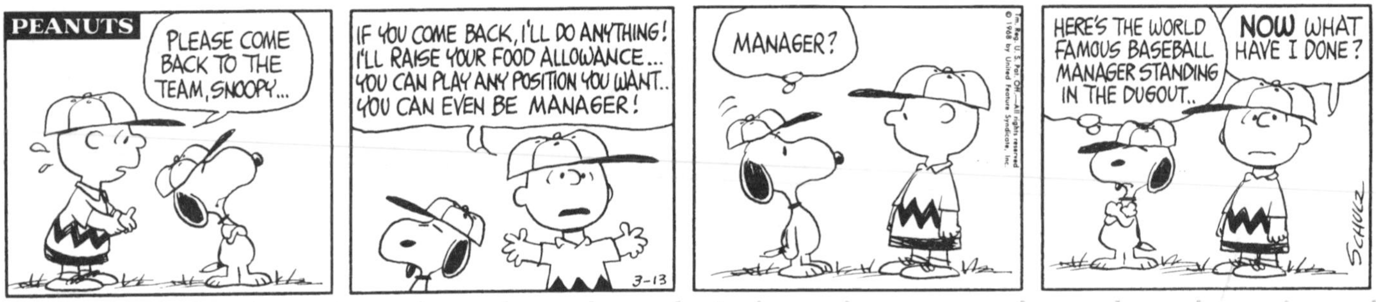
PEANUTS
PLEASE COME BACK TO THE TEAM, SNOOPY...
IF YOU COME BACK, I'LL DO ANYTHING! I'LL RAISE YOUR FOOD ALLOWANCE... YOU CAN PLAY ANY POSITION YOU WANT.. YOU CAN EVEN BE MANAGER!
3-13
MANAGER?
Tm. Reg. U.S. Pat. Off.—All rights reserved © 1968 by United Feature Syndicate, Inc.
HERE'S THE WORLD FAMOUS BASEBALL MANAGER STANDING IN THE DUGOUT..
NOW WHAT HAVE I DONE?
SCHULZ

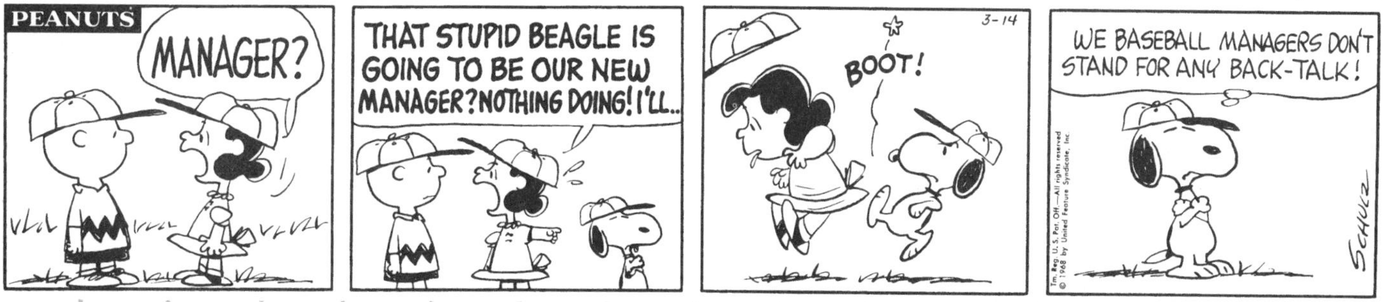
PEANUTS
MANAGER?
THAT STUPID BEAGLE IS GOING TO BE OUR NEW MANAGER? NOTHING DOING! I'LL..
3-14
BOOT!
WE BASEBALL MANAGERS DON'T STAND FOR ANY BACK-TALK!
Tm. Reg. U. S. Pat. Off.—All rights reserved © 1968 by United Feature Syndicate, Inc.
SCHULZ

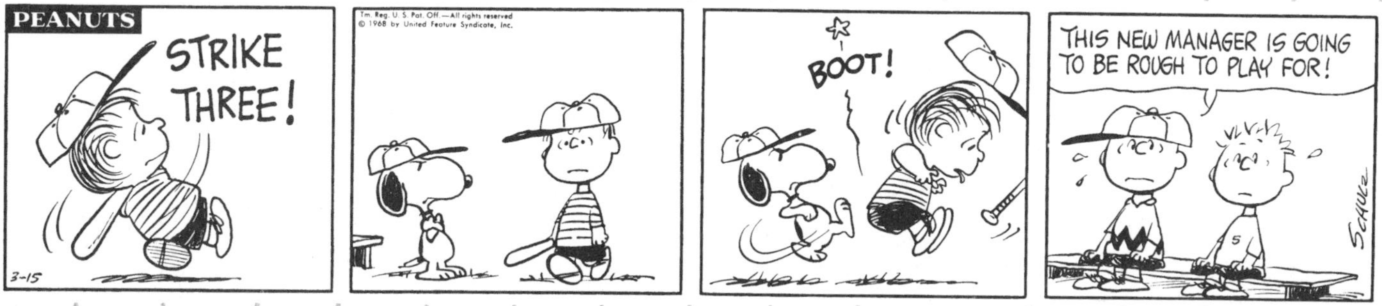
PEANUTS
STRIKE THREE!
3-15
Tm. Reg. U. S. Pat. Off.—All rights reserved © 1968 by United Feature Syndicate, Inc.
BOOT!
THIS NEW MANAGER IS GOING TO BE ROUGH TO PLAY FOR!
SCHULZ

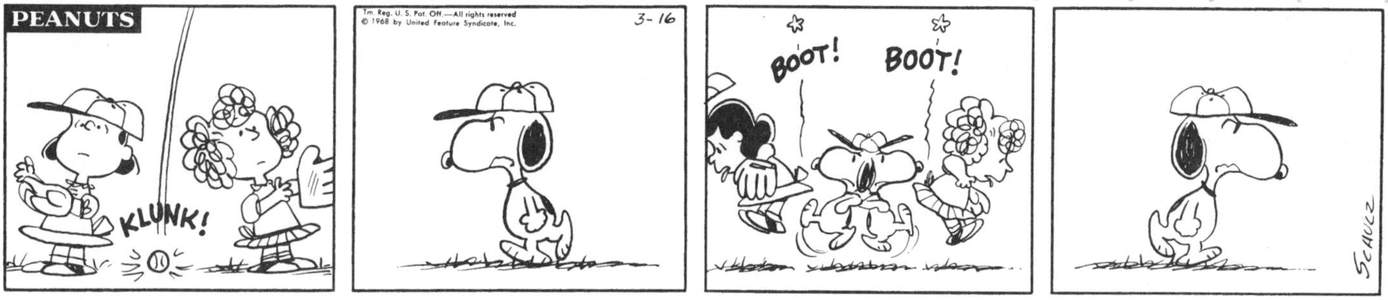
PEANUTS
KLUNK!
Tm. Reg. U. S. Pat. Off.—All rights reserved © 1968 by United Feature Syndicate, Inc.
3-16
BOOT!
BOOT!
SCHULZ

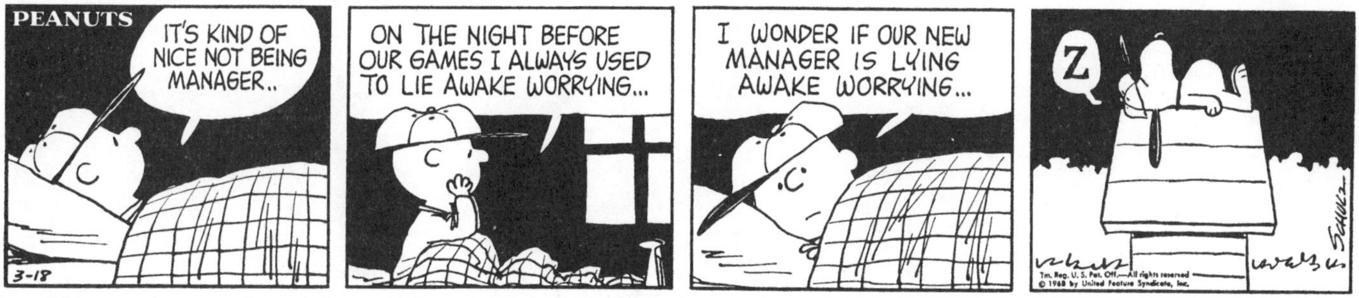
PEANUTS
IT'S KIND OF NICE NOT BEING MANAGER..
3-18
ON THE NIGHT BEFORE OUR GAMES I ALWAYS USED TO LIE AWAKE WORRYING...
I WONDER IF OUR NEW MANAGER IS LYING AWAKE WORRYING...
Z
SCHULZ
Tm. Reg. U. S. Pat. Off.—All rights reserved © 1968 by United Feature Syndicate, Inc.

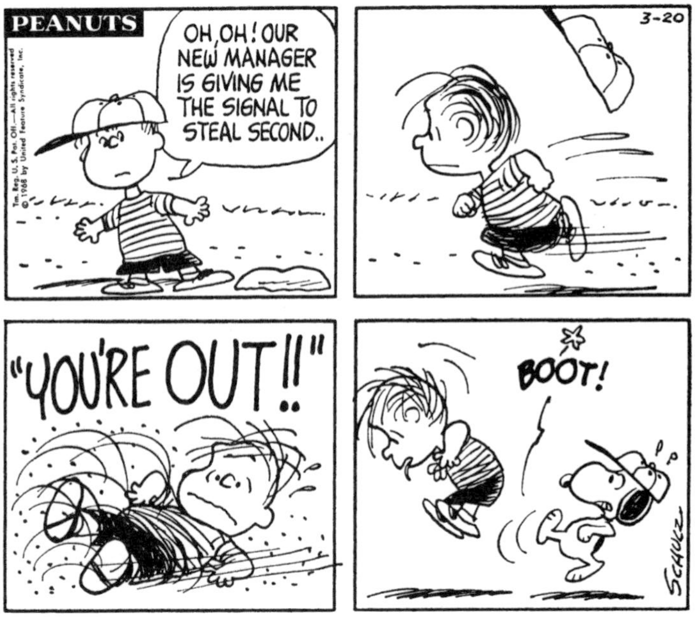
PEANUTS
Tm. Reg. U. S. Pat. Off.—All rights reserved
© 1968 by United Feature Syndicate, Inc.
OH, OH! OUR NEW MANAGER IS GIVING ME THE SIGNAL TO STEAL SECOND..
3-20
"YOU'RE OUT!!"
BOOT!
SCHULZ

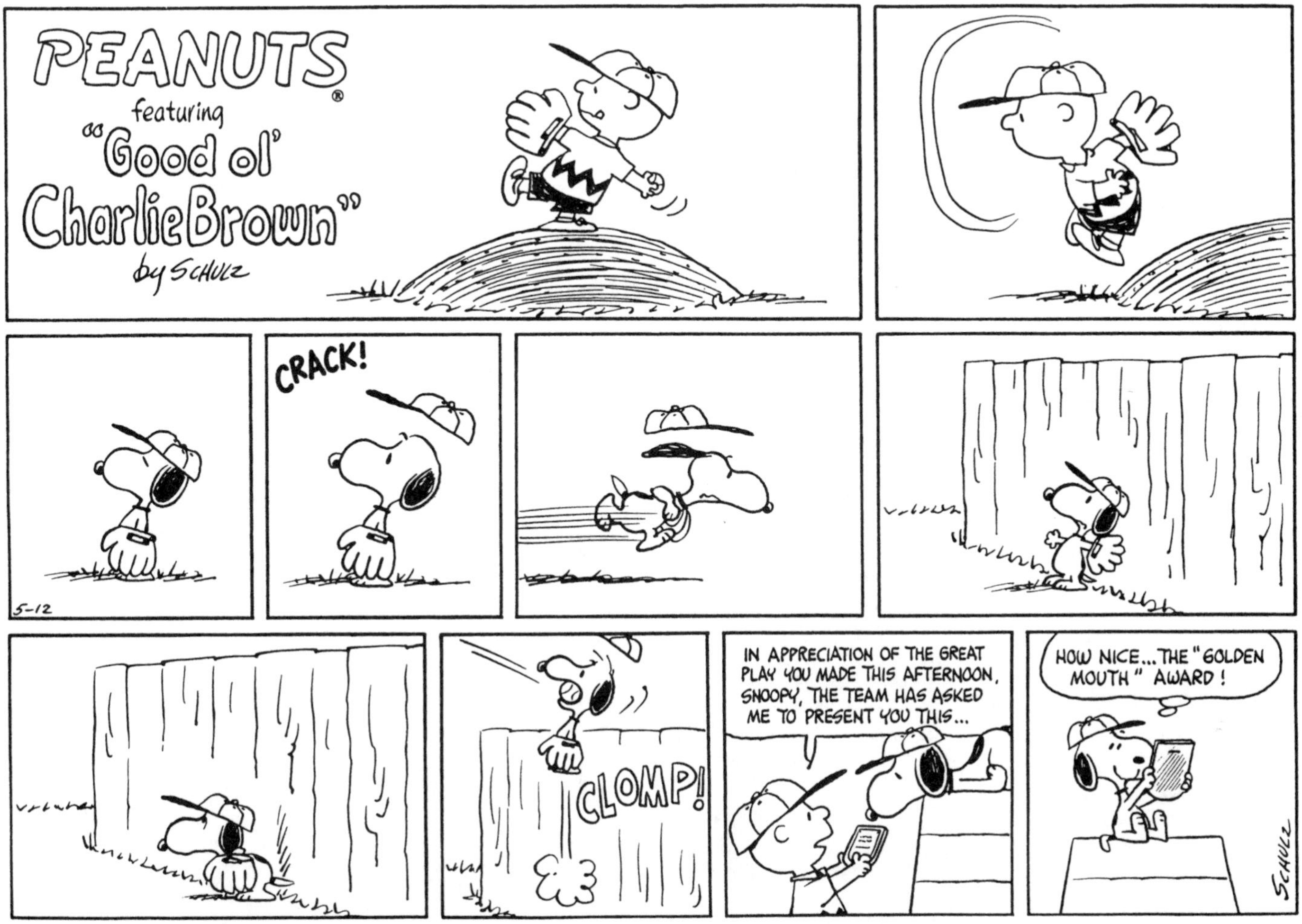
PEANUTS®
featuring
"Good ol' CharlieBrown"
by SCHULZ
5-12
CRACK!
CLOMP!
IN APPRECIATION OF THE GREAT PLAY YOU MADE THIS AFTERNOON, SNOOPY, THE TEAM HAS ASKED ME TO PRESENT YOU THIS...
HOW NICE...THE "GOLDEN MOUTH" AWARD!
SCHULZ

PEANUTS

WHAT ARE YOU DOING, CHARLIE BROWN? WHY DON'T YOU PITCH?

THAT LITTLE RED-HAIRED GIRL..SHE'S WATCHING THE GAME...

OH, GOOD GRIEF!

THIS IS MY BIG CHANCE TO BE A HERO, AND SHE'S WATCHING!

I'M GOING TO BEAR DOWN AND PITCH A GREAT GAME, AND THAT LITTLE RED-HAIRED GIRL WILL BE SO IMPRESSED AND SO EXCITED THAT SHE'LL RUSH OUT HERE TO THE MOUND AND GIVE ME A BIG HUG, AND.....

OH, BROTHER! WHY DO I THINK ABOUT THINGS LIKE THAT?

8-13

PEANUTS

GOOD GRIEF, CHARLIE BROWN, WHEN ARE YOU GOING TO THROW THE FIRST PITCH?

THAT LITTLE RED-HAIRED GIRL IS WATCHING... I CAN'T LET GO OF THE BALL...MY FINGERS ARE NUMB

I'M STARTING TO SHAKE..LOOK AT ME! I'M SHAKING ALL OVER!

I DON'T SUPPOSE THERE'S A NEUROLOGIST IN THE STANDS..

WOULDN'T A GENERAL PRACTITIONER DO?

HOW ABOUT A VET?

8-14

PEANUTS

OKAY, START THE GAME!

I FEEL BETTER! I'VE STOPPED SHAKING!

THE GAME'S OVER, CHARLIE BROWN, AND GUESS WHAT... **WE WON!**

LINUS TOOK YOUR PLACE...HE PITCHED A GREAT GAME...AND THERE WAS THIS LITTLE RED-HAIRED GIRL WATCHING...

SHE GOT SO EXCITED AFTER THE GAME THAT SHE RUSHED OUT TO THE MOUND, AND GAVE LINUS A BIG HUG!

AAUGH!

8-16

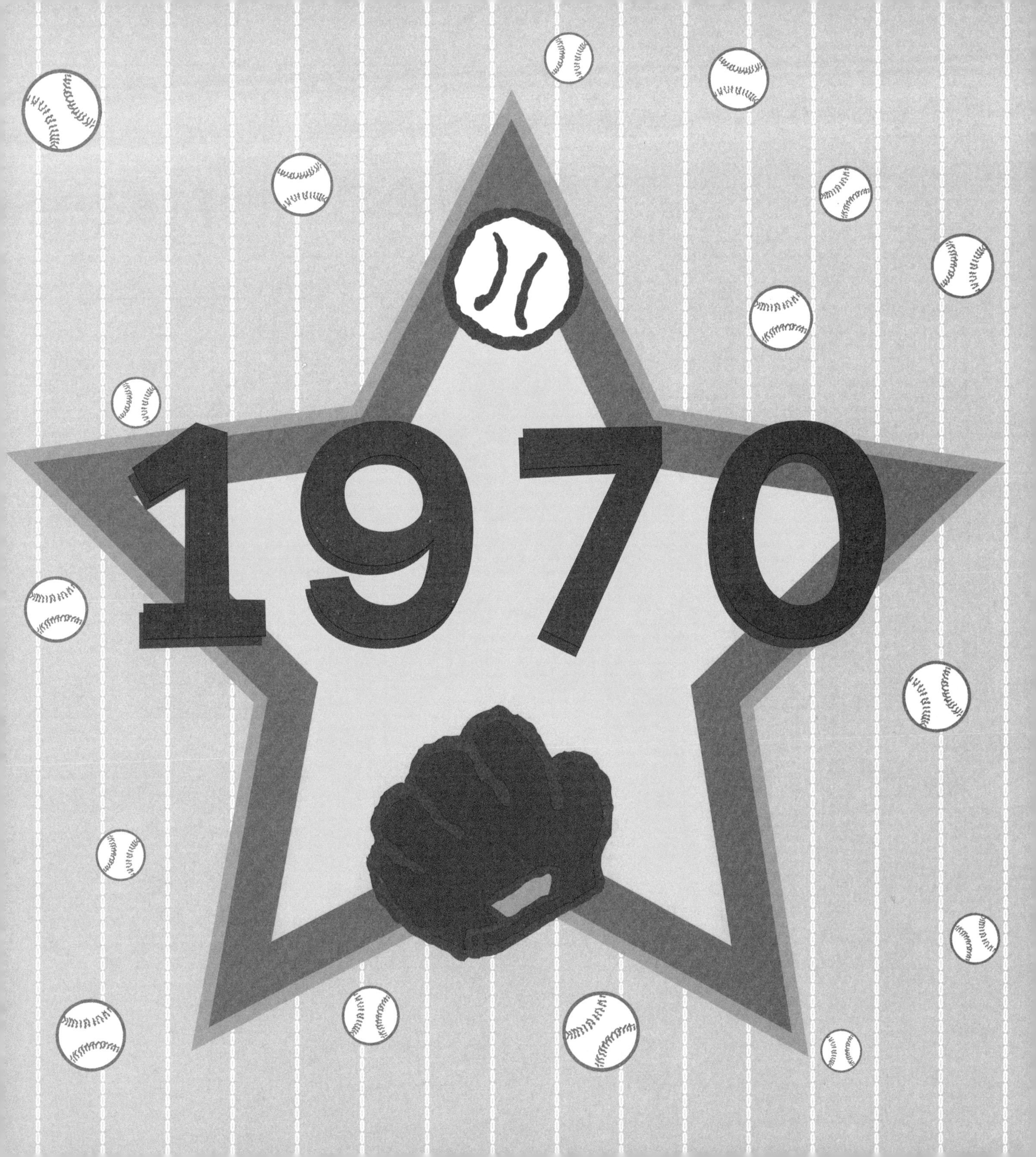
1970

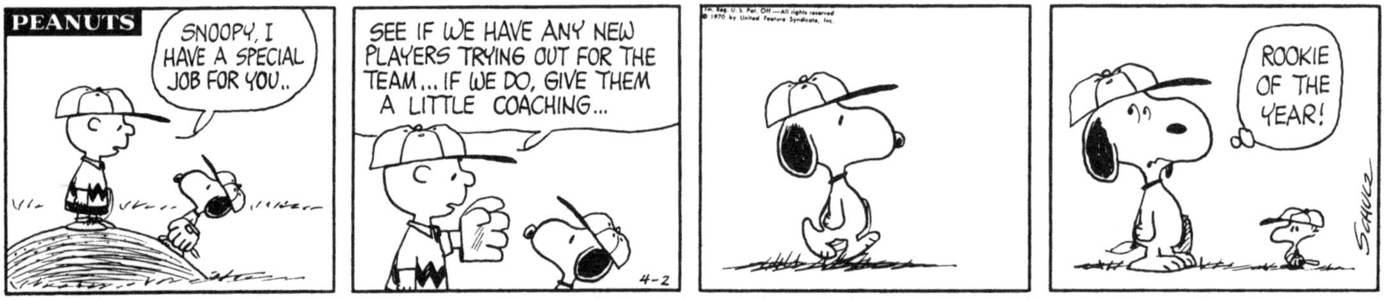
PEANUTS
SNOOPY, I HAVE A SPECIAL JOB FOR YOU..
SEE IF WE HAVE ANY NEW PLAYERS TRYING OUT FOR THE TEAM... IF WE DO, GIVE THEM A LITTLE COACHING...
ROOKIE OF THE YEAR!

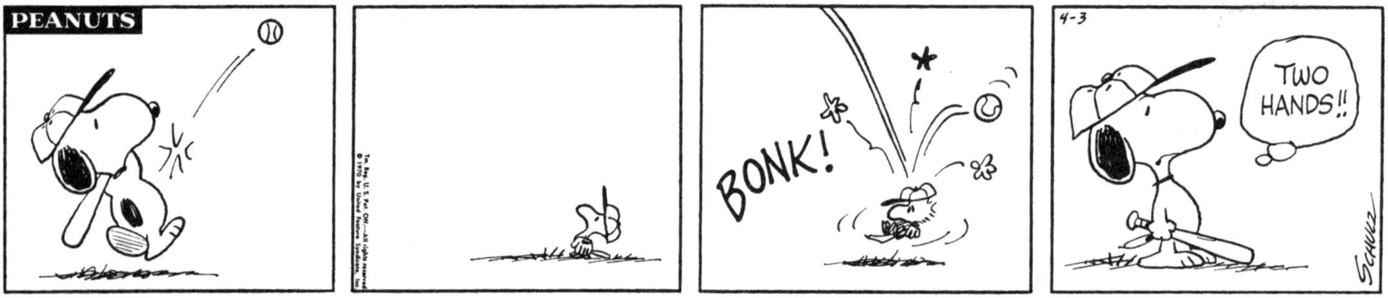
PEANUTS
BONK!
TWO HANDS!!

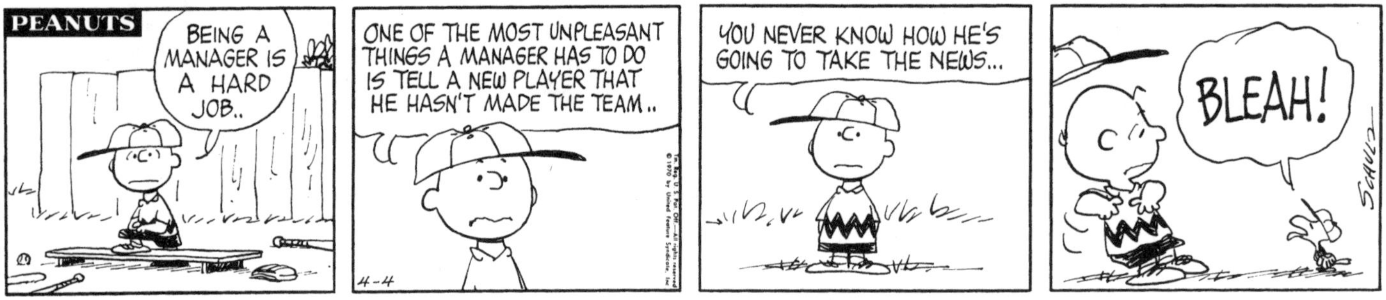
PEANUTS
BEING A MANAGER IS A HARD JOB..
ONE OF THE MOST UNPLEASANT THINGS A MANAGER HAS TO DO IS TELL A NEW PLAYER THAT HE HASN'T MADE THE TEAM..
YOU NEVER KNOW HOW HE'S GOING TO TAKE THE NEWS...
BLEAH!

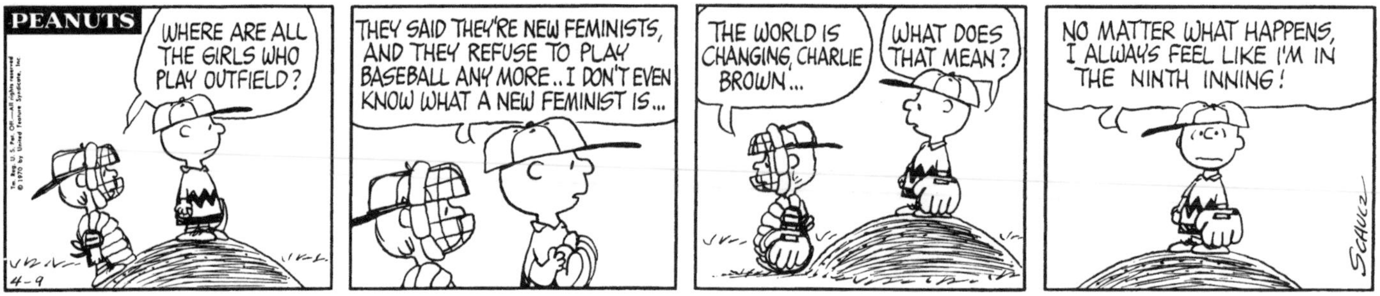
PEANUTS
WHERE ARE ALL THE GIRLS WHO PLAY OUTFIELD?
THEY SAID THEY'RE NEW FEMINISTS, AND THEY REFUSE TO PLAY BASEBALL ANY MORE.. I DON'T EVEN KNOW WHAT A NEW FEMINIST IS...
THE WORLD IS CHANGING, CHARLIE BROWN...
WHAT DOES THAT MEAN?
NO MATTER WHAT HAPPENS, I ALWAYS FEEL LIKE I'M IN THE NINTH INNING!

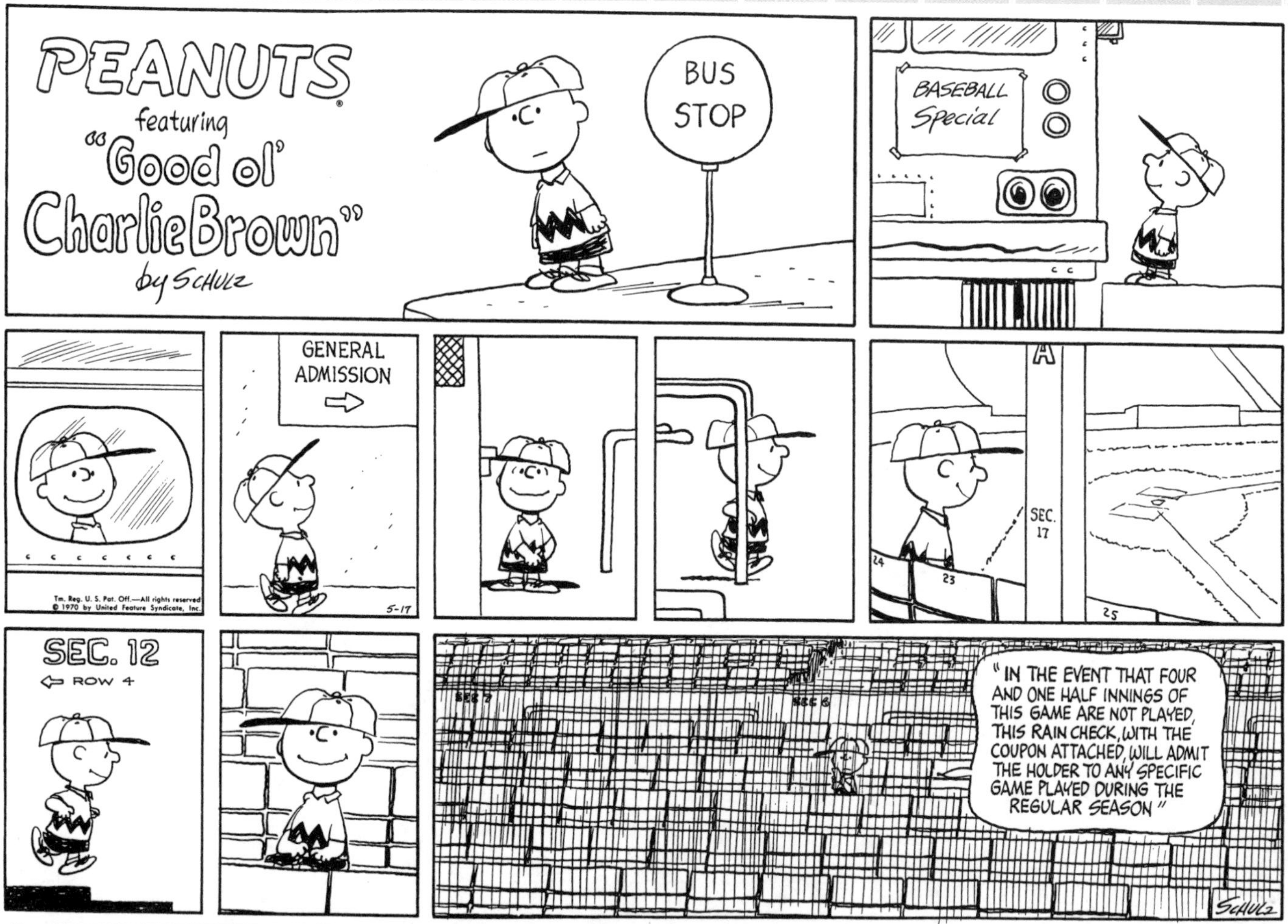
PEANUTS
featuring
"Good ol' CharlieBrown"
by SCHULZ
BUS STOP
BASEBALL Special
Tm. Reg. U. S. Pat. Off.—All rights reserved
© 1970 by United Feature Syndicate, Inc.
GENERAL ADMISSION
5-17
A
SEC. 17
24
23
25
SEC. 12
ROW 4
"IN THE EVENT THAT FOUR AND ONE HALF INNINGS OF THIS GAME ARE NOT PLAYED, THIS RAIN CHECK, WITH THE COUPON ATTACHED, WILL ADMIT THE HOLDER TO ANY SPECIFIC GAME PLAYED DURING THE REGULAR SEASON"
SCHULZ

PEANUTS
RATS! I CAN'T STAND LOSING ALL THE TIME!
Tm. Reg. U. S. Pat. Off.—All rights reserved
© 1970 by United Feature Syndicate, Inc.
THERE MUST BE SOMETHING WRONG WITH ME...
I USED TO COME HOME AND HURL MY GLOVE INTO THE CLOSET..
6-18
NOW, I CAN'T EVEN HIT THE CLOSET!
SCHULZ

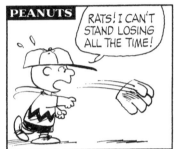

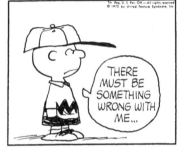

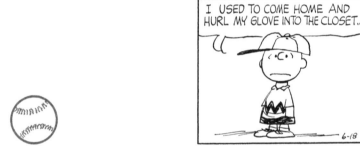

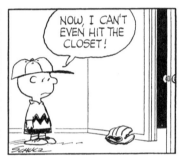

PEANUTS featuring "Good ol' Charlie Brown" by SCHULZ
CLOMP!
CLOMP!
Tm. Reg. U. S. Pat. Off.—All rights reserved © 1970 by United Feature Syndicate, Inc.
7-19
CLOMP!
CLOMP!
CLOMP!
CLOMP!
CLOMP!
I THINK I'LL SLEEP IN TOMORROW MORNING... I HAVE TIRED TEETH!
SCHULZ

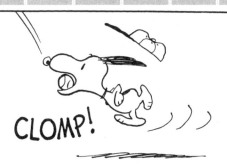

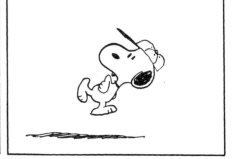

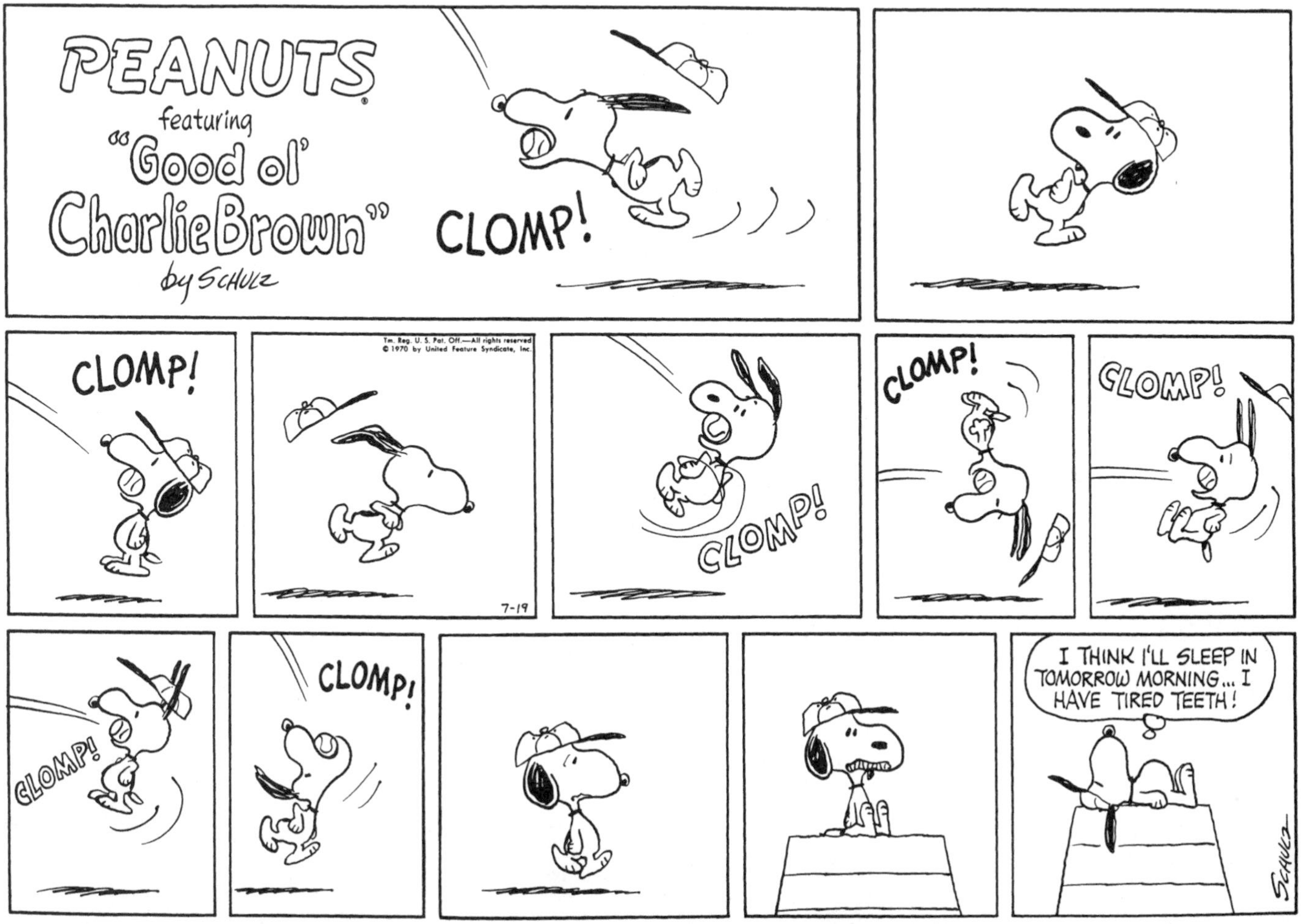

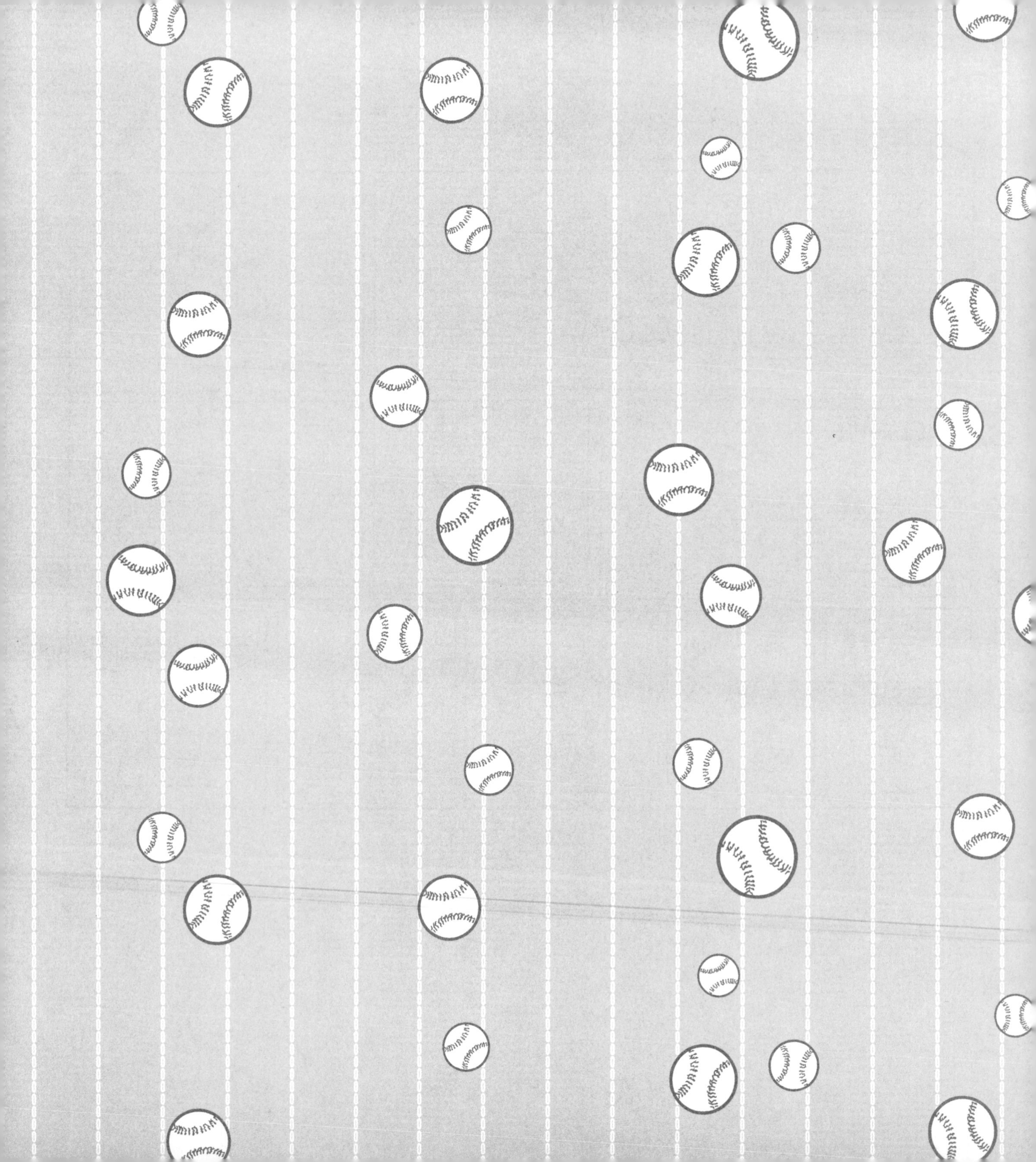

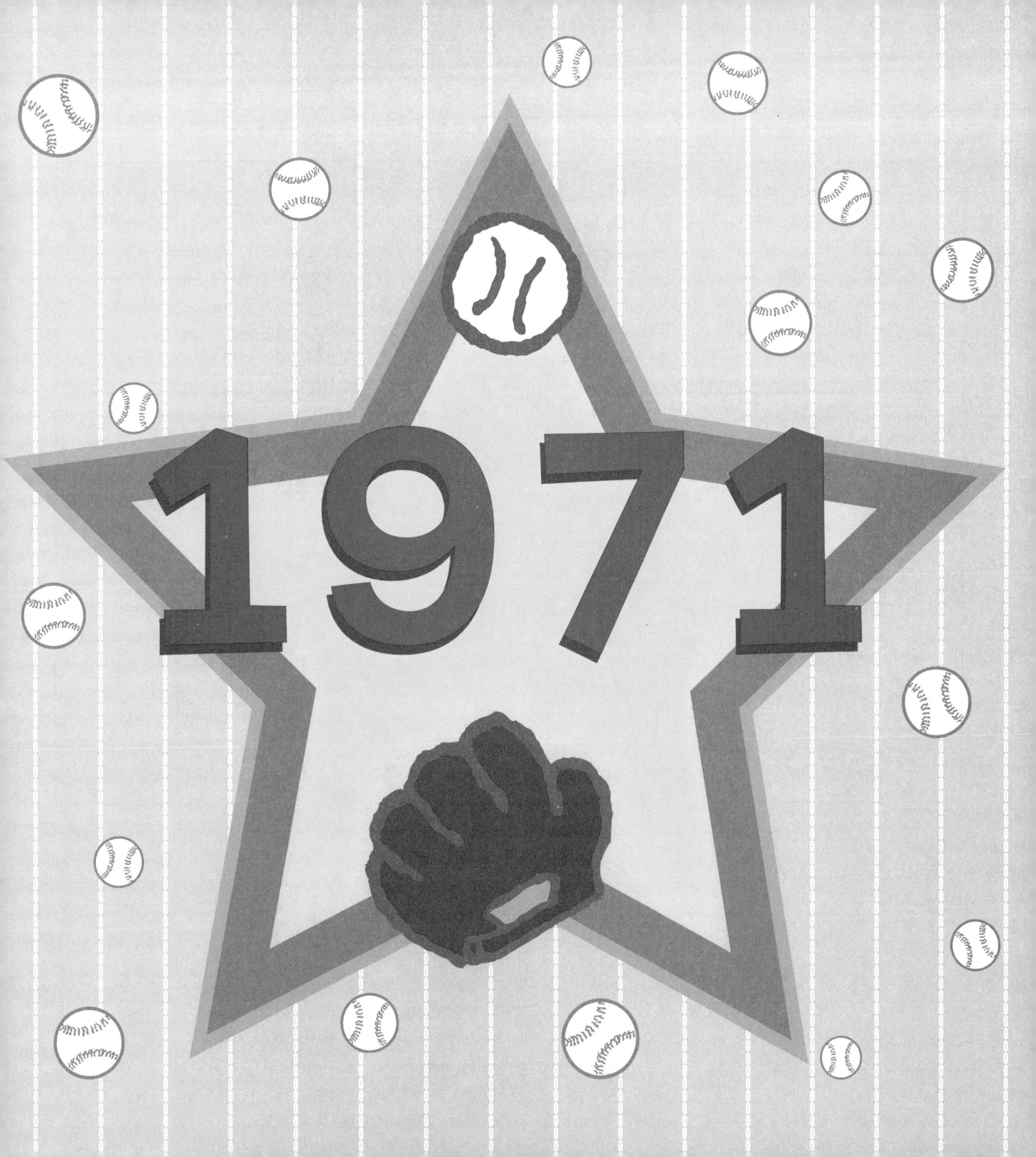
1971

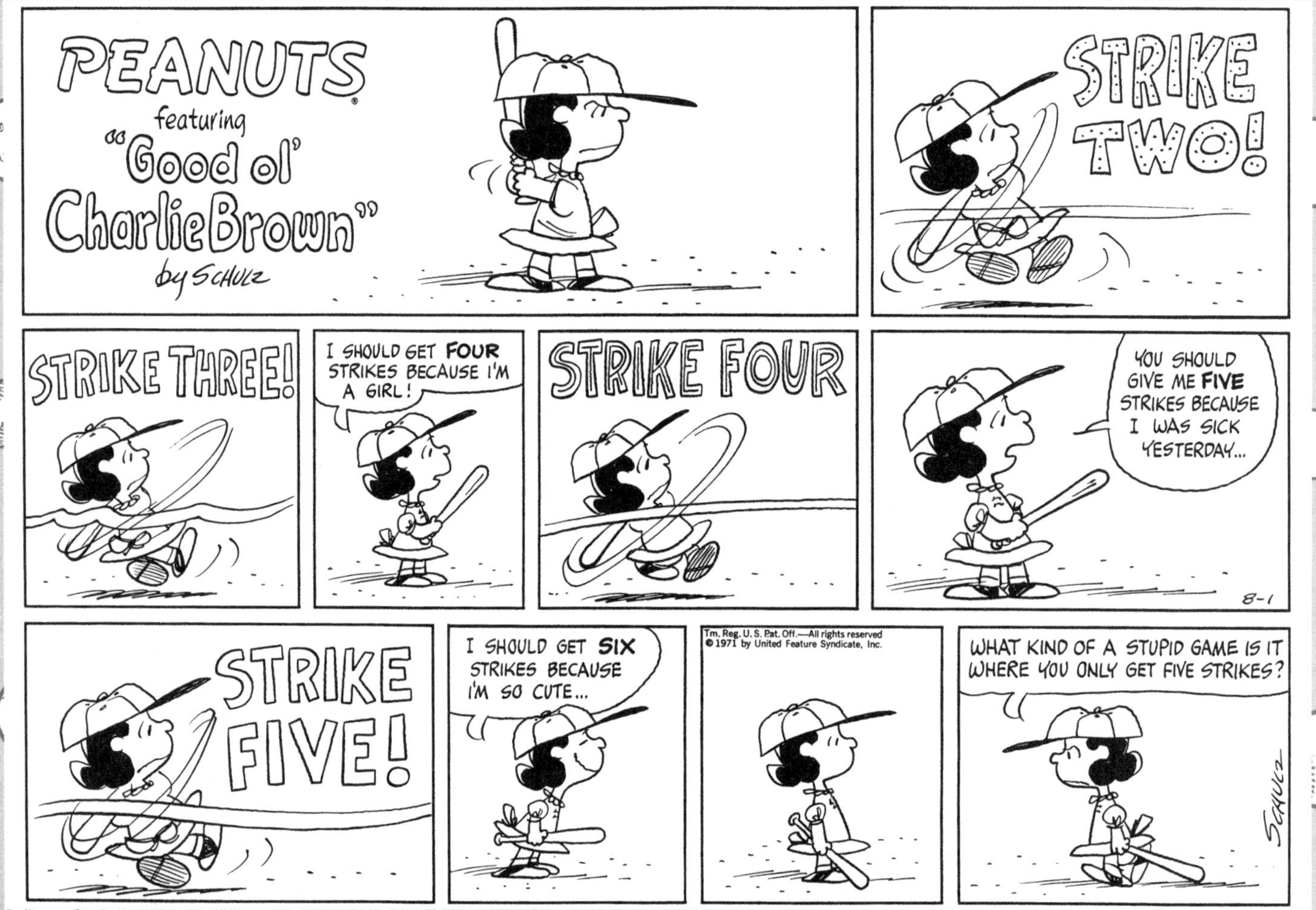
PEANUTS
featuring "Good ol' Charlie Brown"
by SCHULZ
STRIKE TWO!
STRIKE THREE!
I SHOULD GET FOUR STRIKES BECAUSE I'M A GIRL!
STRIKE FOUR
YOU SHOULD GIVE ME FIVE STRIKES BECAUSE I WAS SICK YESTERDAY...
8-1
STRIKE FIVE!
I SHOULD GET SIX STRIKES BECAUSE I'M SO CUTE...
Tm. Reg. U. S. Pat. Off.—All rights reserved
© 1971 by United Feature Syndicate, Inc.
WHAT KIND OF A STUPID GAME IS IT WHERE YOU ONLY GET FIVE STRIKES?
SCHULZ

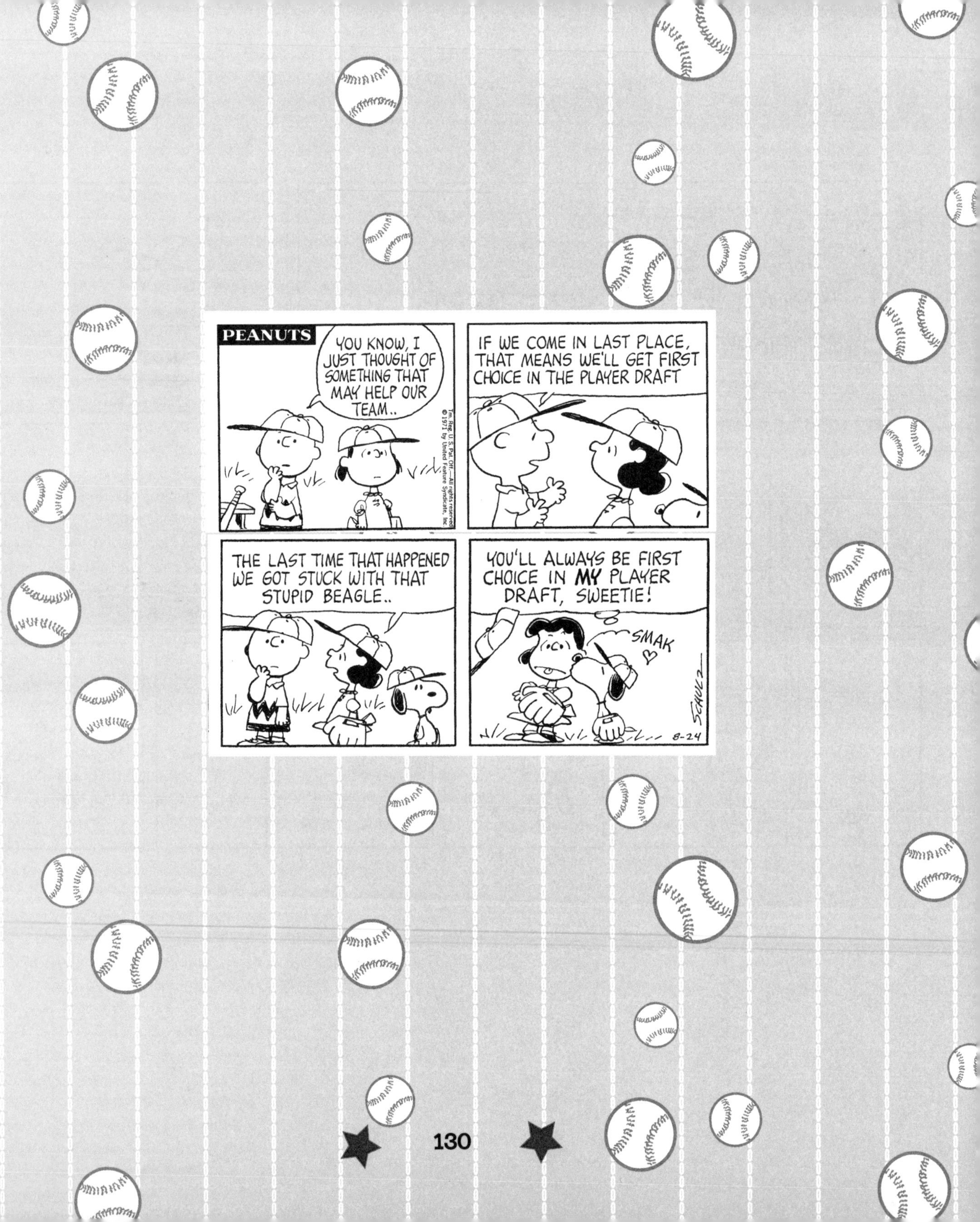
PEANUTS
YOU KNOW, I JUST THOUGHT OF SOMETHING THAT MAY HELP OUR TEAM..
Tm. Reg. U. S. Pat. Off.—All rights reserved
© 1971 by United Feature Syndicate, Inc.
IF WE COME IN LAST PLACE, THAT MEANS WE'LL GET FIRST CHOICE IN THE PLAYER DRAFT
THE LAST TIME THAT HAPPENED WE GOT STUCK WITH THAT STUPID BEAGLE..
YOU'LL ALWAYS BE FIRST CHOICE IN **MY** PLAYER DRAFT, SWEETIE!
SMAK
SCHULZ
8-24

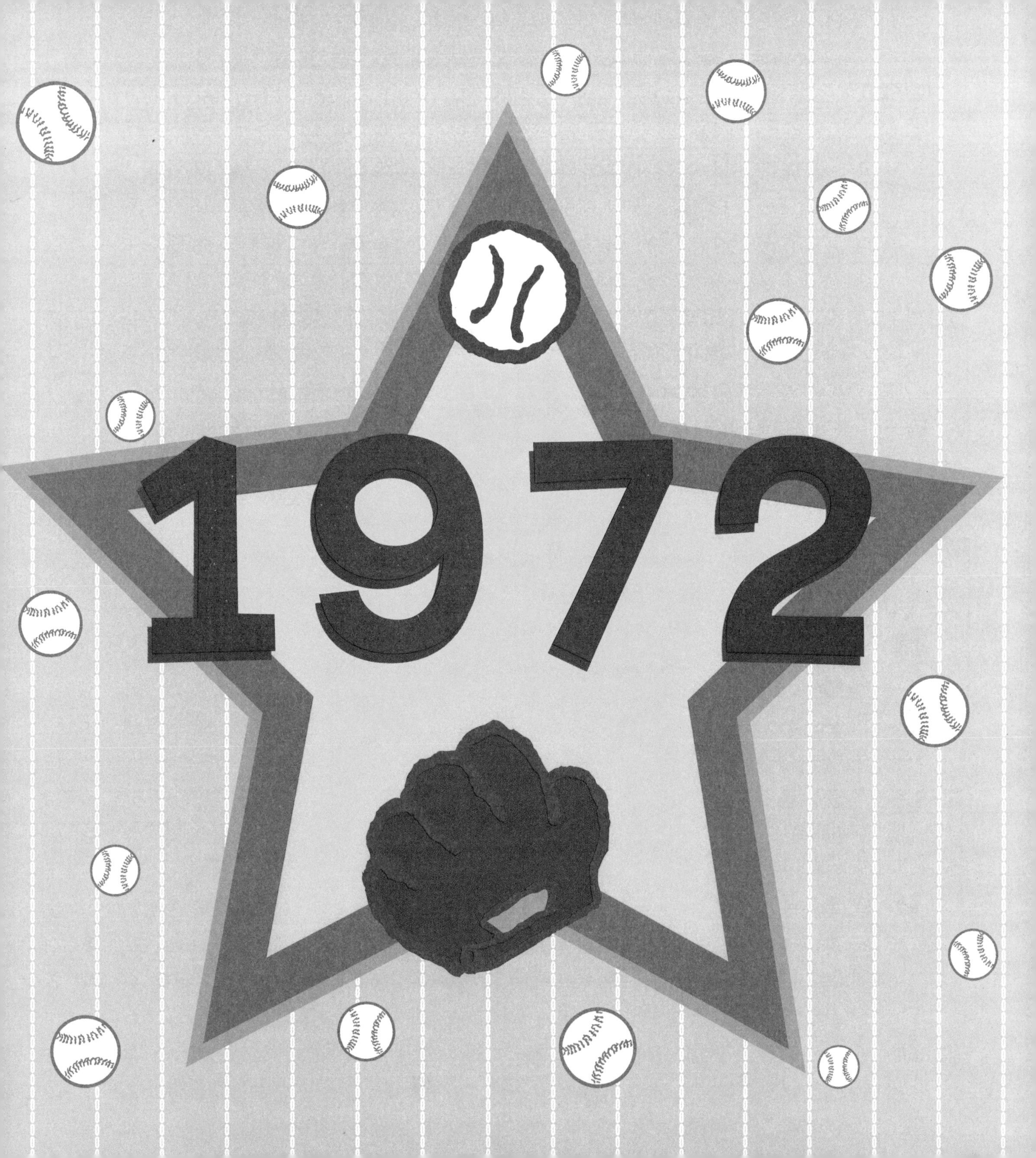
1972

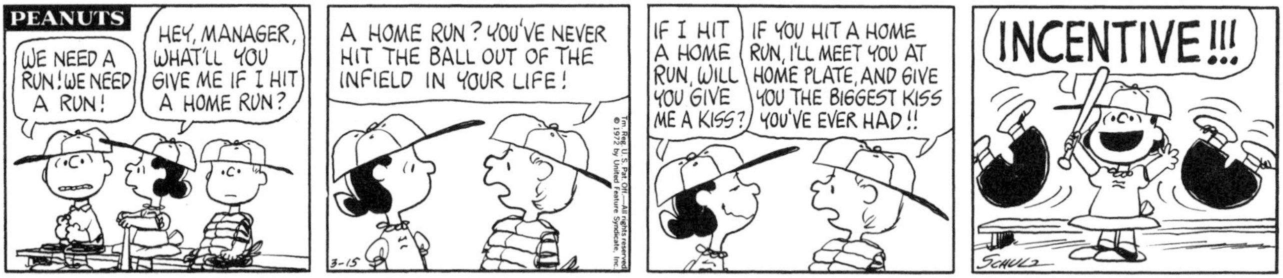
PEANUTS
WE NEED A RUN! WE NEED A RUN!
HEY, MANAGER, WHAT'LL YOU GIVE ME IF I HIT A HOME RUN?
A HOME RUN? YOU'VE NEVER HIT THE BALL OUT OF THE INFIELD IN YOUR LIFE!
3-15
Tm. Reg. U.S. Pat. Off.—All rights reserved © 1972 by United Feature Syndicate, Inc.
IF I HIT A HOME RUN, WILL YOU GIVE ME A KISS?
IF YOU HIT A HOME RUN, I'LL MEET YOU AT HOME PLATE, AND GIVE YOU THE BIGGEST KISS YOU'VE EVER HAD!!
INCENTIVE!!!
SCHULZ

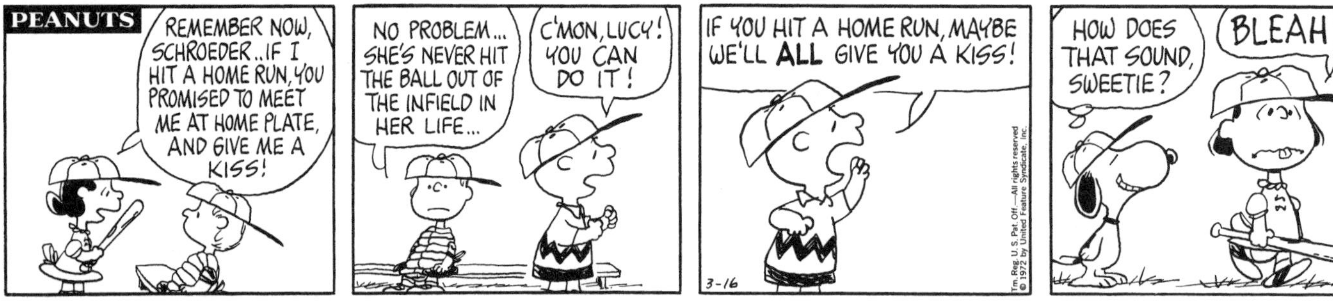
PEANUTS
REMEMBER NOW, SCHROEDER..IF I HIT A HOME RUN, YOU PROMISED TO MEET ME AT HOME PLATE, AND GIVE ME A KISS!
NO PROBLEM... SHE'S NEVER HIT THE BALL OUT OF THE INFIELD IN HER LIFE...
C'MON, LUCY! YOU CAN DO IT!
IF YOU HIT A HOME RUN, MAYBE WE'LL ALL GIVE YOU A KISS!
3-16
Tm. Reg. U.S. Pat. Off.—All rights reserved © 1972 by United Feature Syndicate, Inc.
HOW DOES THAT SOUND, SWEETIE?
BLEAH!!
SCHULZ

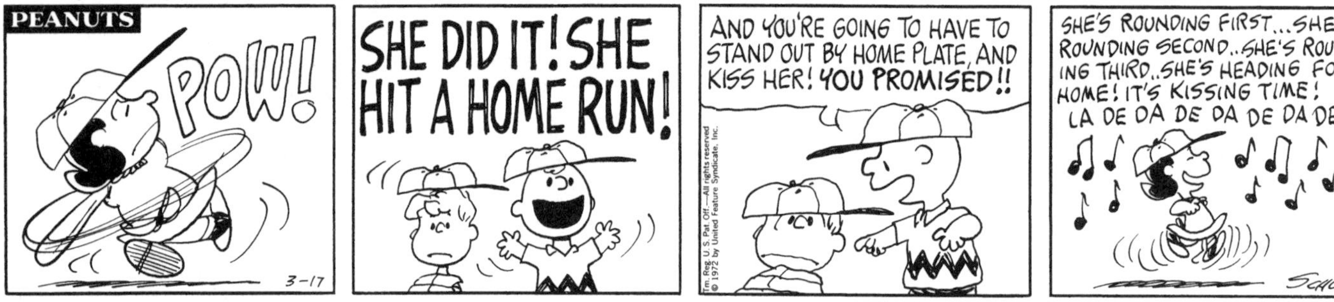
PEANUTS
POW!
3-17
SHE DID IT! SHE HIT A HOME RUN!
Tm. Reg. U.S. Pat. Off.—All rights reserved © 1972 by United Feature Syndicate, Inc.
AND YOU'RE GOING TO HAVE TO STAND OUT BY HOME PLATE, AND KISS HER! YOU PROMISED!!
SHE'S ROUNDING FIRST...SHE'S ROUNDING SECOND..SHE'S ROUNDING THIRD..SHE'S HEADING FOR HOME! IT'S KISSING TIME!
LA DE DA DE DA DE DA DE DA
SCHULZ

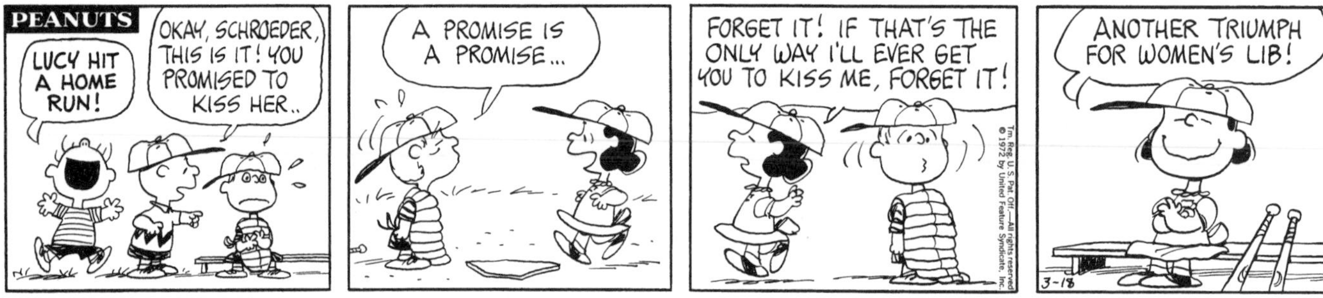
PEANUTS
LUCY HIT A HOME RUN!
OKAY, SCHROEDER, THIS IS IT! YOU PROMISED TO KISS HER..
A PROMISE IS A PROMISE...
FORGET IT! IF THAT'S THE ONLY WAY I'LL EVER GET YOU TO KISS ME, FORGET IT!
Tm. Reg. U.S. Pat. Off.—All rights reserved © 1972 by United Feature Syndicate, Inc.
ANOTHER TRIUMPH FOR WOMEN'S LIB!
3-18
SCHULZ

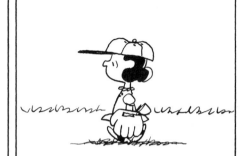

PEANUTS
featuring
"Good ol' CharlieBrown"
by SCHULZ
HEY, MANAGER, I'VE GOT A GREAT IDEA!
WHY DON'T WE SELL OUR TEAM, AND MOVE TO A DIFFERENT CITY? THAT'S WHAT EVERYONE ELSE IS DOING
WE COULD SELL OUR TEAM, AND GET A FRESH START IN A NEW CITY
I'VE GOT A BETTER IDEA...WHY DON'T WE KEEP OUR TEAM, AND JUST SELL YOU?!
Tm. Reg. U.S. Pat. Off.—All rights reserved © 1972 by United Feature Syndicate, Inc.
3-19
THE NEXT TIME I GET A GREAT IDEA, I'LL KEEP IT TO MYSELF!
SCHULZ

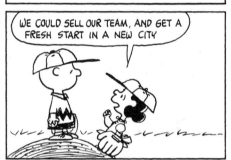

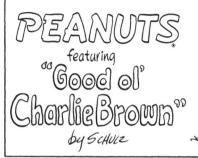

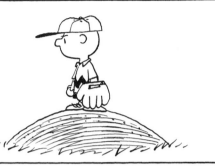

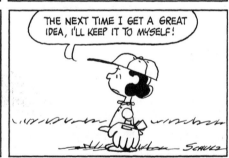

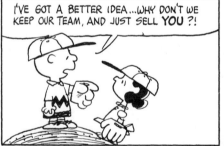

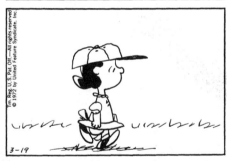

PEANUTS
featuring
"Good ol' Charlie Brown"
by SCHULZ

IN CONFERENCE

HEY, MANAGER!

HAVE YOU EVER NOTICED HOW THE PEOPLE IN THE STANDS REALLY DON'T KNOW WHAT WE'RE SAYING WHEN WE HAVE THESE CONFERENCES ON THE MOUND?

ALL THEY HAVE TO GO BY IS THE WAY WE WAVE OUR ARMS

SEE, I POINT TO THE OUTFIELD, AND THEY THINK I'M TALKING ABOUT SOMETHING OUT THERE...

OR I CAN HOLD UP TWO FINGERS, AND THEY THINK I'M SAYING THAT THERE'S TWO OUTS NOW, AND WE HAVE TO GET THIS NEXT HITTER...

NO ONE IN THE STANDS CAN TELL WHAT I'M REALLY SAYING...

Tm. Reg. U.S. Pat. Off.—All rights reserved
© 1972 by United Feature Syndicate, Inc.

WHAT IS IT THAT YOU'RE REALLY SAYING?

I THINK YOU'RE KIND OF CUTE!

I CAN'T STAND IT!

✳SIGH✳ ♪

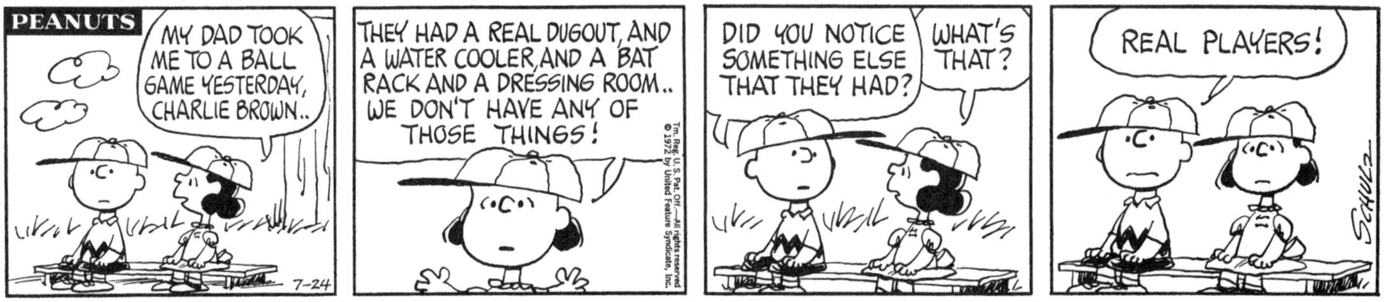
PEANUTS
MY DAD TOOK ME TO A BALL GAME YESTERDAY, CHARLIE BROWN..
7-24
THEY HAD A REAL DUGOUT, AND A WATER COOLER, AND A BAT RACK AND A DRESSING ROOM.. WE DON'T HAVE ANY OF THOSE THINGS!
Tm. Reg. U.S. Pat. Off.—All rights reserved © 1972 by United Feature Syndicate, Inc.
DID YOU NOTICE SOMETHING ELSE THAT THEY HAD?
WHAT'S THAT?
REAL PLAYERS!
SCHULZ

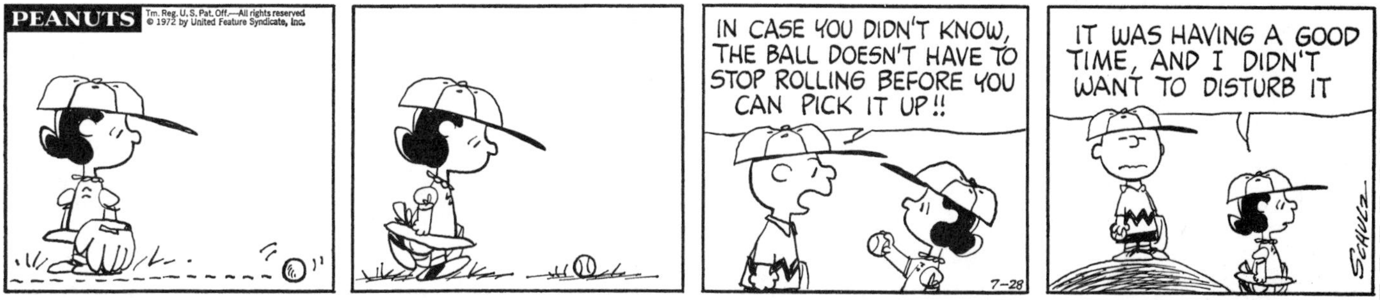
PEANUTS
Tm. Reg. U.S. Pat. Off.—All rights reserved © 1972 by United Feature Syndicate, Inc.
IN CASE YOU DIDN'T KNOW, THE BALL DOESN'T HAVE TO STOP ROLLING BEFORE YOU CAN PICK IT UP!!
7-28
IT WAS HAVING A GOOD TIME, AND I DIDN'T WANT TO DISTURB IT
SCHULZ

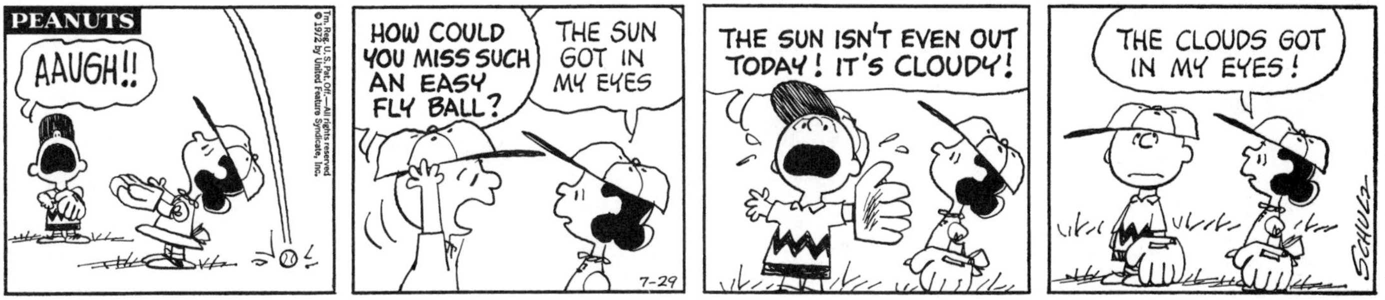
PEANUTS
AAUGH!!
Tm. Reg. U.S. Pat. Off.—All rights reserved © 1972 by United Feature Syndicate, Inc.
HOW COULD YOU MISS SUCH AN EASY FLY BALL?
THE SUN GOT IN MY EYES
7-29
THE SUN ISN'T EVEN OUT TODAY! IT'S CLOUDY!
THE CLOUDS GOT IN MY EYES!
SCHULZ

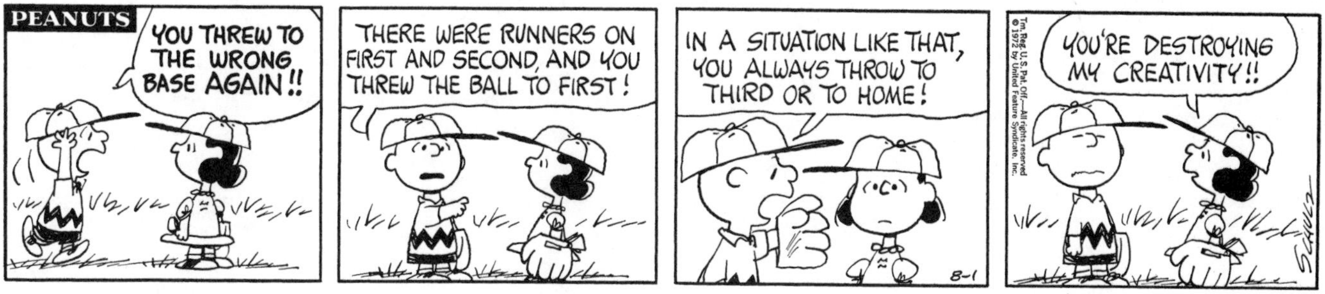
PEANUTS
YOU THREW TO THE WRONG BASE AGAIN!!
THERE WERE RUNNERS ON FIRST AND SECOND, AND YOU THREW THE BALL TO FIRST!
IN A SITUATION LIKE THAT, YOU ALWAYS THROW TO THIRD OR TO HOME!
8-1
Tm. Reg. U.S. Pat. Off.—All rights reserved © 1972 by United Feature Syndicate, Inc.
YOU'RE DESTROYING MY CREATIVITY!!
SCHULZ

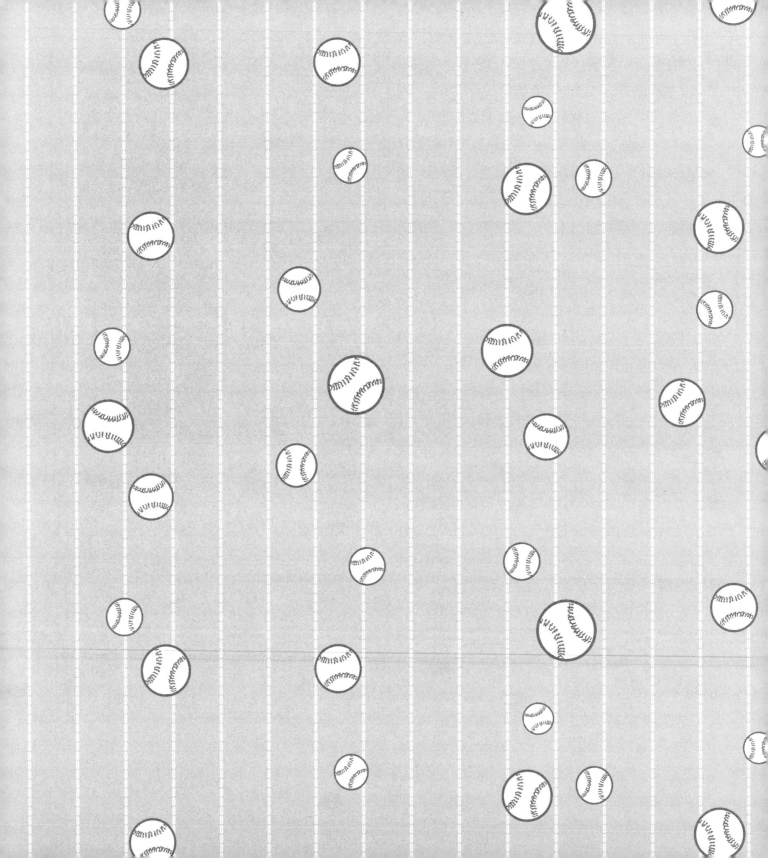

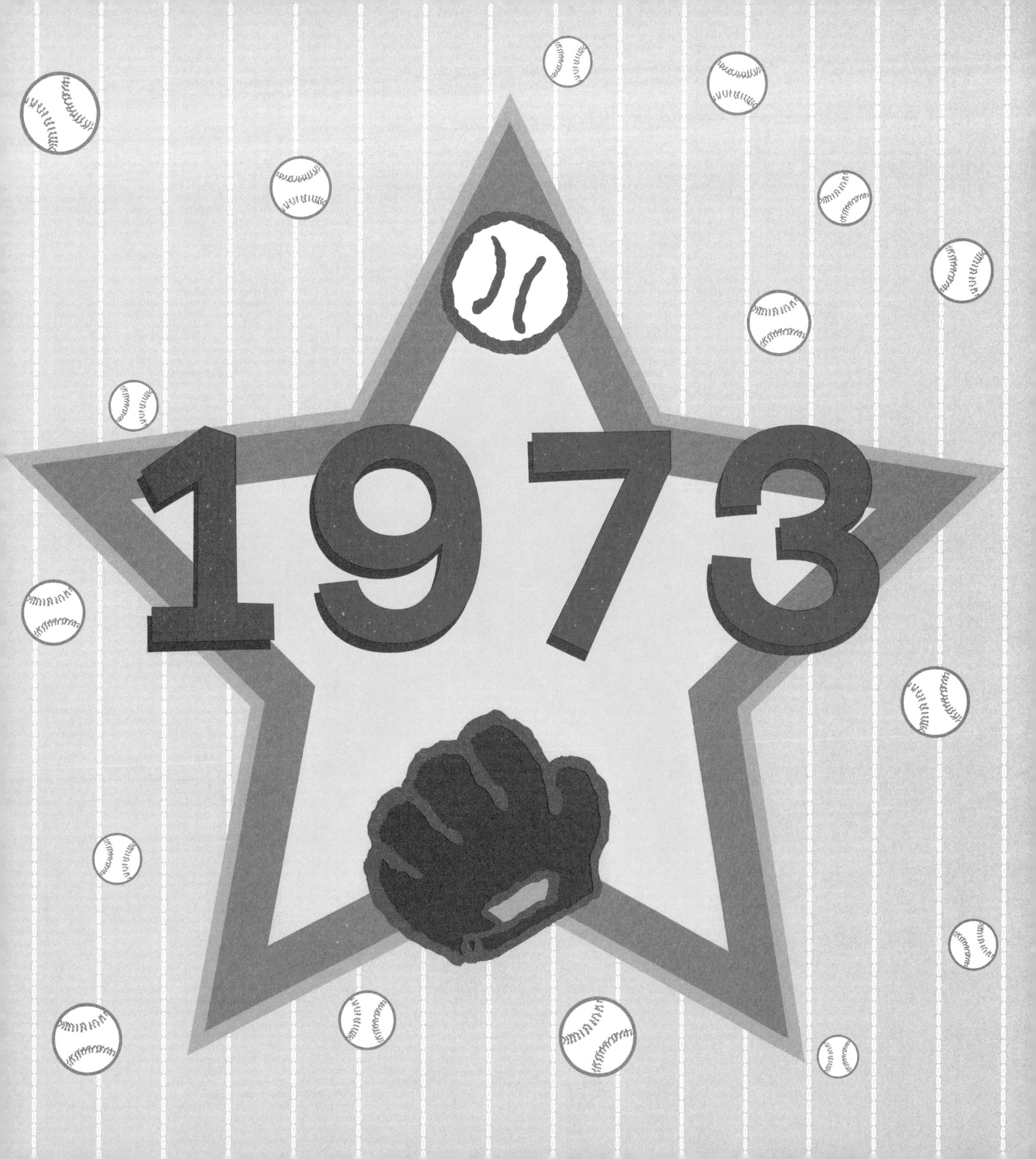
1973

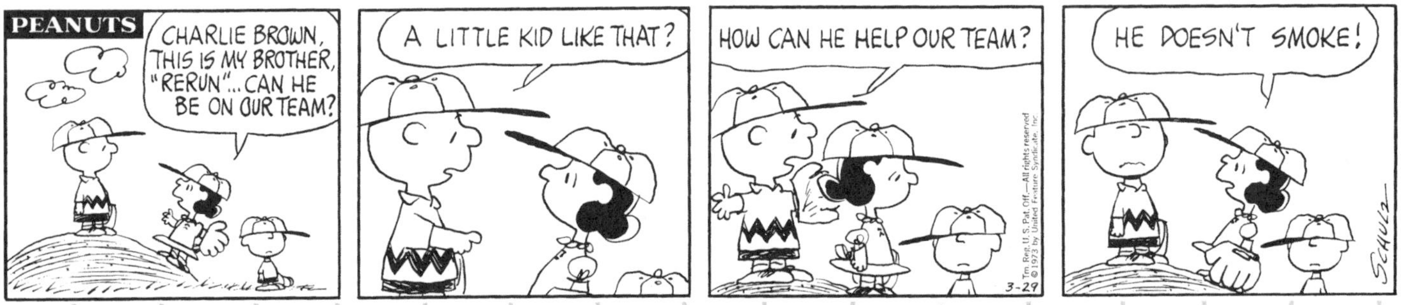
PEANUTS
CHARLIE BROWN, THIS IS MY BROTHER, "RERUN"... CAN HE BE ON OUR TEAM?
A LITTLE KID LIKE THAT?
HOW CAN HE HELP OUR TEAM?
Tm. Reg. U.S. Pat. Off.—All rights reserved © 1973 by United Feature Syndicate, Inc.
3-29
HE DOESN'T SMOKE!
SCHULZ

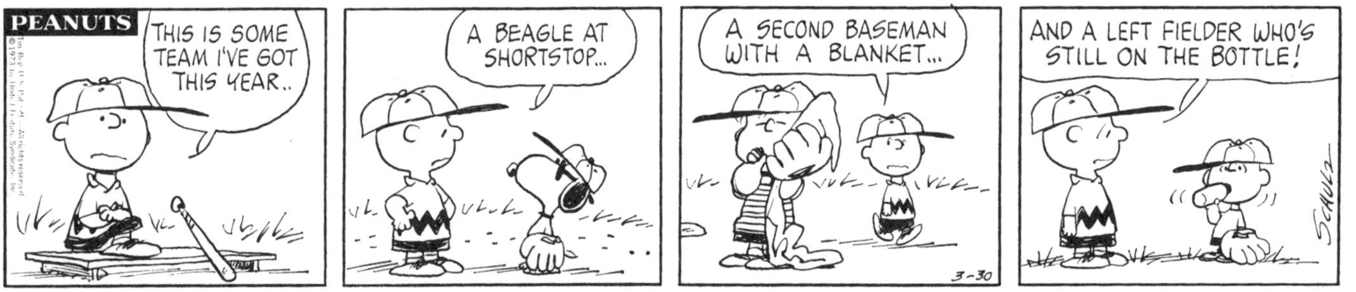
PEANUTS
THIS IS SOME TEAM I'VE GOT THIS YEAR..
A BEAGLE AT SHORTSTOP...
A SECOND BASEMAN WITH A BLANKET...
3-30
AND A LEFT FIELDER WHO'S STILL ON THE BOTTLE!
SCHULZ

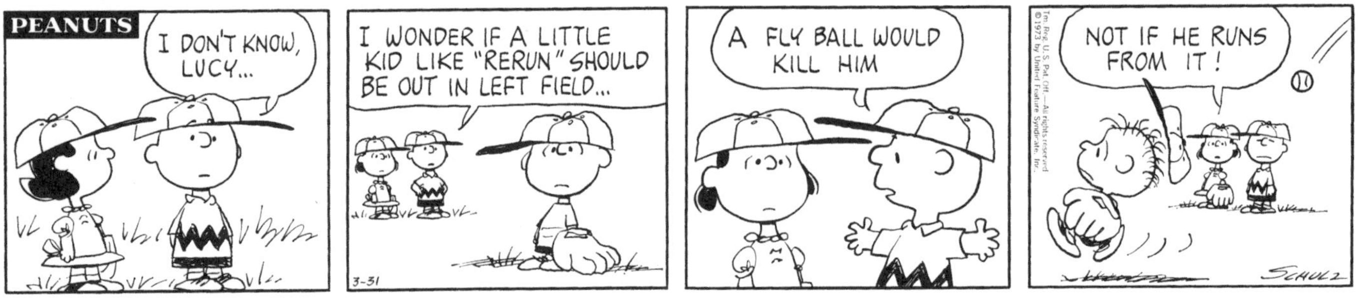
PEANUTS
I DON'T KNOW, LUCY...
I WONDER IF A LITTLE KID LIKE "RERUN" SHOULD BE OUT IN LEFT FIELD...
3-31
A FLY BALL WOULD KILL HIM
NOT IF HE RUNS FROM IT!
SCHULZ

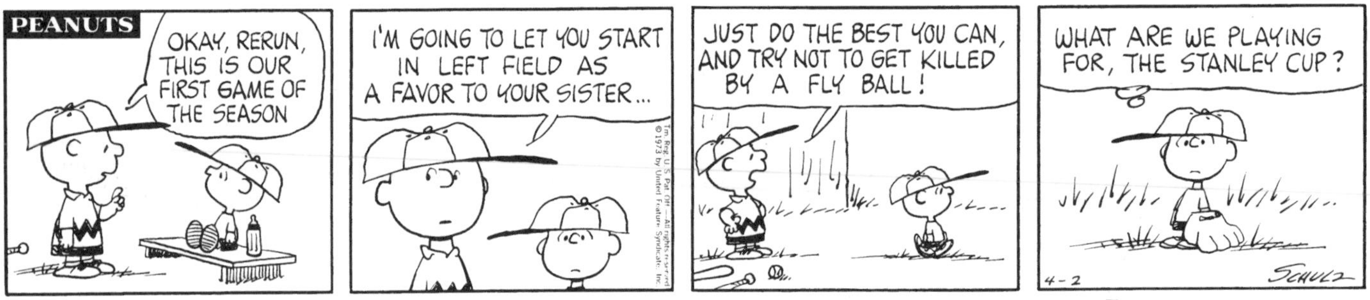
PEANUTS
OKAY, RERUN, THIS IS OUR FIRST GAME OF THE SEASON
I'M GOING TO LET YOU START IN LEFT FIELD AS A FAVOR TO YOUR SISTER...
JUST DO THE BEST YOU CAN, AND TRY NOT TO GET KILLED BY A FLY BALL!
WHAT ARE WE PLAYING FOR, THE STANLEY CUP?
4-2
SCHULZ

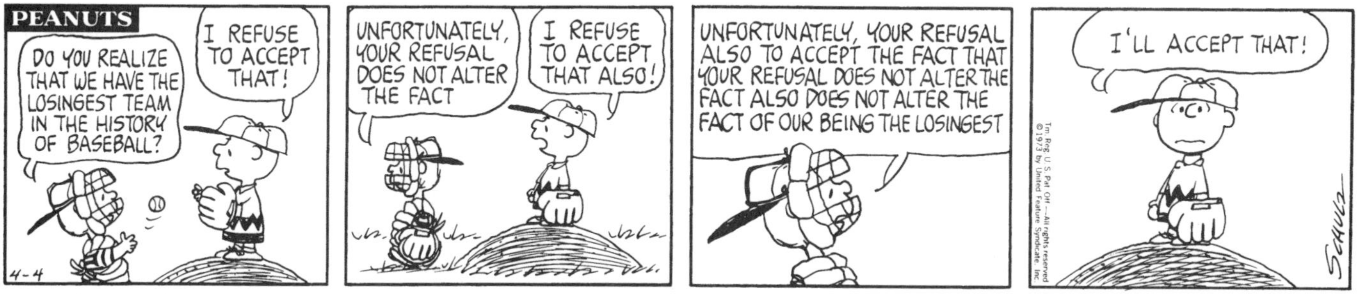
PEANUTS
DO YOU REALIZE THAT WE HAVE THE LOSINGEST TEAM IN THE HISTORY OF BASEBALL?
I REFUSE TO ACCEPT THAT!
4-4
UNFORTUNATELY, YOUR REFUSAL DOES NOT ALTER THE FACT
I REFUSE TO ACCEPT THAT ALSO!
UNFORTUNATELY, YOUR REFUSAL ALSO TO ACCEPT THE FACT THAT YOUR REFUSAL DOES NOT ALTER THE FACT ALSO DOES NOT ALTER THE FACT OF OUR BEING THE LOSINGEST
Tm. Reg. U.S. Pat. Off.—All rights reserved © 1973 by United Feature Syndicate, Inc.
I'LL ACCEPT THAT!
SCHULZ

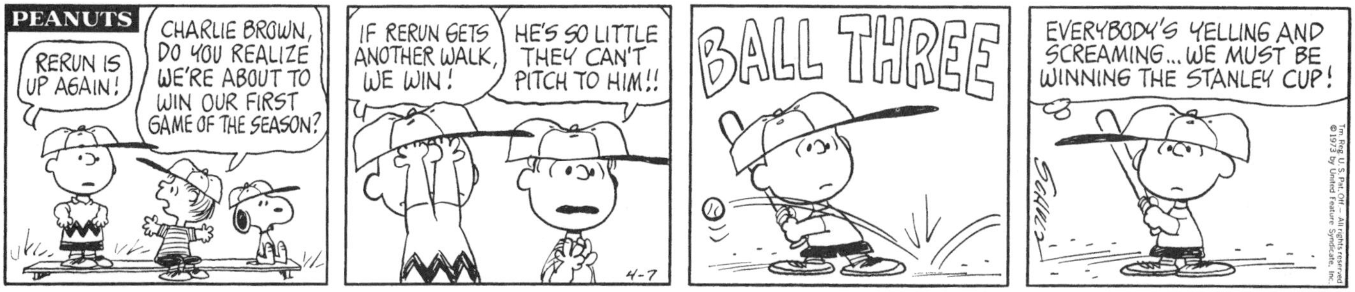
PEANUTS
RERUN IS UP AGAIN!
CHARLIE BROWN, DO YOU REALIZE WE'RE ABOUT TO WIN OUR FIRST GAME OF THE SEASON?
IF RERUN GETS ANOTHER WALK, WE WIN!
HE'S SO LITTLE THEY CAN'T PITCH TO HIM!!
4-7
BALL THREE
SCHULZ
EVERYBODY'S YELLING AND SCREAMING... WE MUST BE WINNING THE STANLEY CUP!
Tm. Reg. U.S. Pat. Off.—All rights reserved © 1973 by United Feature Syndicate, Inc.

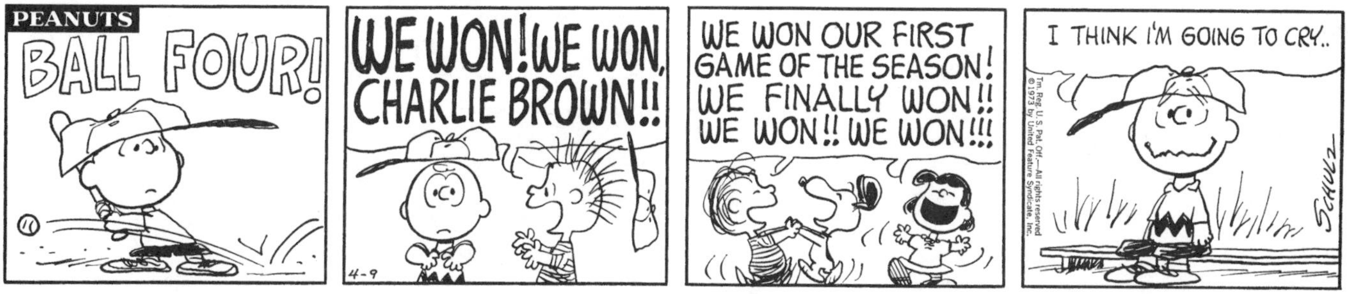
PEANUTS
BALL FOUR!
WE WON! WE WON, CHARLIE BROWN!!
4-9
WE WON OUR FIRST GAME OF THE SEASON! WE FINALLY WON!! WE WON!! WE WON!!!
Tm. Reg. U.S. Pat. Off.—All rights reserved © 1973 by United Feature Syndicate, Inc.
I THINK I'M GOING TO CRY..
SCHULZ

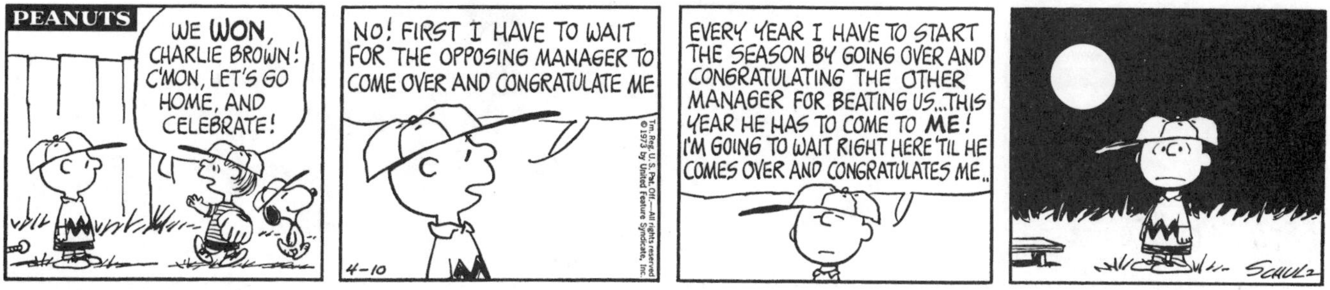
PEANUTS
WE WON, CHARLIE BROWN! C'MON, LET'S GO HOME, AND CELEBRATE!
NO! FIRST I HAVE TO WAIT FOR THE OPPOSING MANAGER TO COME OVER AND CONGRATULATE ME
4-10
Tm. Reg. U.S. Pat. Off.—All rights reserved © 1973 by United Feature Syndicate, Inc.
EVERY YEAR I HAVE TO START THE SEASON BY GOING OVER AND CONGRATULATING THE OTHER MANAGER FOR BEATING US...THIS YEAR HE HAS TO COME TO ME! I'M GOING TO WAIT RIGHT HERE 'TIL HE COMES OVER AND CONGRATULATES ME..
SCHULZ

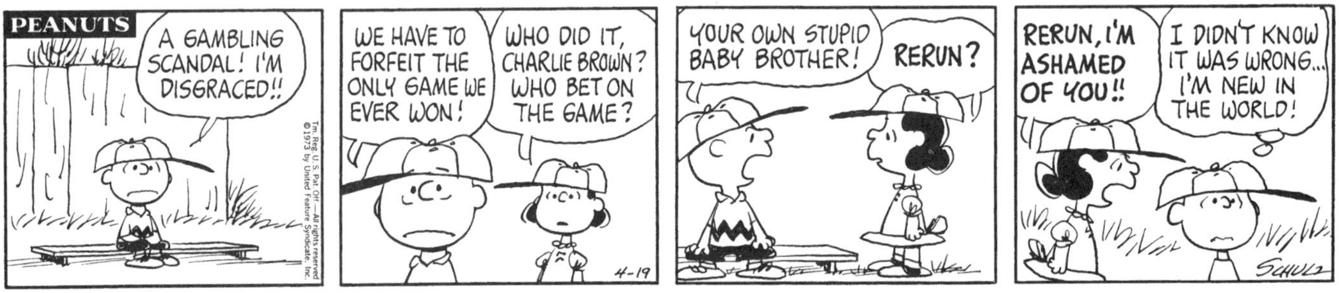
PEANUTS
A GAMBLING SCANDAL! I'M DISGRACED!!
Tm. Reg. U.S. Pat. Off.—All rights reserved © 1973 by United Feature Syndicate, Inc.
WE HAVE TO FORFEIT THE ONLY GAME WE EVER WON!
WHO DID IT, CHARLIE BROWN? WHO BET ON THE GAME?
4-19
YOUR OWN STUPID BABY BROTHER!
RERUN?
RERUN, I'M ASHAMED OF YOU!!
I DIDN'T KNOW IT WAS WRONG... I'M NEW IN THE WORLD!
SCHULZ

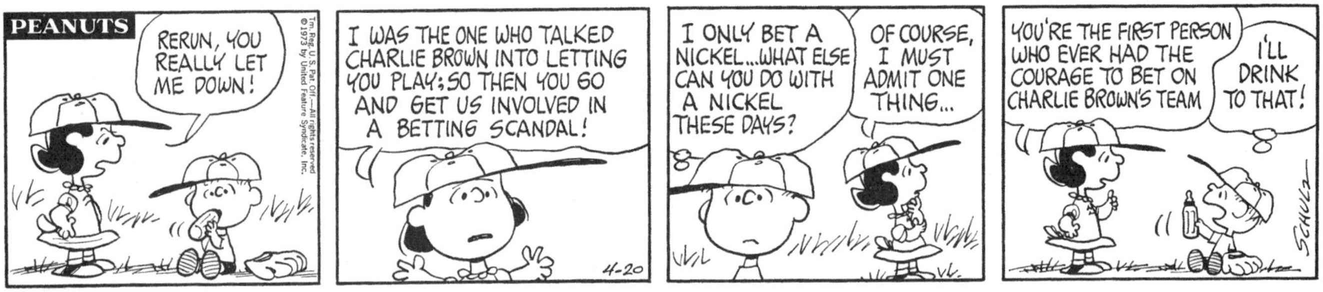
PEANUTS
RERUN, YOU REALLY LET ME DOWN!
Tm. Reg. U.S. Pat. Off.—All rights reserved © 1973 by United Feature Syndicate, Inc.
I WAS THE ONE WHO TALKED CHARLIE BROWN INTO LETTING YOU PLAY; SO THEN YOU GO AND GET US INVOLVED IN A BETTING SCANDAL!
4-20
I ONLY BET A NICKEL...WHAT ELSE CAN YOU DO WITH A NICKEL THESE DAYS?
OF COURSE, I MUST ADMIT ONE THING...
YOU'RE THE FIRST PERSON WHO EVER HAD THE COURAGE TO BET ON CHARLIE BROWN'S TEAM
I'LL DRINK TO THAT!
SCHULZ

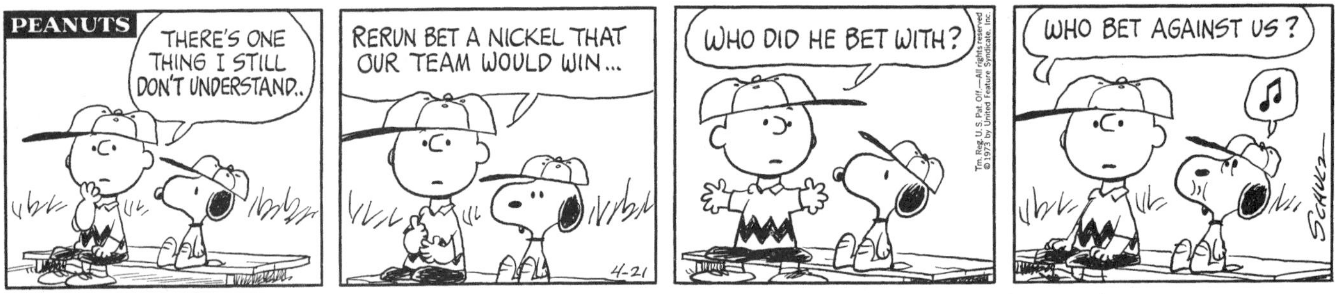
PEANUTS
THERE'S ONE THING I STILL DON'T UNDERSTAND..
RERUN BET A NICKEL THAT OUR TEAM WOULD WIN...
4-21
WHO DID HE BET WITH?
Tm. Reg. U.S. Pat. Off.—All rights reserved © 1973 by United Feature Syndicate, Inc.
WHO BET AGAINST US?
SCHULZ

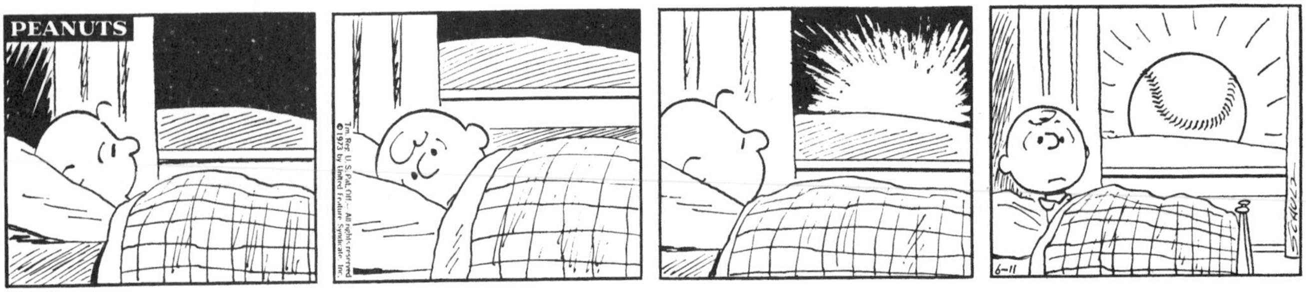
PEANUTS
Tm. Reg. U.S. Pat. Off.—All rights reserved © 1973 by United Feature Syndicate, Inc.
6-11
SCHULZ

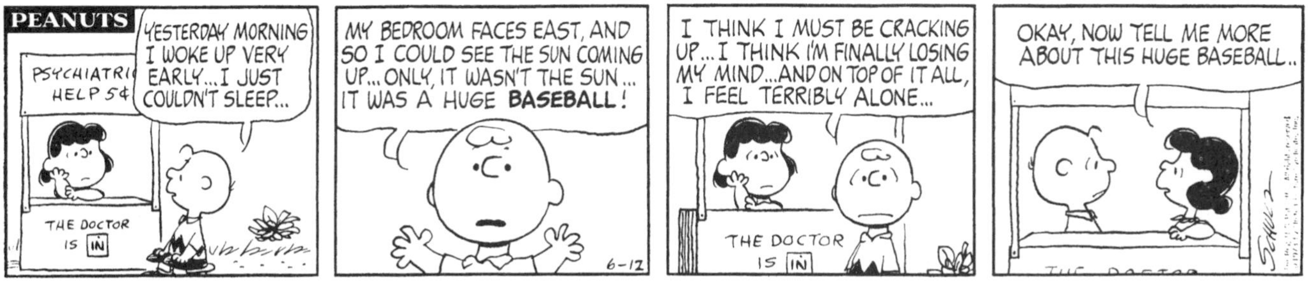
PEANUTS
PSYCHIATRIC HELP 5¢
THE DOCTOR IS IN
YESTERDAY MORNING I WOKE UP VERY EARLY...I JUST COULDN'T SLEEP...
MY BEDROOM FACES EAST, AND SO I COULD SEE THE SUN COMING UP... ONLY, IT WASN'T THE SUN ... IT WAS A HUGE **BASEBALL** !
6-12
I THINK I MUST BE CRACKING UP... I THINK I'M FINALLY LOSING MY MIND...AND ON TOP OF IT ALL, I FEEL TERRIBLY ALONE...
THE DOCTOR IS IN
OKAY, NOW TELL ME MORE ABOUT THIS HUGE BASEBALL..
SCHULZ

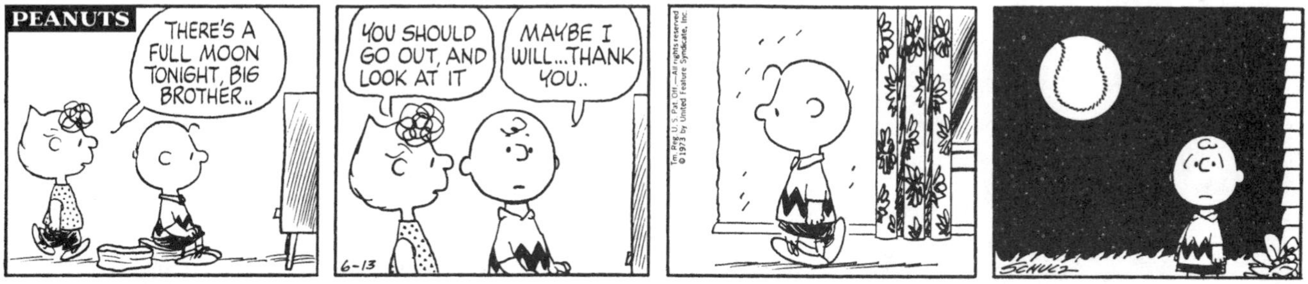
PEANUTS
THERE'S A FULL MOON TONIGHT, BIG BROTHER..
YOU SHOULD GO OUT, AND LOOK AT IT
MAYBE I WILL...THANK YOU..
6-13
Tm. Reg. U. S. Pat. Off.—All rights reserved
© 1973 by United Feature Syndicate, Inc.
SCHULZ

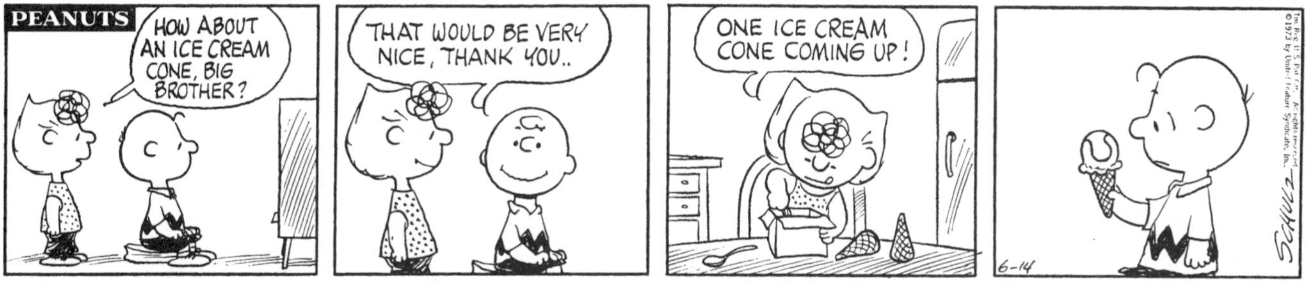
PEANUTS
HOW ABOUT AN ICE CREAM CONE, BIG BROTHER?
THAT WOULD BE VERY NICE, THANK YOU..
ONE ICE CREAM CONE COMING UP!
6-14
SCHULZ

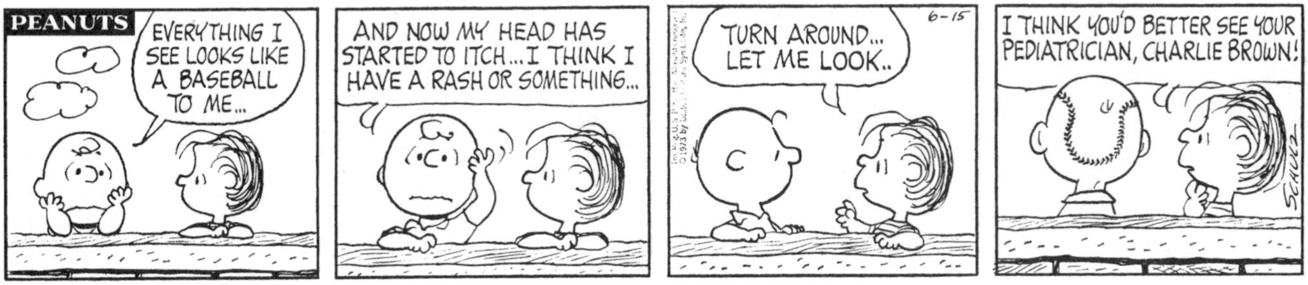
PEANUTS
EVERYTHING I SEE LOOKS LIKE A BASEBALL TO ME...
AND NOW MY HEAD HAS STARTED TO ITCH...I THINK I HAVE A RASH OR SOMETHING...
TURN AROUND... LET ME LOOK..
6-15
I THINK YOU'D BETTER SEE YOUR PEDIATRICIAN, CHARLIE BROWN!
SCHULZ

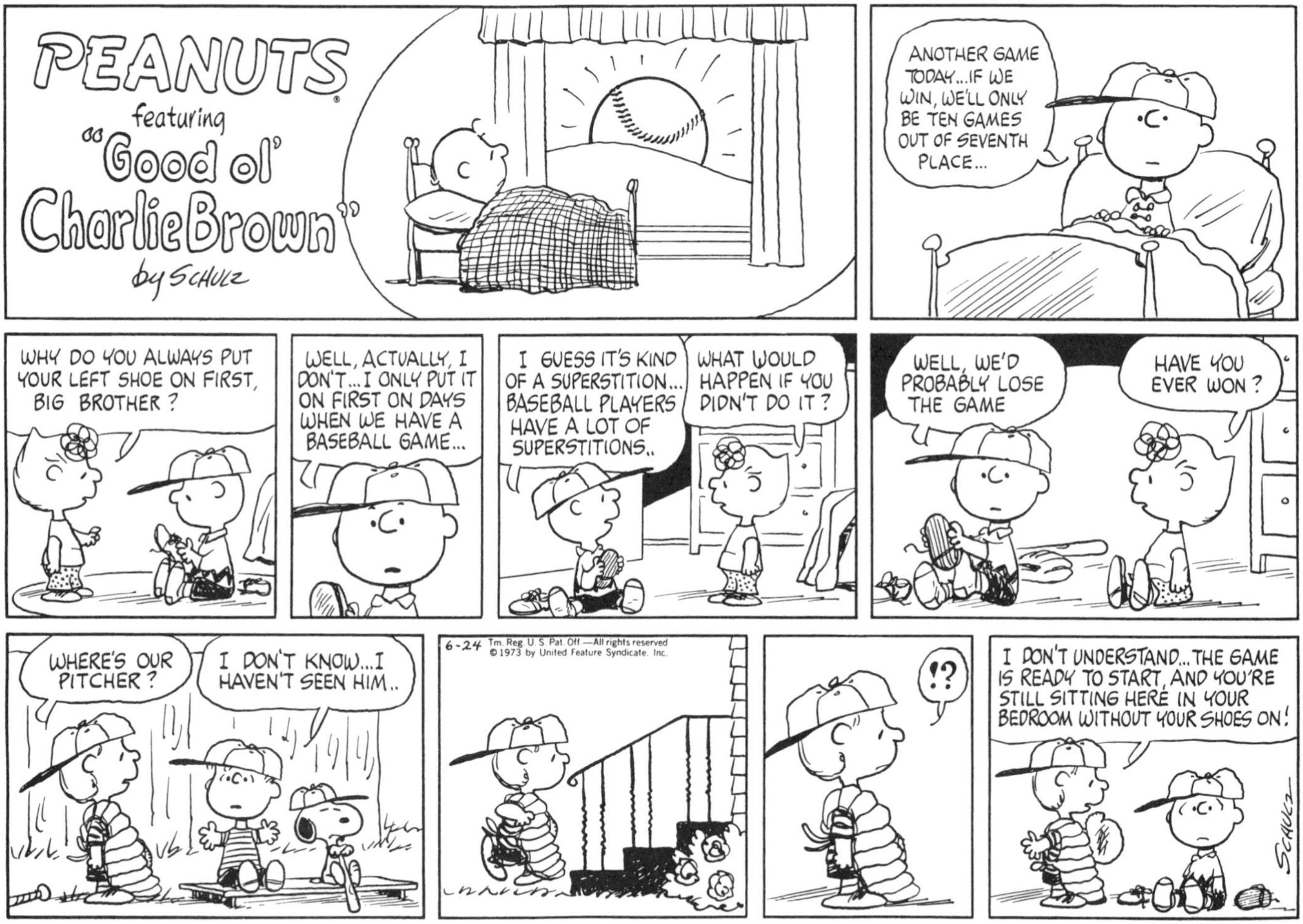
PEANUTS
featuring "Good ol' Charlie Brown"
by SCHULZ
ANOTHER GAME TODAY...IF WE WIN, WE'LL ONLY BE TEN GAMES OUT OF SEVENTH PLACE...
WHY DO YOU ALWAYS PUT YOUR LEFT SHOE ON FIRST, BIG BROTHER ?
WELL, ACTUALLY, I DON'T...I ONLY PUT IT ON FIRST ON DAYS WHEN WE HAVE A BASEBALL GAME...
I GUESS IT'S KIND OF A SUPERSTITION... BASEBALL PLAYERS HAVE A LOT OF SUPERSTITIONS..
WHAT WOULD HAPPEN IF YOU DIDN'T DO IT ?
WELL, WE'D PROBABLY LOSE THE GAME
HAVE YOU EVER WON ?
WHERE'S OUR PITCHER ?
I DON'T KNOW...I HAVEN'T SEEN HIM..
6-24 Tm. Reg. U.S. Pat. Off.—All rights reserved © 1973 by United Feature Syndicate, Inc.
!?
I DON'T UNDERSTAND...THE GAME IS READY TO START, AND YOU'RE STILL SITTING HERE IN YOUR BEDROOM WITHOUT YOUR SHOES ON!
SCHULZ

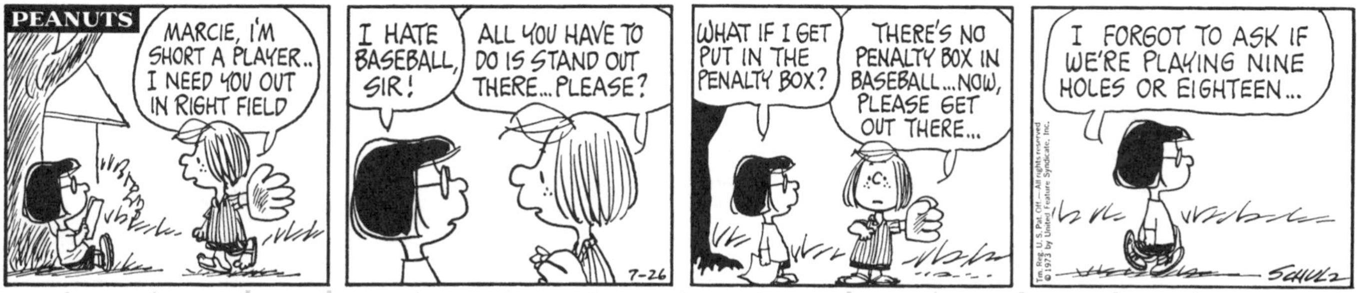
PEANUTS
MARCIE, I'M SHORT A PLAYER.. I NEED YOU OUT IN RIGHT FIELD
I HATE BASEBALL, SIR!
ALL YOU HAVE TO DO IS STAND OUT THERE... PLEASE?
7-26
WHAT IF I GET PUT IN THE PENALTY BOX?
THERE'S NO PENALTY BOX IN BASEBALL... NOW, PLEASE GET OUT THERE...
I FORGOT TO ASK IF WE'RE PLAYING NINE HOLES OR EIGHTEEN...
Tm. Reg. U.S. Pat. Off.—All rights reserved © 1973 by United Feature Syndicate, Inc.
SCHULZ

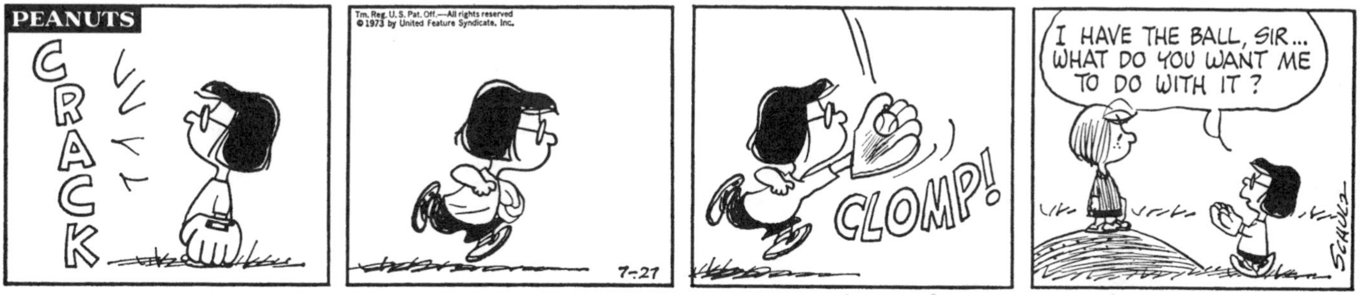
PEANUTS
CRACK
Tm. Reg. U.S. Pat. Off.—All rights reserved © 1973 by United Feature Syndicate, Inc.
7-27
CLOMP!
I HAVE THE BALL, SIR... WHAT DO YOU WANT ME TO DO WITH IT?
SCHULZ

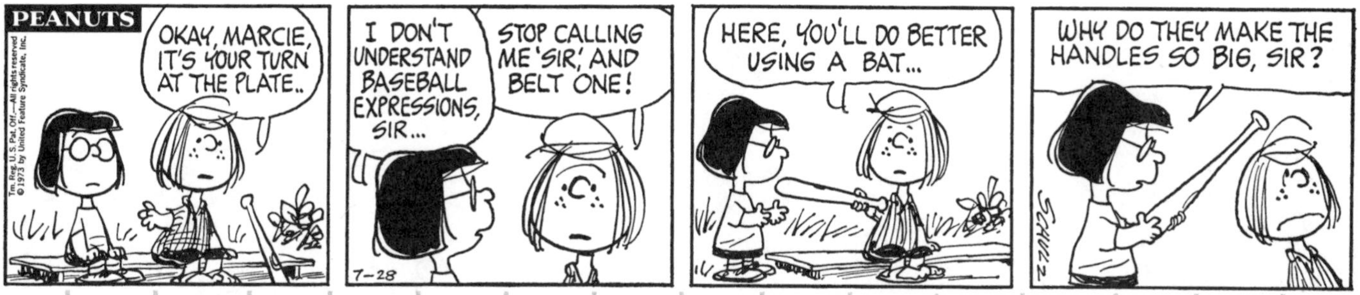
PEANUTS
Tm. Reg. U.S. Pat. Off.—All rights reserved © 1973 by United Feature Syndicate, Inc.
OKAY, MARCIE, IT'S YOUR TURN AT THE PLATE..
I DON'T UNDERSTAND BASEBALL EXPRESSIONS, SIR...
STOP CALLING ME 'SIR,' AND BELT ONE!
7-28
HERE, YOU'LL DO BETTER USING A BAT...
SCHULZ
WHY DO THEY MAKE THE HANDLES SO BIG, SIR?

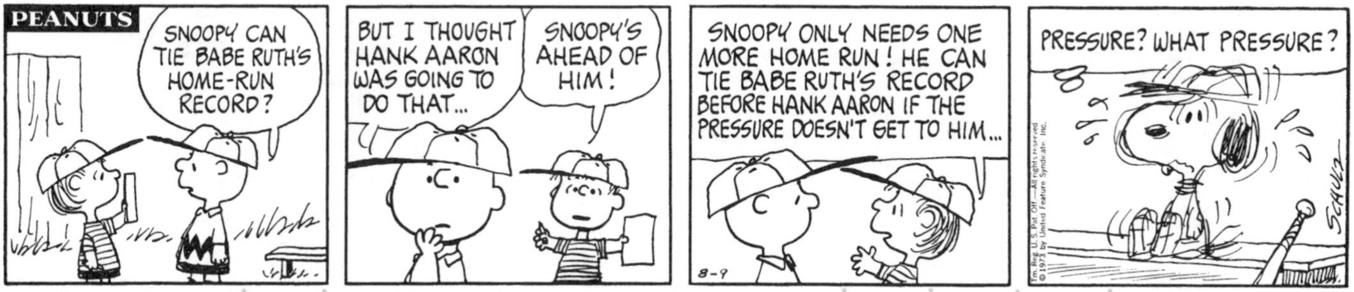
PEANUTS
SNOOPY CAN TIE BABE RUTH'S HOME-RUN RECORD?
BUT I THOUGHT HANK AARON WAS GOING TO DO THAT...
SNOOPY'S AHEAD OF HIM!
SNOOPY ONLY NEEDS ONE MORE HOME RUN! HE CAN TIE BABE RUTH'S RECORD BEFORE HANK AARON IF THE PRESSURE DOESN'T GET TO HIM...
8-9
Tm. Reg. U.S. Pat. Off.—All rights reserved © 1973 by United Feature Syndicate, Inc.
PRESSURE? WHAT PRESSURE?
SCHULZ

PEANUTS
HERE, YOU GOT A LETTER..
8-10
"DEAR STUPID, WHO DO YOU THINK YOU ARE TRYING TO BREAK BABE RUTH'S RECORD?"
Tm. Reg. U.S. Pat. Off.—All rights reserved ©1973 by United Feature Syndicate, Inc.
"WHY DON'T YOU GO BACK WHERE YOU CAME FROM? DROP DEAD! GET LOST! SINCERELY, A TRUE BASEBALL FAN"
IS IT FROM ANYONE YOU KNOW?
ONE OF MY ADMIRERS
SCHULZ

PEANUTS
I HOPE THAT HANK AARON WILL BREAK BABE RUTH'S HOME-RUN RECORD..
HANK AARON IS A GREAT PLAYER.... BUT YOU! IF YOU BREAK BABE RUTH'S RECORD, IT'LL BE A DISGRACE!
8-11
YOU'RE NOT EVEN **HUMAN**!
SMAK!!
THAT'S A POINT IN MY FAVOR, SWEETIE!
SCHULZ

PEANUTS
STRIKE THREE!
IF YOU'RE GOING TO BREAK BABE RUTH'S HOME-RUN RECORD, YOU'RE GOING TO HAVE TO DO BETTER THAN THAT...
8-14
Tm. Reg. U.S. Pat. Off.—All rights reserved ©1973 by United Feature Syndicate, Inc.
AS YOU SEEM TO KNOW...
SCHULZ

PEANUTS
ALL RIGHT, SNOOPY, IT'S THE NINTH INNING...
8-18
THIS WILL BE YOUR LAST TIME AT BAT THIS SEASON..IF YOU'RE GOING TO TIE BABE RUTH'S HOME-RUN RECORD, YOU'VE GOT TO DO IT NOW!
CHARLIE BROWN'S ON SECOND... A HOME RUN WILL TIE THE RECORD AND WIN THE GAME! IT'S HERO TIME, SNOOPY!!
I JUST WANT TO BE A CREDIT TO MY BREED!
Tm. Reg. U.S. Pat. Off.—All rights reserved © 1973 by United Feature Syndicate, Inc.
SCHULZ

PEANUTS
Tm. Reg. U.S. Pat. Off.—All rights reserved © 1973 by United Feature Syndicate, Inc.
C'MON, SNOOPY, HIT A HOME RUN!! TIE THE RECORD! BRING ME HOME! WIN THE GAME!!
8-20
YOU'RE OUT!
CHARLIE BROWN GOT PICKED OFF SECOND!! THE SEASON IS OVER!!!
AAUGHH!!
SCHULZ

PEANUTS
I'M SORRY, SNOOPY...I KNOW I SPOILED YOUR CHANCE TO TIE BABE RUTH'S RECORD...
8-22
BUT I ALSO DON'T THINK YOU SHOULD GET SO MAD AT ME... AFTER ALL, I'M STILL YOUR MASTER...YOU'RE MY DOG...
JUST REMEMBER, ONE LITTLE PHONE CALL AND I COULD HAVE YOU SENT RIGHT BACK WHERE YOU CAME FROM!
Tm. Reg. U.S. Pat. Off.—All rights reserved © 1973 by United Feature Syndicate, Inc.
SCHULZ

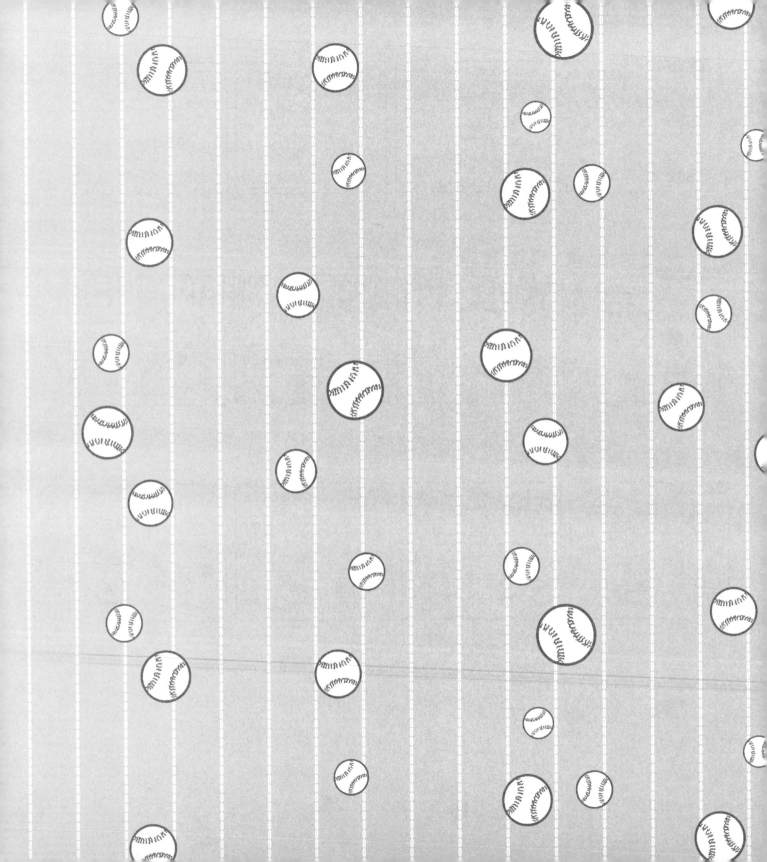

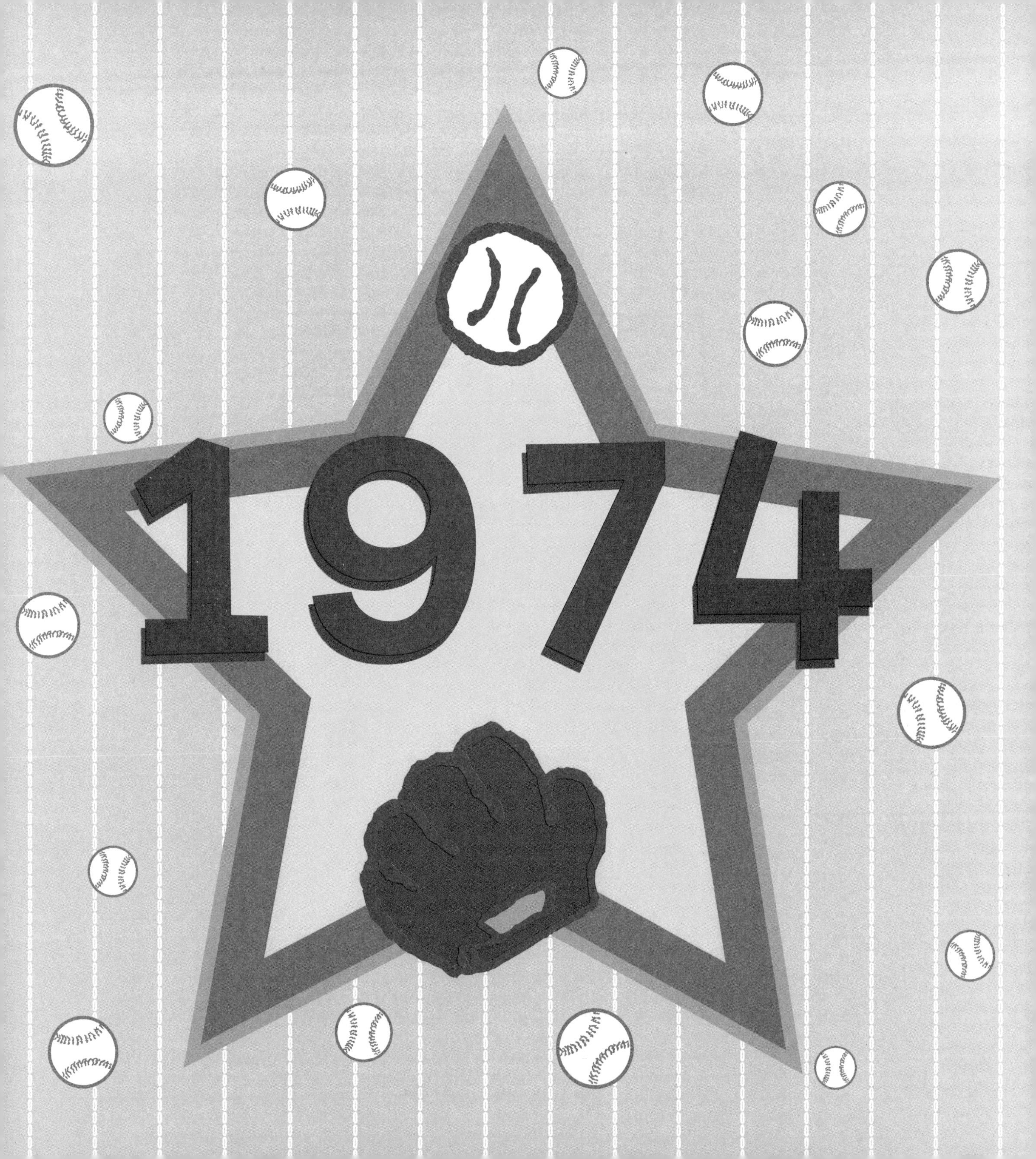
1974

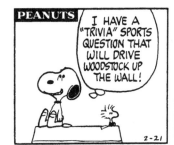

PEANUTS
I HAVE A "TRIVIA" SPORTS QUESTION THAT WILL DRIVE WOODSTOCK UP THE WALL!
2-21
"WHO PLAYED SHORTSTOP FOR ST. PAUL WHEN THEY WON THE AMERICAN ASSOCIATION PENNANT IN NINETEEN THIRTY-EIGHT?"
Tm Reg U.S. Pat Off — All rights reserved
©1974 by United Feature Syndicate, Inc
HOW'D HE EVER HEAR OF OLLIE BEJMA?
SCHULZ

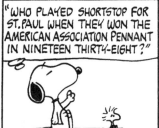

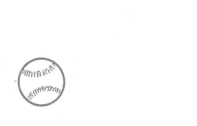

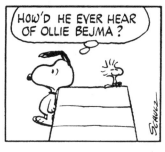

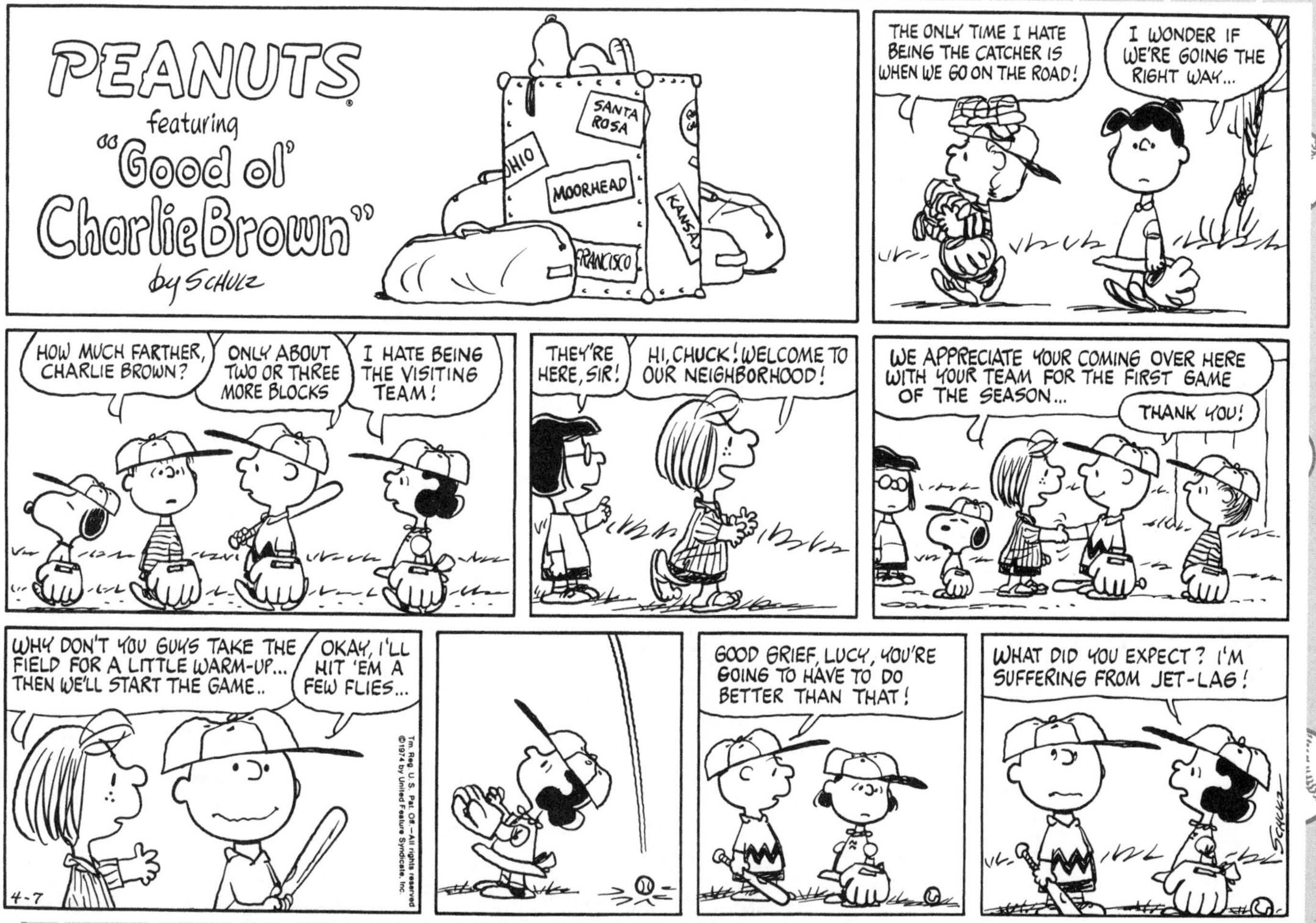
PEANUTS
featuring
"Good ol' CharlieBrown"
by SCHULZ
SANTA ROSA
OHIO
MOORHEAD
KANSAS
FRANCISCO
THE ONLY TIME I HATE BEING THE CATCHER IS WHEN WE GO ON THE ROAD!
I WONDER IF WE'RE GOING THE RIGHT WAY...
HOW MUCH FARTHER, CHARLIE BROWN?
ONLY ABOUT TWO OR THREE MORE BLOCKS
I HATE BEING THE VISITING TEAM!
THEY'RE HERE, SIR!
HI, CHUCK! WELCOME TO OUR NEIGHBORHOOD!
WE APPRECIATE YOUR COMING OVER HERE WITH YOUR TEAM FOR THE FIRST GAME OF THE SEASON...
THANK YOU!
WHY DON'T YOU GUYS TAKE THE FIELD FOR A LITTLE WARM-UP... THEN WE'LL START THE GAME..
OKAY, I'LL HIT 'EM A FEW FLIES...
Tm. Reg. U.S. Pat. Off.—All rights reserved © 1974 by United Feature Syndicate, Inc.
4-7
GOOD GRIEF, LUCY, YOU'RE GOING TO HAVE TO DO BETTER THAN THAT!
WHAT DID YOU EXPECT? I'M SUFFERING FROM JET-LAG!
SCHULZ

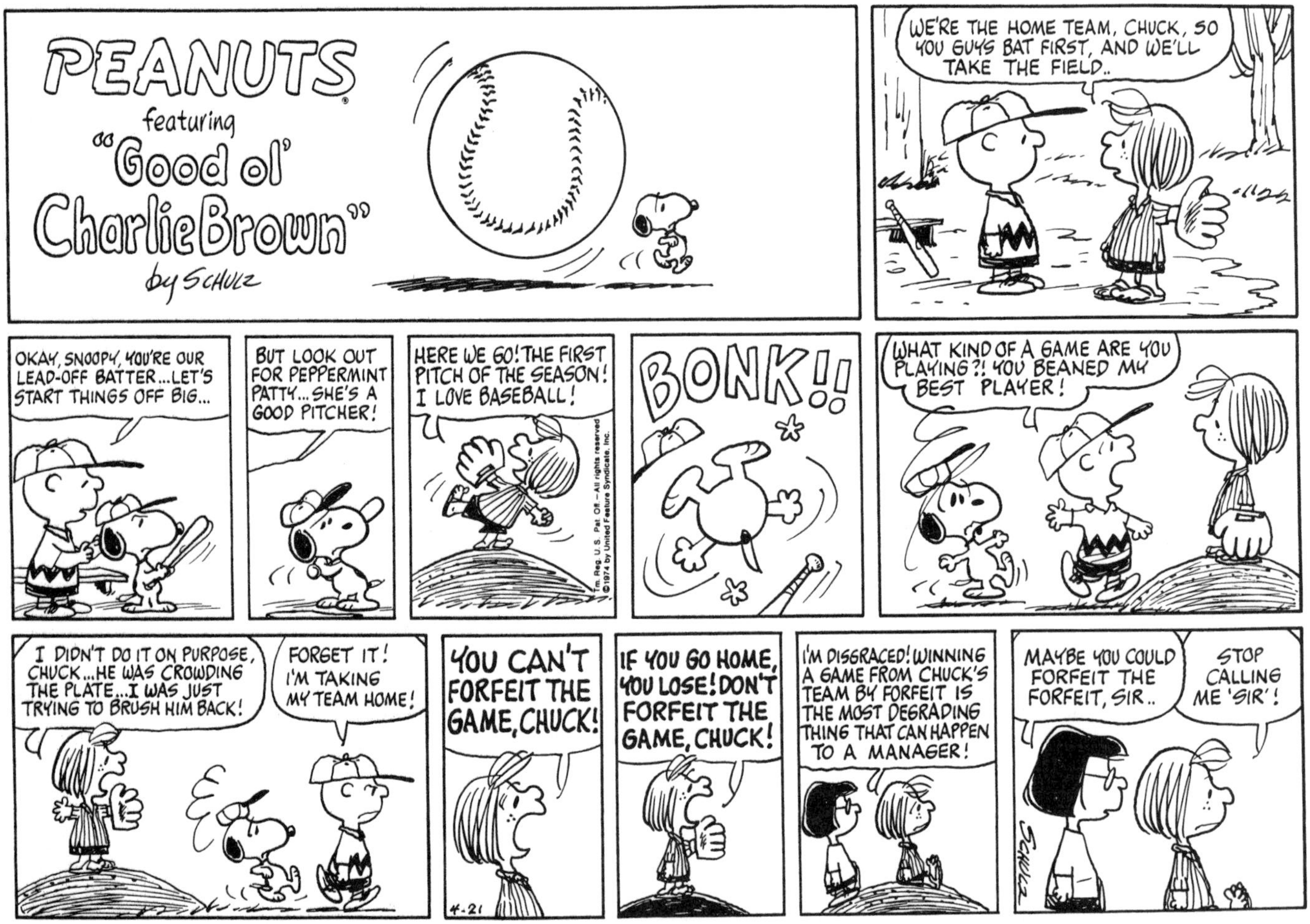
PEANUTS
featuring
"Good ol' CharlieBrown"
by SCHULZ
WE'RE THE HOME TEAM, CHUCK, SO YOU GUYS BAT FIRST, AND WE'LL TAKE THE FIELD..
OKAY, SNOOPY, YOU'RE OUR LEAD-OFF BATTER...LET'S START THINGS OFF BIG...
BUT LOOK OUT FOR PEPPERMINT PATTY...SHE'S A GOOD PITCHER!
HERE WE GO! THE FIRST PITCH OF THE SEASON! I LOVE BASEBALL!
Tm. Reg. U.S. Pat. Off.—All rights reserved
©1974 by United Feature Syndicate, Inc.
BONK!!
WHAT KIND OF A GAME ARE YOU PLAYING?! YOU BEANED MY BEST PLAYER!
I DIDN'T DO IT ON PURPOSE, CHUCK...HE WAS CROWDING THE PLATE...I WAS JUST TRYING TO BRUSH HIM BACK!
FORGET IT! I'M TAKING MY TEAM HOME!
YOU CAN'T FORFEIT THE GAME, CHUCK!
4-21
IF YOU GO HOME, YOU LOSE! DON'T FORFEIT THE GAME, CHUCK!
I'M DISGRACED! WINNING A GAME FROM CHUCK'S TEAM BY FORFEIT IS THE MOST DEGRADING THING THAT CAN HAPPEN TO A MANAGER!
MAYBE YOU COULD FORFEIT THE FORFEIT, SIR..
STOP CALLING ME 'SIR'!
SCHULZ

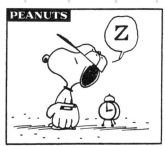

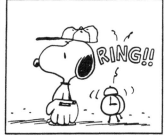

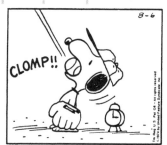

PEANUTS
Z
RING!!
8-6
CLOMP!!
Tm Reg U.S. Pat Off — All rights reserved
©1974 by United Feature Syndicate, Inc.
HOW DO YOU SET THE ALARM FOR A FLY BALL?
SCHULZ

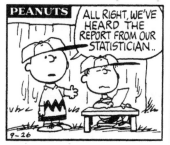

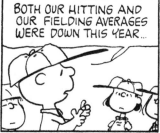

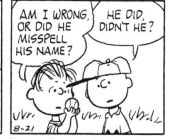

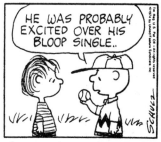

PEANUTS
LOOK! I GOT AN AUTOGRAPHED BASEBALL FROM JOE SHLABOTNIK!
THIS IS THE BALL THAT JOE HIT WHEN HE GOT HIS BLOOP SINGLE IN THE NINTH INNING WITH HIS TEAM LEADING FIFTEEN TO THREE
AM I WRONG, OR DID HE MISSPELL HIS NAME?
HE DID, DIDN'T HE?
8-21
HE WAS PROBABLY EXCITED OVER HIS BLOOP SINGLE..
Tm Reg U.S. Pat Off — All rights reserved
©1974 by United Feature Syndicate, Inc.
SCHULZ

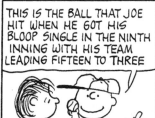

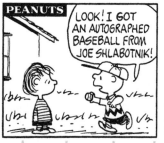

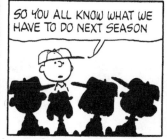

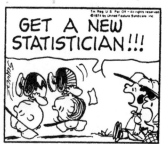

PEANUTS
ALL RIGHT, WE'VE HEARD THE REPORT FROM OUR STATISTICIAN..
9-26
BOTH OUR HITTING AND OUR FIELDING AVERAGES WERE DOWN THIS YEAR...
SO YOU ALL KNOW WHAT WE HAVE TO DO NEXT SEASON
Tm Reg U.S. Pat Off — All rights reserved
©1974 by United Feature Syndicate, Inc.
GET A NEW STATISTICIAN!!!
SCHULZ

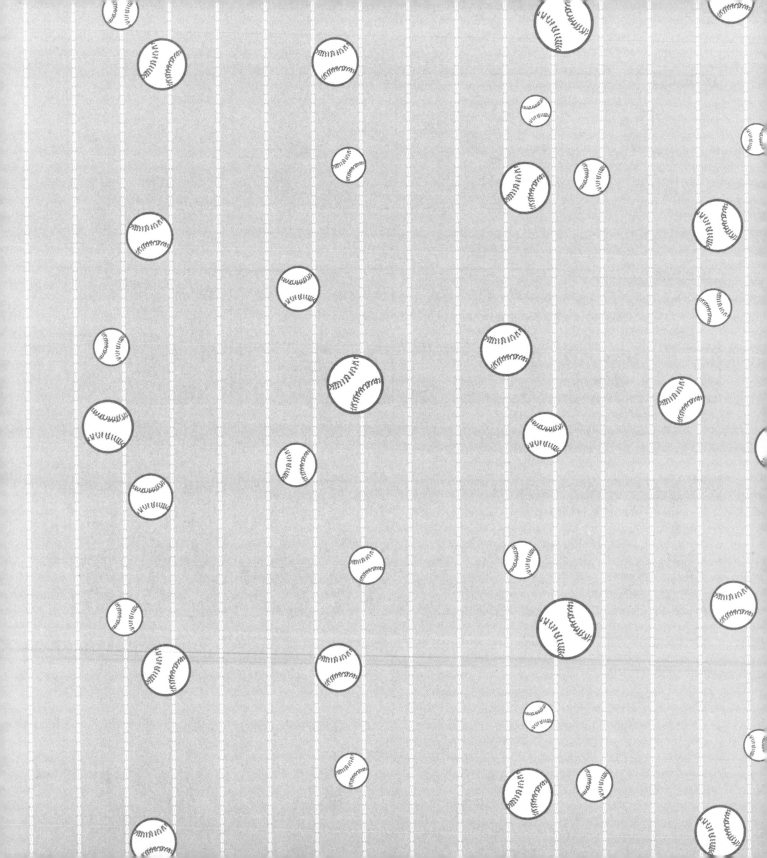

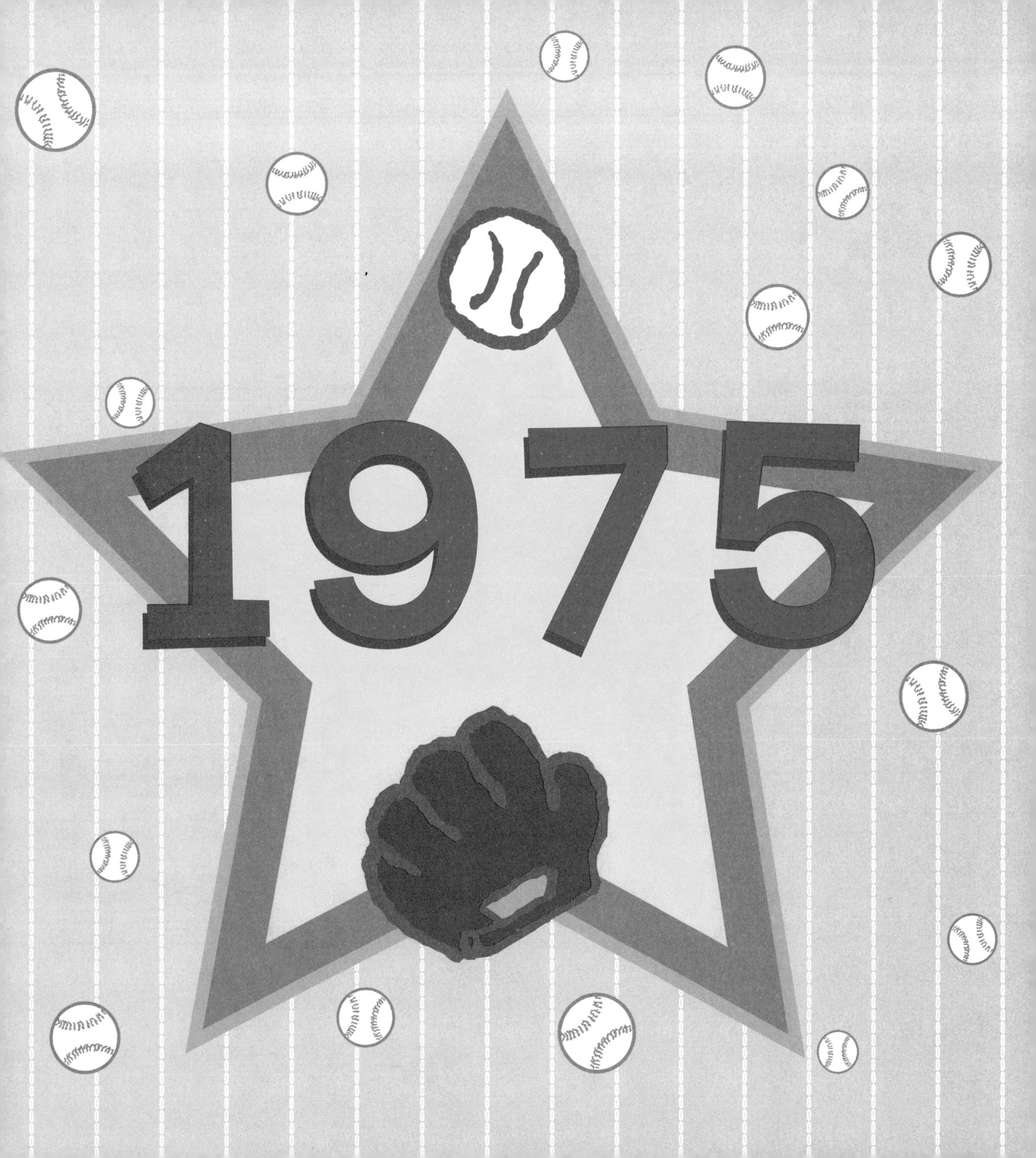
1975

PEANUTS
YOU DON'T LOOK FEROCIOUS ENOUGH WHEN YOU PITCH...
YOU HAVE TO LOOK NASTY, CHARLIE BROWN!
5-2
I CAN'T STAND HERE LOOKING NASTY ALL THE TIME...
NOT ALL THE TIME..
GIVE 'EM THE OL' CHANGE OF FACE!
SCHULZ

PEANUTS
HEY, ROY, LOOK AT THIS!
JOE SHLABOTNIK, MY FAVORITE BALLPLAYER, HAS BEEN MADE MANAGER OF THE WAFFLETOWN SYRUPS! HOW ABOUT THAT?!
SPORTS
6-18
WAFFLETOWN IS ONLY A MILE FROM HERE..
IT IS? I WONDER IF THEY PLAY NIGHT GAMES..
SURE, THEY DO...THE BALLPARK IS NEAR A CORNER, AND THEY PLAY UNDER THE STREET LIGHTS!
SCHULZ

PEANUTS
I'D LIKE A TICKET TO THE BALL GAME, PLEASE
GAME TONITE 8:00
YES, MA'AM...JOE SHLABOTNIK IS THE NEW MANAGER...HE'S MY HERO...I'VE COME TO SEE HIM WORK SOME OF HIS STRATEGY
6-23
GEE! I WISH MY DAD WERE HERE...THIS IS HIS KIND OF BALLPARK...
SEC A
EVERYTHING IS MADE OUT OF WOOD!
SCHULZ

PEANUTS

C'MON, JOE!

WHAT ARE YOU, KID, SOME KIND OF NUT?

I'M JUST CHEERING FOR MY HERO...HE'S THE NEW MANAGER OF THE TEAM...

ALL HE'S DOING IS TAKING THE LINEUP OUT TO THE UMPIRE!

C'MON, JOE! YOU CAN DO IT!!

6-25

PEANUTS

HEY, LOOK! A FOUL BALL COMING THIS WAY!

I GOT IT!

6-27

PEANUTS

CLUB HOUSE

HEY, KID! GET LOST! NO ONE'S ALLOWED BACK HERE!

BUT I CAUGHT A BASEBALL DURING THE GAME, AND I WANTED JOE SHLABOTNIK TO AUTOGRAPH IT FOR ME...

FORGET IT, KID! THEY JUST FIRED HIM..I COULD MANAGE A TEAM BETTER THAN HIM, AND I'M ONLY THE BAT BOY!

HE GOT FIRED ALREADY?

WHO ELSE WOULD SIGNAL FOR A SQUEEZE PLAY WITH NOBODY ON BASE?

6-28

★ 155 ★

PEANUTS
BUS STATION
JOE?
6-30
I'M ONE OF YOUR FANS, JOE! I'M SORRY YOU LOST YOUR JOB... ARE YOU LEAVING TOWN?
BEFORE THE BUS LEAVES, WOULD YOU AUTOGRAPH MY BASEBALL? YOU'LL ALWAYS BE MY HERO!
TRY NOT TO CRY ON THE BALL, JOE... IT MAKES THE INK RUN..
Tm Reg U S Pat Off —All rights reserved ©1975 by United Feature Syndicate, Inc
SCHULZ

PEANUTS
JOE, I THINK THE BUS IS GOING TO LEAVE...
Tm Reg U S Pat Off —All rights reserved ©1975 by United Feature Syndicate, Inc
COULD YOU HURRY UP WITH THE AUTOGRAPH, JOE? THE BUS IS LEAVING! COULD YOU THROW ME THE BALL, JOE?!
THE BUS IS LEAVING! THROW THE BALL, JOE! THROW THE BALL!!!
7-1
BONK!
SCHULZ

PEANUTS
WHAT'RE YOU GUYS TALKING ABOUT?
WE'RE TRYING TO FIGURE OUT SOME STRATEGY
HOW ABOUT TRYING A SQUEEZE PLAY?
Tm Reg U S Pat Off —All rights reserved ©1975 by United Feature Syndicate, Inc
A SQUEEZE PLAY?!
7-24
I'LL SQUEEZE THE CATCHER!
!
SCHULZ

PEANUTS
Tm Reg U S Pat Off —All rights reserved ©1975 by United Feature Syndicate, Inc.
I WONDER WHY I DO THIS...
I WONDER WHY I STAND OUT HERE DAY AFTER DAY LOSING ALL THESE BALL GAMES? WHY DO I DO IT?
PROBABLY BECAUSE IT MAKES YOU HAPPY
YOU ALWAYS HAVE TO BE RIGHT, DON'T YOU?
7-30
SCHULZ

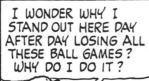

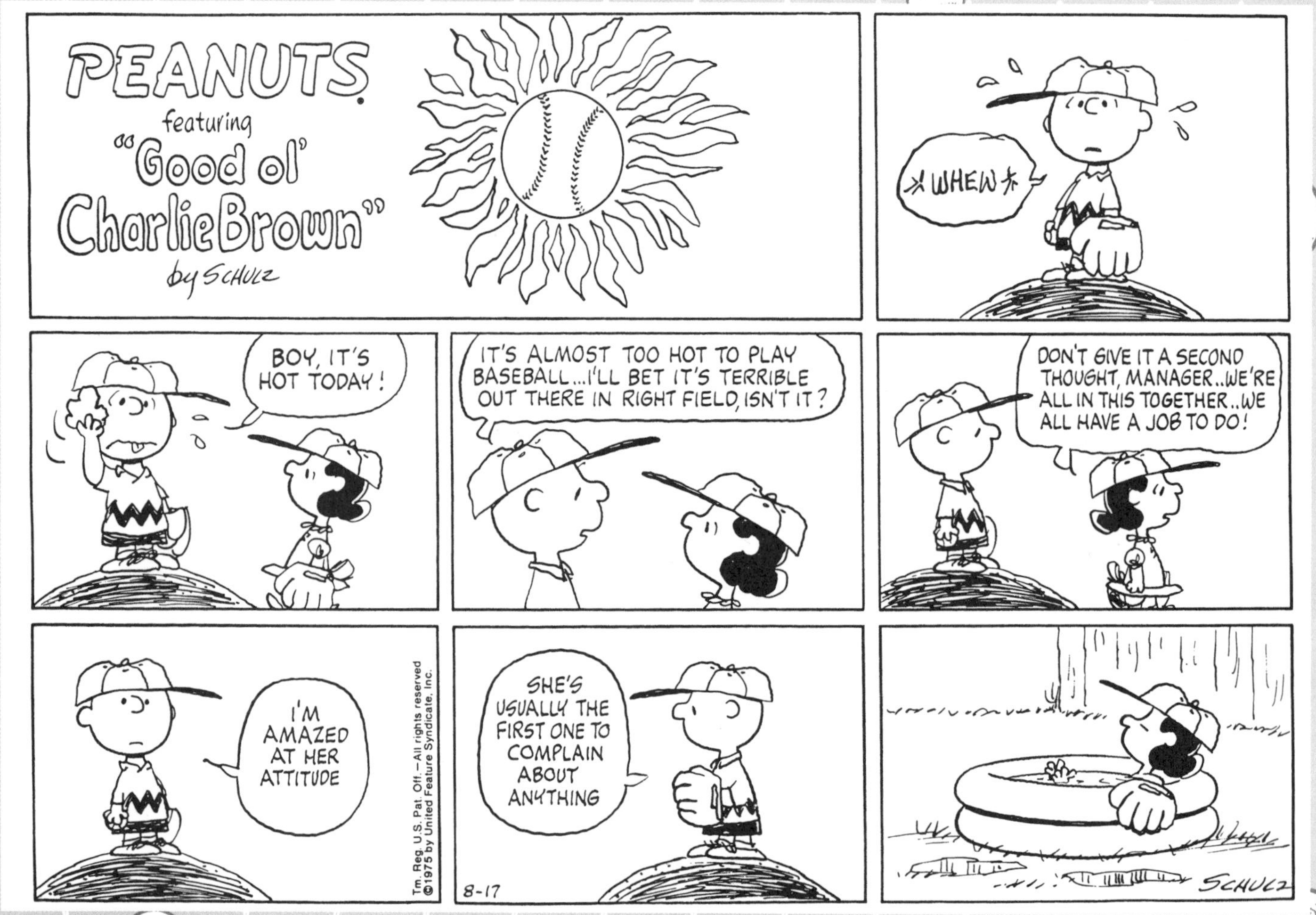
PEANUTS
featuring
"Good ol' Charlie Brown"
by SCHULZ
* WHEW *
BOY, IT'S HOT TODAY!
IT'S ALMOST TOO HOT TO PLAY BASEBALL...I'LL BET IT'S TERRIBLE OUT THERE IN RIGHT FIELD, ISN'T IT?
DON'T GIVE IT A SECOND THOUGHT, MANAGER..WE'RE ALL IN THIS TOGETHER..WE ALL HAVE A JOB TO DO!
I'M AMAZED AT HER ATTITUDE
Tm. Reg. U.S. Pat. Off.—All rights reserved
©1975 by United Feature Syndicate, Inc.
8-17
SHE'S USUALLY THE FIRST ONE TO COMPLAIN ABOUT ANYTHING
SCHULZ

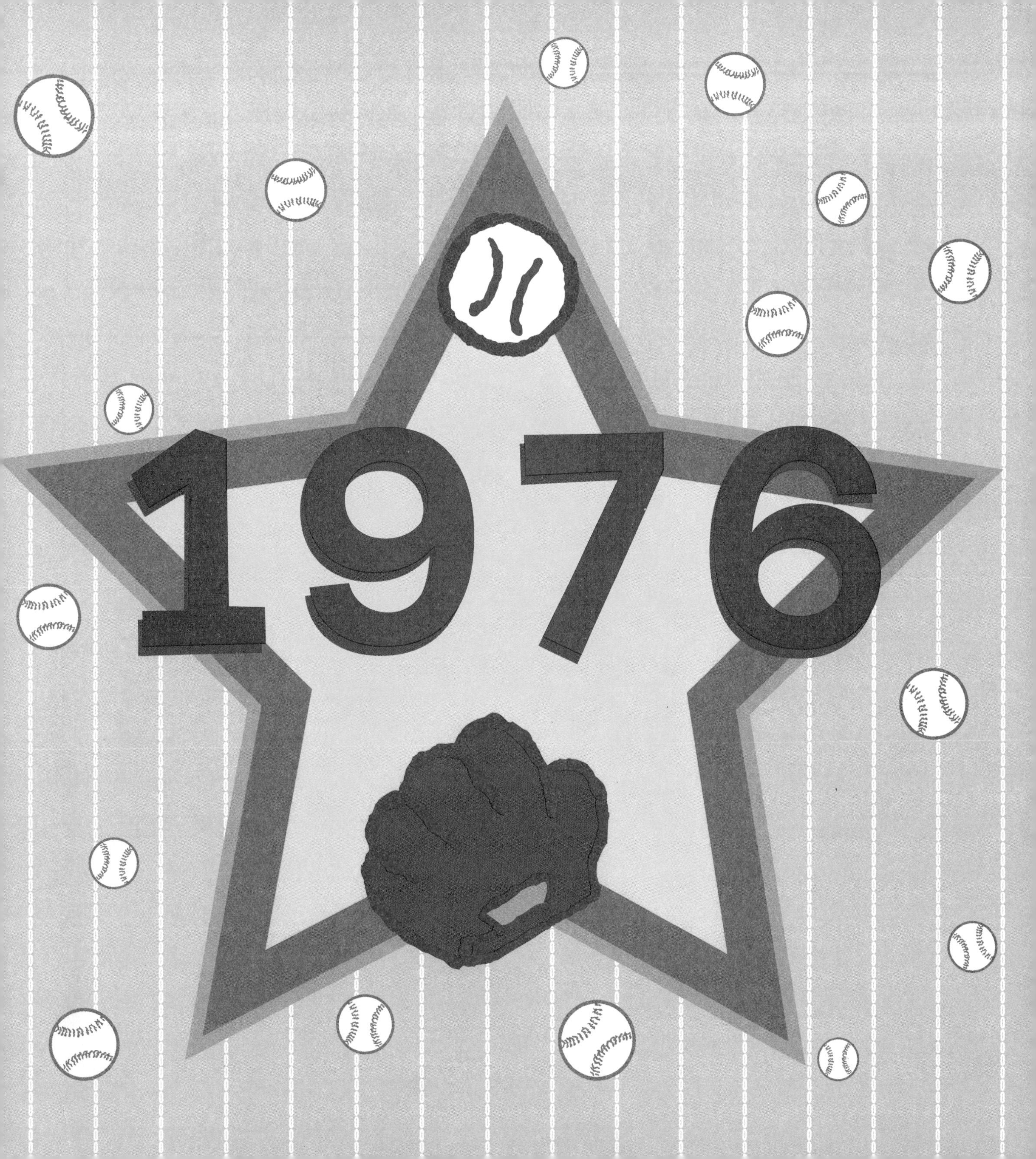
1976

PEANUTS
SIR, HOW COME EVERYONE ON CHUCK'S TEAM HAS A CAP, BUT WE DON'T?
4-6
THEY'RE A BUNCH OF LOSERS, MARCIE! WHICH WOULD YOU RATHER HAVE, A WINNING TEAM OR A CAP?!
WINNING DOESN'T MEAN THAT MUCH TO ME, SIR... I'D RATHER HAVE A CAP
YOU'RE WEIRD, MARCIE!!
Tm. Reg. U.S. Pat. Off.—All rights reserved © 1976 by United Feature Syndicate, Inc.
SCHULZ

PEANUTS
BABE RUTH HAD A CAP! WILLIE MAYS HAD A CAP!
4-9
TED WILLIAMS HAD A CAP! MAURY WILLS HAD A CAP! MICKEY MANTLE HAD A CAP!
MARCIE, WILL YOU SHUT UP?!?
EVEN JOE GARAGIOLA HAD A CAP!
Tm. Reg. U.S. Pat. Off.—All rights reserved © 1976 by United Feature Syndicate, Inc.
SCHULZ

PEANUTS
FRANKLIN, MARCIE SEEMS TO THINK OUR TEAM NEEDS BASEBALL CAPS..
I SURE WOULD LIKE A CAP! JUST THINK HOW GREAT I'D LOOK STEALING THIRD BASE WITH MY CAP FLYING IN THE AIR!
4-10
WHEN WAS THE LAST TIME YOU STOLE THIRD BASE, FRANKLIN?
MAYBE MY CAP WOULD FLY IN THE AIR IF I GOT A WALK...
Tm. Reg. U.S. Pat. Off.—All rights reserved © 1976 by United Feature Syndicate, Inc.
SCHULZ

PEANUTS
HEY, CHUCK, I HAVE TO ASK YOU SOMETHING..
EVERYONE ON MY TEAM SUDDENLY THINKS WE NEED BASEBALL CAPS...WHERE DID YOU GUYS GET YOURS?
WE JUST WENT OUT AND BOUGHT THEM OURSELVES...
ALL EXCEPT OUR SHORTSTOP... HE GOT HIMSELF A SPONSOR!
JOE'S PET SHOP
4-12
Tm Reg U S Pat Off — All rights reserved
© 1976 by United Feature Syndicate, Inc
SCHULZ

PEANUTS
WHAT ARE YOU DOING, CHARLIE BROWN?
GO ON HOME! THE GAME HAS BEEN CALLED!
DON'T YOU THINK I KNOW THAT?
Tm Reg U.S. Pat. Off.—All rights reserved
© 1976 by United Feature Syndicate, Inc
5-5
I'M HERE FOR TOMORROW'S GAME!
SCHULZ

PEANUTS
COME BACK, EVERYBODY! WE CAN STILL PLAY!
A LITTLE WATER DOESN'T HURT!
Tm Reg U S Pat Off – All rights reserved
© 1976 by United Feature Syndicate Inc
THE WAVES AREN'T THAT HIGH!
5-6
THERE AREN'T EVEN ANY WHITE CAPS!
SCHULZ

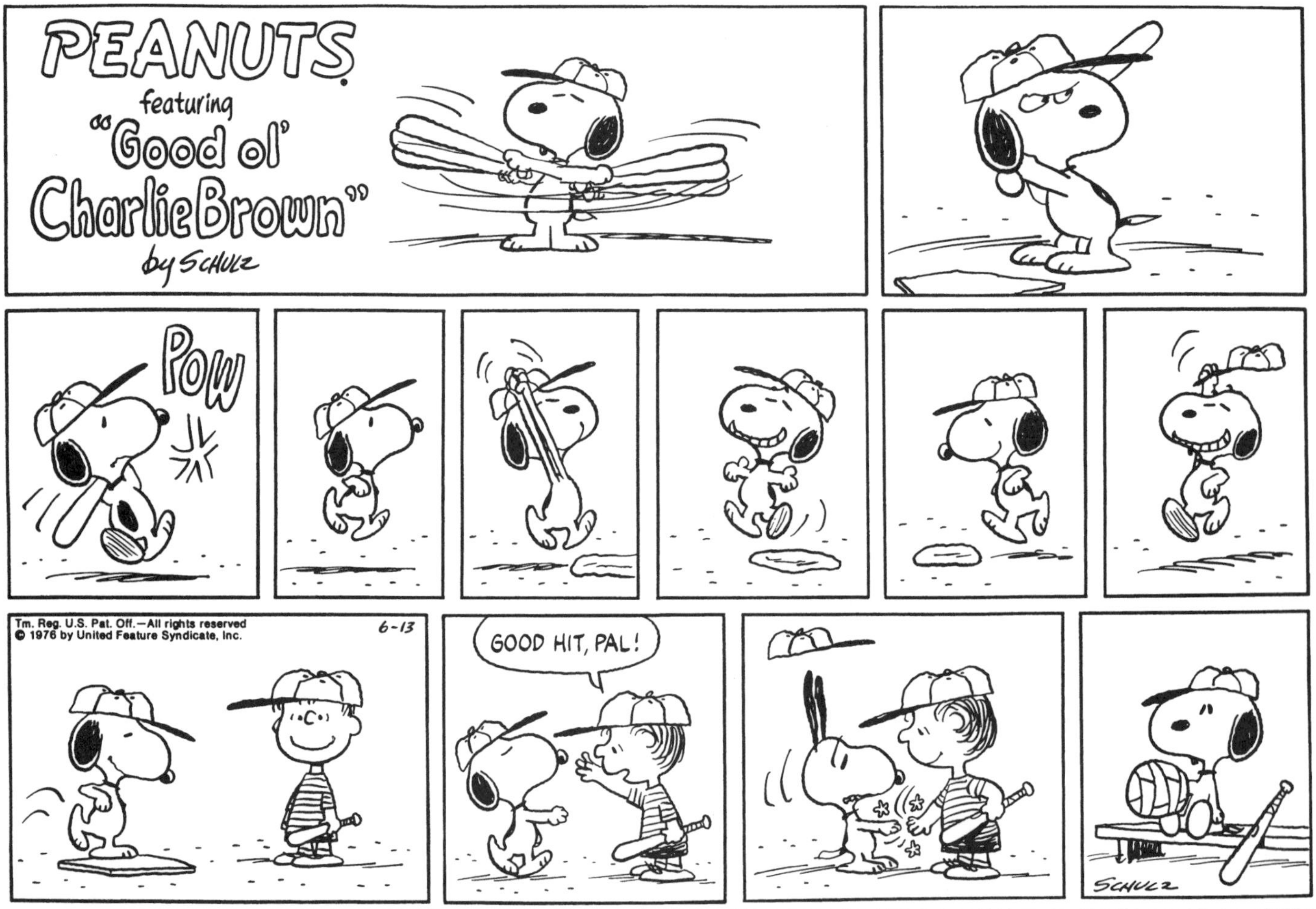
PEANUTS
featuring
"Good ol' Charlie Brown"
by SCHULZ
POW
Tm. Reg. U.S. Pat. Off.—All rights reserved
© 1976 by United Feature Syndicate, Inc.
6-13
GOOD HIT, PAL!
SCHULZ

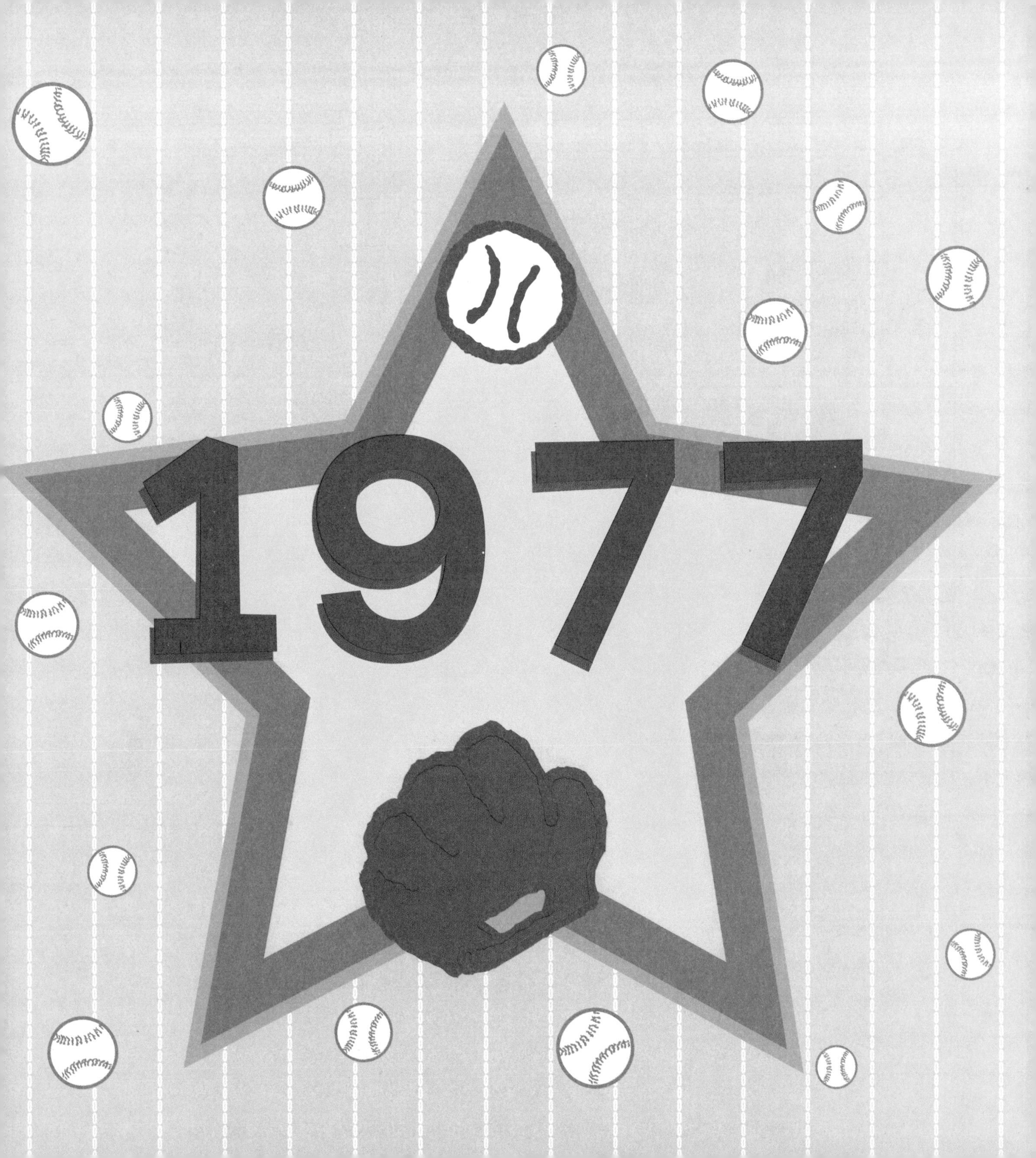
1977

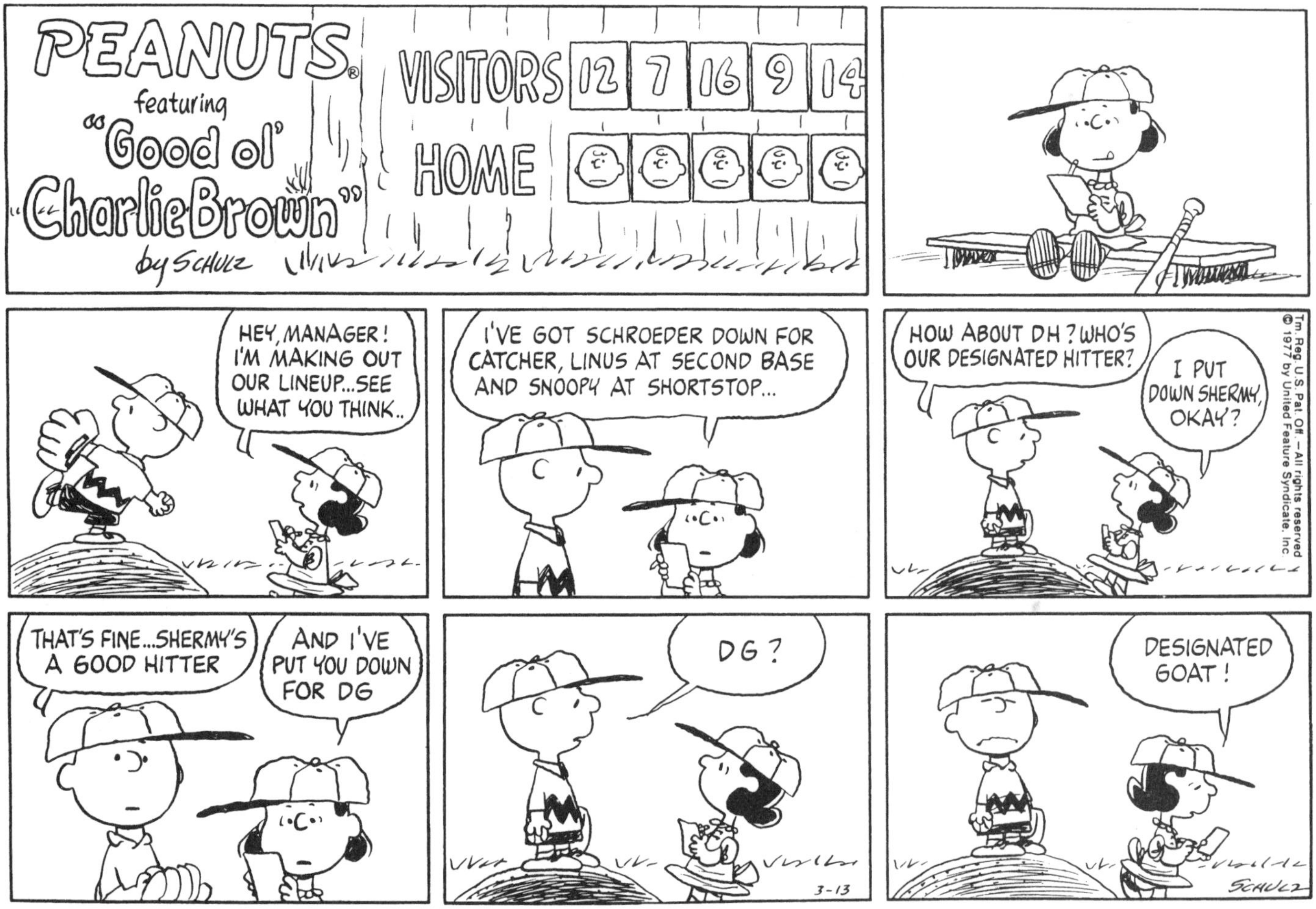
PEANUTS®
featuring
"Good ol' Charlie Brown"
by SCHULZ
VISITORS 12 7 16 9 14
HOME
HEY, MANAGER! I'M MAKING OUT OUR LINEUP...SEE WHAT YOU THINK..
I'VE GOT SCHROEDER DOWN FOR CATCHER, LINUS AT SECOND BASE AND SNOOPY AT SHORTSTOP...
HOW ABOUT DH? WHO'S OUR DESIGNATED HITTER?
I PUT DOWN SHERMY, OKAY?
Tm. Reg U.S. Pat. Off.—All rights reserved
© 1977 by United Feature Syndicate, Inc.
THAT'S FINE...SHERMY'S A GOOD HITTER
AND I'VE PUT YOU DOWN FOR DG
DG?
3-13
DESIGNATED GOAT!
SCHULZ

PEANUTS
featuring
"Good ol' CharlieBrown"
by SCHULZ
TIME OUT!
NOW WHAT?
HEY, MANAGER, I HAVE A GREAT IDEA!
AFTER WE'VE LOST A GAME, WHY DON'T WE RUN AN AD IN THE NEWSPAPER?
AN AD?
SURE, WE COULD OFFER A REWARD FOR THE LOST GAME!
5-15
WHEN THE LOST GAME WAS FOUND, IT WOULDN'T BE A LOST GAME ANY MORE!
IF I GET ANOTHER GREAT IDEA, I'LL LET YOU KNOW..
© 1977 United Feature Syndicate, Inc.
MAYBE OUTFIELDERS SPEND TOO MUCH TIME STANDING IN THE SUN...
SCHULZ

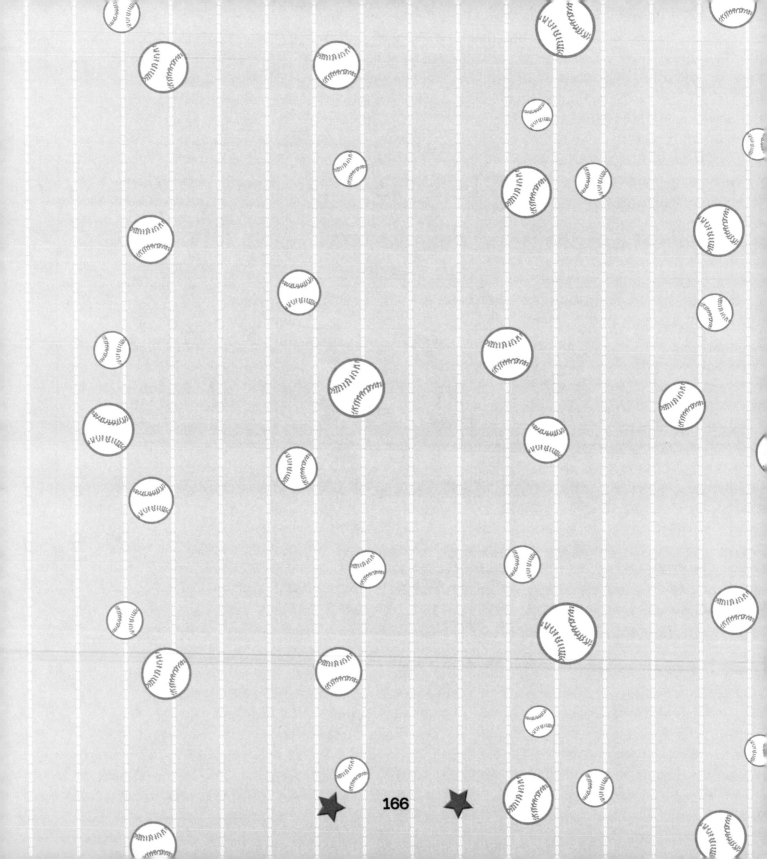

166

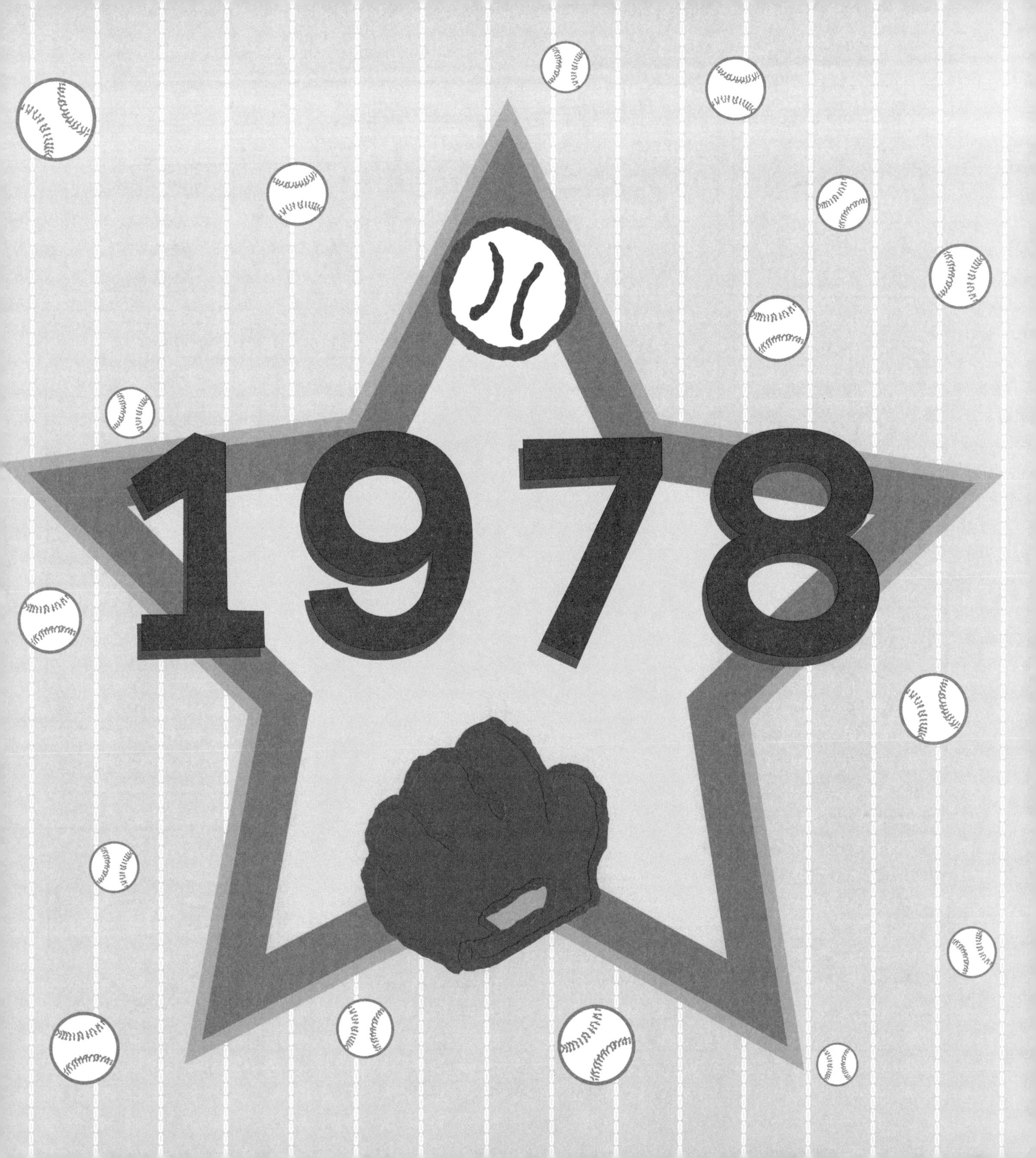
1978

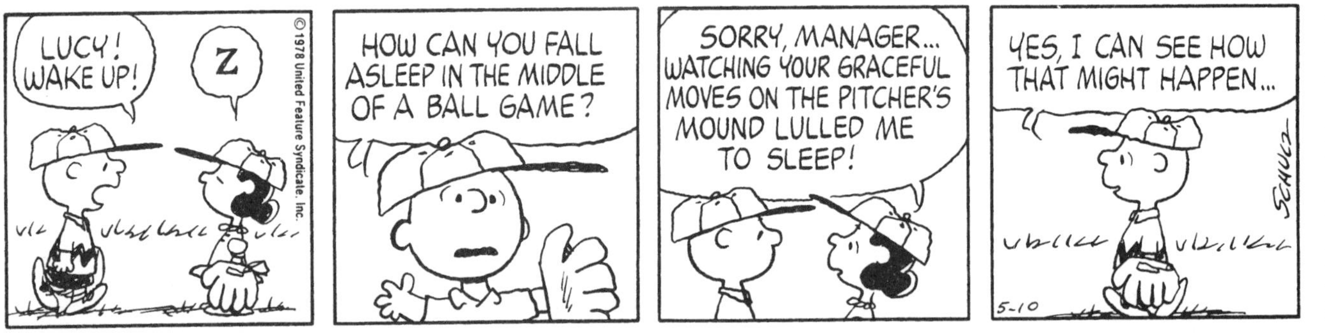
LUCY! WAKE UP!
Z
© 1978 United Feature Syndicate, Inc.
HOW CAN YOU FALL ASLEEP IN THE MIDDLE OF A BALL GAME?
SORRY, MANAGER... WATCHING YOUR GRACEFUL MOVES ON THE PITCHER'S MOUND LULLED ME TO SLEEP!
YES, I CAN SEE HOW THAT MIGHT HAPPEN...
SCHULZ
5-10

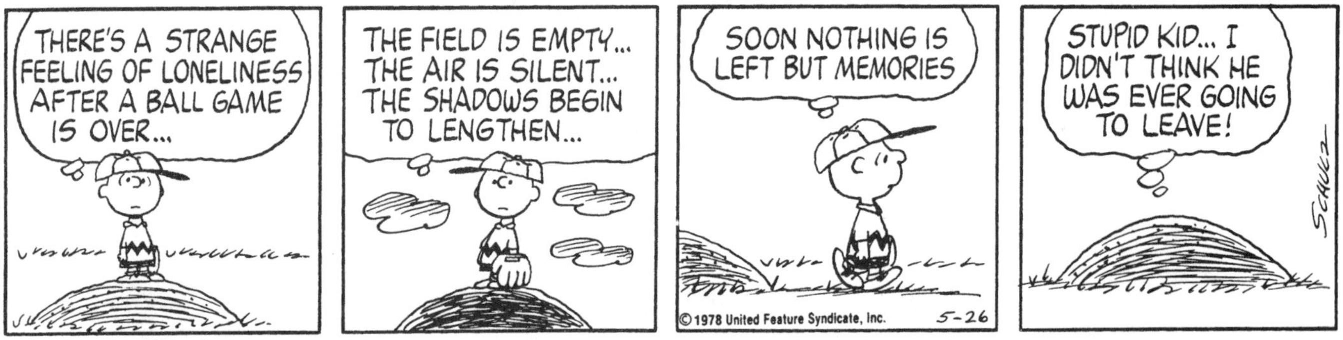
THERE'S A STRANGE FEELING OF LONELINESS AFTER A BALL GAME IS OVER...
THE FIELD IS EMPTY... THE AIR IS SILENT... THE SHADOWS BEGIN TO LENGTHEN...
SOON NOTHING IS LEFT BUT MEMORIES
© 1978 United Feature Syndicate, Inc.
5-26
STUPID KID... I DIDN'T THINK HE WAS EVER GOING TO LEAVE!
SCHULZ

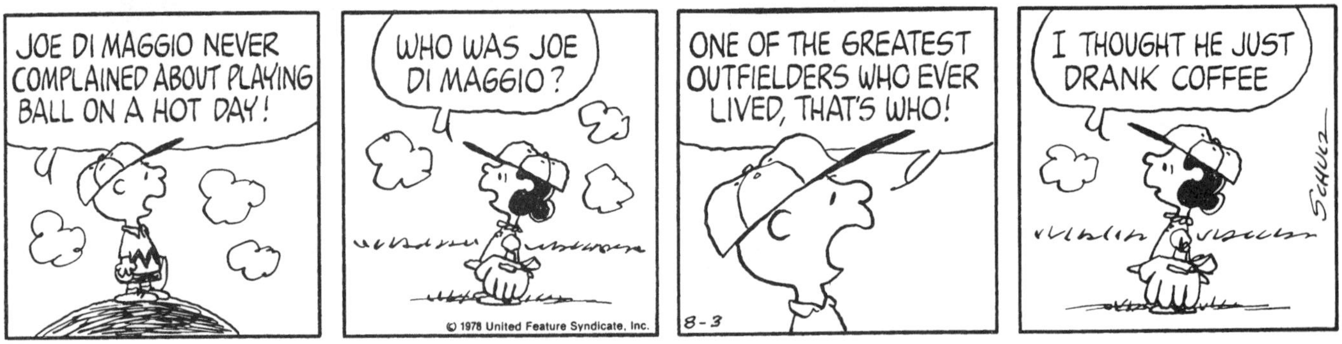
JOE DI MAGGIO NEVER COMPLAINED ABOUT PLAYING BALL ON A HOT DAY!
WHO WAS JOE DI MAGGIO?
© 1978 United Feature Syndicate, Inc.
ONE OF THE GREATEST OUTFIELDERS WHO EVER LIVED, THAT'S WHO!
8-3
I THOUGHT HE JUST DRANK COFFEE
SCHULZ

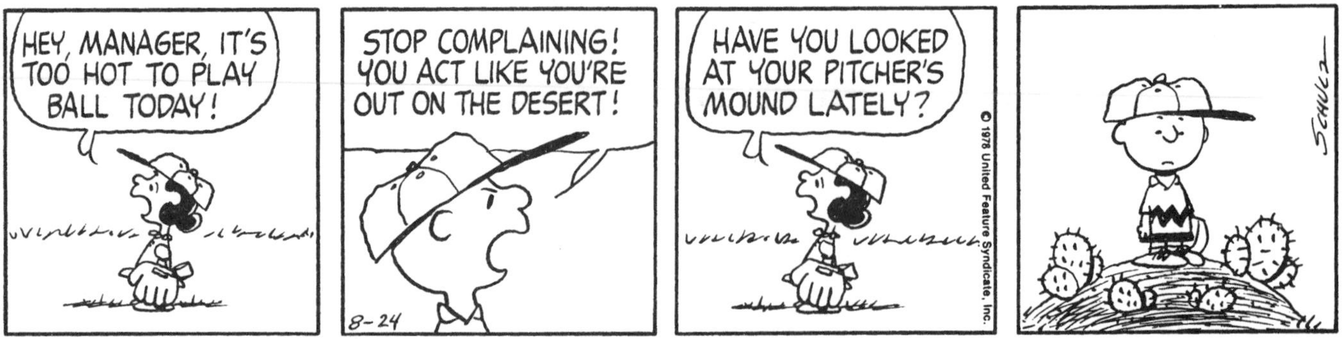
HEY, MANAGER, IT'S TOO HOT TO PLAY BALL TODAY!
STOP COMPLAINING! YOU ACT LIKE YOU'RE OUT ON THE DESERT!
8-24
HAVE YOU LOOKED AT YOUR PITCHER'S MOUND LATELY?
© 1978 United Feature Syndicate, Inc.
SCHULZ

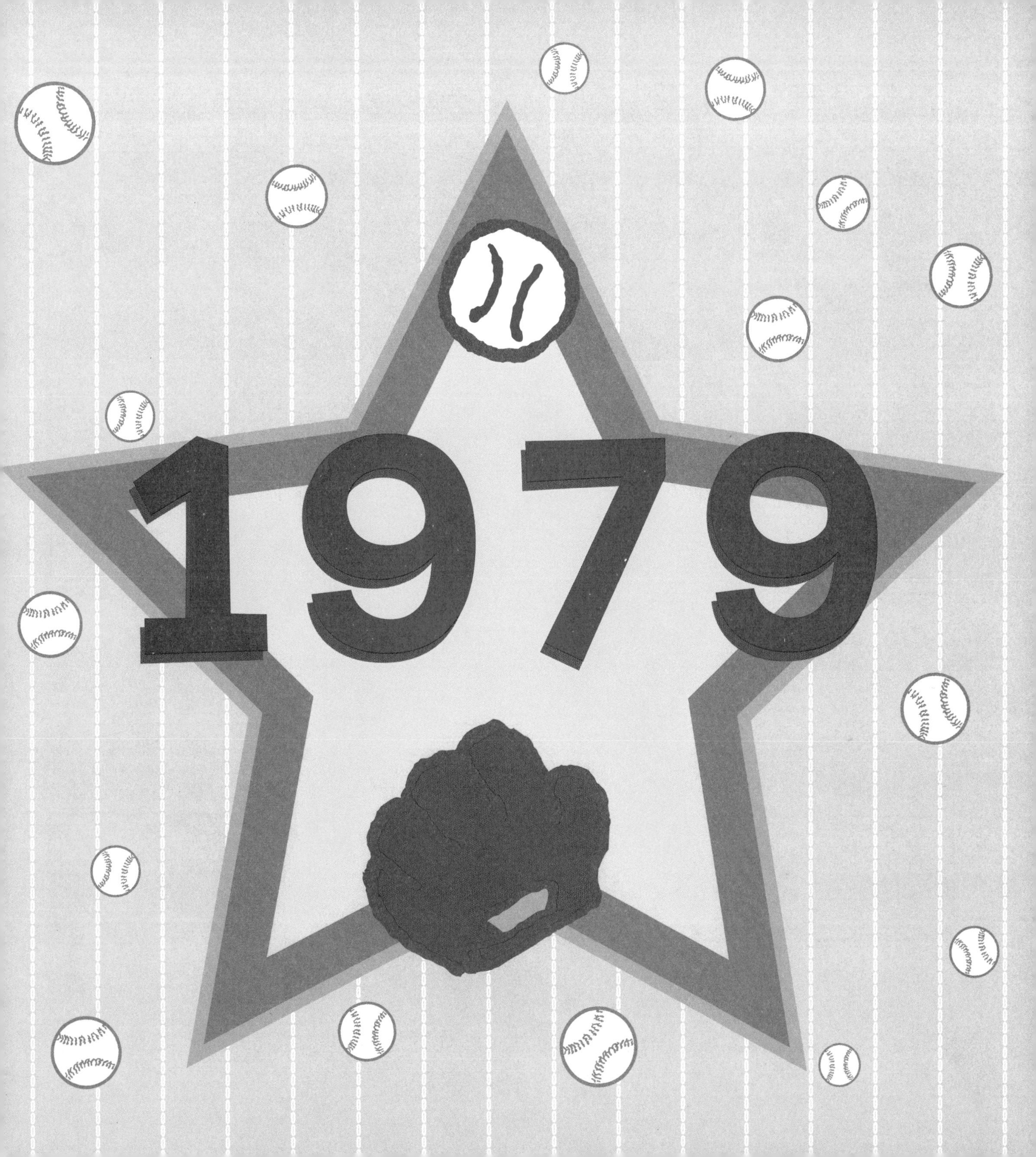
1979

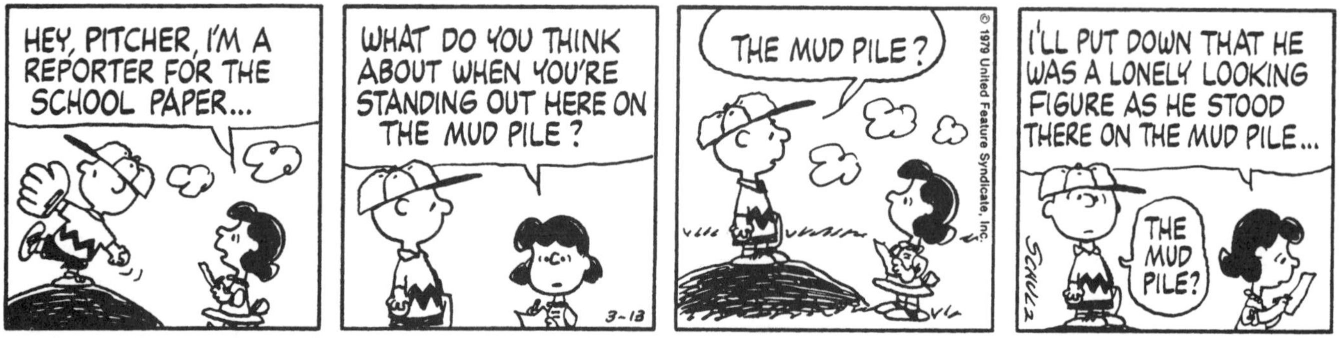
HEY, PITCHER, I'M A REPORTER FOR THE SCHOOL PAPER...
WHAT DO YOU THINK ABOUT WHEN YOU'RE STANDING OUT HERE ON THE MUD PILE?
3-13
THE MUD PILE?
© 1979 United Feature Syndicate, Inc.
I'LL PUT DOWN THAT HE WAS A LONELY LOOKING FIGURE AS HE STOOD THERE ON THE MUD PILE...
THE MUD PILE?
SCHULZ

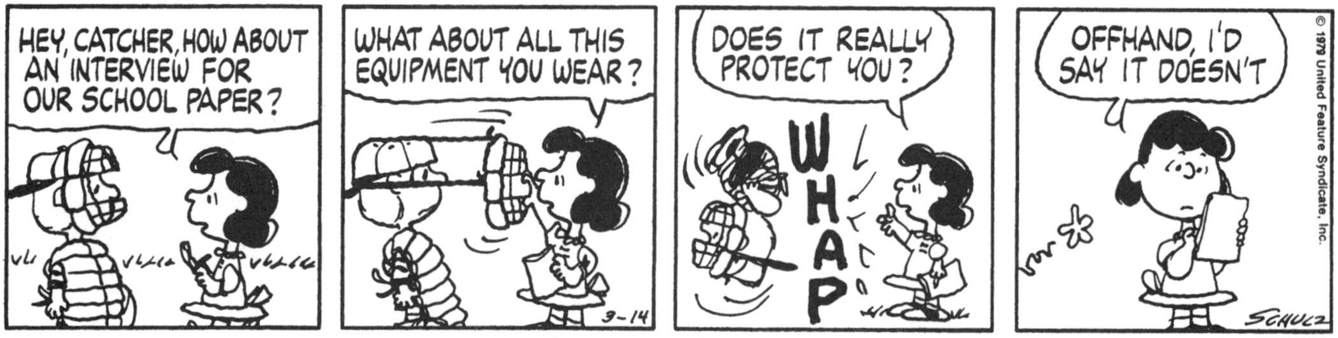
HEY, CATCHER, HOW ABOUT AN INTERVIEW FOR OUR SCHOOL PAPER?
WHAT ABOUT ALL THIS EQUIPMENT YOU WEAR?
3-14
DOES IT REALLY PROTECT YOU?
WHAP
OFFHAND, I'D SAY IT DOESN'T
© 1979 United Feature Syndicate, Inc.
SCHULZ

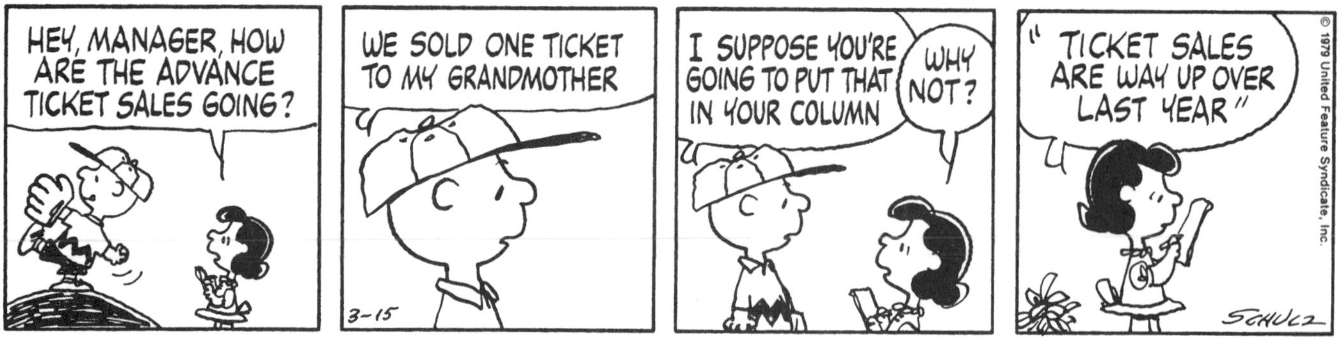
HEY, MANAGER, HOW ARE THE ADVANCE TICKET SALES GOING?
WE SOLD ONE TICKET TO MY GRANDMOTHER
3-15
I SUPPOSE YOU'RE GOING TO PUT THAT IN YOUR COLUMN
WHY NOT?
"TICKET SALES ARE WAY UP OVER LAST YEAR"
© 1979 United Feature Syndicate, Inc.
SCHULZ

HEY, YOU STUPID BEAGLE, I'M DOING INTERVIEWS FOR OUR SCHOOL PAPER...
HOW ABOUT A GOOD QUOTE FOR OUR READERS?
3-16
BLEAH!
"HE SAID HE EXPECTS TO HAVE ONE OF HIS BEST SEASONS EVER"
© 1979 United Feature Syndicate, Inc.
SCHULZ

YOU KNOW WHAT SOMEBODY SAID, CHARLIE BROWN?
SOMEBODY SAID THAT SPORTS ARE SORT OF A CARICATURE OF LIFE
5-24
THAT'S A RELIEF
I WAS AFRAID IT **WAS** LIFE!
© 1979 United Feature Syndicate, Inc.
SCHULZ

PEANUTS featuring "Good ol' Charlie Brown" by Schulz

POW!

HEY, MANAGER, I'M WORKING ON A SPECIAL PROJECT

I'M TRYING TO WRITE AN ARTICLE ABOUT SOME OF THE FUNNY THINGS THAT HAPPEN IN BASEBALL GAMES...

IF YOU CAN THINK OF ANYTHING FUNNY, LET ME KNOW

I DOUBT THAT I'LL COME UP WITH A THING!

5-27

© 1979 United Feature Syndicate, Inc.

NEXT YEAR I'M GONNA BE A FREE AGENT

© 1979 United Feature Syndicate, Inc.

YOU ARE, HUH?

8-21

DO YOU KNOW WHAT A FREE AGENT IS?

NOPE

BUT I'M GONNA BE ONE!!

SCHULZ

DISTANCES ON A BASEBALL DIAMOND ARE DECEIVING...

WHEN YOU WALK FROM THE BENCH TO THE PLATE, IT'S ABOUT THIRTY FEET...

STRIKE THREE!

8-24

WHEN YOU WALK FROM THE PLATE TO THE BENCH, IT'S FOUR MILES!

SCHULZ

© 1979 United Feature Syndicate, Inc.

173

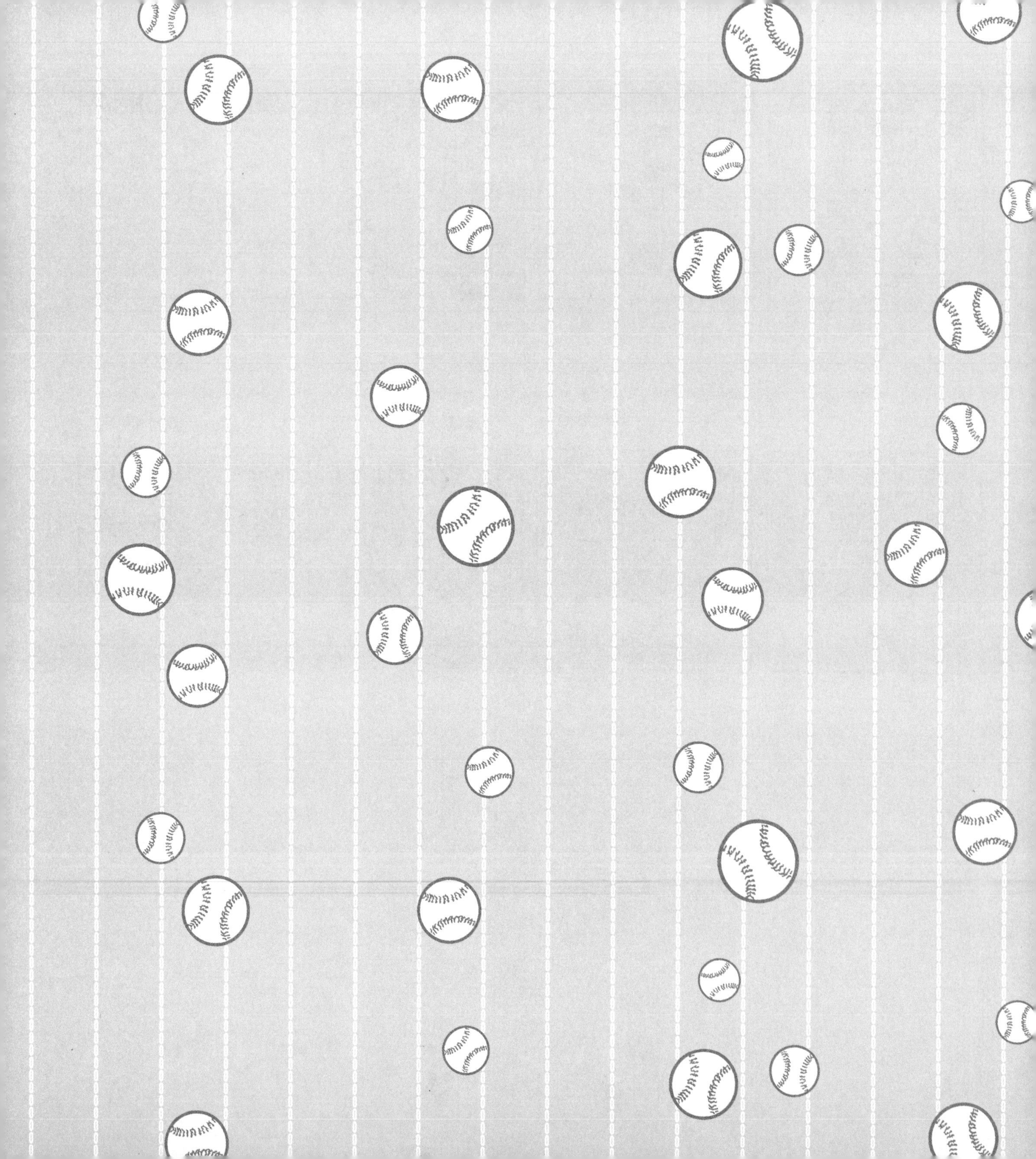

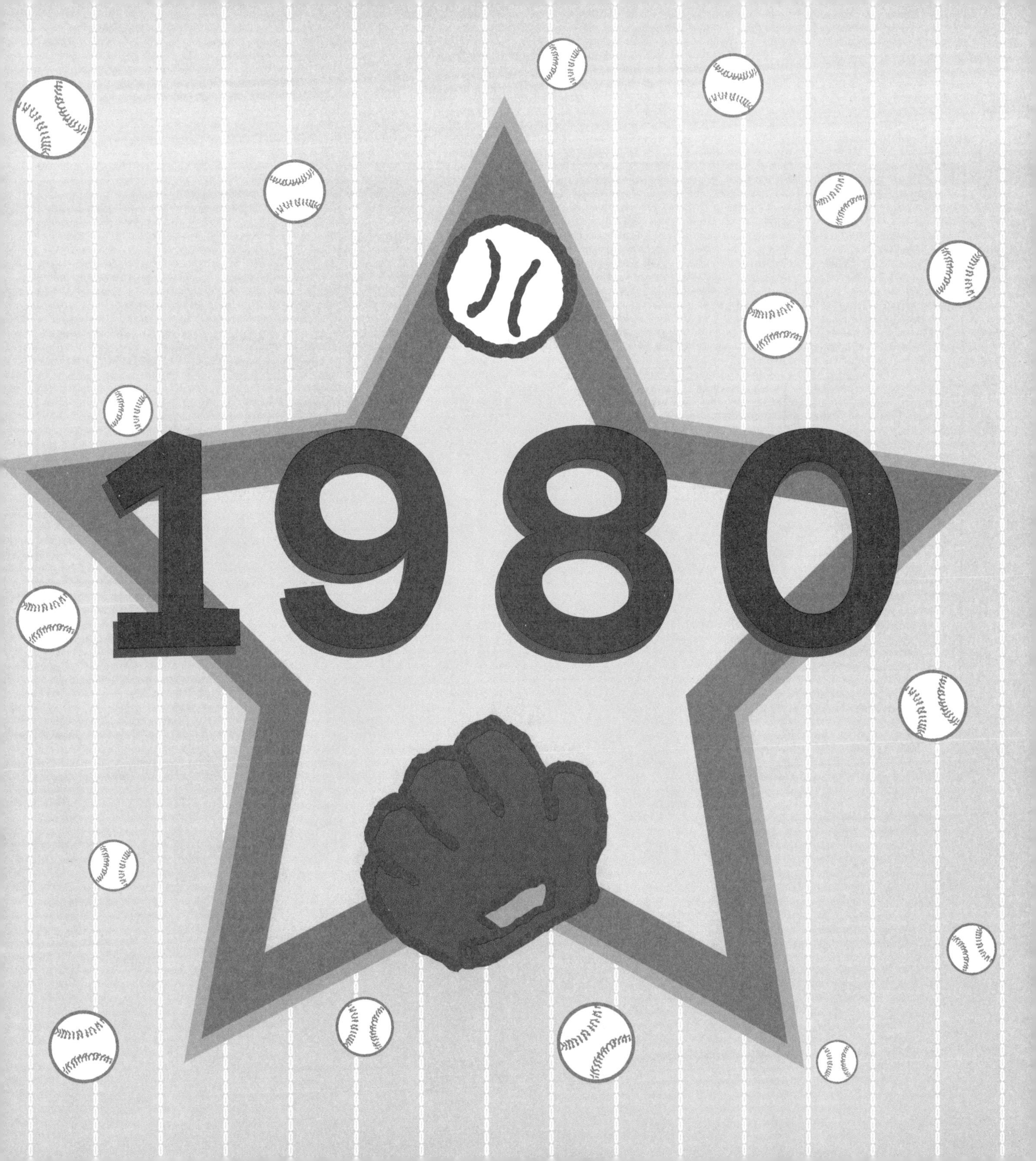
1980

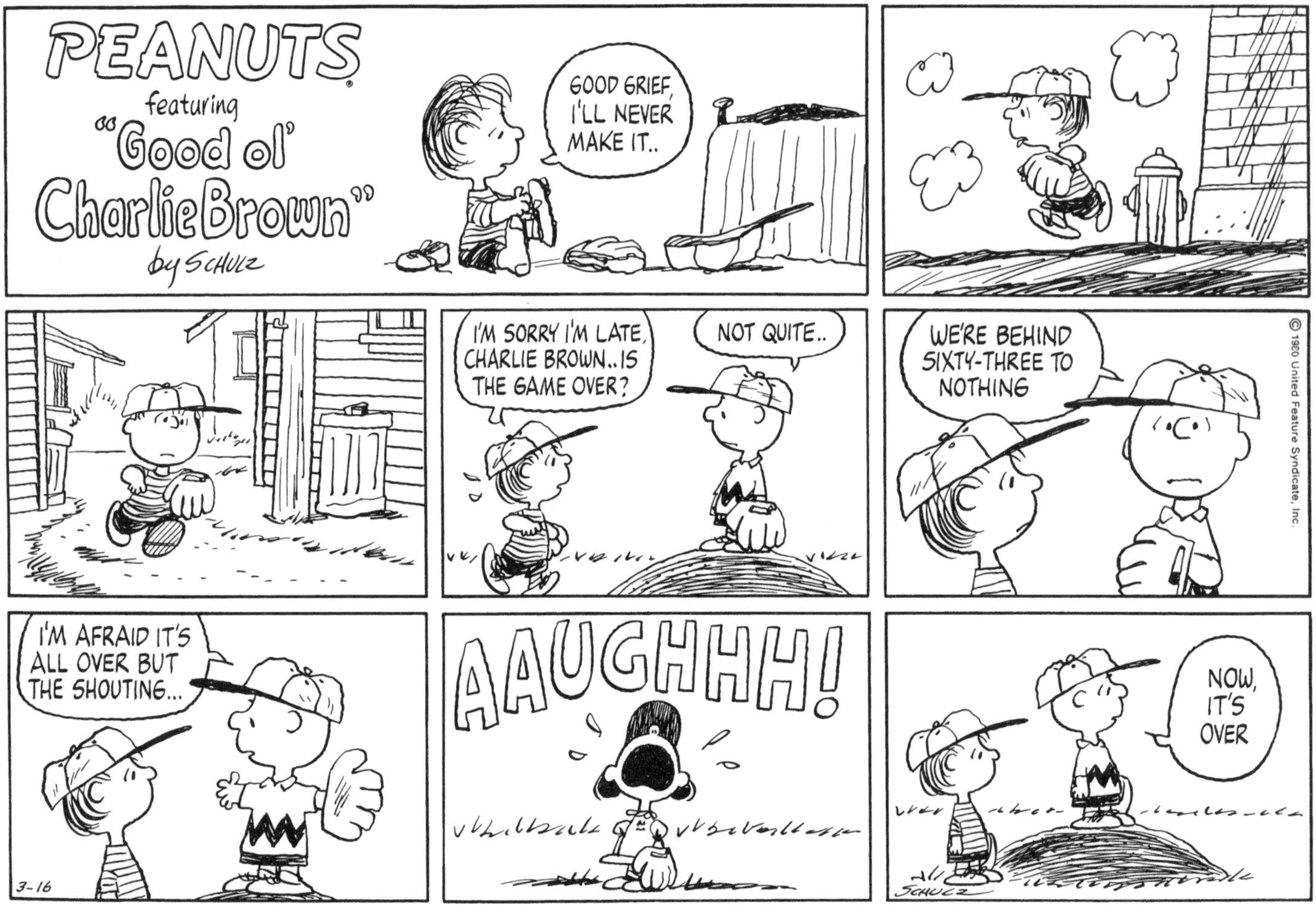
PEANUTS
featuring
"Good ol' CharlieBrown"
by SCHULZ
GOOD GRIEF, I'LL NEVER MAKE IT..
I'M SORRY I'M LATE, CHARLIE BROWN..IS THE GAME OVER?
NOT QUITE..
WE'RE BEHIND SIXTY-THREE TO NOTHING
© 1960 United Feature Syndicate, Inc.
I'M AFRAID IT'S ALL OVER BUT THE SHOUTING...
3-16
AAUGHHH!
NOW, IT'S OVER
SCHULZ

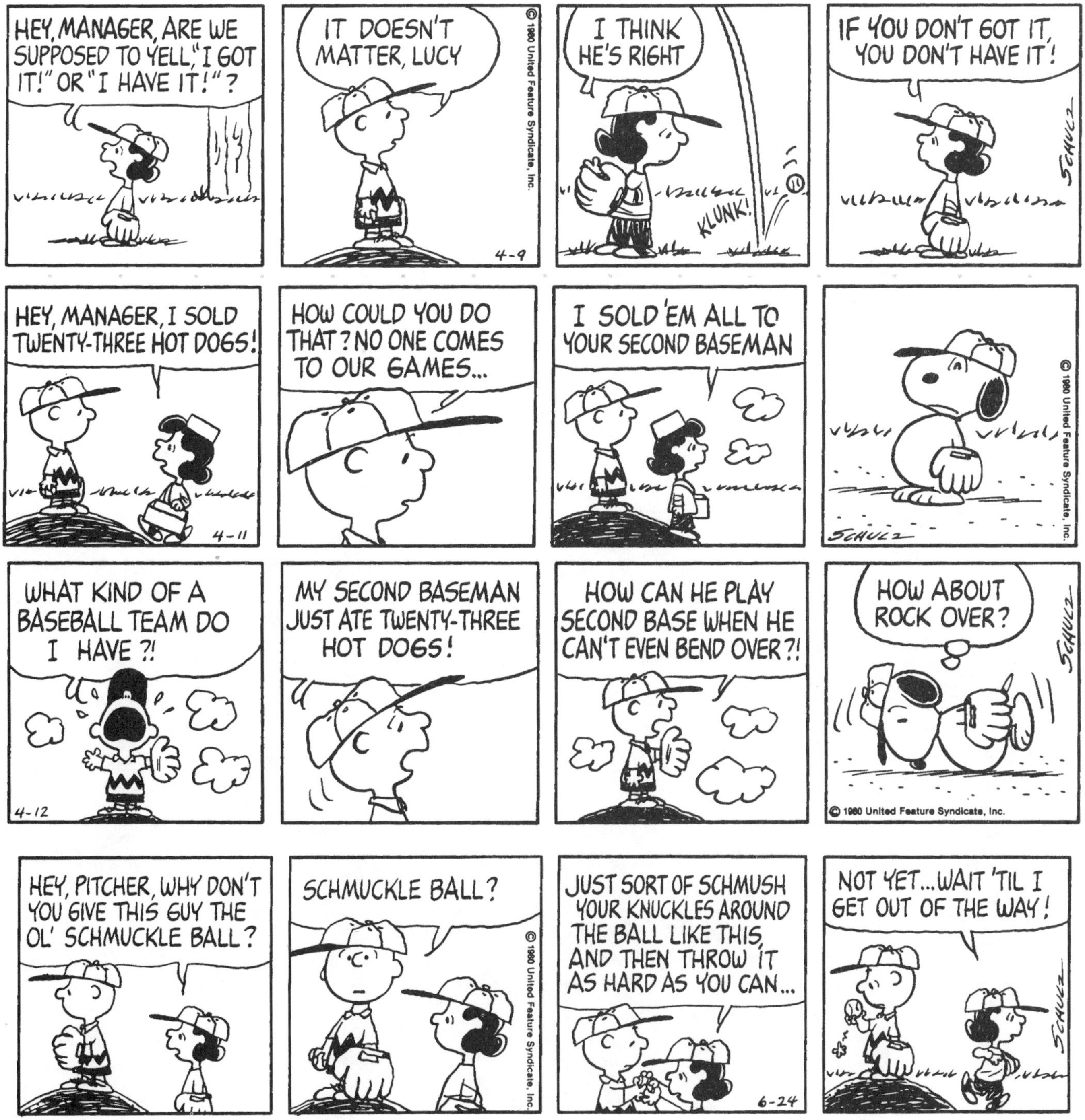
HEY, MANAGER, ARE WE SUPPOSED TO YELL, "I GOT IT!" OR "I HAVE IT!"?
IT DOESN'T MATTER, LUCY
I THINK HE'S RIGHT
KLUNK!
IF YOU DON'T GOT IT, YOU DON'T HAVE IT!
HEY, MANAGER, I SOLD TWENTY-THREE HOT DOGS!
HOW COULD YOU DO THAT? NO ONE COMES TO OUR GAMES...
I SOLD 'EM ALL TO YOUR SECOND BASEMAN
WHAT KIND OF A BASEBALL TEAM DO I HAVE ?!
MY SECOND BASEMAN JUST ATE TWENTY-THREE HOT DOGS!
HOW CAN HE PLAY SECOND BASE WHEN HE CAN'T EVEN BEND OVER?!
HOW ABOUT ROCK OVER?
HEY, PITCHER, WHY DON'T YOU GIVE THIS GUY THE OL' SCHMUCKLE BALL?
SCHMUCKLE BALL?
JUST SORT OF SCHMUSH YOUR KNUCKLES AROUND THE BALL LIKE THIS, AND THEN THROW IT AS HARD AS YOU CAN...
NOT YET...WAIT 'TIL I GET OUT OF THE WAY!
© 1980 United Feature Syndicate, Inc.

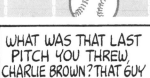

WHAT WAS THAT LAST PITCH YOU THREW, CHARLIE BROWN? THAT GUY MISSED IT A MILE!
THAT WAS THE OL' SCHMUCKLE BALL..LUCY INVENTED IT...
YOU JUST SORT OF SCHMUSH YOUR KNUCKLES AROUND THE BALL LIKE THIS, AND THEN THROW IT AS HARD AS YOU CAN
6-25
EVERY TIME IT WORKS I GET A ROYALTY!
© 1980 United Feature Syndicate, Inc.
SCHULZ

C'MON, CHARLIE BROWN, GIVE 'IM THE OL' SCHMUCKLE BALL!
6-26
© 1980 United Feature Syndicate, Inc.
HOW CAN I FOOL THIS GUY WITH A SECRET PITCH IF YOU'RE GOING TO YELL IT ALL OVER THE NEIGHBORHOOD?
YOU'RE RIGHT, CHARLIE BROWN...I SHOULD HAVE THOUGHT OF THAT...
PSST!! GIVE 'IM THE OL' SCHMUCKLE BALL!
SCHULZ

© 1980 United Feature Syndicate, Inc.
POW!
I THOUGHT YOU WERE GONNA GIVE 'IM THE OL' SCHMUCKLE BALL...
6-27
HE GAVE IT BACK!
SCHULZ

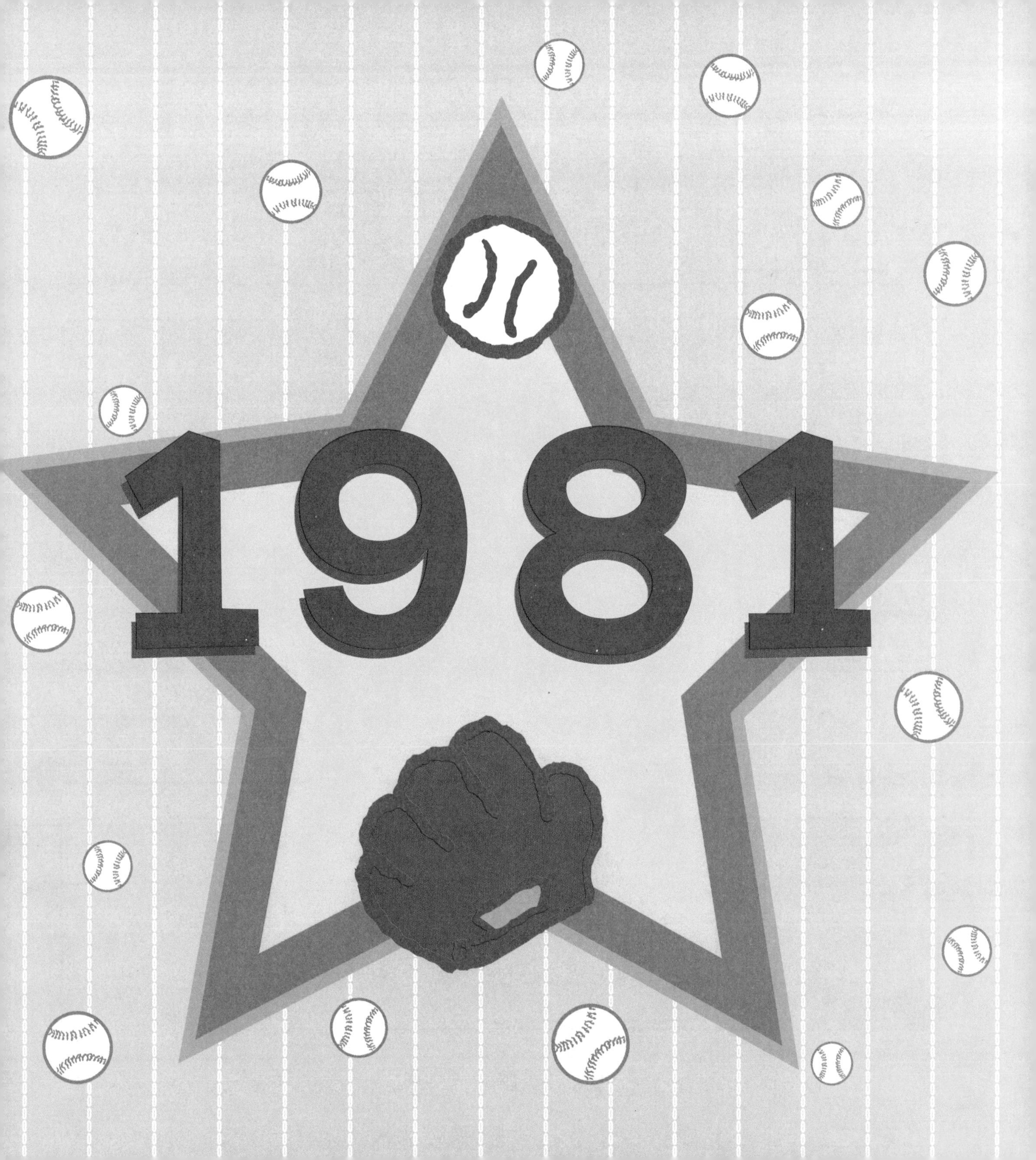
1981

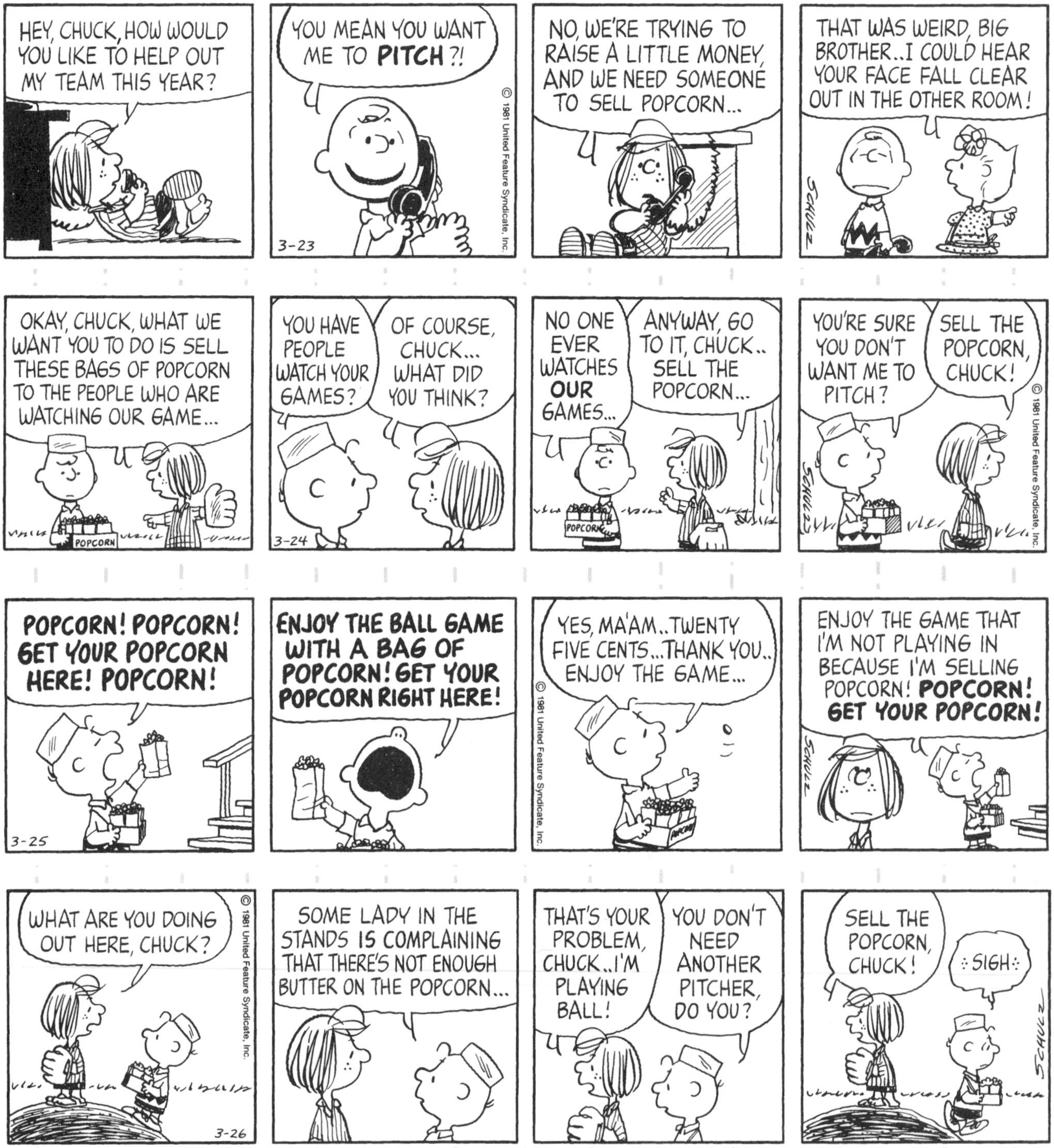
HEY, CHUCK, HOW WOULD YOU LIKE TO HELP OUT MY TEAM THIS YEAR?
YOU MEAN YOU WANT ME TO **PITCH**?!
3-23
© 1981 United Feature Syndicate, Inc.
NO, WE'RE TRYING TO RAISE A LITTLE MONEY, AND WE NEED SOMEONE TO SELL POPCORN...
THAT WAS WEIRD, BIG BROTHER..I COULD HEAR YOUR FACE FALL CLEAR OUT IN THE OTHER ROOM!
SCHULZ
OKAY, CHUCK, WHAT WE WANT YOU TO DO IS SELL THESE BAGS OF POPCORN TO THE PEOPLE WHO ARE WATCHING OUR GAME...
POPCORN
YOU HAVE PEOPLE WATCH YOUR GAMES?
OF COURSE, CHUCK... WHAT DID YOU THINK?
3-24
NO ONE EVER WATCHES **OUR** GAMES...
ANYWAY, GO TO IT, CHUCK.. SELL THE POPCORN...
POPCORN
YOU'RE SURE YOU DON'T WANT ME TO PITCH?
SELL THE POPCORN, CHUCK!
SCHULZ
© 1981 United Feature Syndicate, Inc.
POPCORN! POPCORN! GET YOUR POPCORN HERE! POPCORN!
3-25
ENJOY THE BALL GAME WITH A BAG OF POPCORN! GET YOUR POPCORN RIGHT HERE!
© 1981 United Feature Syndicate, Inc.
YES, MA'AM..TWENTY FIVE CENTS...THANK YOU.. ENJOY THE GAME...
ENJOY THE GAME THAT I'M NOT PLAYING IN BECAUSE I'M SELLING POPCORN! **POPCORN! GET YOUR POPCORN!**
SCHULZ
WHAT ARE YOU DOING OUT HERE, CHUCK?
© 1981 United Feature Syndicate, Inc.
3-26
SOME LADY IN THE STANDS IS COMPLAINING THAT THERE'S NOT ENOUGH BUTTER ON THE POPCORN...
THAT'S YOUR PROBLEM, CHUCK..I'M PLAYING BALL!
YOU DON'T NEED ANOTHER PITCHER, DO YOU?
SELL THE POPCORN, CHUCK!
SIGH
SCHULZ

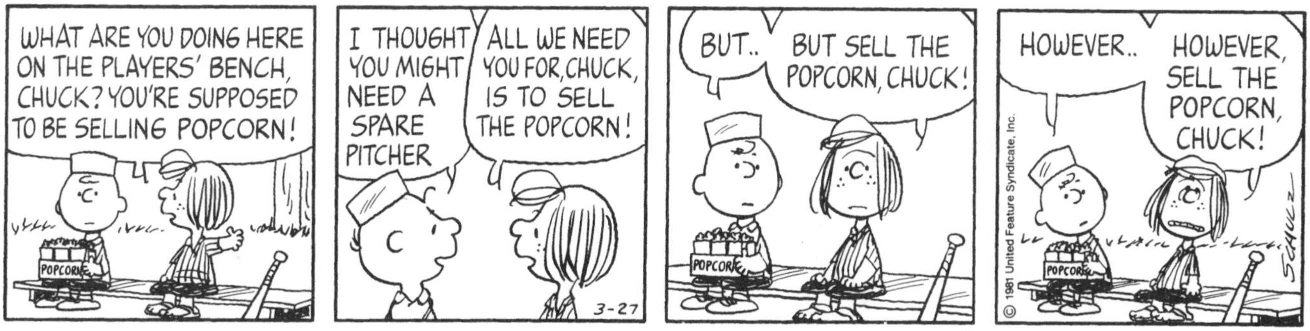
WHAT ARE YOU DOING HERE ON THE PLAYERS' BENCH, CHUCK? YOU'RE SUPPOSED TO BE SELLING POPCORN!
POPCORN
I THOUGHT YOU MIGHT NEED A SPARE PITCHER
ALL WE NEED YOU FOR, CHUCK, IS TO SELL THE POPCORN!
3-27
BUT..
BUT SELL THE POPCORN, CHUCK!
HOWEVER..
HOWEVER, SELL THE POPCORN, CHUCK!
© 1981 United Feature Syndicate, Inc.
SCHULZ

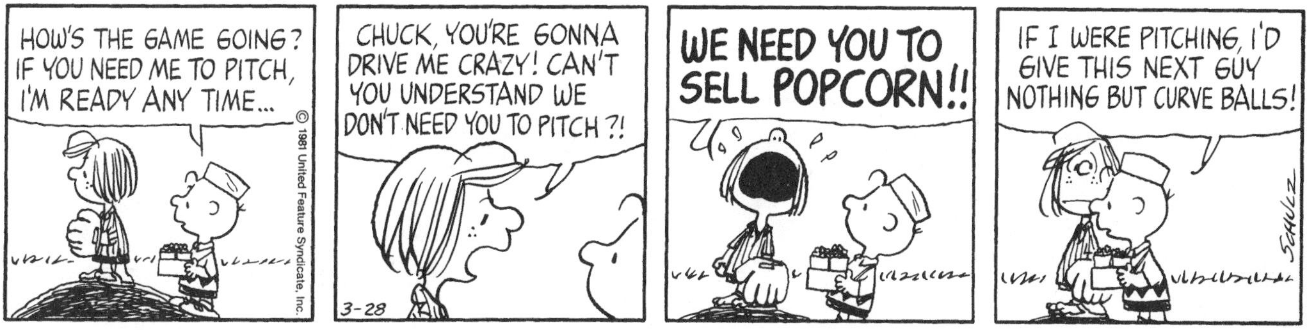
HOW'S THE GAME GOING? IF YOU NEED ME TO PITCH, I'M READY ANY TIME...
© 1981 United Feature Syndicate, Inc.
CHUCK, YOU'RE GONNA DRIVE ME CRAZY! CAN'T YOU UNDERSTAND WE DON'T NEED YOU TO PITCH?!
3-28
WE NEED YOU TO SELL POPCORN!!
IF I WERE PITCHING, I'D GIVE THIS NEXT GUY NOTHING BUT CURVE BALLS!
SCHULZ

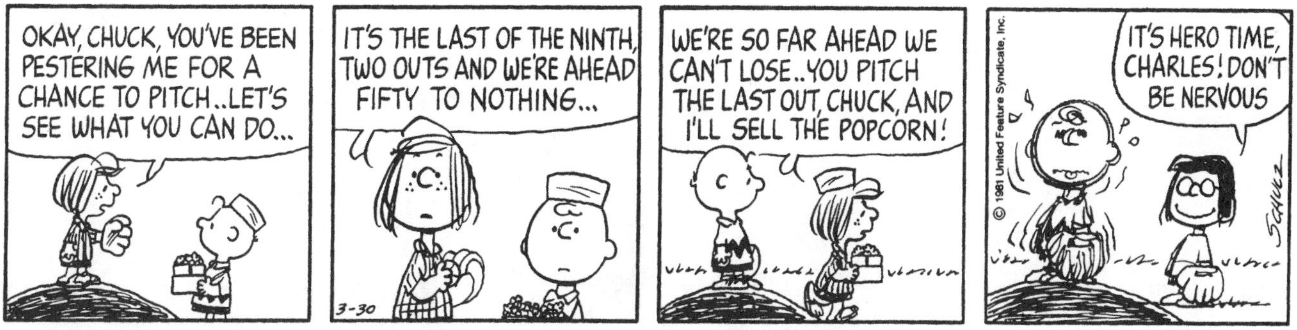
OKAY, CHUCK, YOU'VE BEEN PESTERING ME FOR A CHANCE TO PITCH..LET'S SEE WHAT YOU CAN DO...
IT'S THE LAST OF THE NINTH, TWO OUTS AND WE'RE AHEAD FIFTY TO NOTHING...
3-30
WE'RE SO FAR AHEAD WE CAN'T LOSE..YOU PITCH THE LAST OUT, CHUCK, AND I'LL SELL THE POPCORN!
IT'S HERO TIME, CHARLES! DON'T BE NERVOUS
© 1981 United Feature Syndicate, Inc.
SCHULZ

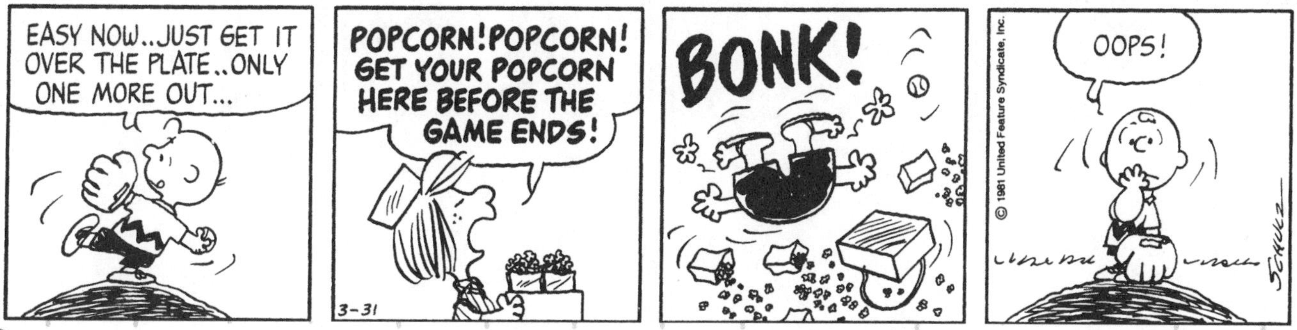
EASY NOW..JUST GET IT OVER THE PLATE..ONLY ONE MORE OUT...
POPCORN! POPCORN! GET YOUR POPCORN HERE BEFORE THE GAME ENDS!
3-31
BONK!
OOPS!
© 1981 United Feature Syndicate, Inc.
SCHULZ

MARCIE! WHAT HAPPENED? WHERE AM I?

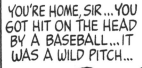
YOU'RE HOME, SIR... YOU GOT HIT ON THE HEAD BY A BASEBALL... IT WAS A WILD PITCH...

© 1981 United Feature Syndicate, Inc. 4-1

CHUCK THREW A WILD PITCH? BUT WE WON, DIDN'T WE? WE WERE AHEAD FIFTY TO NOTHING..

WE LOST, SIR... FIFTY-ONE TO FIFTY!

ALL RIGHT, CHUCK, WHAT HAPPENED?!

© 1981 United Feature Syndicate, Inc.

I LEFT YOU WITH A FIFTY RUN LEAD! HOW COULD YOU BLOW A FIFTY RUN LEAD?

4-2

THERE WERE TWO OUTS IN THE NINTH INNING! EXPLAIN YOURSELF, CHUCK! WHAT HAPPENED?

I'M SORRY.. MR. BROWN IS NOT IN... IF YOU'D CARE TO LEAVE YOUR NUMBER, HE'LL TRY TO GET BACK TO YOU SOMETIME NEXT YEAR...

COME ON OUT, CHUCK! ALL IS FORGIVEN!! I KNOW YOU DIDN'T MEAN TO LOSE THE GAME!

COME OUT, CHUCK! I WON'T HIT YOU! I'M NOT MAD ANY MORE... I FORGIVE YOU! I'M REALLY NOT MAD ANY MORE...

4-3

© 1981 United Feature Syndicate, Inc.

YOU'RE RIGHT, CHUCK! I'M LYING!!

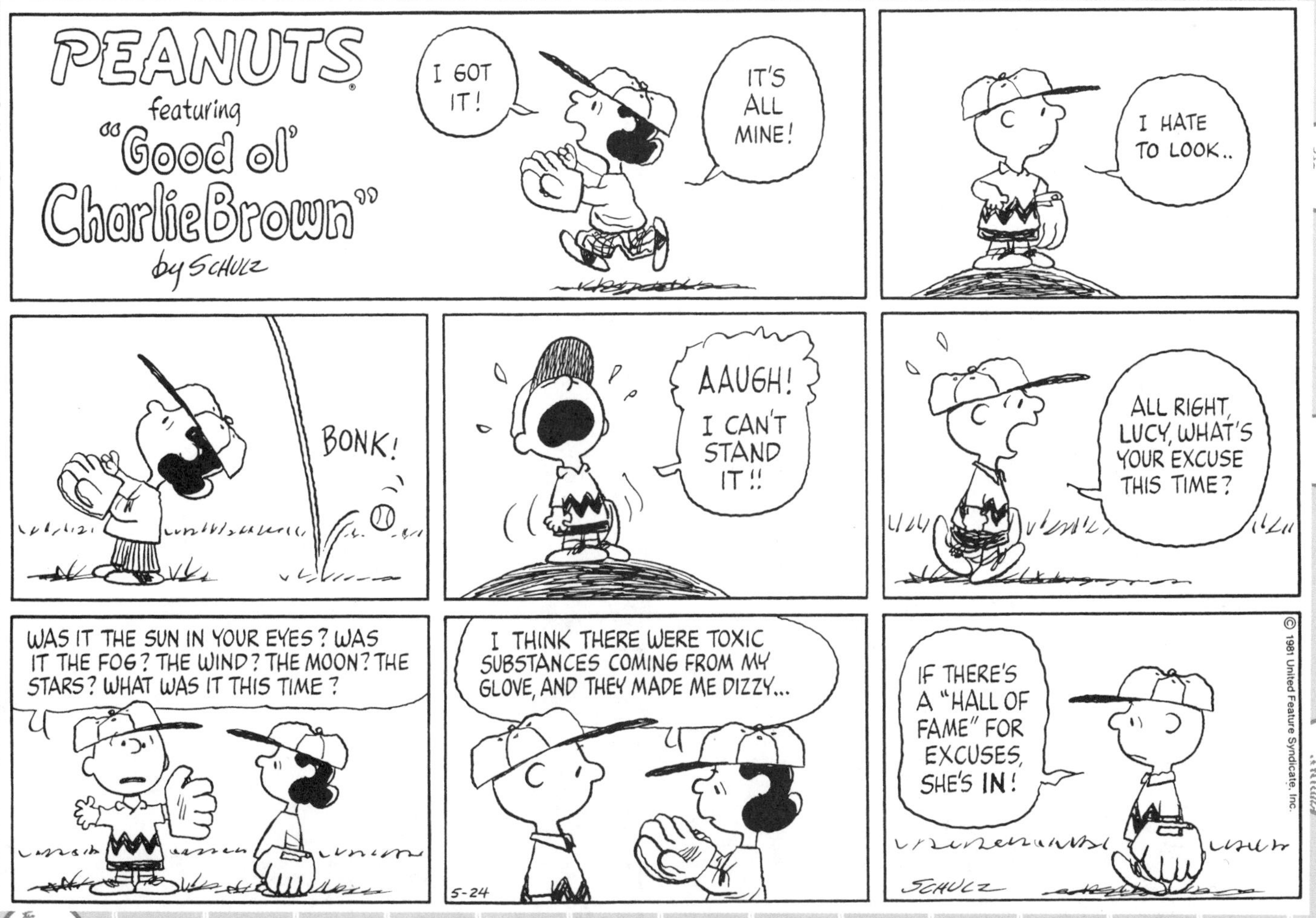
PEANUTS®
featuring "Good ol' CharlieBrown"
by SCHULZ
I GOT IT!
IT'S ALL MINE!
I HATE TO LOOK..
BONK!
AAUGH! I CAN'T STAND IT!!
ALL RIGHT, LUCY, WHAT'S YOUR EXCUSE THIS TIME?
WAS IT THE SUN IN YOUR EYES? WAS IT THE FOG? THE WIND? THE MOON? THE STARS? WHAT WAS IT THIS TIME?
I THINK THERE WERE TOXIC SUBSTANCES COMING FROM MY GLOVE, AND THEY MADE ME DIZZY...
5-24
IF THERE'S A "HALL OF FAME" FOR EXCUSES, SHE'S IN!
SCHULZ
© 1981 United Feature Syndicate, Inc.

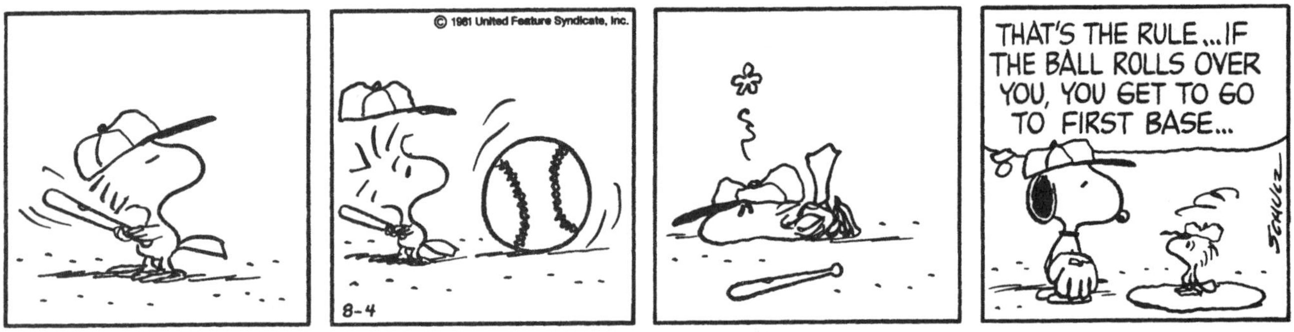
© 1981 United Feature Syndicate, Inc.
8-4
THAT'S THE RULE...IF THE BALL ROLLS OVER YOU, YOU GET TO GO TO FIRST BASE...
SCHULZ

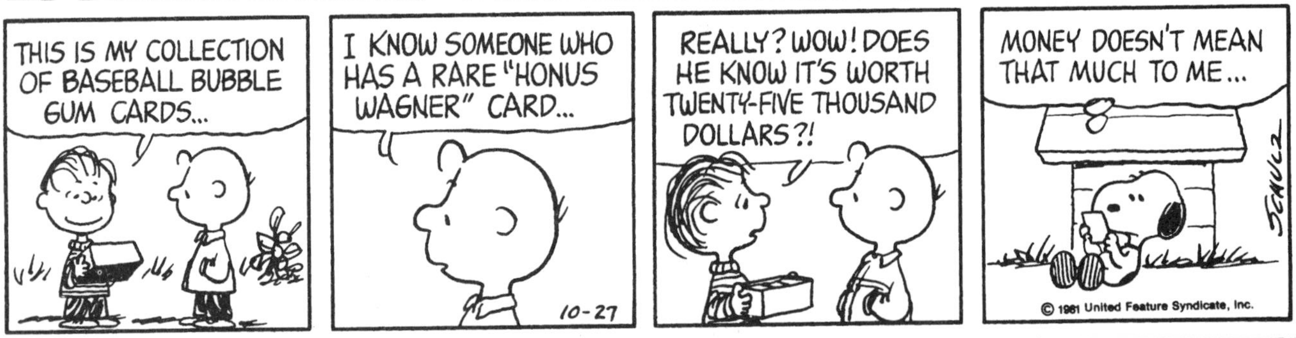
THIS IS MY COLLECTION OF BASEBALL BUBBLE GUM CARDS...
I KNOW SOMEONE WHO HAS A RARE "HONUS WAGNER" CARD...
10-27
REALLY? WOW! DOES HE KNOW IT'S WORTH TWENTY-FIVE THOUSAND DOLLARS?!
MONEY DOESN'T MEAN THAT MUCH TO ME...
SCHULZ
© 1981 United Feature Syndicate, Inc.

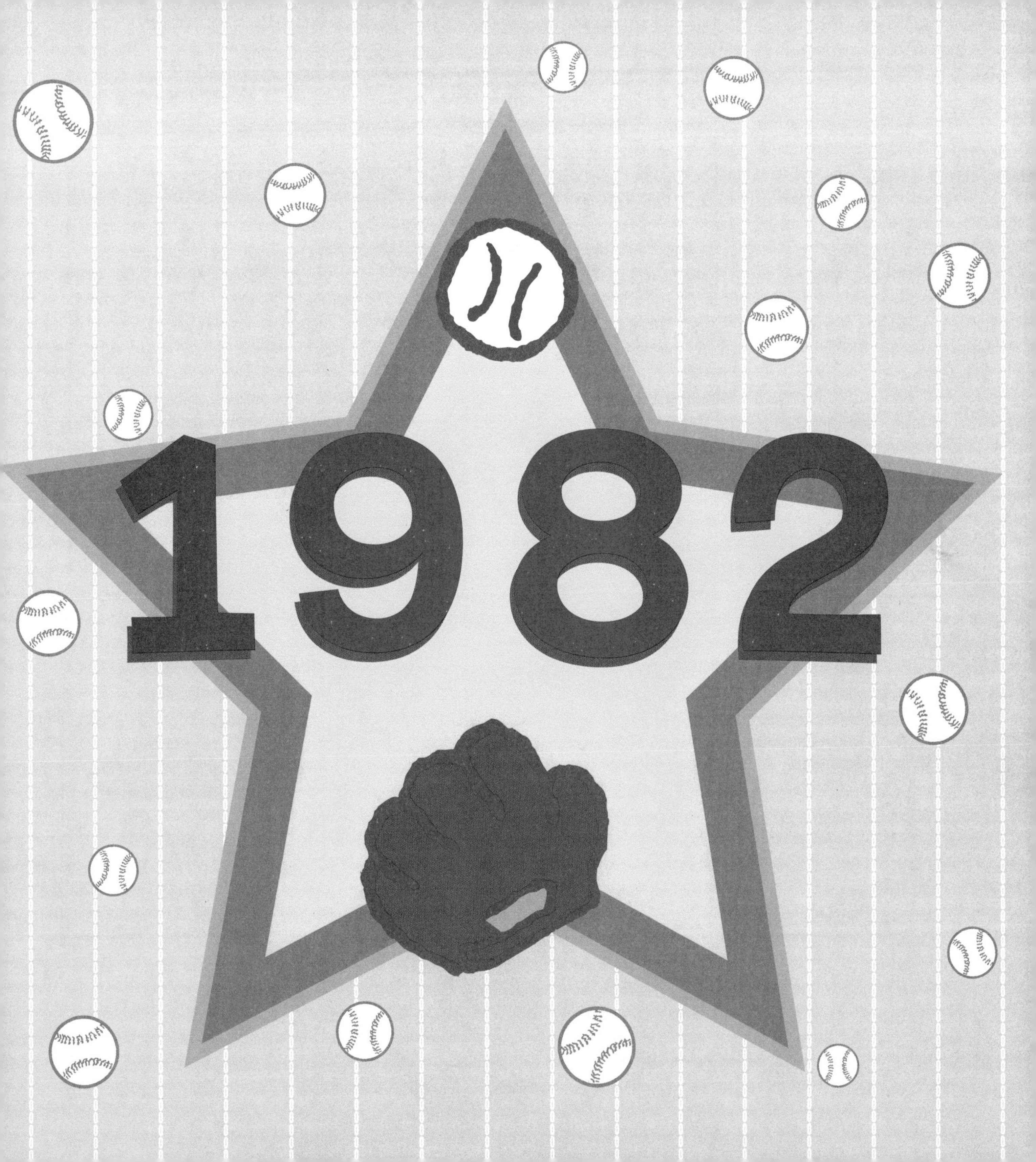
1982

ALL RIGHT, TEAM, THIS YEAR THINGS ARE GOING TO BE DIFFERENT!
3-29
© 1982 United Feature Syndicate, Inc.
POW!
SEE? THEY ONLY KNOCKED ONE SHOE OFF!
SCHULZ

LUCY, WE'VE GOT TO GET A RUNNER ON BASE...
I DON'T SUPPOSE YOU'D LET YOURSELF GET HIT ON THE HEAD WITH THE BALL, WOULD YOU?
3-30
© 1982 United Feature Syndicate, Inc.
THIS IS THE FIRST TIME I'VE EVER LOOKED DIRECTLY INTO THE EYES OF SOMEONE WHO IS TOTALLY OUT OF HIS MIND!
SCHULZ

C'MON, DAD! YOU SAID WE WERE GOING TO PLAY CATCH...
OH.... NO, THAT'S ALL RIGHT... I UNDERSTAND..
4-10
© 1982 United Feature Syndicate, Inc.
WHAT'S HE DOING?
TAKING DOWN OUR OUTSIDE CHRISTMAS LIGHTS...
SCHULZ

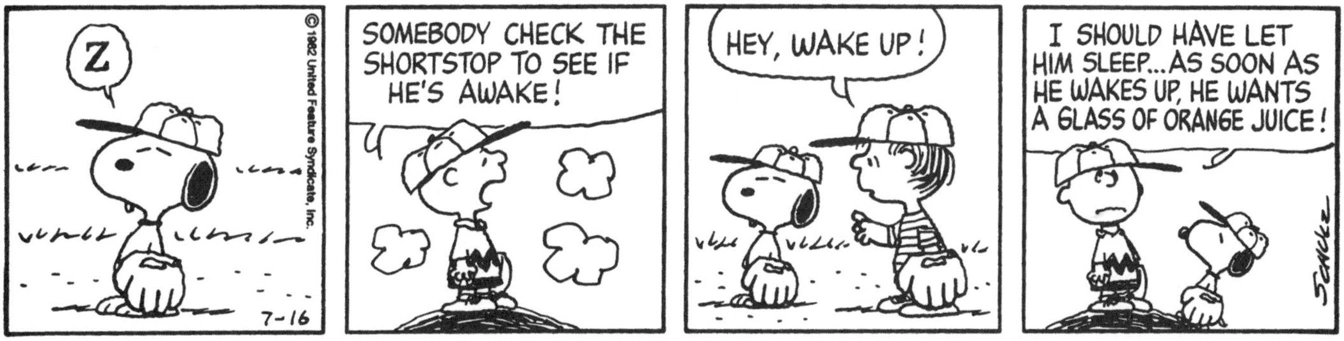
Z
© 1982 United Feature Syndicate, Inc.
7-16
SOMEBODY CHECK THE SHORTSTOP TO SEE IF HE'S AWAKE!
HEY, WAKE UP!
I SHOULD HAVE LET HIM SLEEP...AS SOON AS HE WAKES UP, HE WANTS A GLASS OF ORANGE JUICE!
SCHULZ

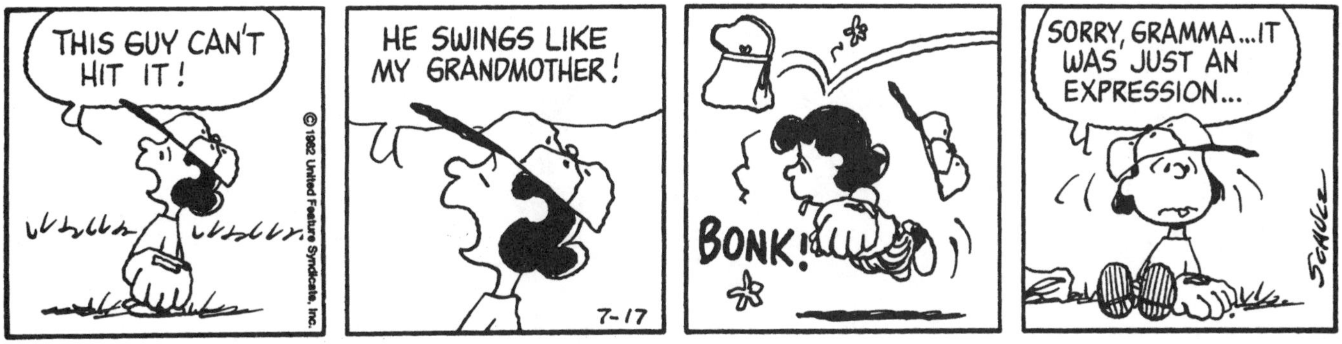
THIS GUY CAN'T HIT IT!
© 1982 United Feature Syndicate, Inc.
HE SWINGS LIKE MY GRANDMOTHER!
7-17
BONK!
SORRY, GRAMMA...IT WAS JUST AN EXPRESSION...
SCHULZ

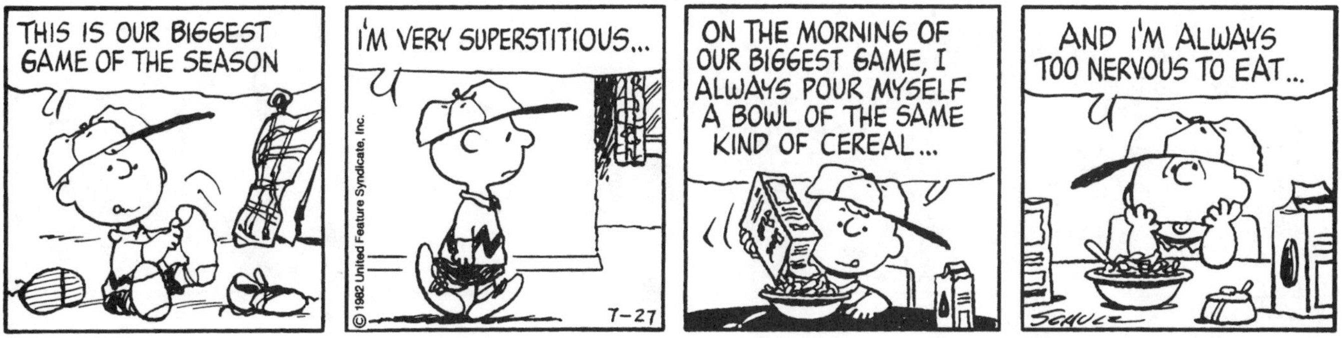
THIS IS OUR BIGGEST GAME OF THE SEASON
I'M VERY SUPERSTITIOUS...
© 1982 United Feature Syndicate, Inc.
7-27
ON THE MORNING OF OUR BIGGEST GAME, I ALWAYS POUR MYSELF A BOWL OF THE SAME KIND OF CEREAL...
AND I'M ALWAYS TOO NERVOUS TO EAT...
SCHULZ

LUCY! HAVE YOU SEEN CHARLIE BROWN?
I'M TRYING TO FIND HIM BEFORE HE GETS TO THE BALL FIELD...
SOMETHING TERRIBLE HAS HAPPENED!
LIKE WHAT? DID THE OTHER TEAM SHOW UP?
© 1982 United Feature Syndicate, Inc.
7-30

HI, CHARLIE BROWN... I GOT HERE TO THE FIELD BEFORE YOU TO PREPARE YOU FOR THE SHOCK...
7-31
SOMETHING
TERRIBLE
© 1982 United Feature Syndicate, Inc.
HAS HAPPENED

WHAT'S THIS?
KEEP OFF!
8-2
© 1982 United Feature Syndicate, Inc.
IT'S THE OWNER, CHARLIE BROWN...HE WAS TOLD NOT TO LET US PLAY BALL ON HIS VACANT LOT ANY MORE
THEY SAID IF ONE OF US GOT HURT, HE MIGHT BE LIABLE...
WHAT'S HAPPENING TO THE WORLD?
SCHULZ

I WONDER IF WE COULD PLAY OUR GAMES AT THE SCHOOL YARD...
KEEP OFF!
8-4
I DON'T THINK SO.. "NO ONE ALLOWED ON THE PLAYGROUND AFTER SCHOOL IS OUT"
HOW ABOUT THE CITY PARK?
ONLY IF WE PAY TWENTY DOLLARS APIECE AND JOIN THE LEAGUE
WHAT HAPPENED TO FUN?
OUR INSURANCE DOESN'T COVER IT!
SCHULZ
© 1982 United Feature Syndicate, Inc.

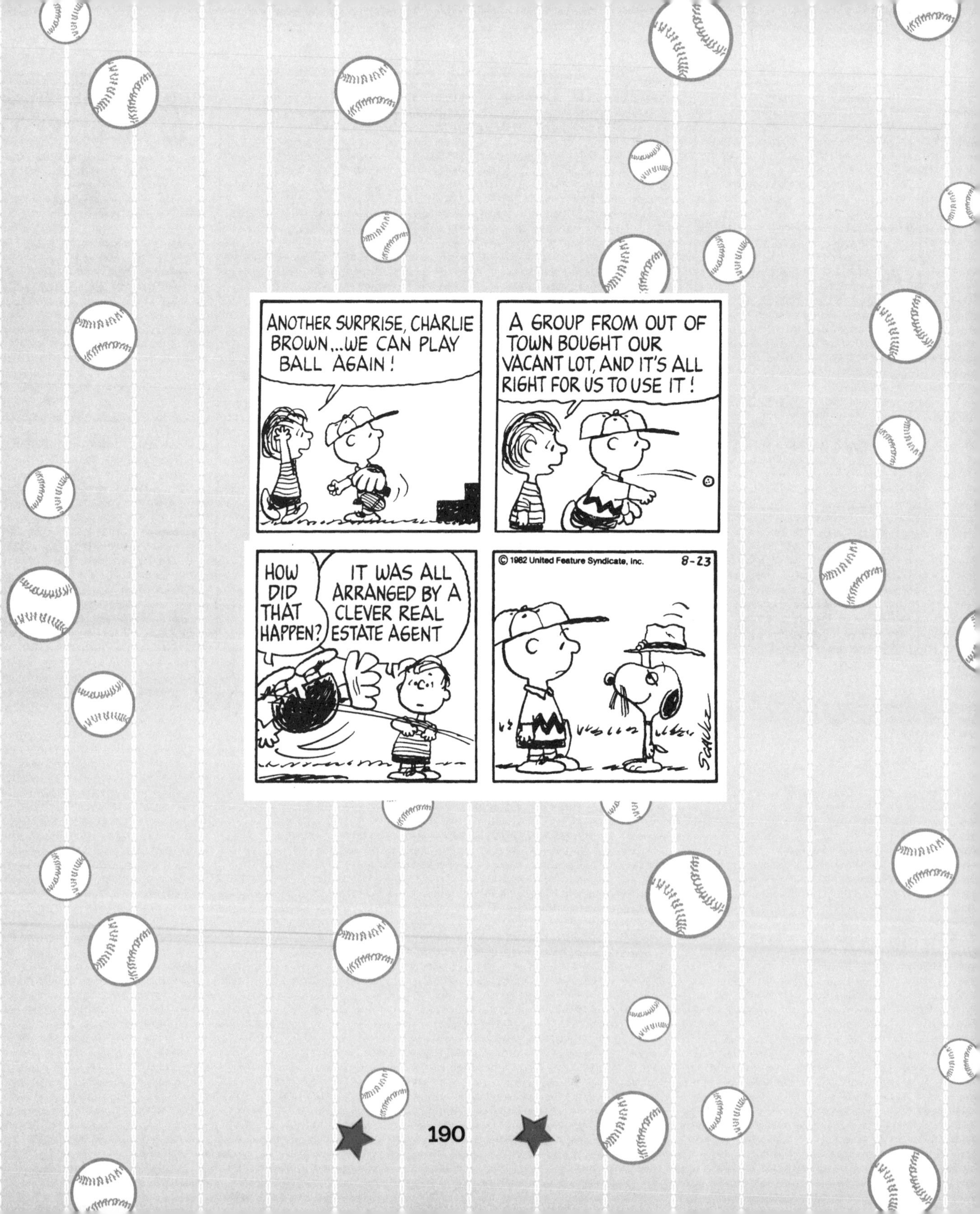
ANOTHER SURPRISE, CHARLIE BROWN...WE CAN PLAY BALL AGAIN!
A GROUP FROM OUT OF TOWN BOUGHT OUR VACANT LOT, AND IT'S ALL RIGHT FOR US TO USE IT!
HOW DID THAT HAPPEN?
IT WAS ALL ARRANGED BY A CLEVER REAL ESTATE AGENT
© 1982 United Feature Syndicate, Inc.
8-23
SCHULZ

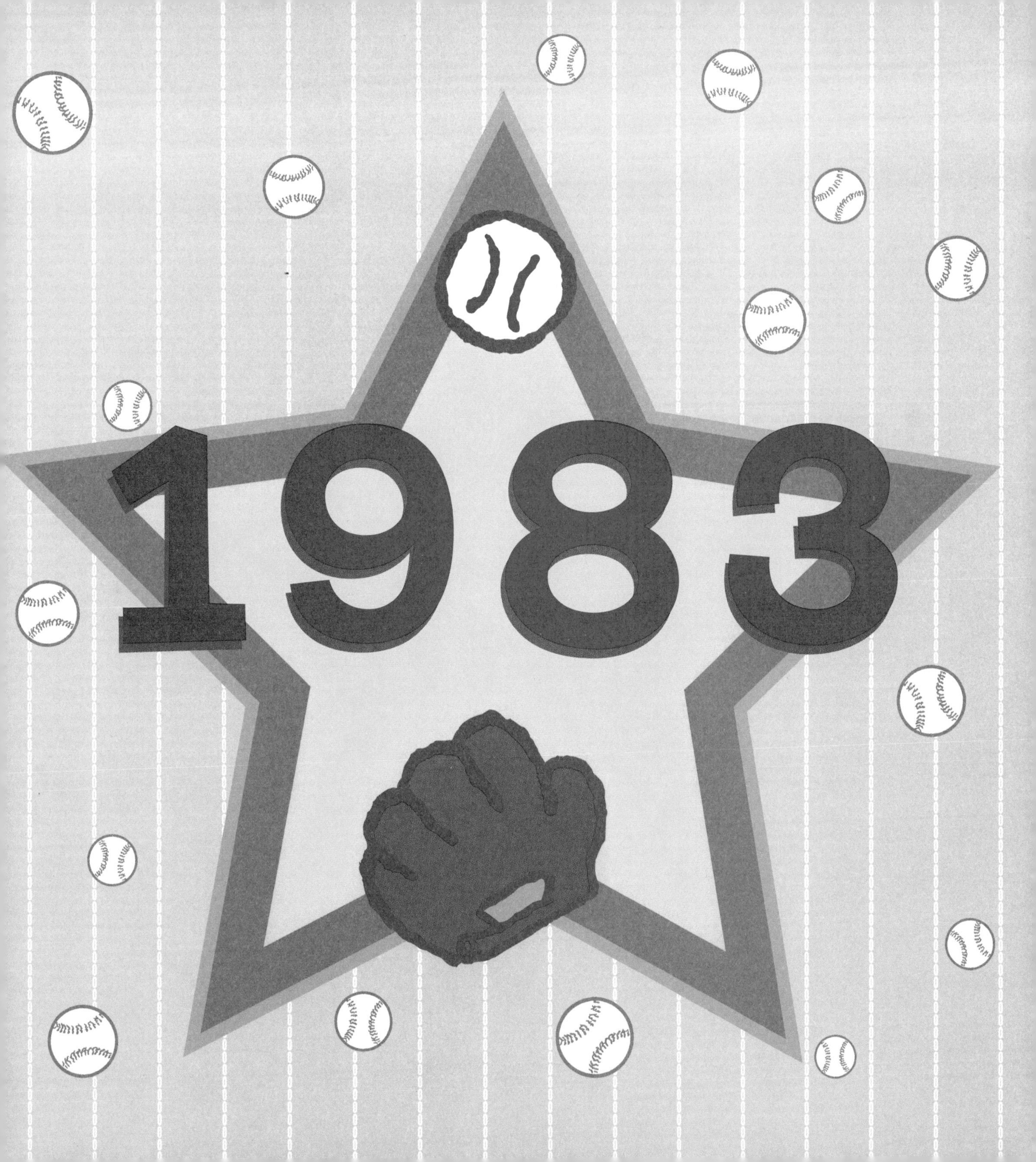
1983

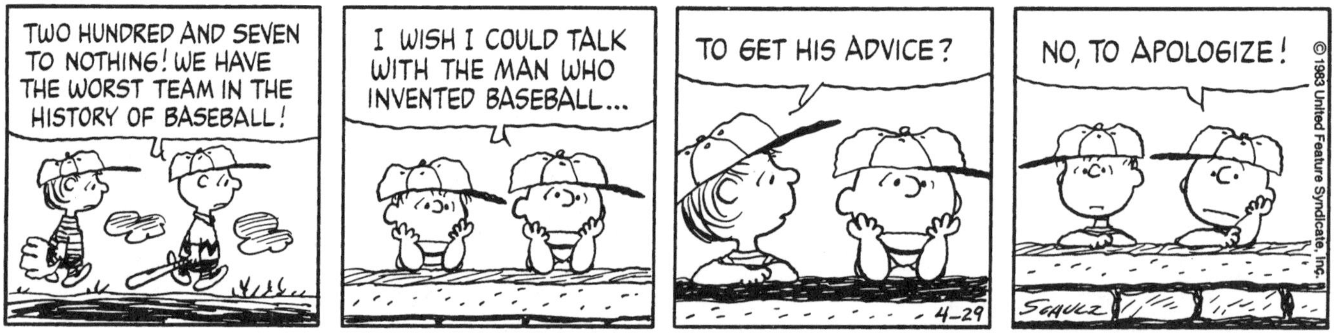
TWO HUNDRED AND SEVEN TO NOTHING! WE HAVE THE WORST TEAM IN THE HISTORY OF BASEBALL!
I WISH I COULD TALK WITH THE MAN WHO INVENTED BASEBALL...
TO GET HIS ADVICE?
NO, TO APOLOGIZE!
4-29
SCHULZ
© 1983 United Feature Syndicate, Inc.

6-8
© 1983 United Feature Syndicate, Inc.
HEY, MANAGER..
NOW WHAT?
I THINK YOUR DOG IS AFRAID OF THUNDER
SCHULZ

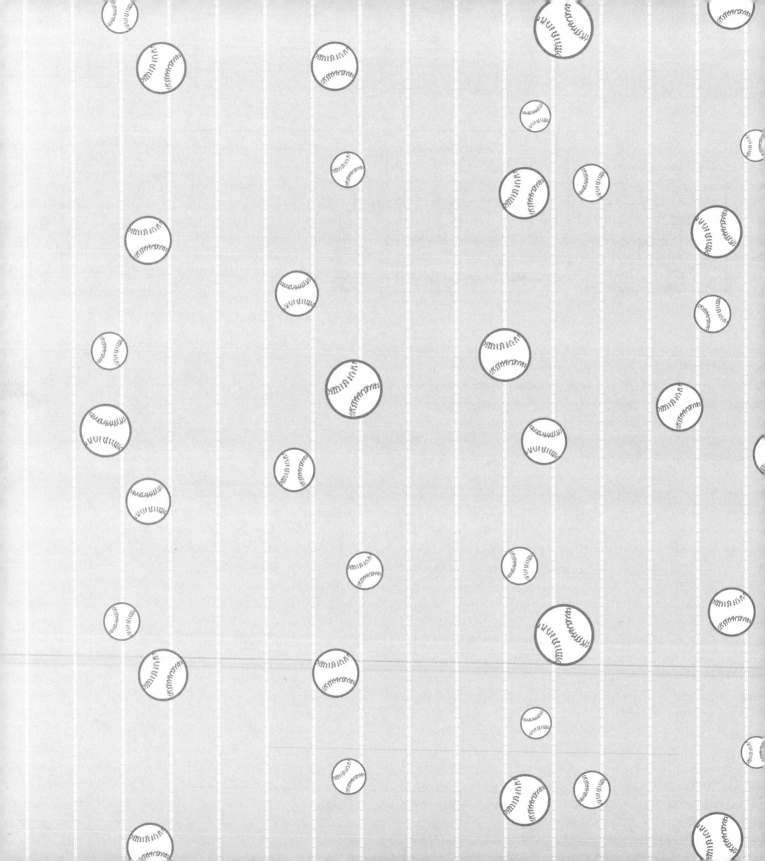

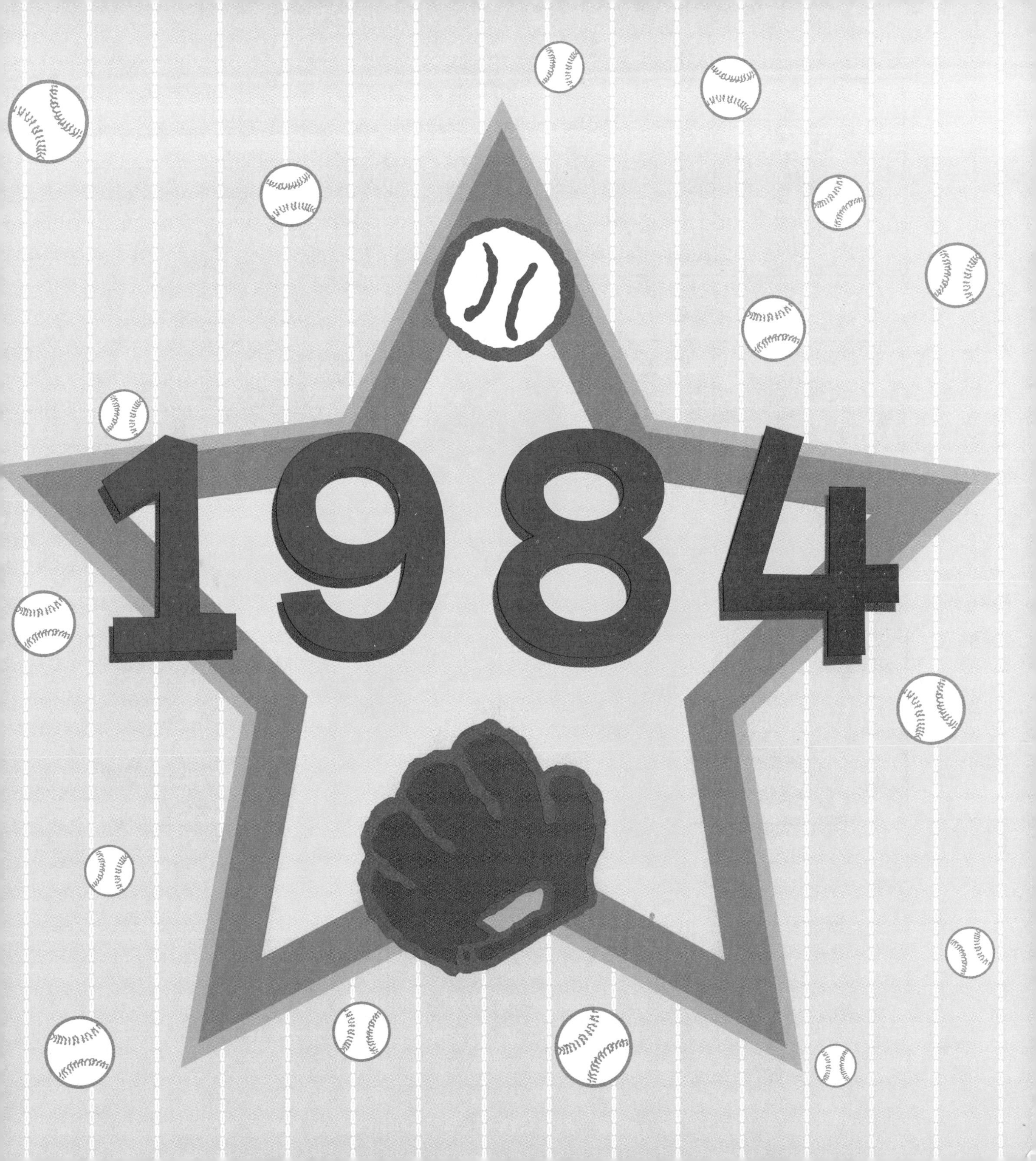
1984

© 1984 United Feature Syndicate, Inc. 3-12
WHEN YOU'RE PLAYING IN THE OUTFIELD, NEVER BLOW BUBBLE GUM ON A WINDY DAY...
SCHULZ

I WAS JUST READING ABOUT WHEN CASEY STENGEL WAS A MANAGER
HE ONCE TIPPED HIS CAP TO AN UMPIRE AND A BIRD FLEW OUT!
THAT MUST HAVE BEEN FUNNY.. I WISH I HAD SEEN THAT...
4-2
SCHULZ
© 1984 United Feature Syndicate, Inc.

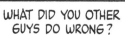

STRIKE THREE!
4-6
THAT'S FOR SWINGING AT A PITCH THAT WAS SIX FEET OVER YOUR HEAD!
© 1984 United Feature Syndicate, Inc.
WHAT DID YOU OTHER GUYS DO WRONG?
I MISSED AN EASY FLY BALL
ME TOO
I SLEPT THROUGH THE THIRD INNING
SCHULZ

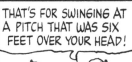

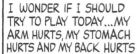

I WONDER IF I SHOULD TRY TO PLAY TODAY...MY ARM HURTS, MY STOMACH HURTS AND MY BACK HURTS
PLAY ANYWAY
© 1984 United Feature Syndicate,Inc.
DON'T LET YOUR BODY PUSH YOU AROUND!
5-8

6-25
© 1984 United Feature Syndicate,Inc.

HEY, MANAGER! HAVE YOU EVER READ WHAT IT SAYS ON YOUR GLOVE?
" TRAP POCKET... NYLON STITCHED... TOP GRADE COWHIDE.. SNAP ACTION...MADE IN TAIWAN..."
BONK!
© 1984 United Feature Syndicate,Inc.
THEY LEFT OUT "PAY ATTENTION"
7-25

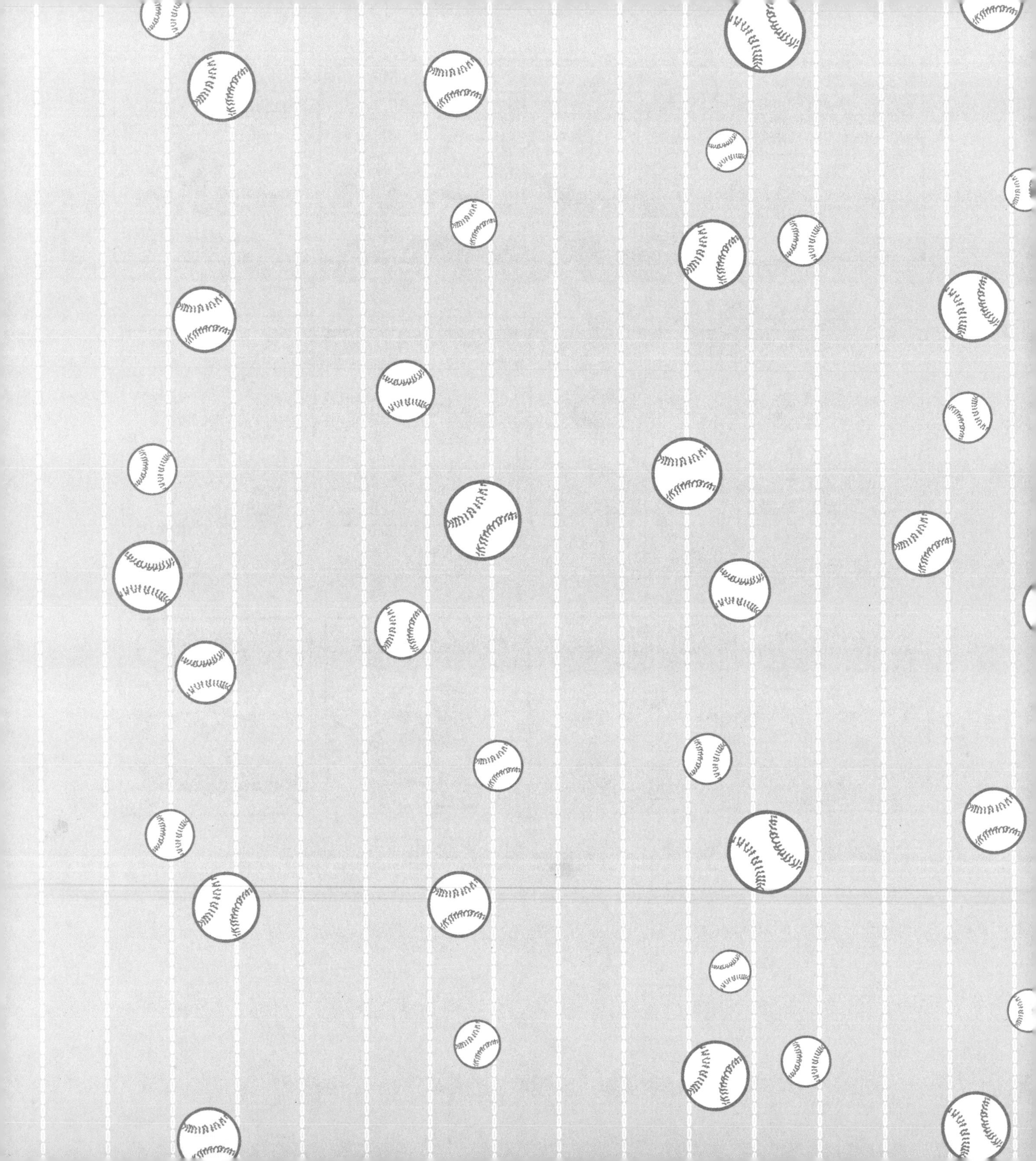

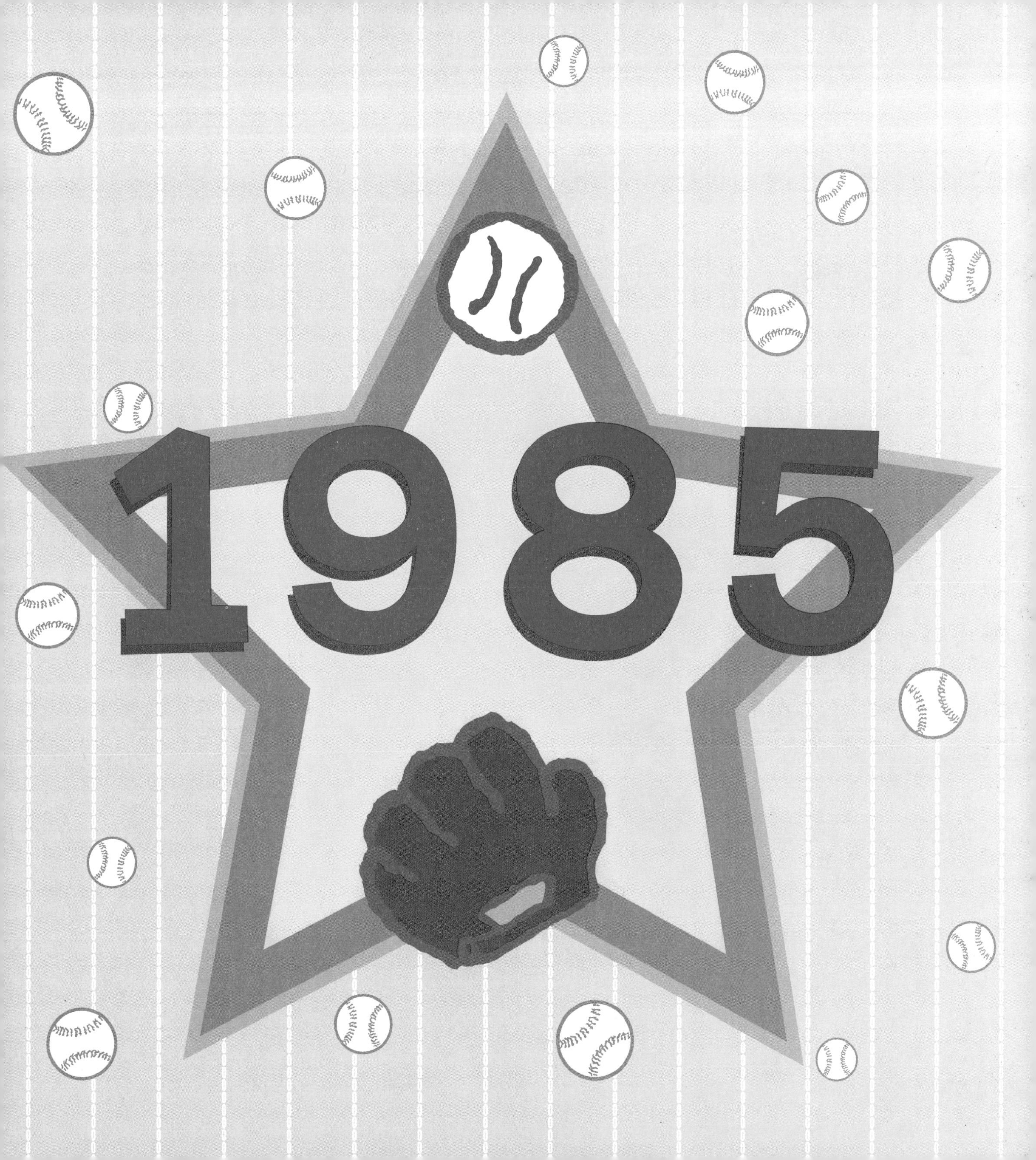
1985

I LOVE THE SOUNDS OF BASEBALL..
THE CRACK OF THE BAT...
© 1985 United Feature Syndicate, Inc.
BONK!
AND THE BONK OF THE OUTFIELDER'S HEAD
SCHULZ
3-27

I ALWAYS WEAR MY CAP TO BED ON THE NIGHT BEFORE A BIG GAME...
I GUESS IT'S JUST A SUPERSTITION
© 1985 United Feature Syndicate, Inc.
I WONDER IF ANY OF MY OTHER PLAYERS WEAR THEIR CAPS TO BED...
SCHULZ
4/10

I STILL CAN'T FIND THE BALL!
YOU'D BETTER GO HELP HER..
I'M SENDING OUR SHORTSTOP OUT TO HELP YOU...
YOU SHOULD HAVE SENT THE TALLSTOP
© 1985 United Feature Syndicate, Inc.
4-17
SCHULZ

HAVE YOU FOUND THE BALL YET?
YES, I FOUND IT! HERE IT IS! I FOUND IT!
WAIT A MINUTE...
I WAS WRONG..
© 1985 United Feature Syndicate, Inc.
4-18
SCHULZ

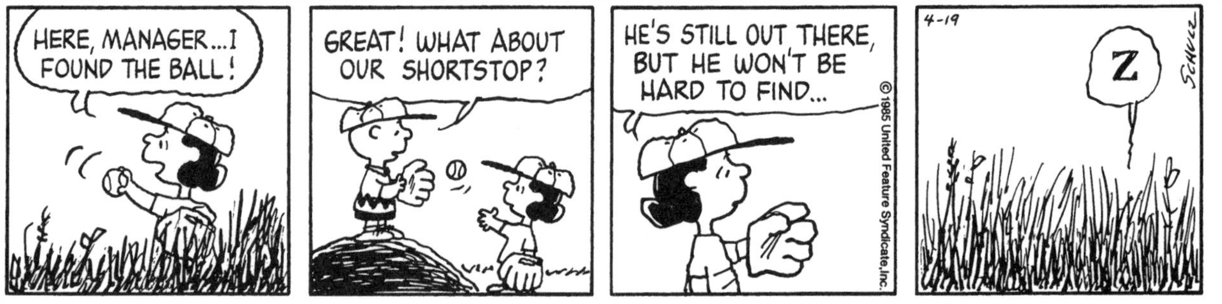
HERE, MANAGER...I FOUND THE BALL!
GREAT! WHAT ABOUT OUR SHORTSTOP?
HE'S STILL OUT THERE, BUT HE WON'T BE HARD TO FIND...
© 1985 United Feature Syndicate, Inc.
4-19
Z
SCHULZ

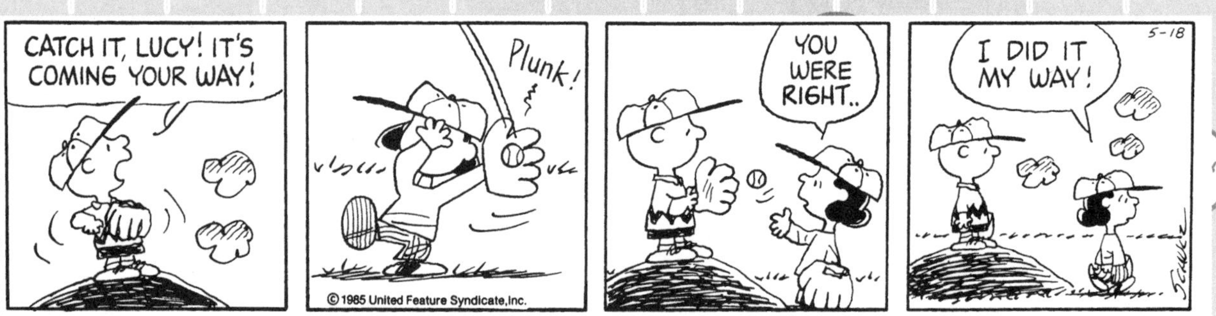
CATCH IT, LUCY! IT'S COMING YOUR WAY!
Plunk!
© 1985 United Feature Syndicate, Inc.
YOU WERE RIGHT..
5-18
I DID IT MY WAY!
SCHULZ

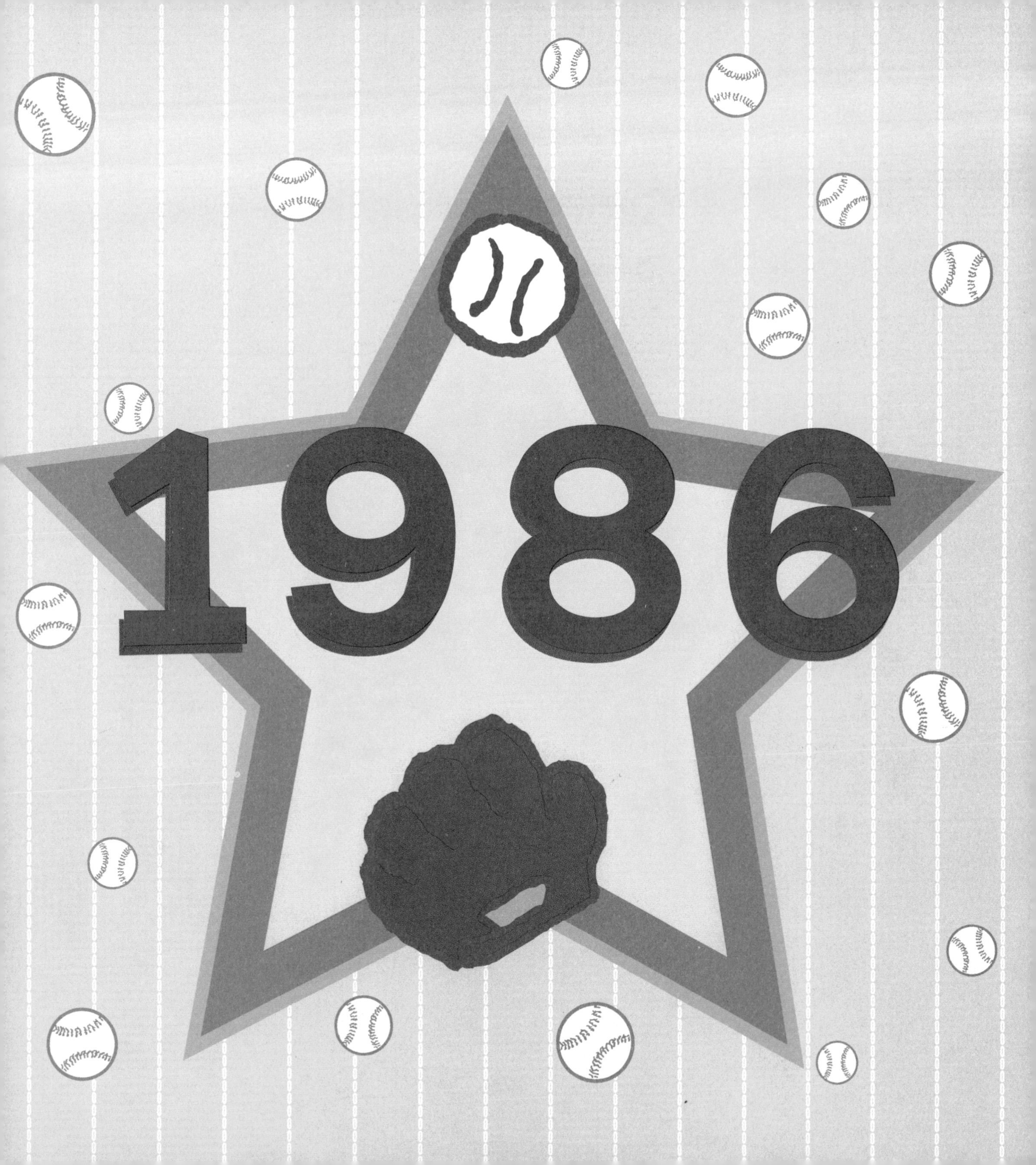
1986

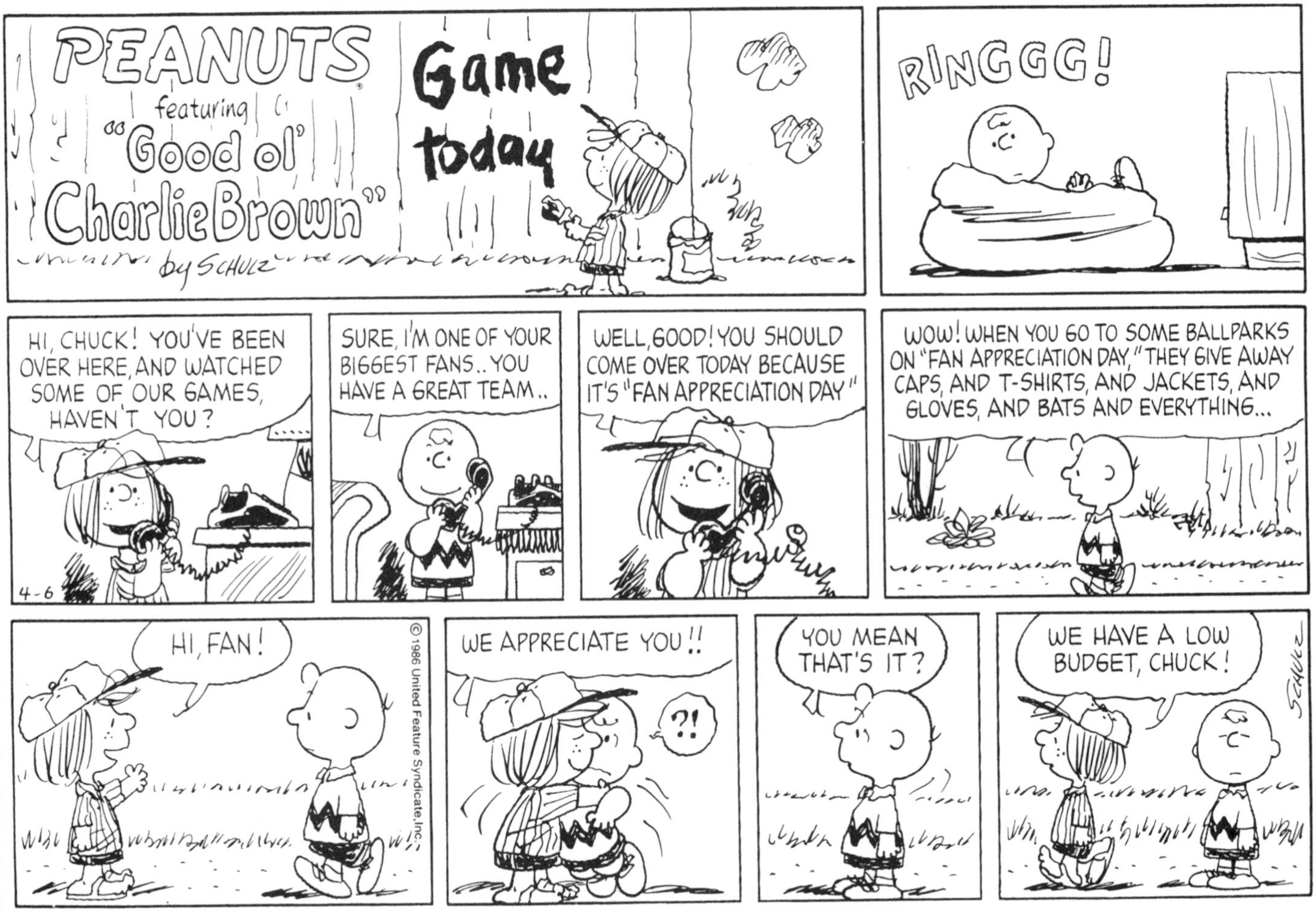
PEANUTS
featuring "Good ol' CharlieBrown"
by SCHULZ
Game today
RINGGG!
HI, CHUCK! YOU'VE BEEN OVER HERE, AND WATCHED SOME OF OUR GAMES, HAVEN'T YOU?
4-6
SURE, I'M ONE OF YOUR BIGGEST FANS.. YOU HAVE A GREAT TEAM..
WELL, GOOD! YOU SHOULD COME OVER TODAY BECAUSE IT'S "FAN APPRECIATION DAY"
WOW! WHEN YOU GO TO SOME BALLPARKS ON "FAN APPRECIATION DAY," THEY GIVE AWAY CAPS, AND T-SHIRTS, AND JACKETS, AND GLOVES, AND BATS AND EVERYTHING...
HI, FAN!
© 1986 United Feature Syndicate, Inc.
WE APPRECIATE YOU!!
?!
YOU MEAN THAT'S IT?
WE HAVE A LOW BUDGET, CHUCK!
SCHULZ

I FEEL RIDICULOUS!
HOLD IT!
THIS IS FOR OUR SCHOOL PAPER, CHARLIE BROWN.. IT'S OUR ANNUAL SWIMSUIT ISSUE...
5-28
WHO'D WANT TO SEE PICTURES OF BASEBALL PLAYERS IN SWIMSUITS?
IT'LL BE A SELLOUT!
© 1986 United Feature Syndicate, Inc.

TWAK!
8-16
OOOO! MY HANDS!! THAT STUNG!!!
KISS MY HANDS, MANAGER...THEY HURT...
IF JOE GARAGIOLA SEES THIS, I'LL NEVER LIVE IT DOWN..
© 1986 United Feature Syndicate, Inc.

HERE'S AN ARTICLE ABOUT WHAT YOU SHOULD DO WITH YOUR BASEBALL GLOVE FOR THE WINTER...
"PUT YOUR GLOVE AWAY IN A DRY PLACE WHERE THE DOG CAN'T FIND IT"
10-20
© 1986 United Feature Syndicate, Inc.
"IF YOU'RE A DOG, PUT YOUR GLOVE AWAY IN A DRY PLACE WHERE THE KIDS CAN'T FIND IT"

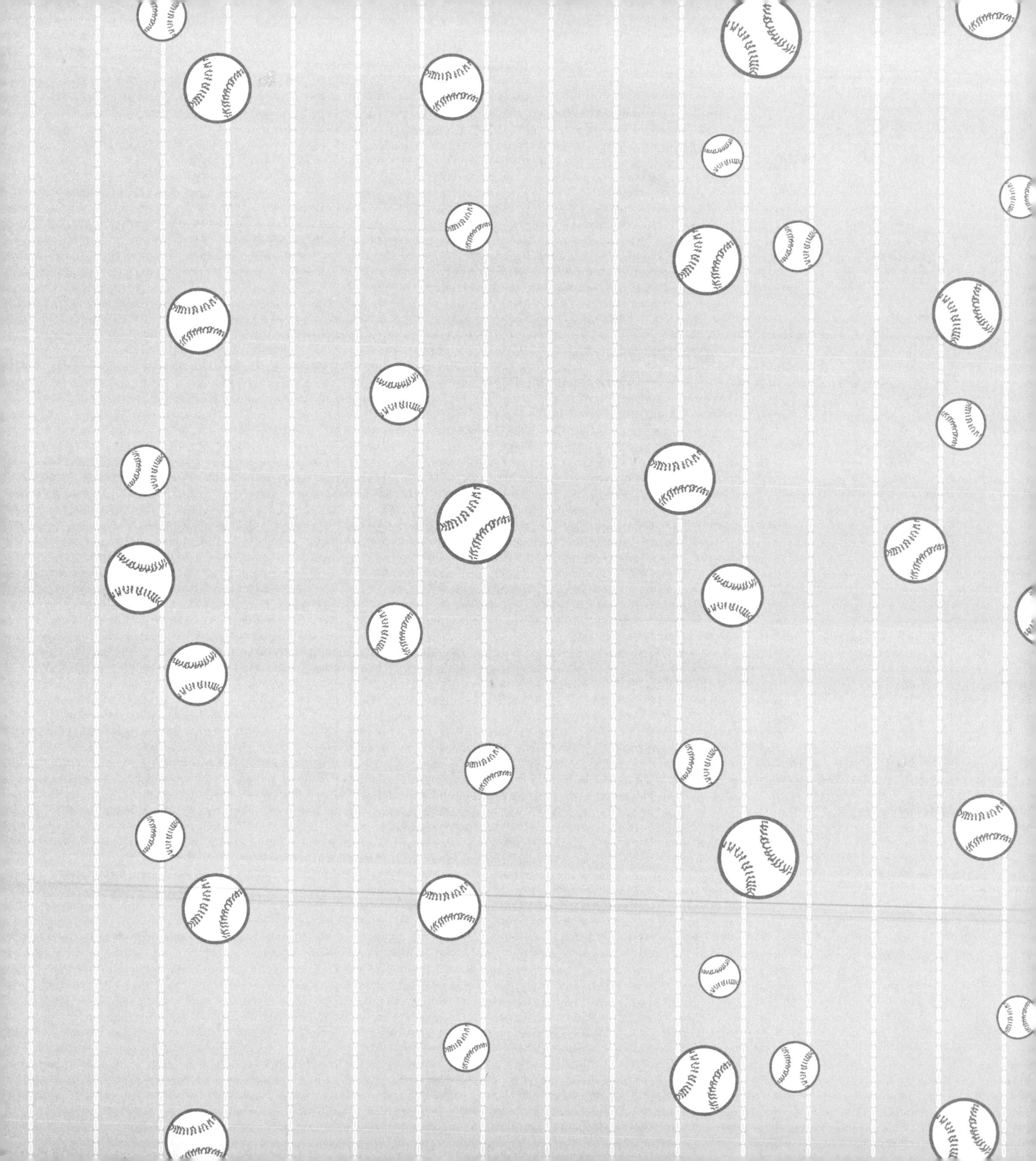

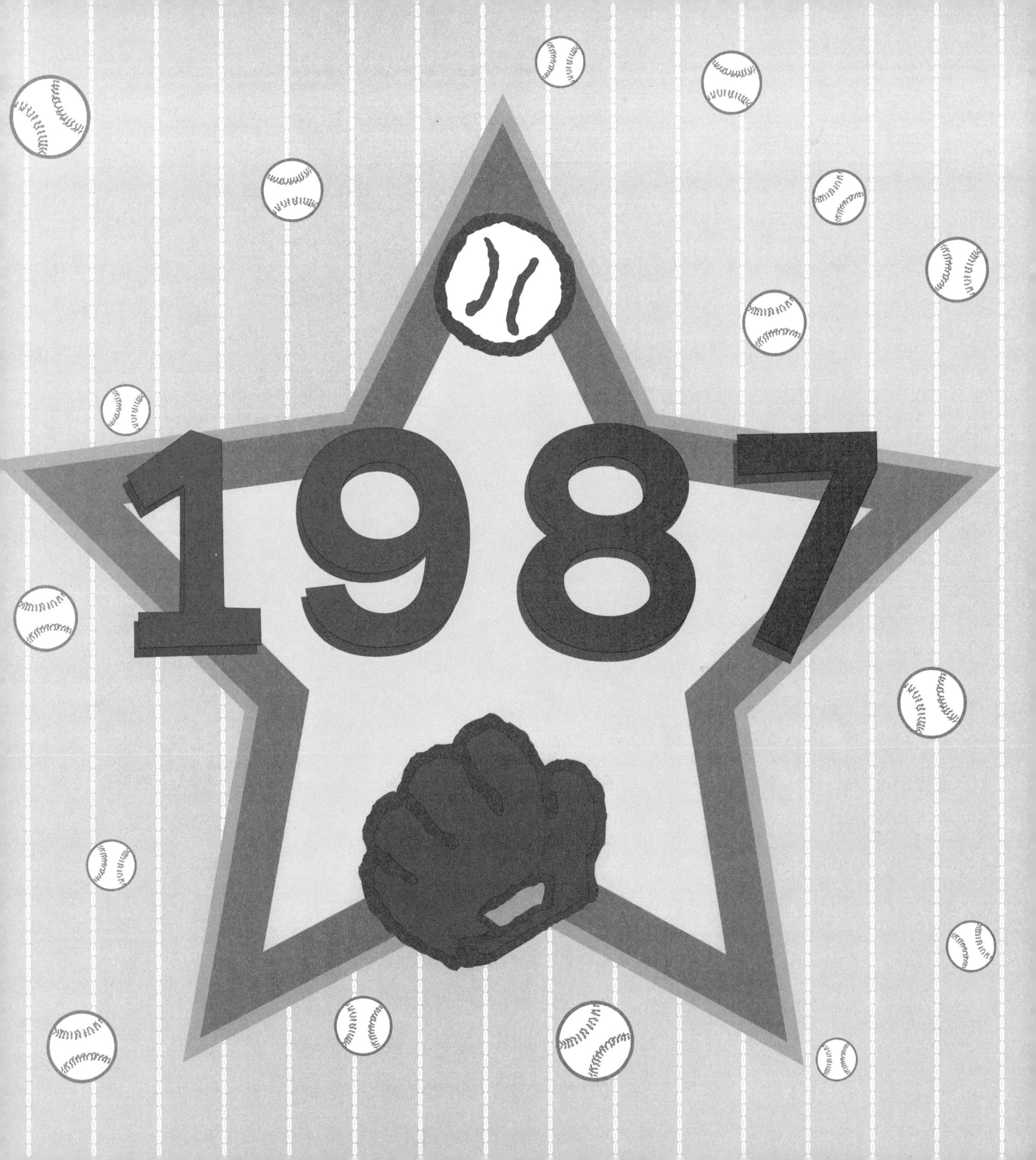
1987

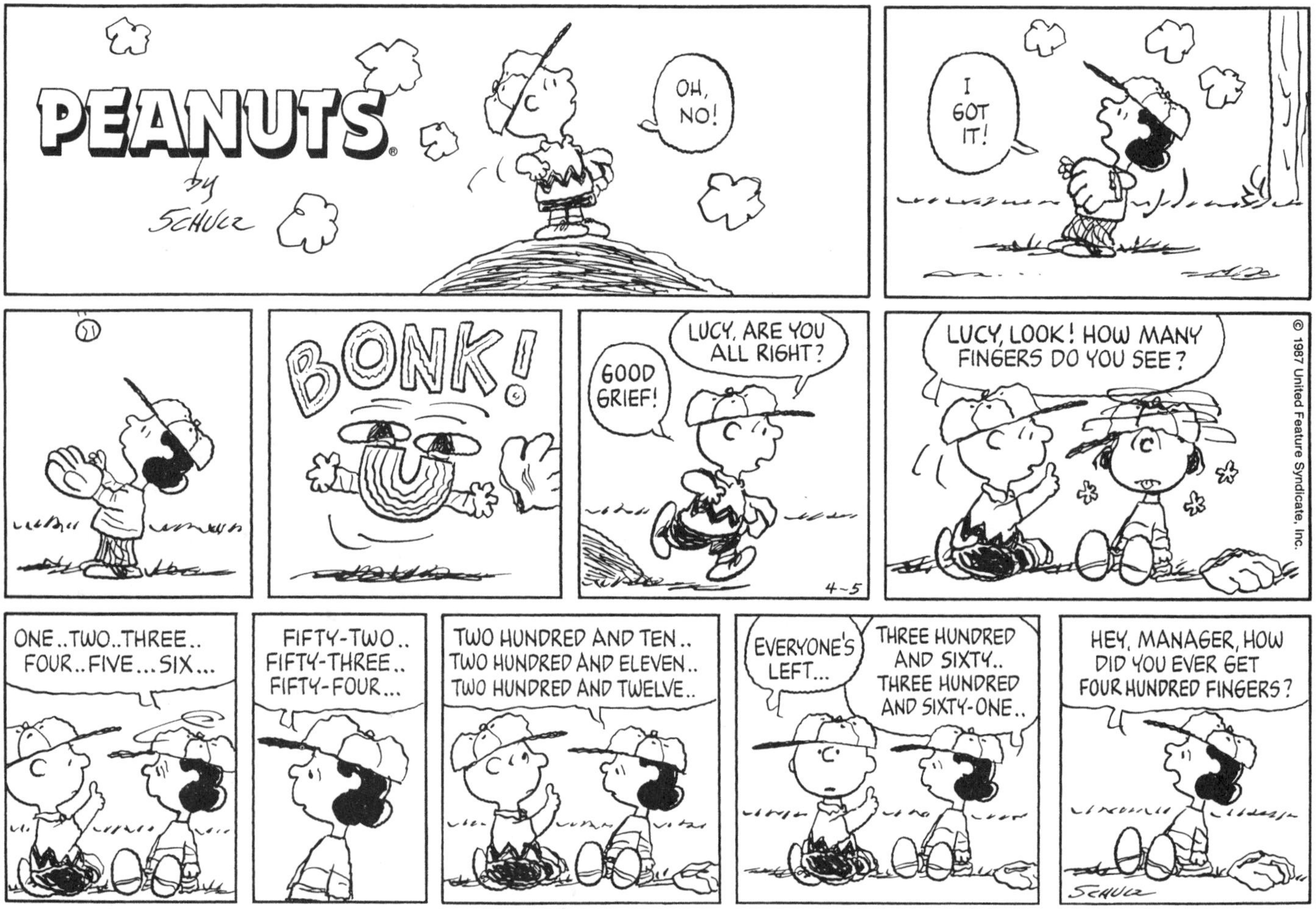
PEANUTS
by SCHULZ
OH, NO!
I GOT IT!
BONK!
GOOD GRIEF!
LUCY, ARE YOU ALL RIGHT?
4-5
LUCY, LOOK! HOW MANY FINGERS DO YOU SEE?
© 1987 United Feature Syndicate, Inc.
ONE..TWO..THREE.. FOUR..FIVE...SIX...
FIFTY-TWO.. FIFTY-THREE.. FIFTY-FOUR...
TWO HUNDRED AND TEN.. TWO HUNDRED AND ELEVEN.. TWO HUNDRED AND TWELVE..
EVERYONE'S LEFT...
THREE HUNDRED AND SIXTY.. THREE HUNDRED AND SIXTY-ONE..
HEY, MANAGER, HOW DID YOU EVER GET FOUR HUNDRED FINGERS?
SCHULZ

HEY, MANAGER..WE HAVE A PROBLEM...
I THINK THE FARMER WANTS US OFF THE FIELD..
FARMER? WHAT FARMER?!
© 1987 United Feature Syndicate, Inc.
5-2
SCHULZ

OH, NO..DON'T TELL ME IT'S GOING TO RAIN!
THE FARMERS NEED THE RAIN!
FARMERS? WHAT FARMERS?
OH, YES..I KEEP FORGETTING...
© 1987 United Feature Syndicate, Inc.
5-4
SCHULZ

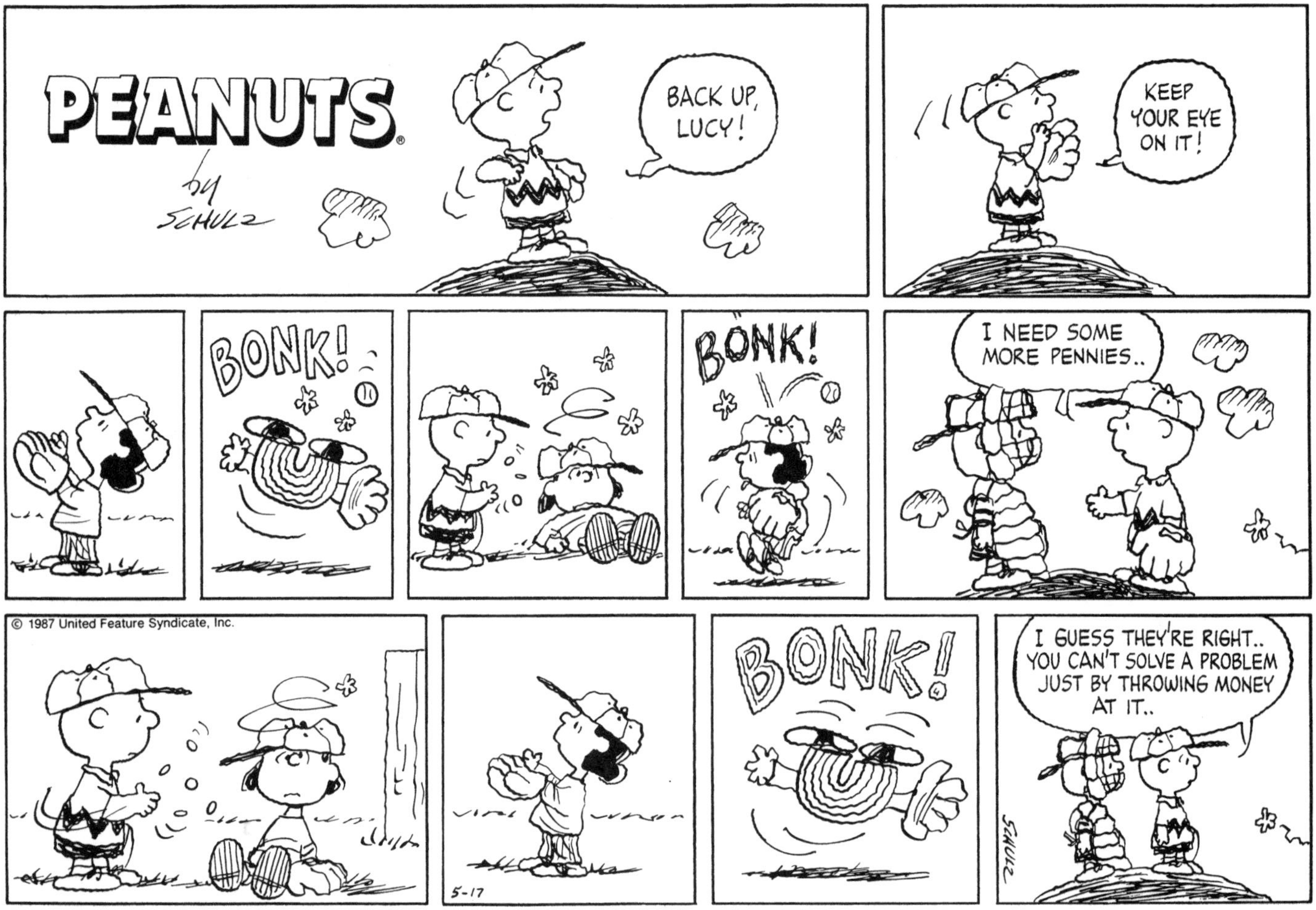
PEANUTS
by SCHULZ
BACK UP, LUCY!
KEEP YOUR EYE ON IT!
BONK!
BONK!
I NEED SOME MORE PENNIES..
© 1987 United Feature Syndicate, Inc.
5-17
BONK!
I GUESS THEY'RE RIGHT.. YOU CAN'T SOLVE A PROBLEM JUST BY THROWING MONEY AT IT..
SCHULZ

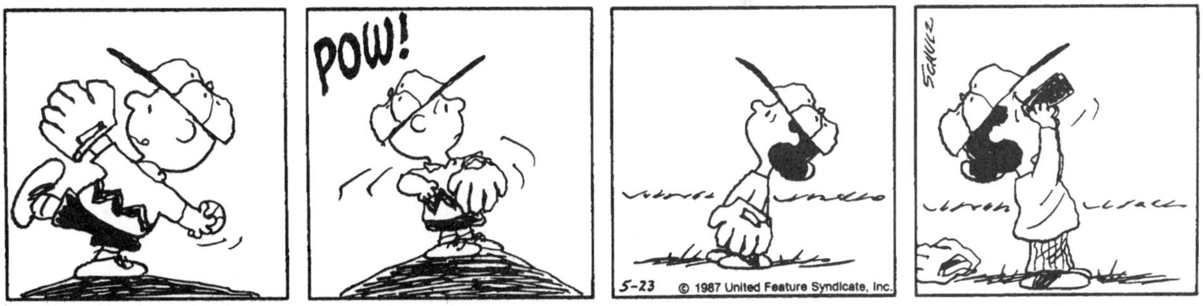
POW!
5-23
© 1987 United Feature Syndicate, Inc.
SCHULZ

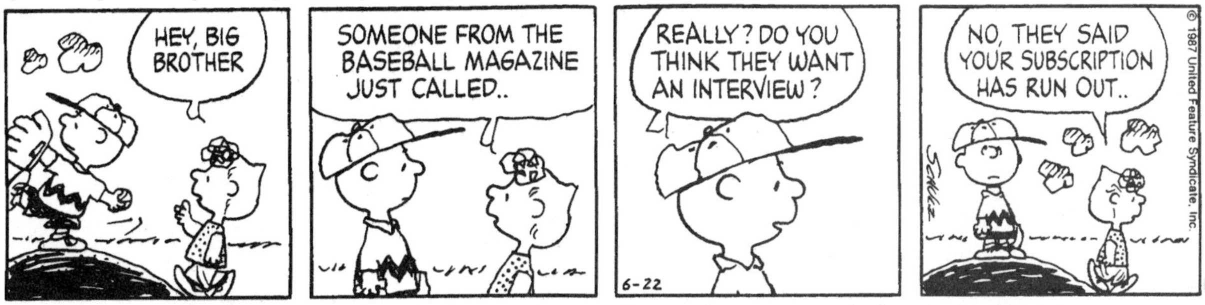
HEY, BIG BROTHER
SOMEONE FROM THE BASEBALL MAGAZINE JUST CALLED..
REALLY? DO YOU THINK THEY WANT AN INTERVIEW?
6-22
NO, THEY SAID YOUR SUBSCRIPTION HAS RUN OUT..
SCHULZ
© 1987 United Feature Syndicate, Inc.

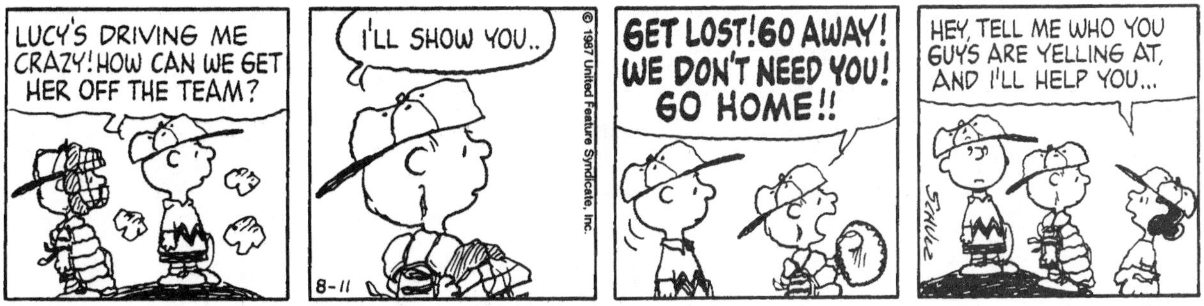
LUCY'S DRIVING ME CRAZY! HOW CAN WE GET HER OFF THE TEAM?
I'LL SHOW YOU..
8-11
© 1987 United Feature Syndicate, Inc.
GET LOST! GO AWAY! WE DON'T NEED YOU! GO HOME!!
HEY, TELL ME WHO YOU GUYS ARE YELLING AT, AND I'LL HELP YOU...
SCHULZ

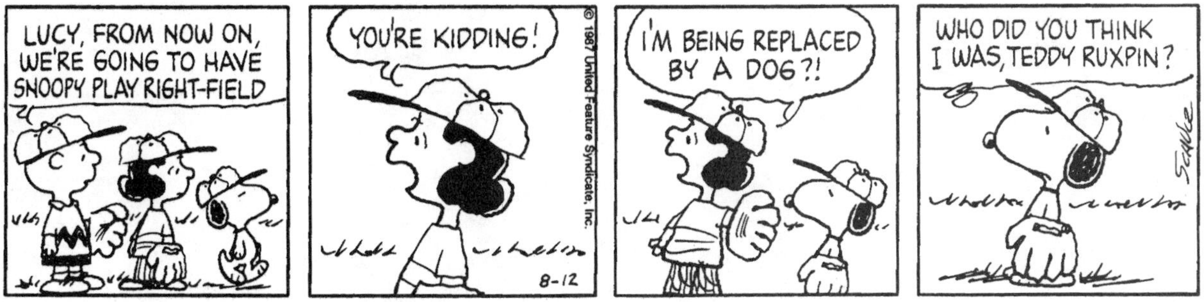
LUCY, FROM NOW ON, WE'RE GOING TO HAVE SNOOPY PLAY RIGHT-FIELD
YOU'RE KIDDING!
8-12
© 1987 United Feature Syndicate, Inc.
I'M BEING REPLACED BY A DOG?!
WHO DID YOU THINK I WAS, TEDDY RUXPIN?
SCHULZ

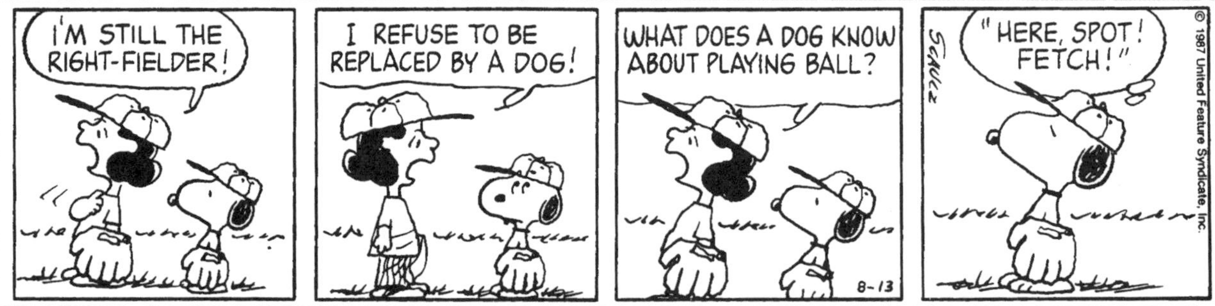
I'M STILL THE RIGHT-FIELDER!
I REFUSE TO BE REPLACED BY A DOG!
WHAT DOES A DOG KNOW ABOUT PLAYING BALL?
"HERE, SPOT! FETCH!"
© 1987 United Feature Syndicate, Inc.

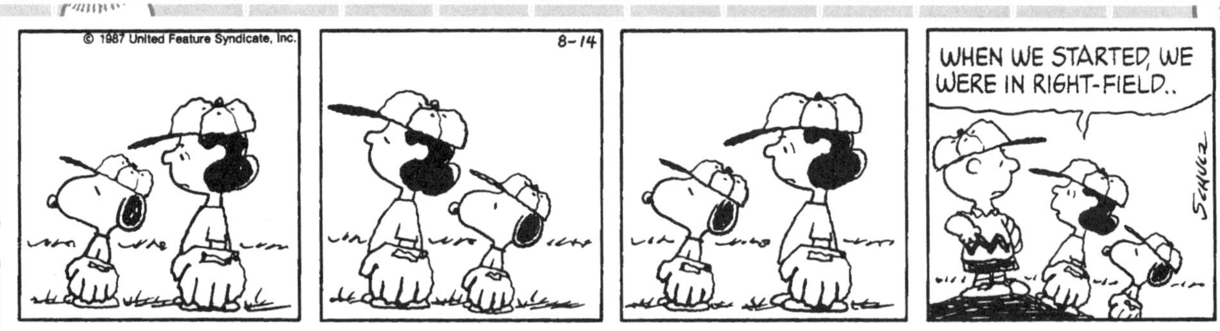
© 1987 United Feature Syndicate, Inc.
WHEN WE STARTED, WE WERE IN RIGHT-FIELD..

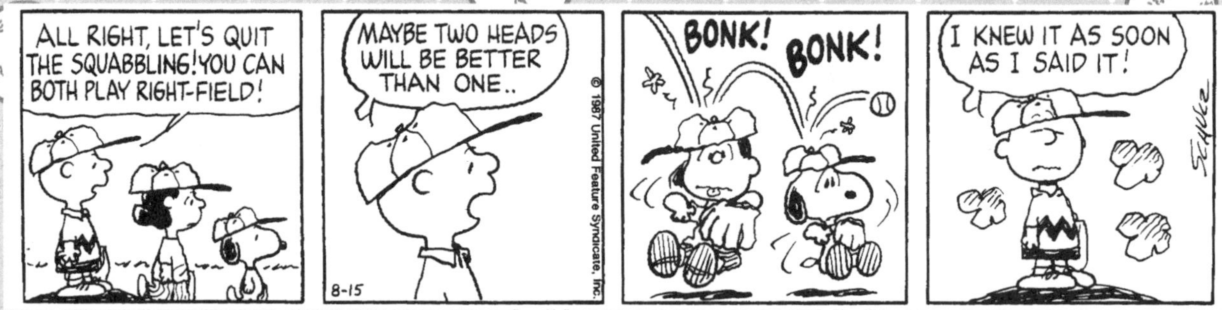
ALL RIGHT, LET'S QUIT THE SQUABBLING! YOU CAN BOTH PLAY RIGHT-FIELD!
MAYBE TWO HEADS WILL BE BETTER THAN ONE..
© 1987 United Feature Syndicate, Inc.
BONK!
BONK!
I KNEW IT AS SOON AS I SAID IT!

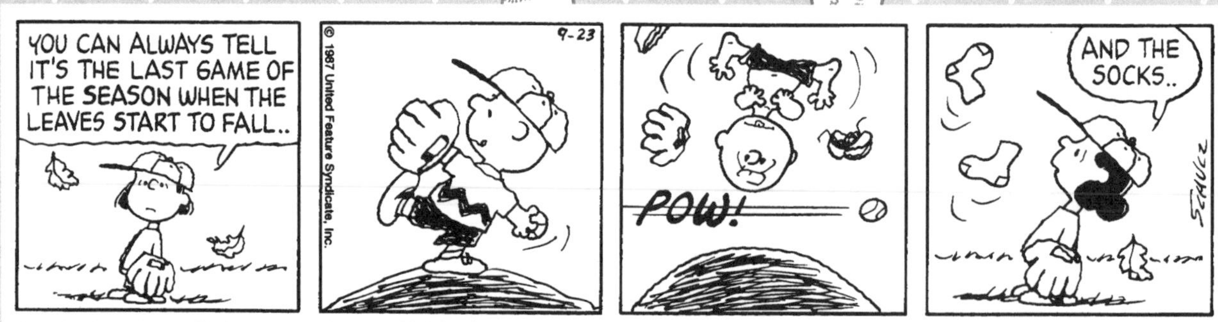
YOU CAN ALWAYS TELL IT'S THE LAST GAME OF THE SEASON WHEN THE LEAVES START TO FALL..
© 1987 United Feature Syndicate, Inc.
POW!
AND THE SOCKS..

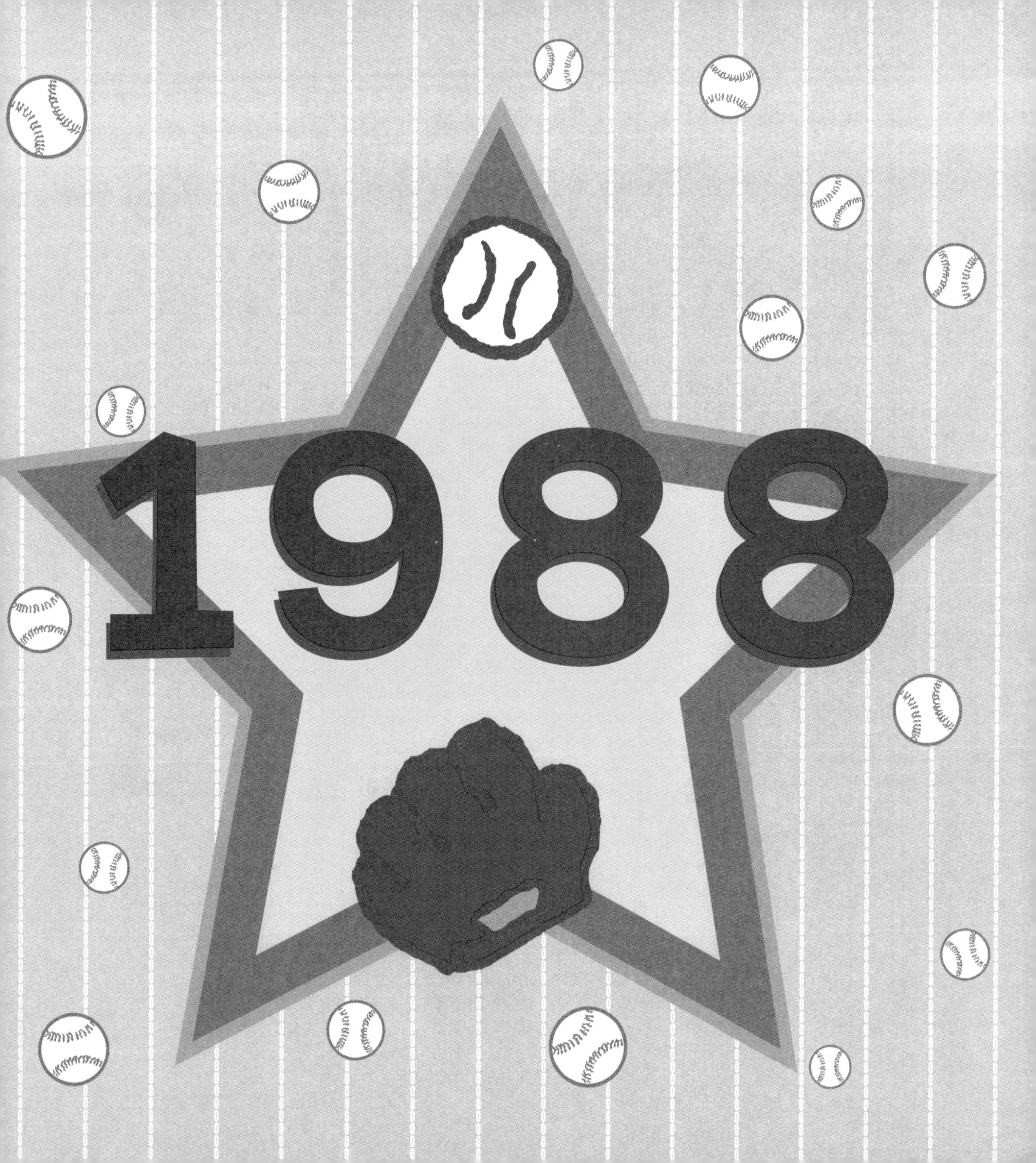
1988

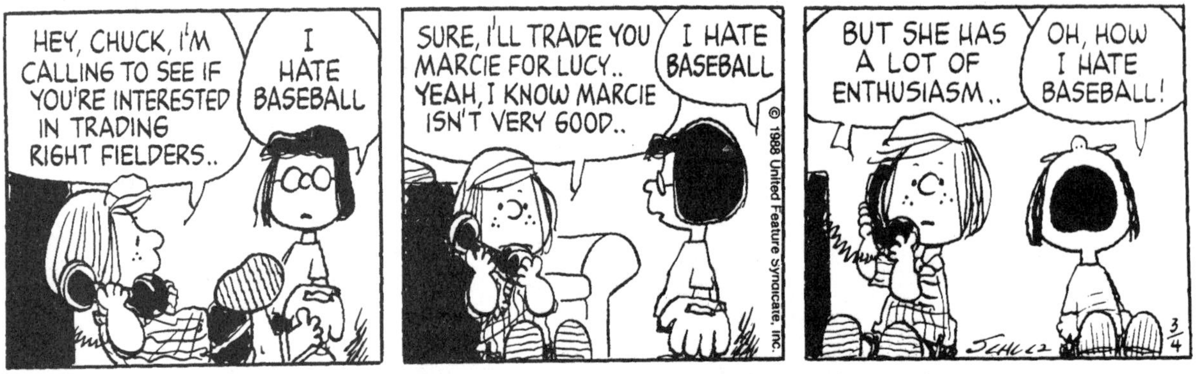
HEY, CHUCK, I'M CALLING TO SEE IF YOU'RE INTERESTED IN TRADING RIGHT FIELDERS..
I HATE BASEBALL
SURE, I'LL TRADE YOU MARCIE FOR LUCY.. YEAH, I KNOW MARCIE ISN'T VERY GOOD..
I HATE BASEBALL
© 1988 United Feature Syndicate, Inc.
BUT SHE HAS A LOT OF ENTHUSIASM..
OH, HOW I HATE BASEBALL!
SCHULZ
3/4

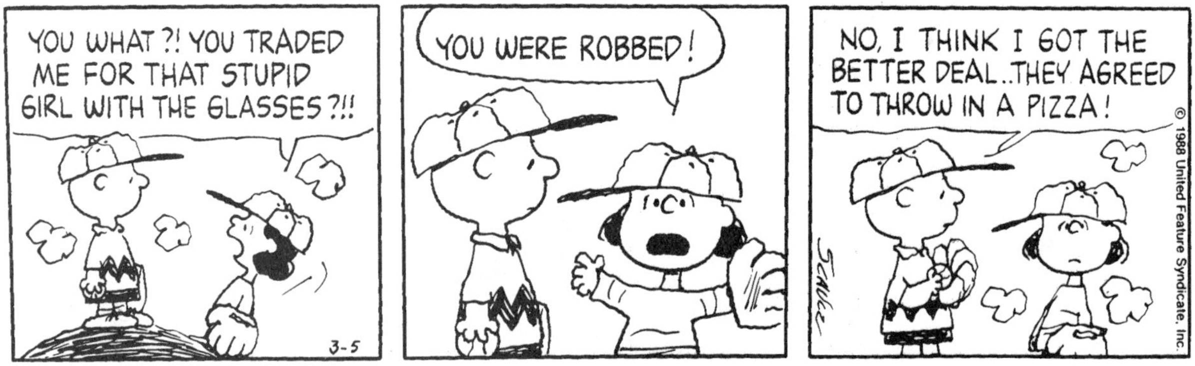
YOU WHAT?! YOU TRADED ME FOR THAT STUPID GIRL WITH THE GLASSES?!!
3-5
YOU WERE ROBBED!
NO, I THINK I GOT THE BETTER DEAL..THEY AGREED TO THROW IN A PIZZA!
SCHULZ
© 1988 United Feature Syndicate, Inc.

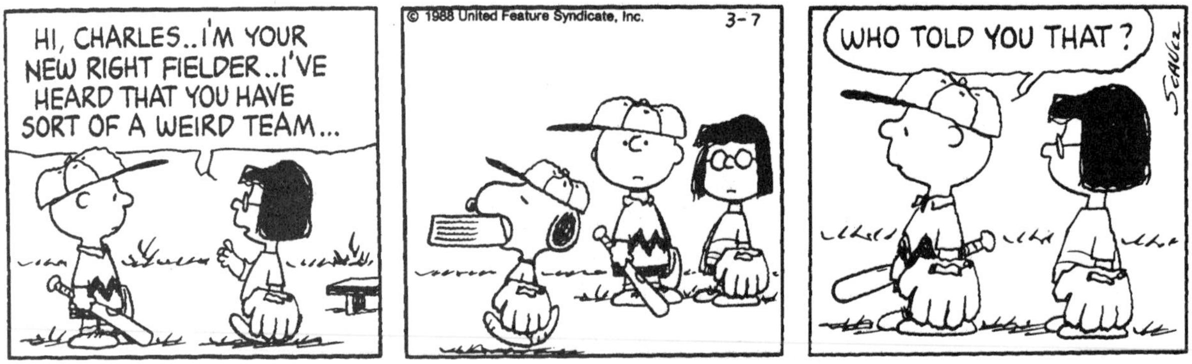
HI, CHARLES..I'M YOUR NEW RIGHT FIELDER..I'VE HEARD THAT YOU HAVE SORT OF A WEIRD TEAM...
© 1988 United Feature Syndicate, Inc.
3-7
WHO TOLD YOU THAT?
SCHULZ

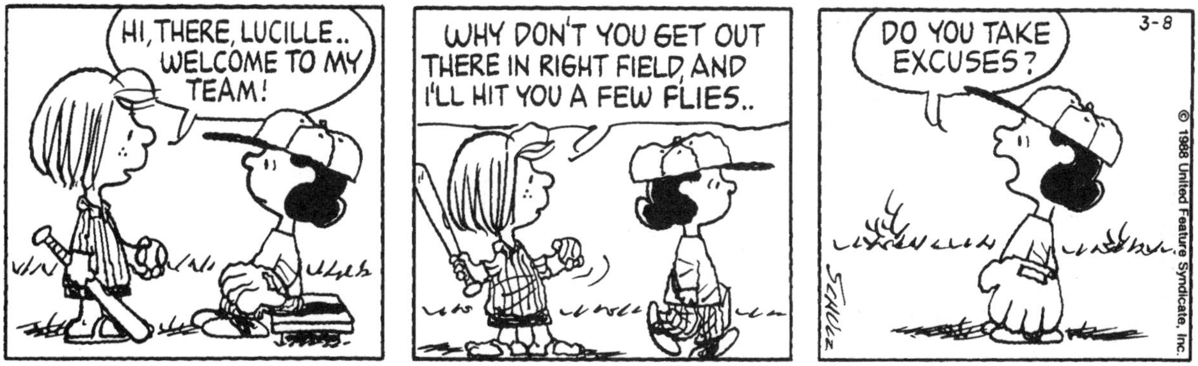
HI, THERE, LUCILLE.. WELCOME TO MY TEAM!
WHY DON'T YOU GET OUT THERE IN RIGHT FIELD, AND I'LL HIT YOU A FEW FLIES..
3-8
DO YOU TAKE EXCUSES?
© 1988 United Feature Syndicate, Inc.
SCHULZ

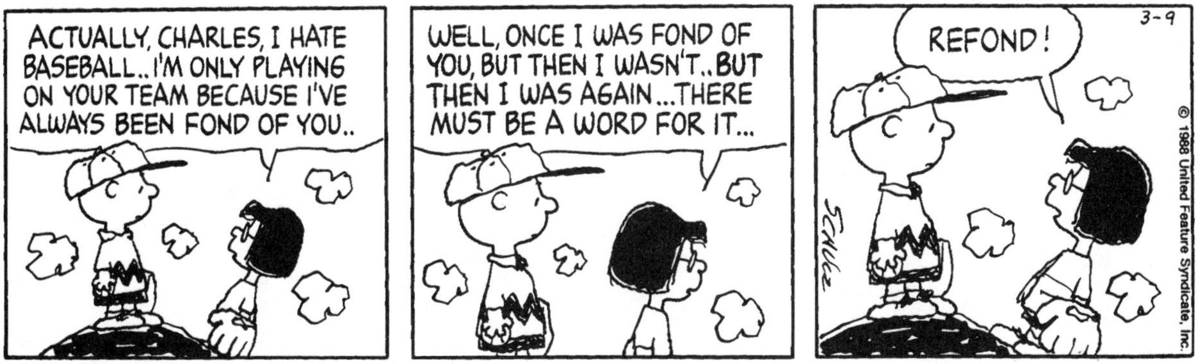
ACTUALLY, CHARLES, I HATE BASEBALL.. I'M ONLY PLAYING ON YOUR TEAM BECAUSE I'VE ALWAYS BEEN FOND OF YOU..
WELL, ONCE I WAS FOND OF YOU, BUT THEN I WASN'T.. BUT THEN I WAS AGAIN...THERE MUST BE A WORD FOR IT...
3-9
REFOND!
© 1988 United Feature Syndicate, Inc.
SCHULZ

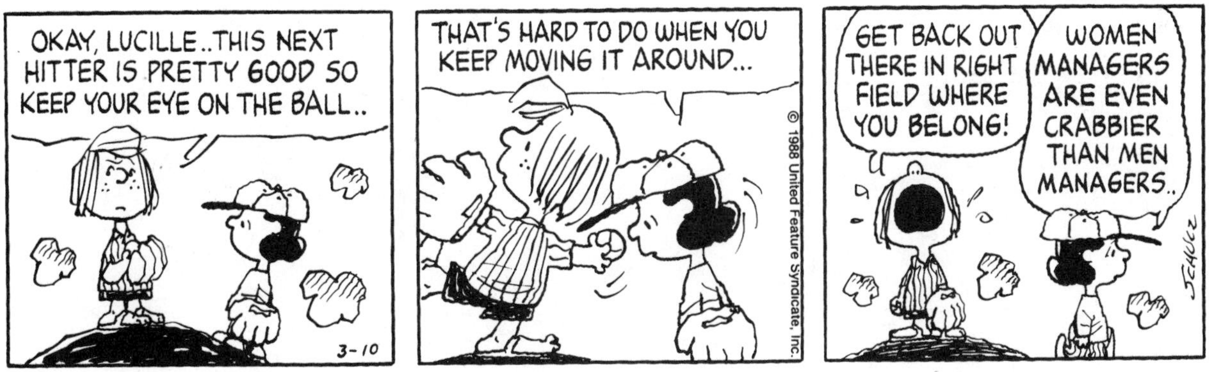
OKAY, LUCILLE..THIS NEXT HITTER IS PRETTY GOOD SO KEEP YOUR EYE ON THE BALL..
3-10
THAT'S HARD TO DO WHEN YOU KEEP MOVING IT AROUND...
© 1988 United Feature Syndicate, Inc.
GET BACK OUT THERE IN RIGHT FIELD WHERE YOU BELONG!
WOMEN MANAGERS ARE EVEN CRABBIER THAN MEN MANAGERS..
SCHULZ

SORRY I MISSED THAT ONE, MANAGER..MAYBE MY GLOVE ISN'T BIG ENOUGH...
BIG ENOUGH?! HA! YOU KNOW WHAT YOU NEED?
© 1988 United Feature Syndicate, Inc.
3-11
SCHULZ

MARCIE, YOU SHOULD BE OUT IN RIGHT FIELD..
I'M HAPPIER STANDING HERE WITH YOU, CHARLES...
BUT WHAT IF SOMEONE HITS A BALL TO RIGHT FIELD?
WHO CARES? I'M HAPPY JUST STANDING HERE NEXT TO YOU, CHARLES
3-12
WE DON'T WIN ANY GAMES, BUT I HAVE HAPPY PLAYERS..
SCHULZ
© 1988 United Feature Syndicate, Inc.

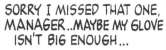

I MADE A MISTAKE, CHUCK.. I ADMIT IT... LUCY IS THE WORST PLAYER I'VE EVER SEEN! YOU GOTTA TAKE HER BACK..
I KNOW YOU TRADED HER TO ME FOR MARCIE AND A PIZZA, BUT NOW I WANNA CALL THE DEAL OFF..WADDYA SAY, CHUCK?
3-14
© 1988 United Feature Syndicate, Inc.
I ALREADY ATE THE PIZZA..
SCHULZ

4-9
© 1988 United Feature Syndicate, Inc.
SORRY, BUT IT'S HARD TO HIT 'EM RIGHT TO YOU..
SCHULZ

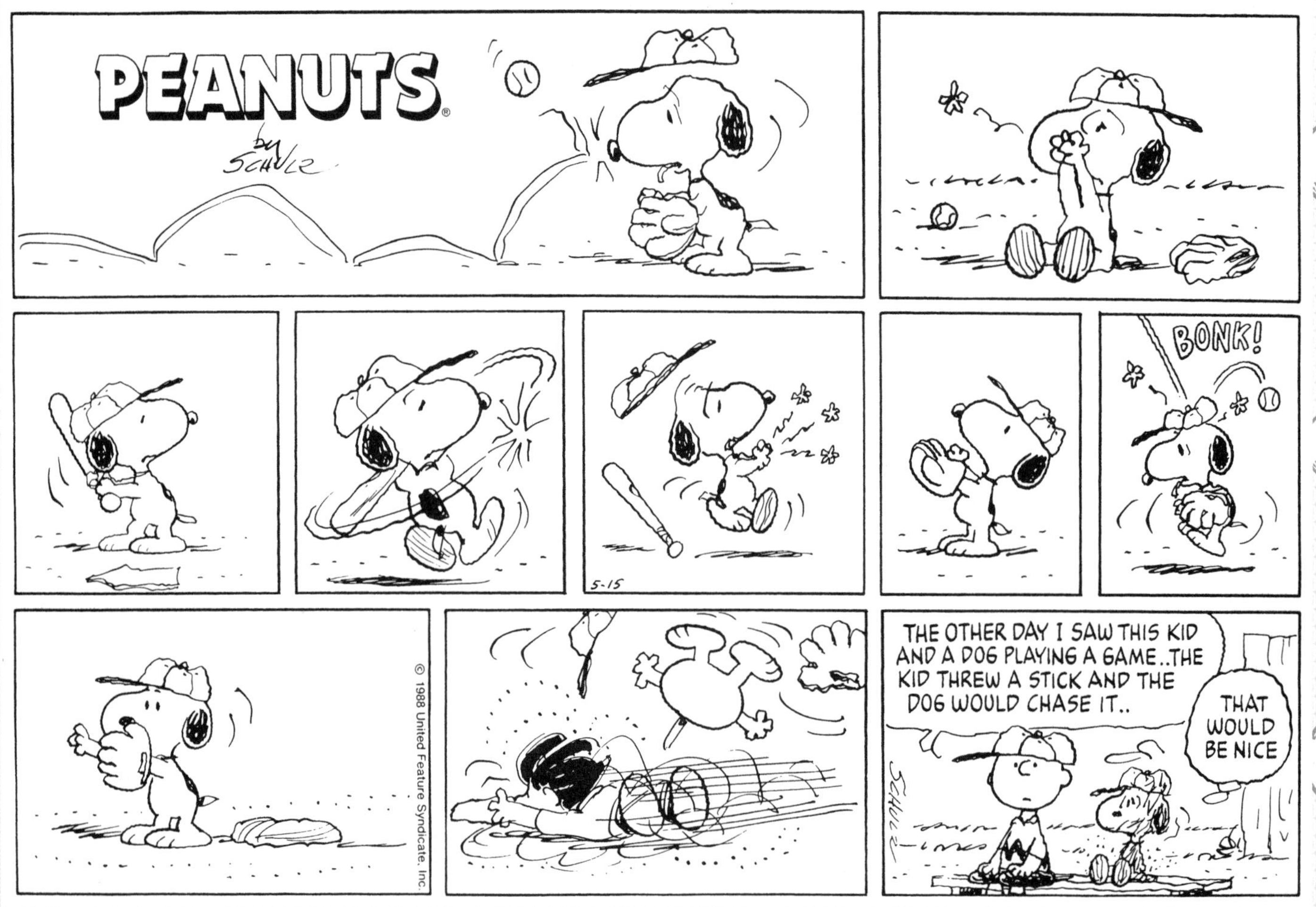
PEANUTS
by SCHULZ
BONK!
5-15
© 1988 United Feature Syndicate, Inc.
THE OTHER DAY I SAW THIS KID AND A DOG PLAYING A GAME..THE KID THREW A STICK AND THE DOG WOULD CHASE IT..
THAT WOULD BE NICE
SCHULZ

HEY, PITCHER! IT HURTS MY NECK WATCHING THE OTHER TEAM HIT HOME RUNS OVER MY HEAD!
MAYBE I'LL JUST FACE THE OTHER WAY, AND THEN I WON'T HAVE TO TURN AROUND EVERY TIME...YES, THIS IS GOING TO BE MUCH BETTER..
6-4
IT'S A NICE FEELING KNOWING THAT YOUR PLAYERS ARE COMFORTABLE
SCHULZ
© 1988 United Feature Syndicate, Inc.

© 1988 United Feature Syndicate, Inc.
I GOT IT! I GOT IT!
WHAT ARE YOU YELLING ABOUT? I HAVEN'T EVEN PITCHED YET!
DON'T HIT IT TO ME! DON'T HIT IT TO ME!
SCHULZ
6-25

PSST, MANAGER..DON'T LOOK NOW, BUT I'M PULLING THE OL' HIDDEN BAT PLAY..
I HID THE OTHER TEAM'S BAT SO THEY CAN'T GET ANY HITS!
8-15
NO WONDER I STRUCK THAT LAST GUY OUT..
SCHULZ
© 1988 United Feature Syndicate, Inc.

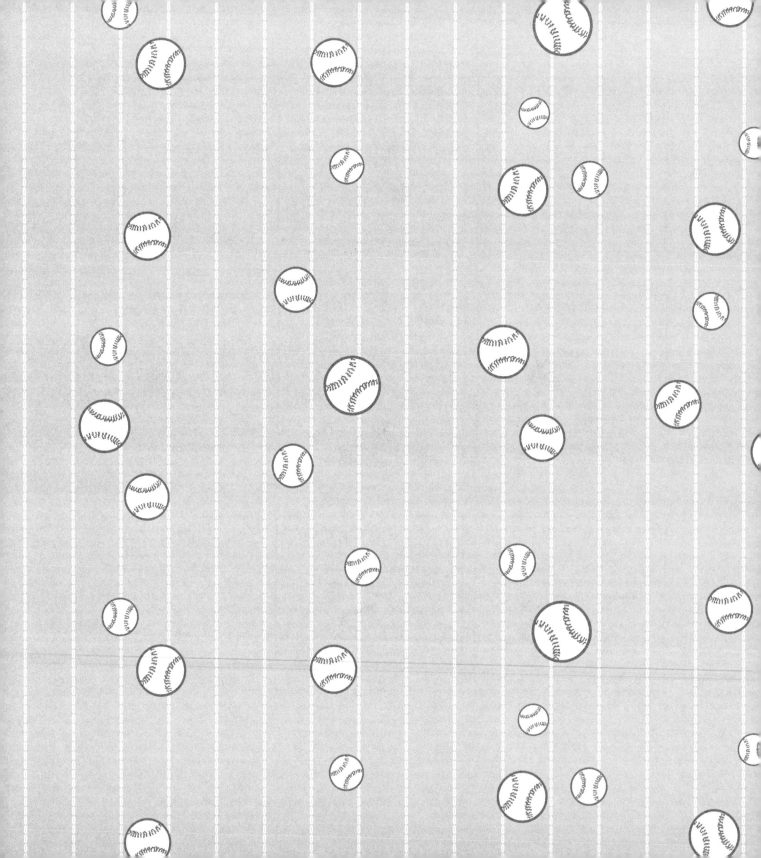

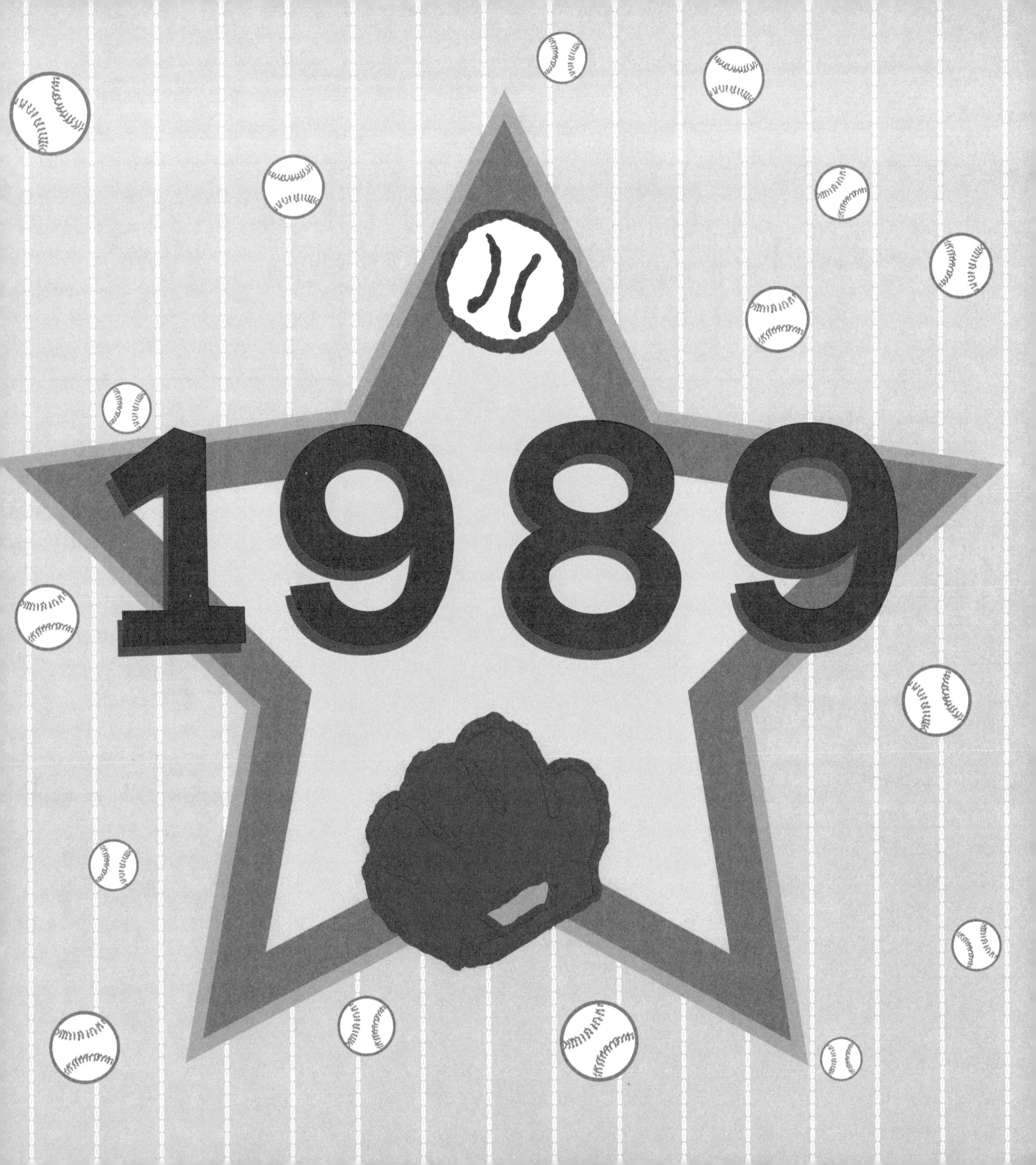
1989

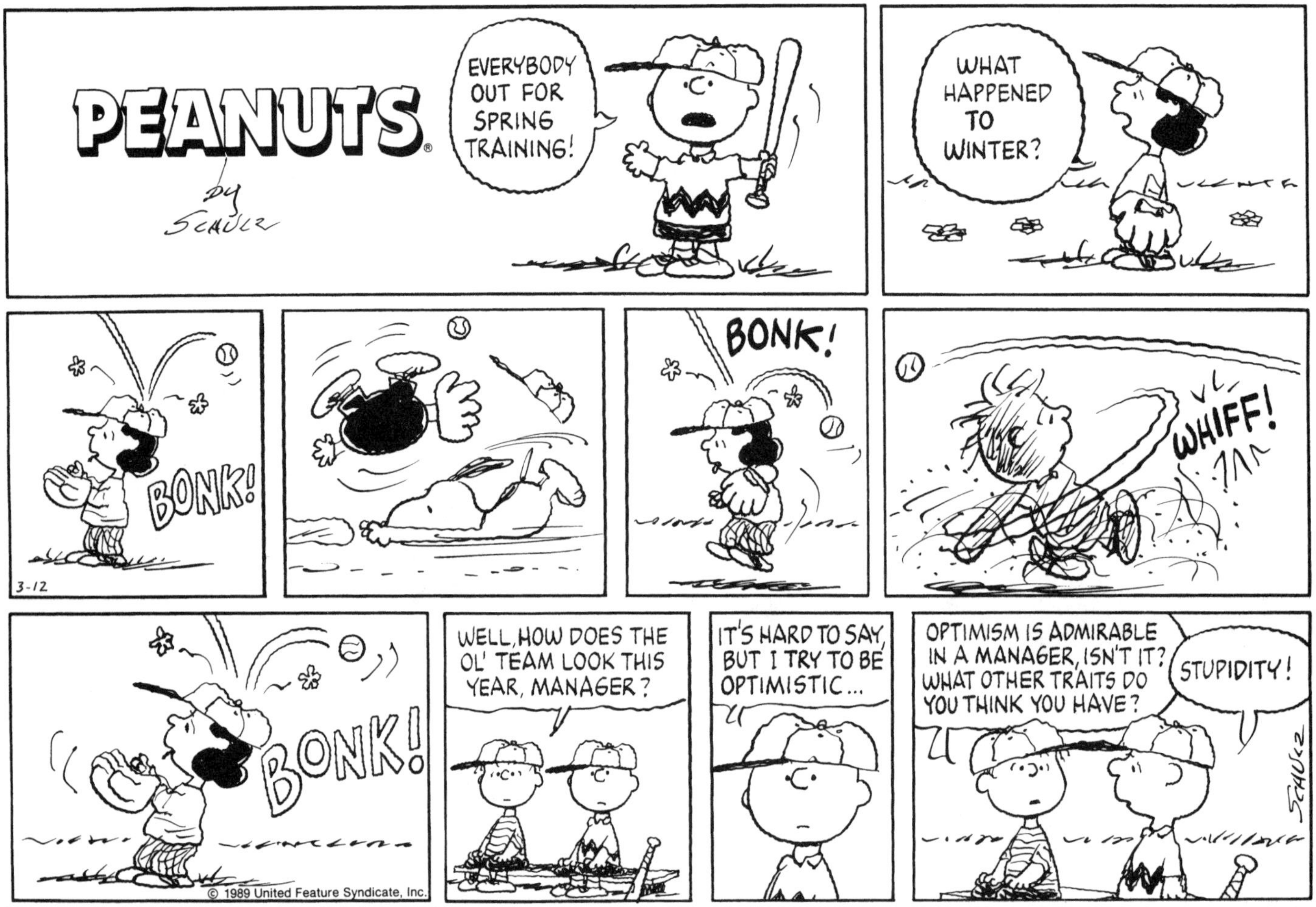
PEANUTS
by Schulz
EVERYBODY OUT FOR SPRING TRAINING!
WHAT HAPPENED TO WINTER?
BONK!
BONK!
WHIFF!
BONK!
WELL, HOW DOES THE OL' TEAM LOOK THIS YEAR, MANAGER?
IT'S HARD TO SAY, BUT I TRY TO BE OPTIMISTIC...
OPTIMISM IS ADMIRABLE IN A MANAGER, ISN'T IT? WHAT OTHER TRAITS DO YOU THINK YOU HAVE?
STUPIDITY!
© 1989 United Feature Syndicate, Inc.

REMEMBER, WE'RE OUT HERE TO HAVE FUN..
© 1989 United Feature Syndicate, Inc.
LET'S TRY TO MAKE IT A NICE FRIENDLY GAME...
4-18
GOOD! I'LL HUG THE CATCHER!
SCHULZ

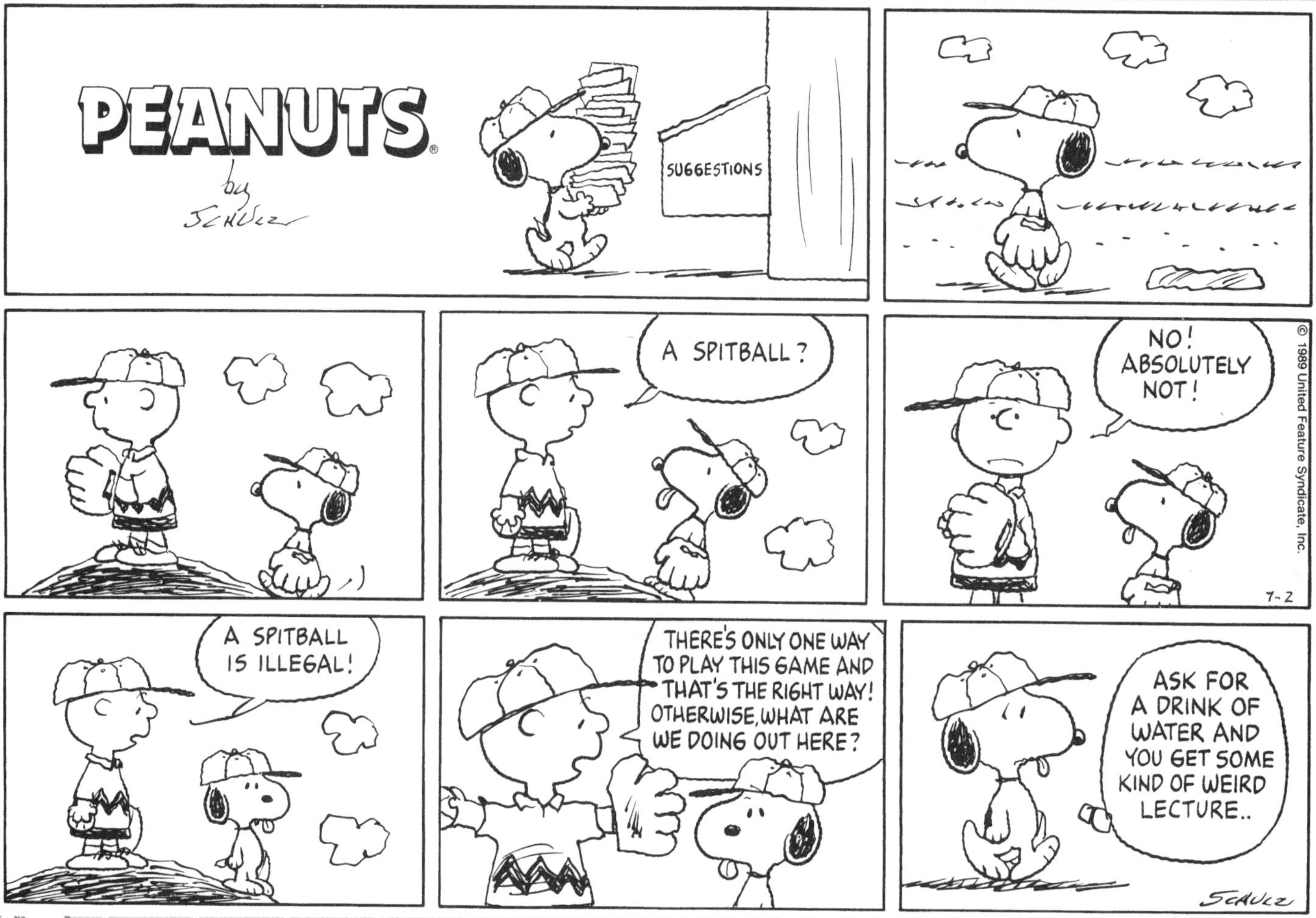
PEANUTS
by SCHULZ
SUGGESTIONS
A SPITBALL ?
NO! ABSOLUTELY NOT!
© 1989 United Feature Syndicate, Inc.
7-2
A SPITBALL IS ILLEGAL!
THERE'S ONLY ONE WAY TO PLAY THIS GAME AND THAT'S THE RIGHT WAY! OTHERWISE, WHAT ARE WE DOING OUT HERE?
ASK FOR A DRINK OF WATER AND YOU GET SOME KIND OF WEIRD LECTURE..
SCHULZ

STRIKE THREE!

Z

7-14

JUST WHAT I NEED.. A PLAYER WHO STRIKES OUT WHILE HE'S ASLEEP!

© 1989 United Feature Syndicate, Inc.

HE'D BE EVEN MADDER IF HE KNEW I DREAMED I WAS HITTING A HOME RUN..

IT'S GOING TO COST ME THIRTY DOLLARS, BUT I'M GOING TO GET JOE DiMAGGIO'S AUTOGRAPH!

HOW MUCH FOR A TED WILLIAMS?

TWENTY-FIVE DOLLARS

STEVE GARVEY IS NINE AND MAURY WILLS IS FIVE..

ISN'T JOE SHLABOTNIK YOUR FAVORITE PLAYER, CHARLIE BROWN?

I GOT HIS AUTOGRAPH, AND HE GAVE ME A DOLLAR!

© 1989 United Feature Syndicate, Inc.

8-14

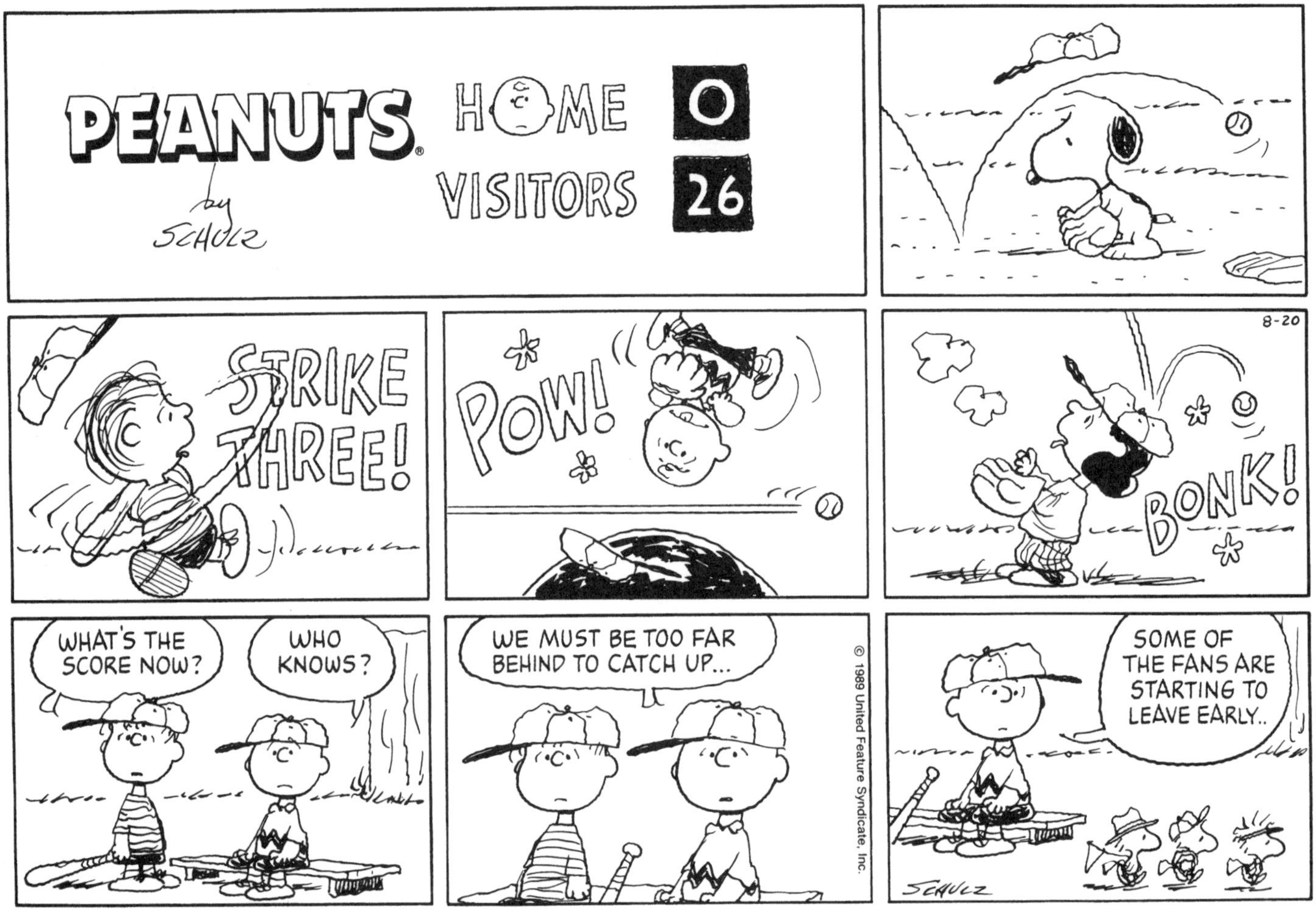
PEANUTS
by SCHULZ
HOME 0
VISITORS 26
STRIKE THREE!
POW!
8-20
BONK!
WHAT'S THE SCORE NOW?
WHO KNOWS?
WE MUST BE TOO FAR BEHIND TO CATCH UP...
© 1989 United Feature Syndicate, Inc.
SOME OF THE FANS ARE STARTING TO LEAVE EARLY..
SCHULZ

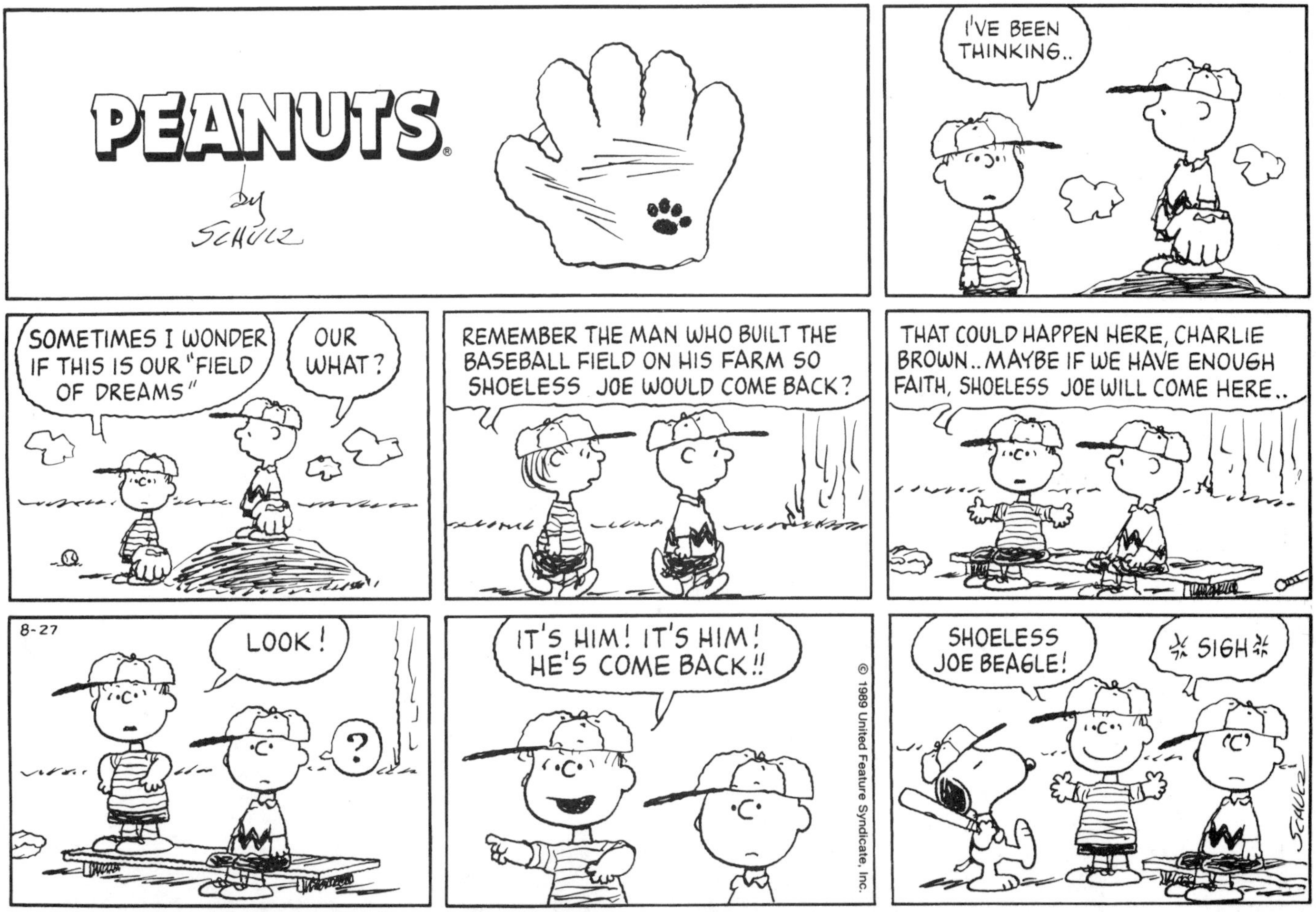
PEANUTS
by SCHULZ
I'VE BEEN THINKING..
SOMETIMES I WONDER IF THIS IS OUR "FIELD OF DREAMS"
OUR WHAT?
REMEMBER THE MAN WHO BUILT THE BASEBALL FIELD ON HIS FARM SO SHOELESS JOE WOULD COME BACK?
THAT COULD HAPPEN HERE, CHARLIE BROWN.. MAYBE IF WE HAVE ENOUGH FAITH, SHOELESS JOE WILL COME HERE..
8-27
LOOK!
?
IT'S HIM! IT'S HIM! HE'S COME BACK!!
© 1989 United Feature Syndicate, Inc.
SHOELESS JOE BEAGLE!
SIGH
SCHULZ

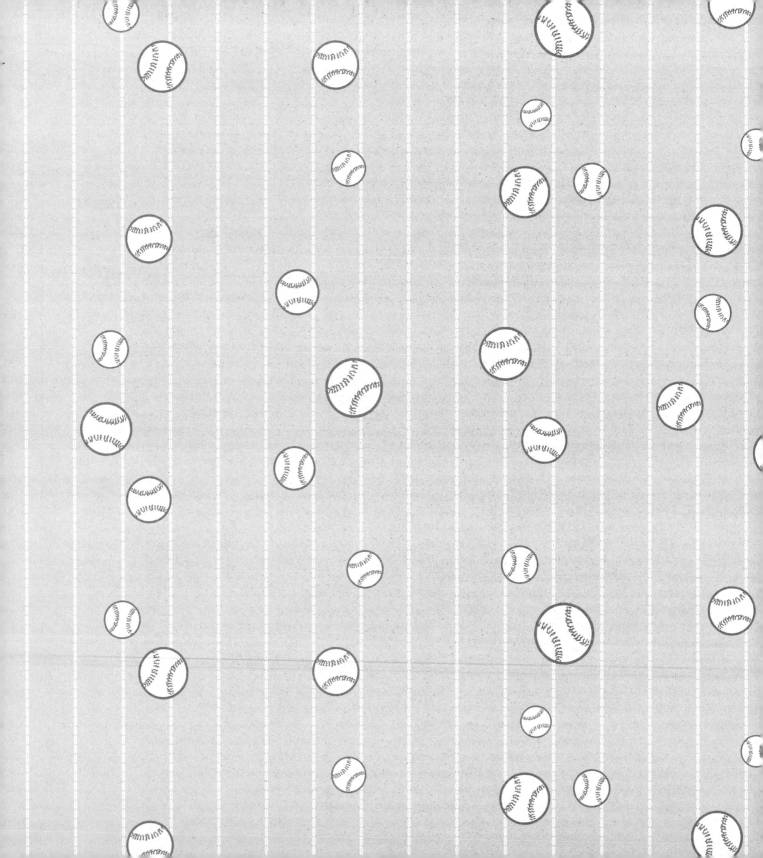

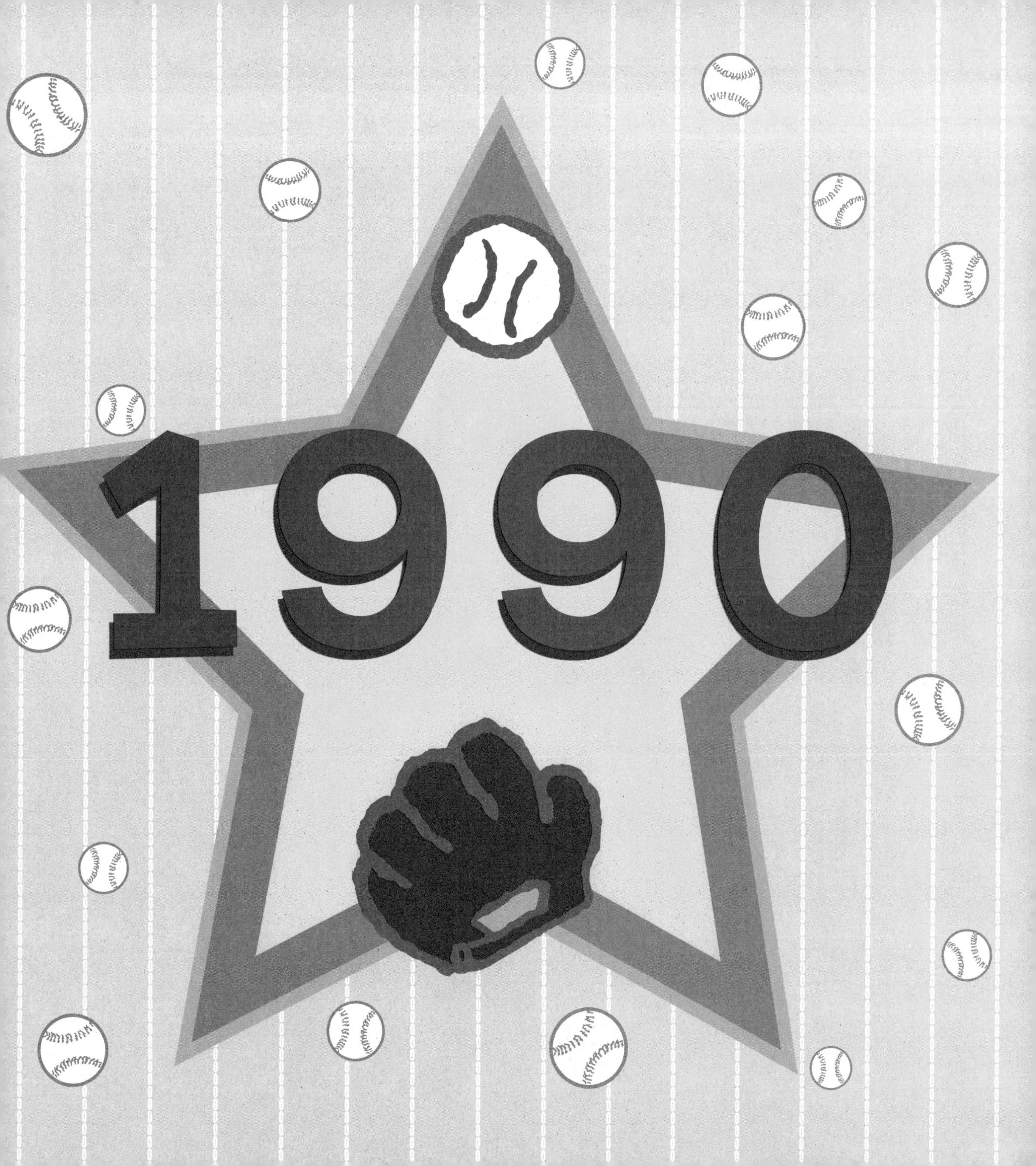
1990

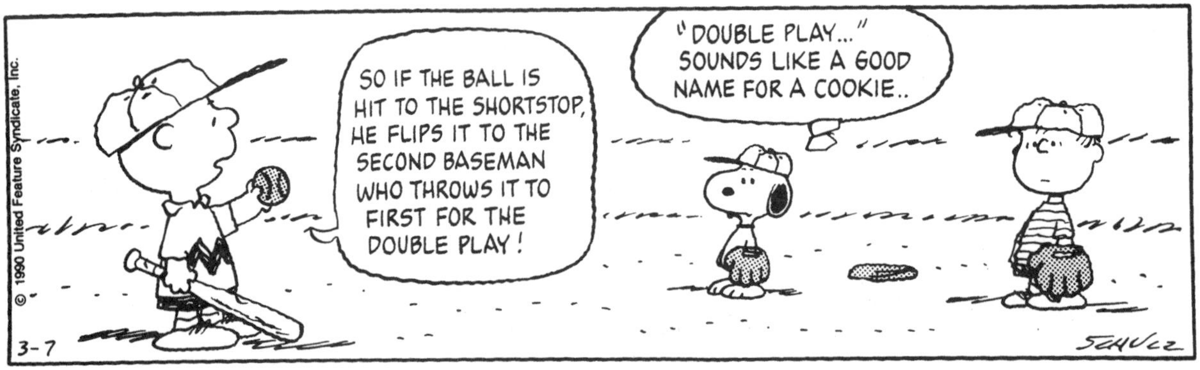
© 1990 United Feature Syndicate, Inc.
SO IF THE BALL IS HIT TO THE SHORTSTOP, HE FLIPS IT TO THE SECOND BASEMAN WHO THROWS IT TO FIRST FOR THE DOUBLE PLAY!
"DOUBLE PLAY..." SOUNDS LIKE A GOOD NAME FOR A COOKIE..
3-7
SCHULZ

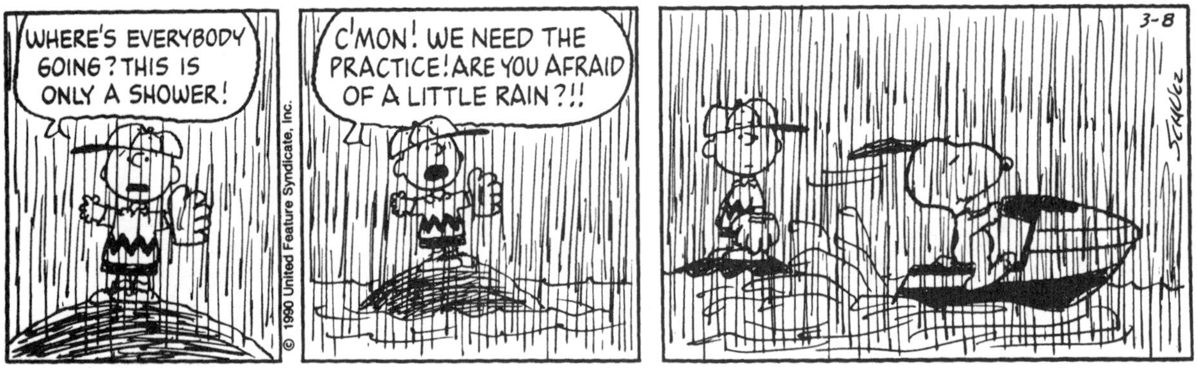
WHERE'S EVERYBODY GOING? THIS IS ONLY A SHOWER!
C'MON! WE NEED THE PRACTICE! ARE YOU AFRAID OF A LITTLE RAIN?!!
© 1990 United Feature Syndicate, Inc.
3-8
SCHULZ

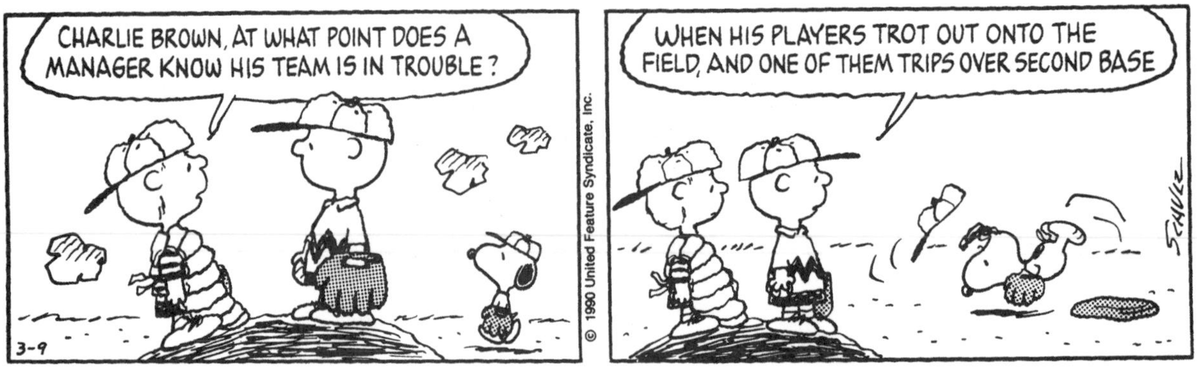
CHARLIE BROWN, AT WHAT POINT DOES A MANAGER KNOW HIS TEAM IS IN TROUBLE?
WHEN HIS PLAYERS TROT OUT ONTO THE FIELD, AND ONE OF THEM TRIPS OVER SECOND BASE
3-9
© 1990 United Feature Syndicate, Inc.
SCHULZ

© 1990 United Feature Syndicate, Inc.
WHAT KIND OF A SHORTSTOP ARE YOU?! THAT BALL WENT RIGHT BY YOU, AND YOU DIDN'T EVEN MOVE!
3-29
YOU DIDN'T SAY, "FETCH"
SCHULZ

© 1990 United Feature Syndicate, Inc.
JUST REMEMBER, THE BETTER THE PLAYER, THE MORE IMPORTANT THE MENTAL GAME BECOMES..
7-10
GOOD! THAT MEANS I DON'T HAVE TO THINK AT ALL!
SCHULZ

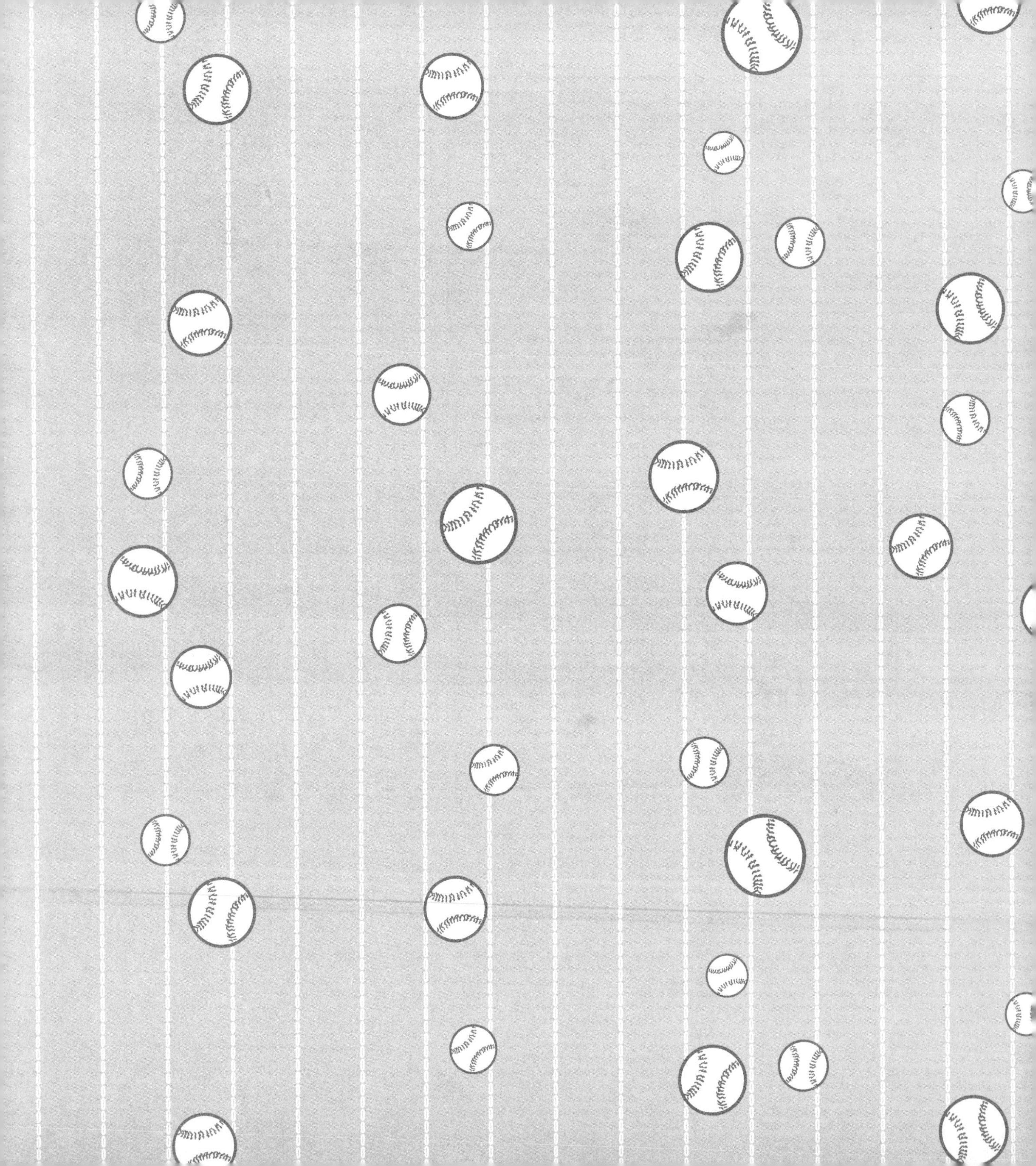

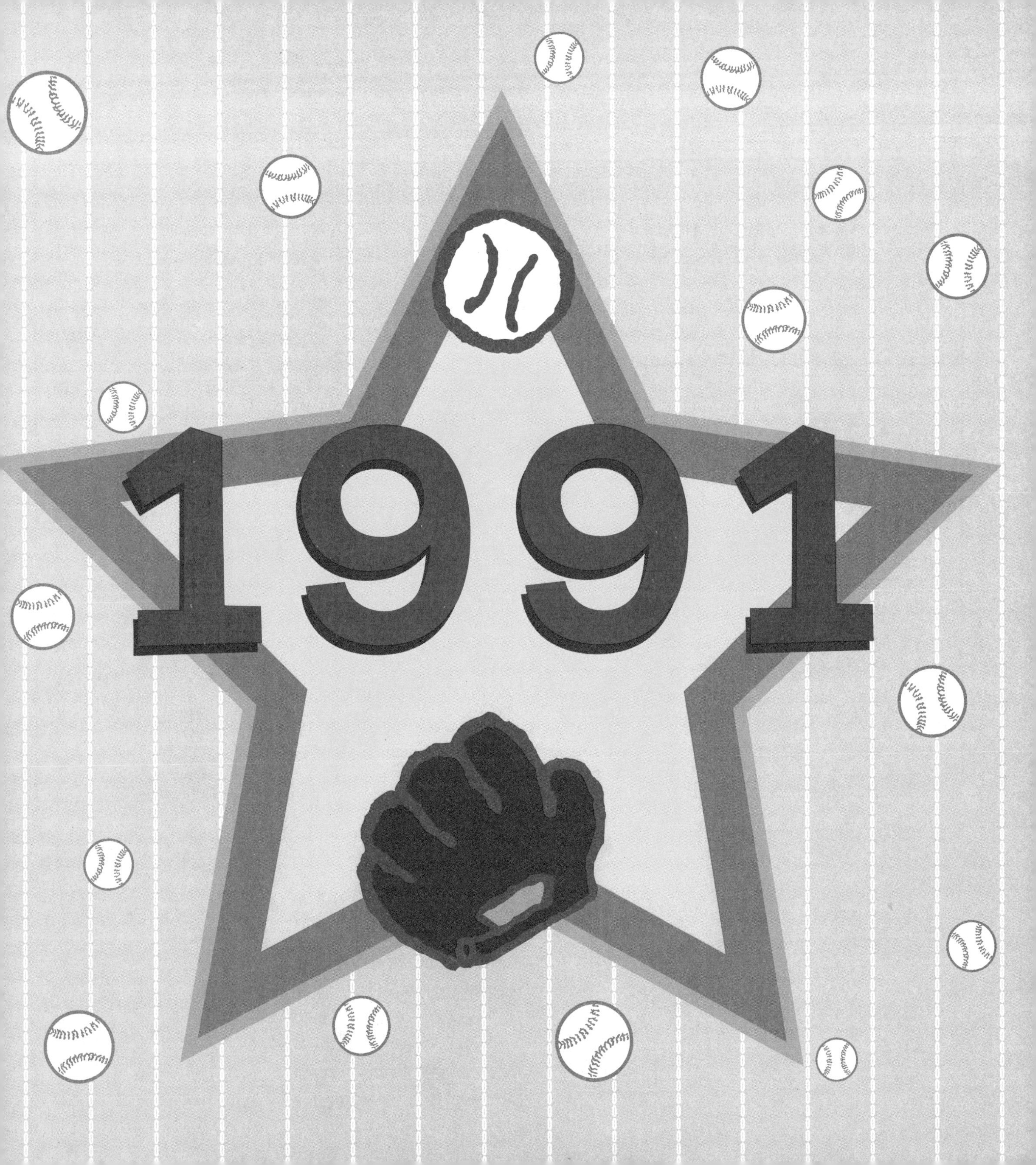
1991

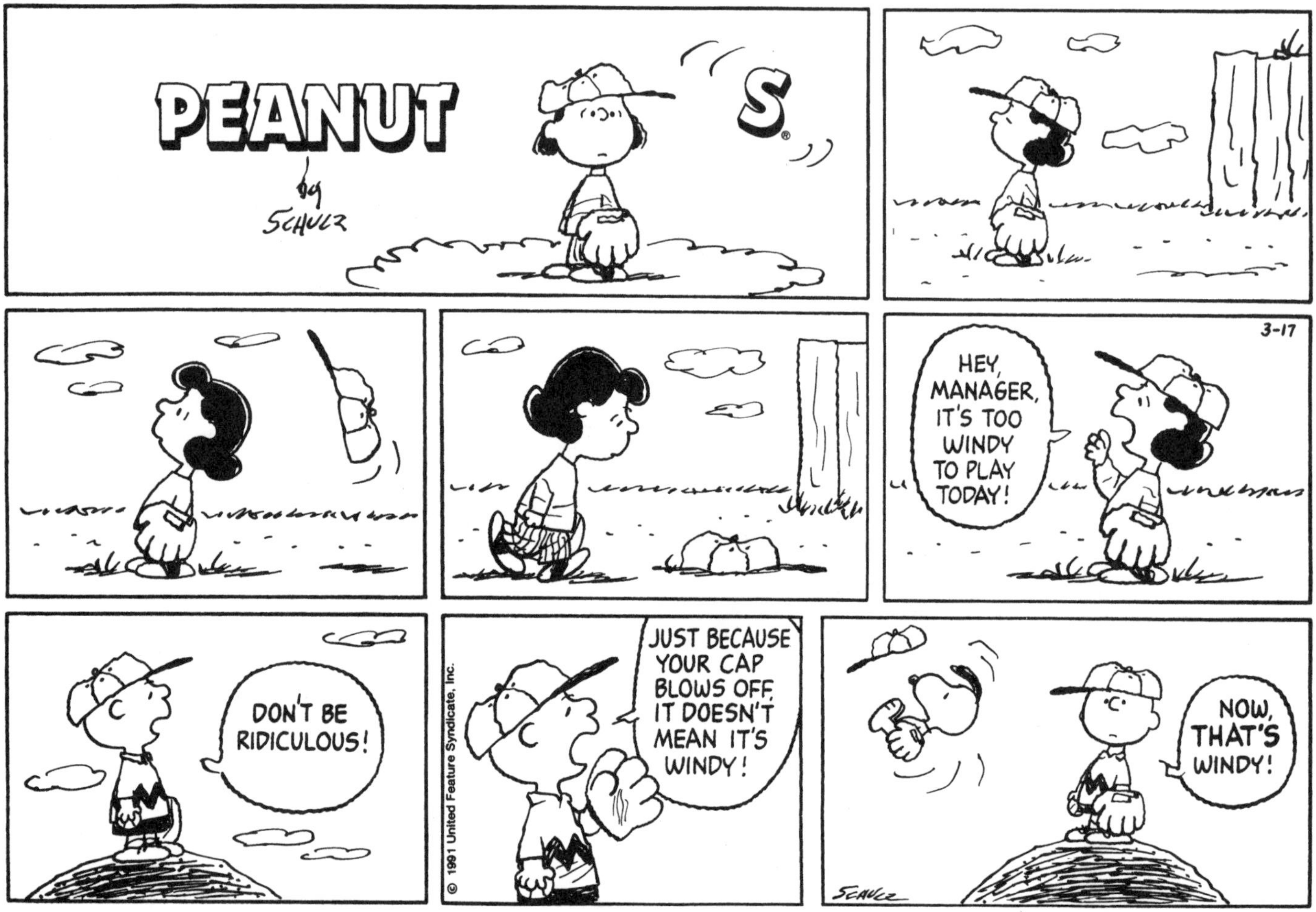
PEANUTS®
by SCHULZ
3-17
HEY, MANAGER, IT'S TOO WINDY TO PLAY TODAY!
DON'T BE RIDICULOUS!
JUST BECAUSE YOUR CAP BLOWS OFF, IT DOESN'T MEAN IT'S WINDY!
NOW, THAT'S WINDY!
SCHULZ
© 1991 United Feature Syndicate, Inc.

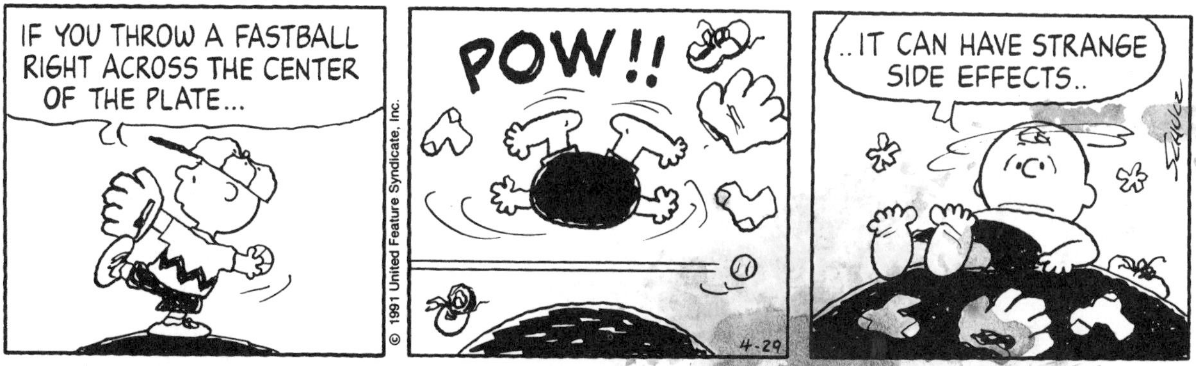
IF YOU THROW A FASTBALL RIGHT ACROSS THE CENTER OF THE PLATE...
POW!!
..IT CAN HAVE STRANGE SIDE EFFECTS..
© 1991 United Feature Syndicate, Inc.
4-29

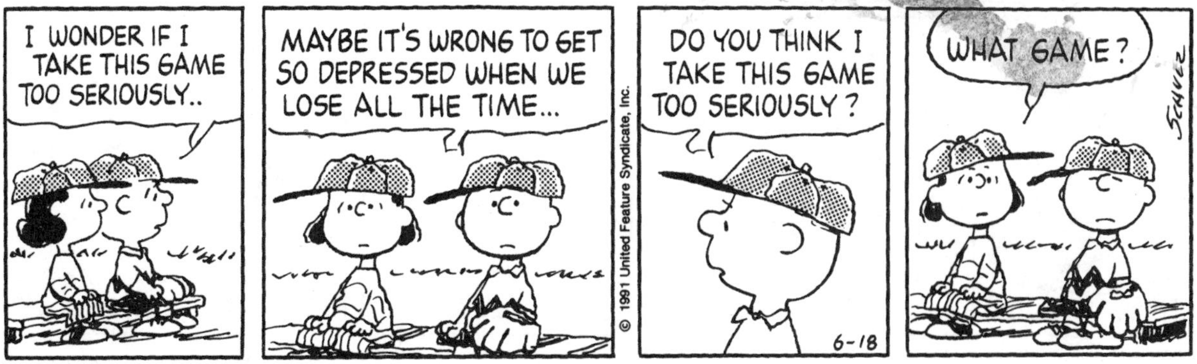
I WONDER IF I TAKE THIS GAME TOO SERIOUSLY..
MAYBE IT'S WRONG TO GET SO DEPRESSED WHEN WE LOSE ALL THE TIME...
DO YOU THINK I TAKE THIS GAME TOO SERIOUSLY?
WHAT GAME?
© 1991 United Feature Syndicate, Inc.
6-18

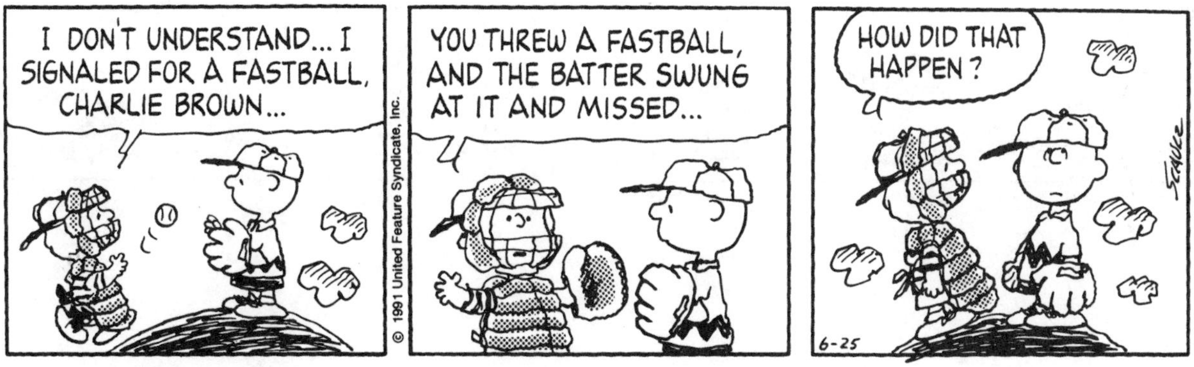
I DON'T UNDERSTAND... I SIGNALED FOR A FASTBALL, CHARLIE BROWN...
YOU THREW A FASTBALL, AND THE BATTER SWUNG AT IT AND MISSED...
HOW DID THAT HAPPEN?
© 1991 United Feature Syndicate, Inc.
6-25

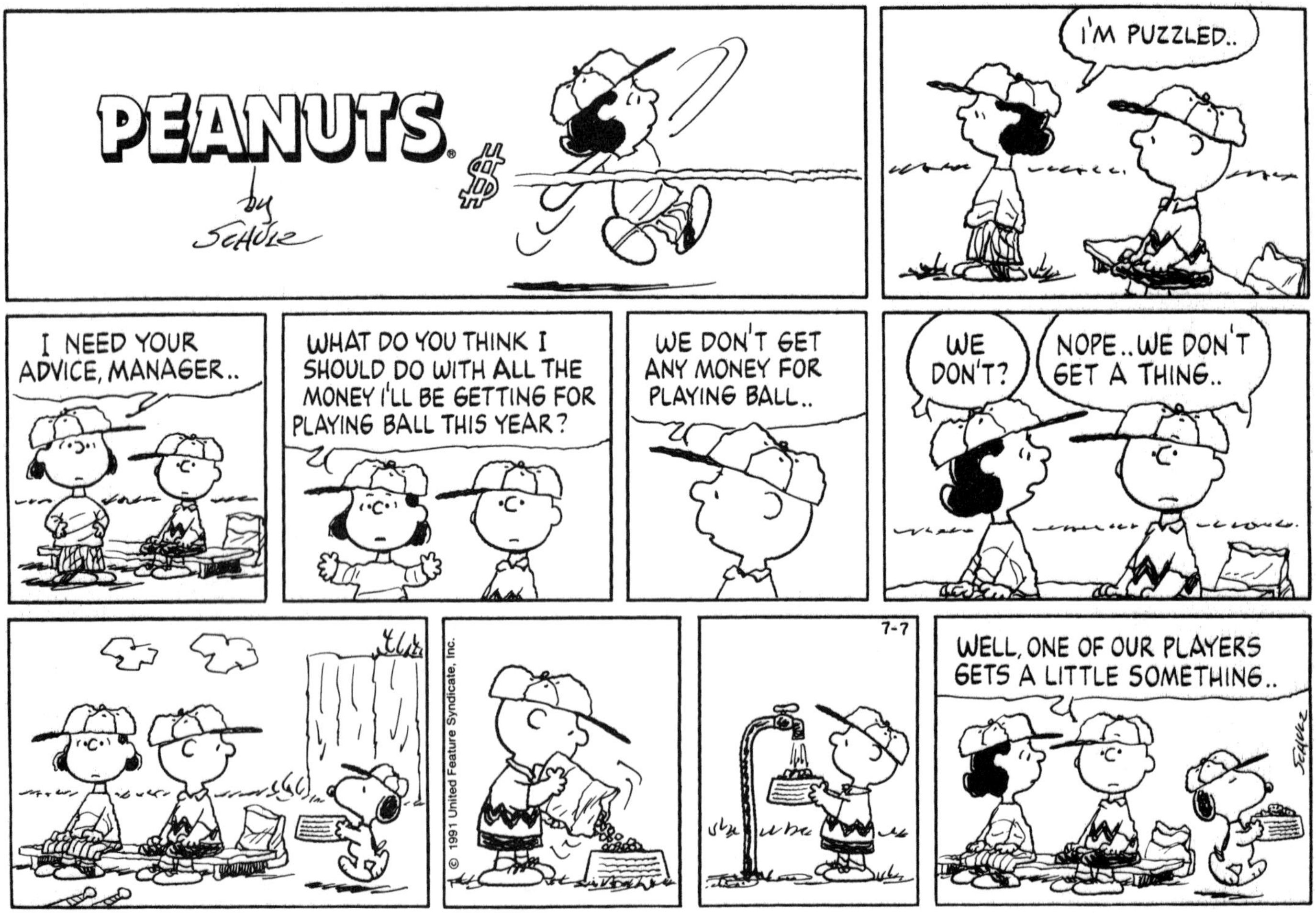
PEANUTS
by SCHULZ
I'M PUZZLED..
I NEED YOUR ADVICE, MANAGER..
WHAT DO YOU THINK I SHOULD DO WITH ALL THE MONEY I'LL BE GETTING FOR PLAYING BALL THIS YEAR?
WE DON'T GET ANY MONEY FOR PLAYING BALL..
WE DON'T?
NOPE..WE DON'T GET A THING..
© 1991 United Feature Syndicate, Inc.
7-7
WELL, ONE OF OUR PLAYERS GETS A LITTLE SOMETHING..
SCHULZ

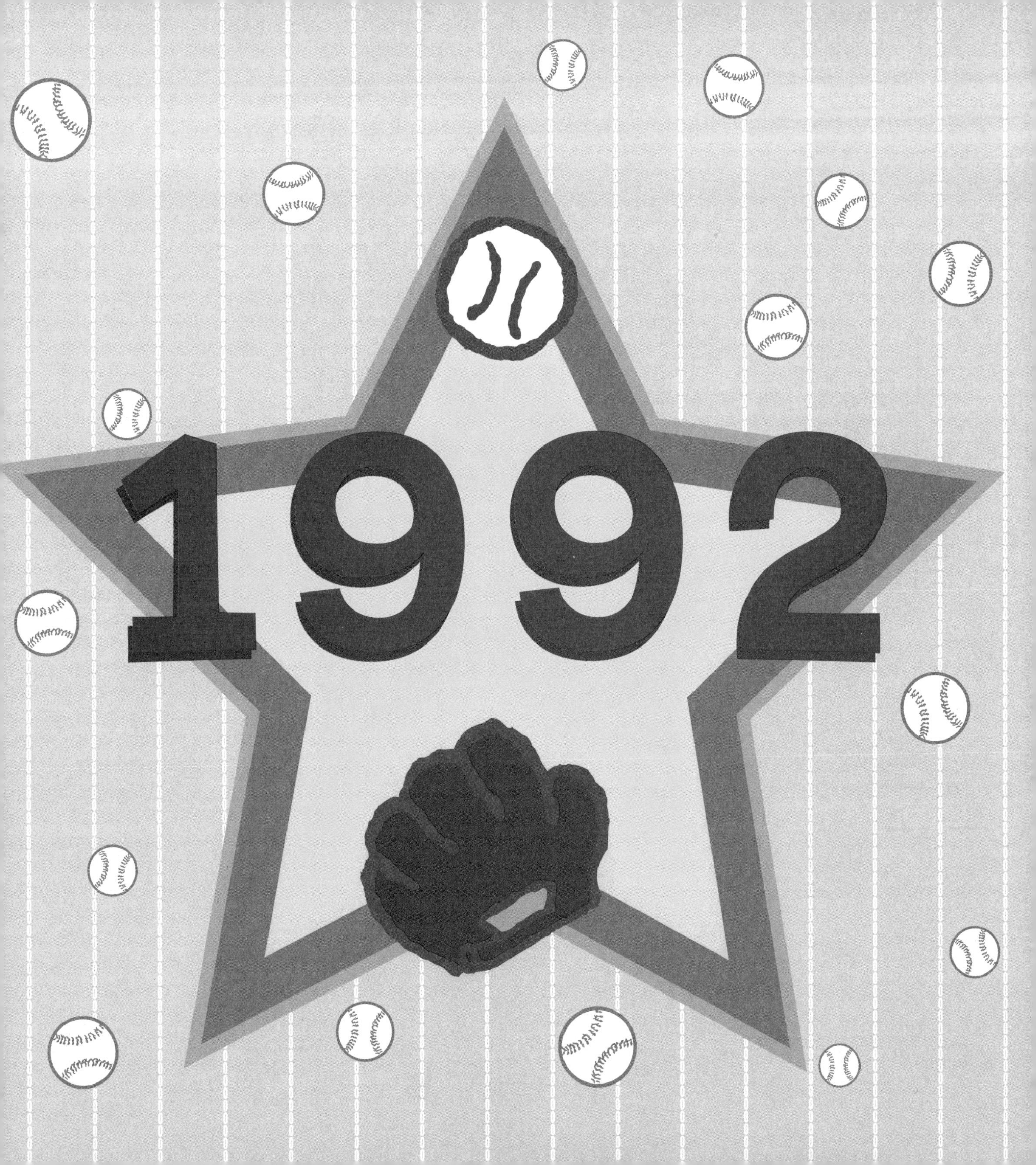
1992

THEY SAY THAT A BALL DROPPED FROM WAIST HEIGHT WILL HIT THE GROUND AT A SPEED OF 9.45 MILES PER HOUR
© 1992 United Feature Syndicate, Inc.
3-6
SO?
SO, INSTEAD OF PITCHING IT, WHY DON'T YOU JUST DROP IT?
SCHULZ

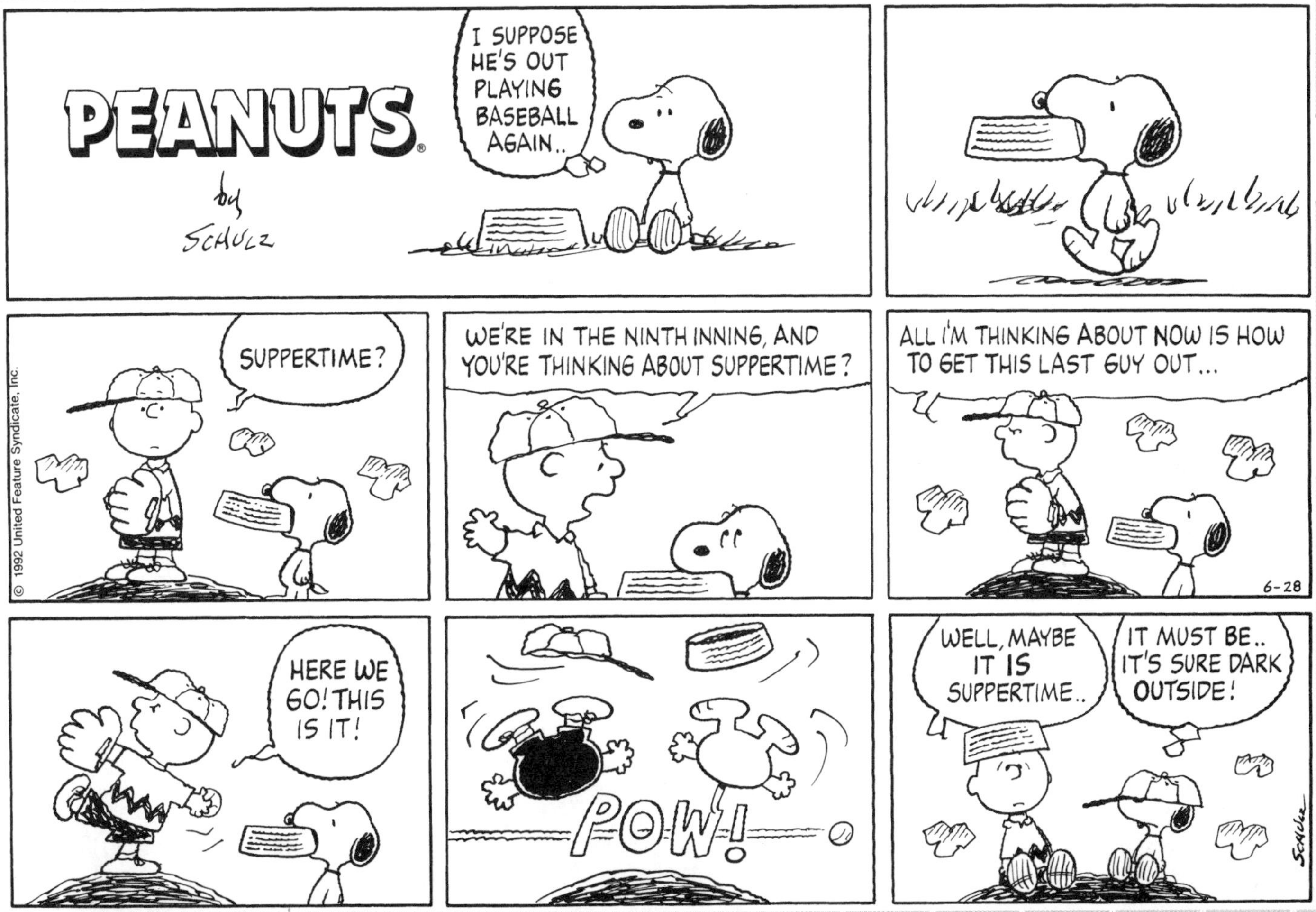
PEANUTS
by SCHULZ
I SUPPOSE HE'S OUT PLAYING BASEBALL AGAIN..
© 1992 United Feature Syndicate, Inc.
SUPPERTIME?
WE'RE IN THE NINTH INNING, AND YOU'RE THINKING ABOUT SUPPERTIME?
ALL I'M THINKING ABOUT NOW IS HOW TO GET THIS LAST GUY OUT...
6-28
HERE WE GO! THIS IS IT!
POW!
WELL, MAYBE IT IS SUPPERTIME..
IT MUST BE.. IT'S SURE DARK OUTSIDE!
SCHULZ

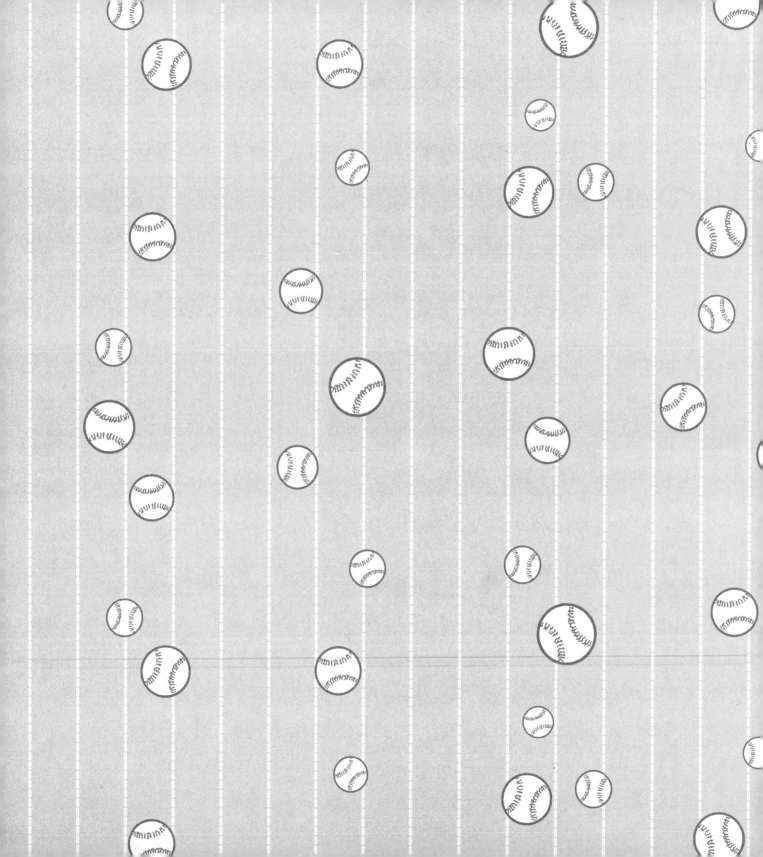

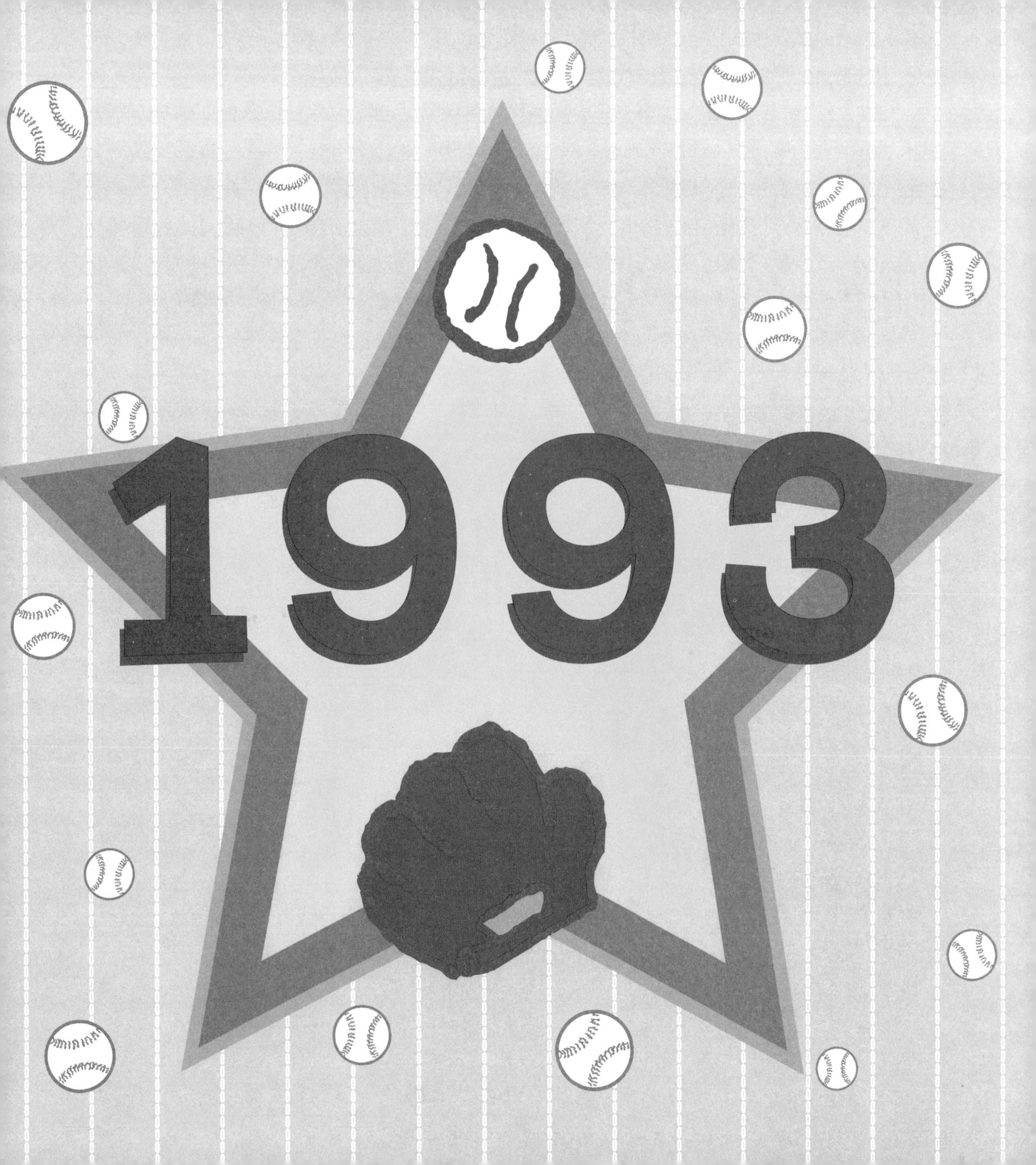
1993

DON'T TELL ME YOU'RE GOING TO TRY PLAYING BASEBALL AGAIN..

I HAVE TO.. IT'S MY DESTINY...

WHEN SPRING COMES, I'M DRAWN TO THE BALL FIELD! I FORGET EVERYTHING ELSE..

3-15

DON'T FORGET TO FEED THE DOG..

NOW, WHEN WE ASK HIM IF YOU CAN PLAY, DON'T LET HIM KNOW YOU'RE SO SHORT

YOU HAVE A FRIEND WHO WANTS TO PLAY ON OUR TEAM?

3-17

WHERE?

HOW COULD HE PLAY ON OUR TEAM? HE'S TOO SHORT!

SNIF!

3-18

WELL, ASK HIM IF MAYBE HE'D LIKE TO BE OUR BAT BIRD..

Panel 1: HOW ARE THINGS IN LEFT FIELD, PIGPEN?

Panel 2: I PUT BURNT CORK UNDER MY EYES JUST LIKE THE PROS..

Panel 3: "PAINTING THE LILY," HUH?

PAINTING THE WHAT?

Panel 4: MANAGERS ARE ALWAYS SAYING STRANGE THINGS..

3-19

Panel 5: ALL RIGHT, EVERYONE OVER HERE FOR THE TEAM PHOTO!

Panel 6: YOU HAVE YOUR CHOICE.. YOU CAN SIT WITH EITHER PIGPEN OR THE DOG...

Panel 7: WHAT KIND OF A CHOICE IS THAT?

I SHOULD THINK IT WOULD BE OBVIOUS

Panel 8: I'LL TAKE TEN 5×7, TWELVE 8×10, AND TWENTY WALLET SIZE..

3-20

© 1993 United Feature Syndicate, Inc.

PEANUTS
by SCHULZ
CAPS
WHAT'S GOING ON?
..AND EVERYONE WHO MADE THE TEAM THIS YEAR GETS A NEW CAP!
HERE YOU GO, SCHROEDER.. YOU DESERVE IT..
HERE YOU ARE, PIGPEN.. TRY TO KEEP IT CLEAN...
3-21
THIS IS FOR YOU, SNOOPY, OL' PAL!
HERE YOU GO, LINUS.. A BRAND NEW CAP!
© 1993 United Feature Syndicate, Inc.
I DON'T KNOW IF I MADE THE TEAM OR NOT..
SCHULZ

I CAN'T BELIEVE IT..
OUR BASEBALL SEASON STARTS TODAY, AND WE HAVEN'T LOST YET..
OF COURSE, I HAVEN'T GOTTEN OUT OF BED YET, EITHER..
3-23
© 1993 United Feature Syndicate, Inc.

THIS IS IT, CHARLIE BROWN..LAST INNING.. TWO OUTS... AND YOU'RE UP!
ALL THE PRESSURE IS ON ME, BUT I CAN DO IT! I KNOW I CAN DO IT...
3-29
JUST DON'T GET NERVOUS..
© 1993 United Feature Syndicate, Inc.
HERE, YOU'D BETTER USE A BAT..

I HIT A HOME RUN IN THE NINTH INNING, AND WE WON! I WAS THE HERO!!
YOU?!
3-30
© 1993 United Feature Syndicate, Inc.

THE BALL CAME RIGHT OVER THE PLATE..
3-31
THEN, POW! YOU HIT IT OVER THE FENCE, AND WE WON THE GAME!
THEIR PITCHER WAS IN TOTAL SHOCK..
© 1993 United Feature Syndicate, Inc.
YEAH, I CAN STILL SEE THE LOOK ON HER FACE!
SCHULZ

ARE YOU THE KID WHO HIT THE HOME RUN OFF ME YESTERDAY?
4-1
WELL, I HOPE YOU'RE SATISFIED! YOU RUINED MY WHOLE LIFE!
YOU CAME CLEAR OVER HERE TO TELL ME THAT?
© 1993 United Feature Syndicate, Inc.
NO, I WAS JUST KIND OF CURIOUS TO SEE WHERE YOU LIVE..YOU PROBABLY HAVE A DOG, TOO, DON'T YOU?
SORT OF..
WHAT DO YOU MEAN, SORT OF?
SCHULZ

HEY, KID! WAIT A MINUTE! I DON'T KNOW YOUR NAME!
4-2
ROY HOBBS WAS MY GREAT-GRANDFATHER..WHEN YOU HIT THAT HOME RUN YESTERDAY, YOU RUINED MY LIFE!
© 1993 United Feature Syndicate, Inc.
I JUST MET THE GREAT-GRANDDAUGHTER OF ROY HOBBS!
I NEVER KNOW WHAT YOU'RE TALKING ABOUT..
SCHULZ

HEY, KID.. REMEMBER ME? I'M ROY HOBBS' GREAT-GRANDDAUGHTER

I KNOW.. I'M VERY IMPRESSED

THE LAST TIME WE PLAYED, YOU HIT A HOME RUN OFF ME, AND RUINED MY LIFE!

6-21

I WAS JUST LUCKY

I SUPPOSE YOU THINK YOU'RE GONNA DO IT AGAIN..

WHAT'RE YOU TRYIN' TO DO NEXT, RUIN MY AFTERLIFE?

© 1993 United Feature Syndicate, Inc.

YOU'RE UP NEXT, CHARLIE BROWN.. YOU CAN HIT THIS PITCHER! THE LAST TIME YOU FACED HER, YOU HIT A HOME RUN!

6-22

YOU CAN DO IT! YOU'RE THE HERO TYPE!

OR THE GOAT TYPE..

© 1993 United Feature Syndicate, Inc.

THAT ROUND-HEADED KID IS UP NEXT, ISN'T HE?

6-23

SO WHAT? HE WAS JUST LUCKY THE LAST TIME WE PLAYED...

YOU'RE ROY HOBBS' GREAT-GRANDDAUGHTER, AREN'T YOU? WELL, SHOW 'IM WHO YOU ARE!

THROW IT IN HERE, ROYANNE!

ROYANNE?

© 1993 United Feature Syndicate, Inc.

6-24
STRIKE ONE!
© 1993 United Feature Syndicate, Inc.
C'MON, CHARLIE BROWN! SHE'S NO PITCHER! SHE'S ONLY A GIRL!
ONLY A GIRL?!
WELL, I'M ONLY YOUR SISTER, YOU BLOCKHEAD!!
SCHULZ

HEY, I THOUGHT I FELT A DROP OF RAIN..
6-25
I DID! IT'S RAINING!
STRIKE TWO!
© 1993 United Feature Syndicate, Inc.
HA! YOU'RE DOOMED, KID! YOU'RE GONNA STRIKE OUT!!
NO, I'M GONNA DROWN..
SCHULZ

© 1993 United Feature Syndicate, Inc.
TWO STRIKES ON THAT ROUND-HEADED KID, AND IT STARTS RAINING!
MAYBE IT'LL STOP SOON..
YOU CAN GET A HIT, CHARLIE BROWN..DON'T LET THAT GIRL STRIKE YOU OUT!
SHE THROWS PRETTY HARD..
I'M A HOUSE DOG.. HOUSE DOGS AREN'T SUPPOSED TO GET WET
SCHULZ
6-26

OKAY, KID, IT'S STOPPED RAINING, AND YOU GOT TWO STRIKES AGAINST YOU!
TIME OUT! ONE OF MY PLAYERS WANTS TO TALK TO ME...
THEY'RE HAVING A CONFERENCE, AREN'T THEY? THEY'RE PLANNING SOME CLEVER STRATEGY.. I JUST FEEL IT...
NO, LAST NIGHT YOU HAD YOUR SUPPER IN THE RED DISH AND WATER IN THE YELLOW DISH..
© 1993 United Feature Syndicate, Inc.
6-28
SCHULZ

CRACK!
HE HIT IT! CHARLIE BROWN HIT IT! THE BALL IS GOING TO THE FENCE! RUN, CHARLIE BROWN! RUN!
OH, NO! THE WORLD IS COMING TO AN END! I ALWAYS KNEW IT WOULD END THIS WAY!
© 1993 United Feature Syndicate, Inc.
6-29
SCHULZ

CHARLIE BROWN IS ROUNDING FIRST! HE'S ROUNDING SECOND! HE'S ROUNDING THIRD...
BUT ROY HOBBS' GREAT-GRANDDAUGHTER HAS THE BALL!! SHE'S BLOCKING THE PLATE!!!
6-30 © 1993 United Feature Syndicate, Inc.
SCHULZ

SLIDE, CHARLIE BROWN, SLIDE!!
7-1
© 1993 United Feature Syndicate, Inc.
SCHULZ

YOU DID IT, CHARLIE BROWN! YOU HIT ANOTHER HOME RUN, AND WE WON THE GAME!
YOU MEAN I WAS SAFE?
I'M ROY HOBBS' GREAT-GRANDDAUGHTER.. WHERE AM I? WHAT HAPPENED?
YOU WERE BLOCKING THE PLATE, SWEETIE.. HERE, I COULD ONLY FIND ONE SHOE..
7-2 © 1993 United Feature Syndicate, Inc.
SCHULZ

WELL, YOU DID IT AGAIN, DIDN'T YOU? YOU HIT ANOTHER HOME RUN, AND RUINED MY LIFE!
I WAS LUCKY
© 1993 United Feature Syndicate, Inc.
YOU ALMOST KILLED ME WHEN YOU SLID INTO HOME..
YOU WERE BLOCKING THE PLATE, SWEETIE..
I STILL CAN'T FIND MY OTHER SHOE...
I'M SORRY
7-3
I HATE GOING THE REST OF MY LIFE WEARING ONLY ONE SHOE

ROYANNE! WHAT A SURPRISE!
I NEED TO TALK TO YOU, CHARLES..DO YOU HAVE TIME TO GO GET A CHOCOLATE SUNDAE?
8-17
© 1993 United Feature Syndicate, Inc.
OKAY, ROYANNE, WHAT'S UP?
DO YOU LIKE ME, CHARLES?
OH, GOOD GRIEF!

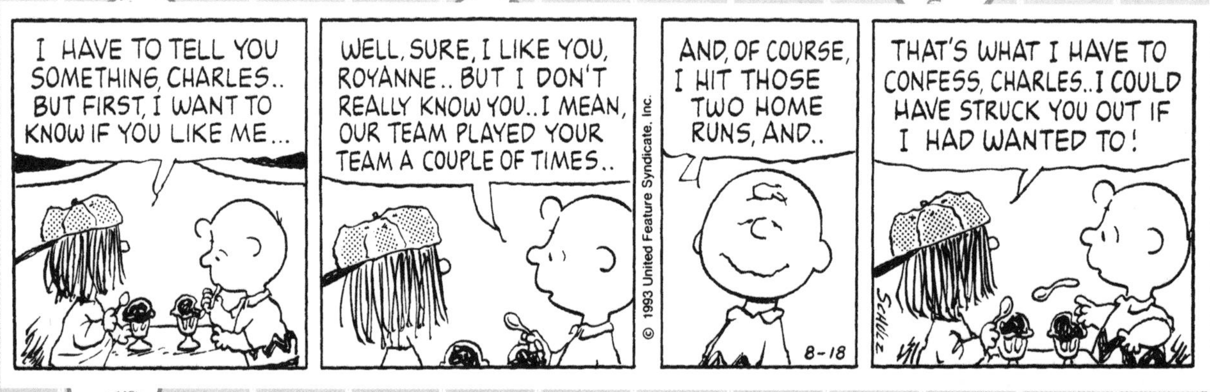
I HAVE TO TELL YOU SOMETHING, CHARLES.. BUT FIRST, I WANT TO KNOW IF YOU LIKE ME...
WELL, SURE, I LIKE YOU, ROYANNE.. BUT I DON'T REALLY KNOW YOU.. I MEAN, OUR TEAM PLAYED YOUR TEAM A COUPLE OF TIMES..
© 1993 United Feature Syndicate, Inc.
AND, OF COURSE, I HIT THOSE TWO HOME RUNS, AND..
8-18
THAT'S WHAT I HAVE TO CONFESS, CHARLES.. I COULD HAVE STRUCK YOU OUT IF I HAD WANTED TO!
SCHULZ

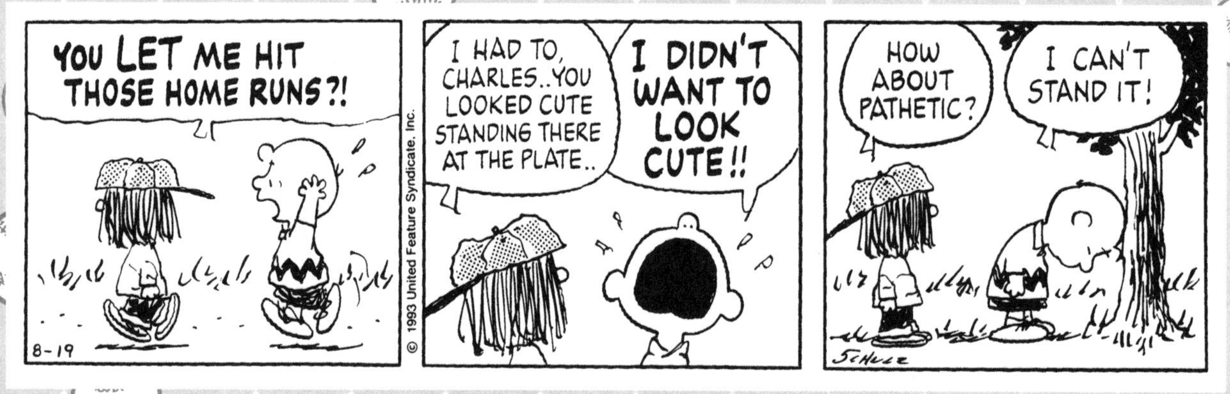
YOU LET ME HIT THOSE HOME RUNS?!
8-19
© 1993 United Feature Syndicate, Inc.
I HAD TO, CHARLES.. YOU LOOKED CUTE STANDING THERE AT THE PLATE..
I DIDN'T WANT TO LOOK CUTE!!
HOW ABOUT PATHETIC?
I CAN'T STAND IT!
SCHULZ

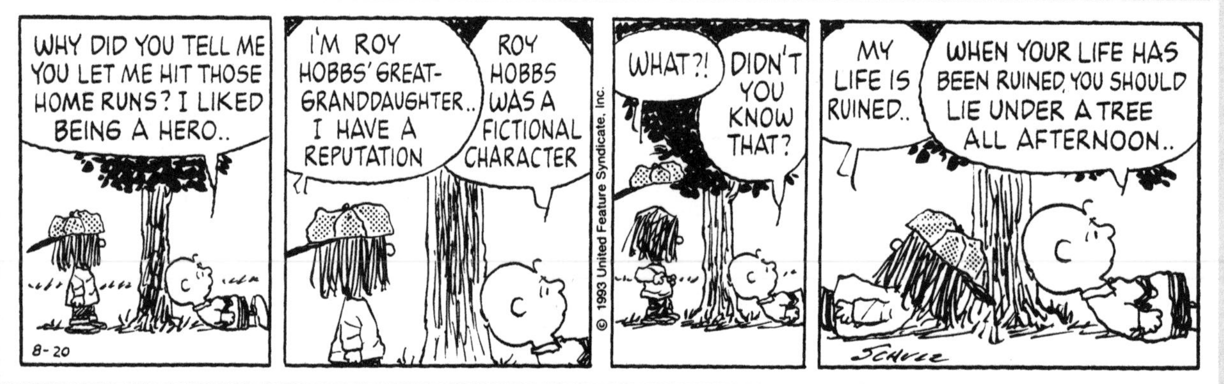
WHY DID YOU TELL ME YOU LET ME HIT THOSE HOME RUNS? I LIKED BEING A HERO..
8-20
I'M ROY HOBBS' GREAT-GRANDDAUGHTER.. I HAVE A REPUTATION
ROY HOBBS WAS A FICTIONAL CHARACTER
© 1993 United Feature Syndicate, Inc.
WHAT?!
DIDN'T YOU KNOW THAT?
MY LIFE IS RUINED..
WHEN YOUR LIFE HAS BEEN RUINED, YOU SHOULD LIE UNDER A TREE ALL AFTERNOON..
SCHULZ

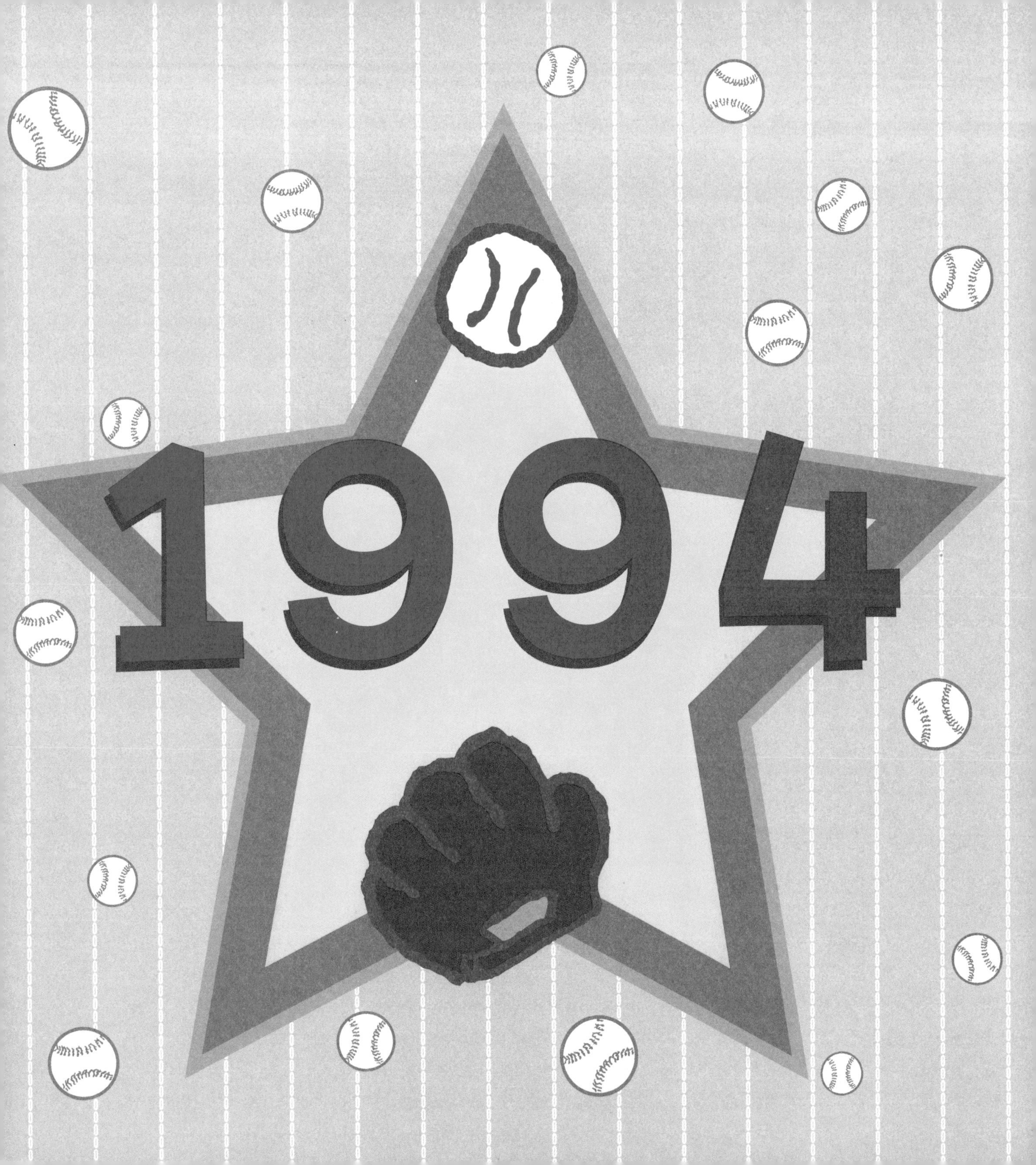
1994

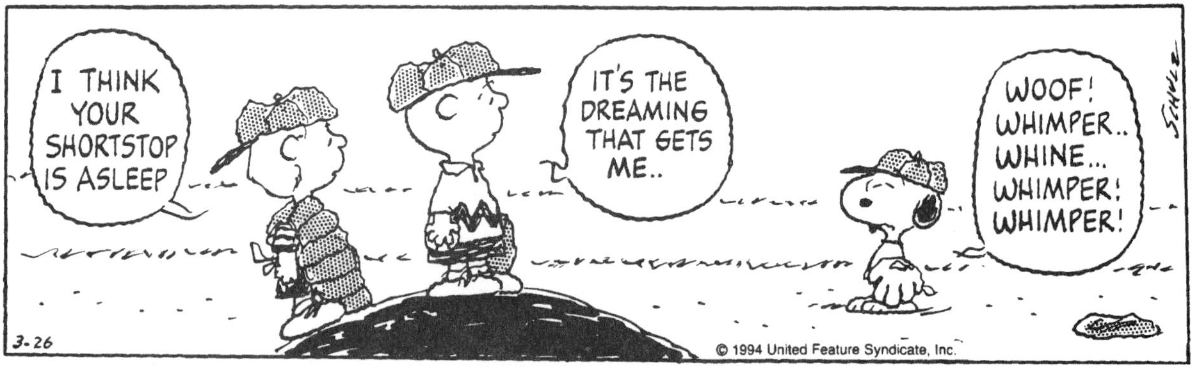
I THINK YOUR SHORTSTOP IS ASLEEP
IT'S THE DREAMING THAT GETS ME..
WOOF! WHIMPER.. WHINE... WHIMPER! WHIMPER!
3-26
© 1994 United Feature Syndicate, Inc.

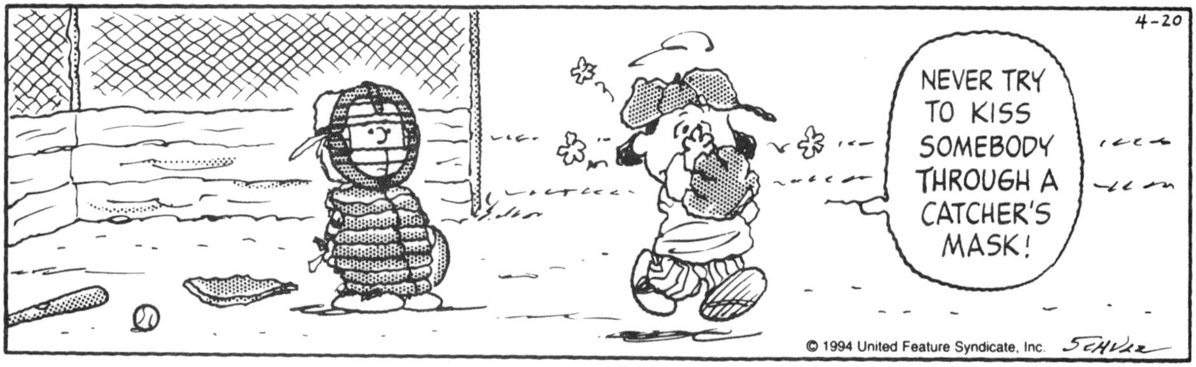
4-20
NEVER TRY TO KISS SOMEBODY THROUGH A CATCHER'S MASK!
© 1994 United Feature Syndicate, Inc.

© 1994 United Feature Syndicate, Inc. 5-11
ALL RIGHT, TEAM, WE'RE ONLY ONE RUN BEHIND..WE CAN WIN IF WE CONCENTRATE!
WE'RE CONCENTRATING!
WE'RE ALL CONCENTRATING..
Z
KLUNK!
SCHULZ

© 1994 United Feature Syndicate, Inc.
8-13
SCHULZ

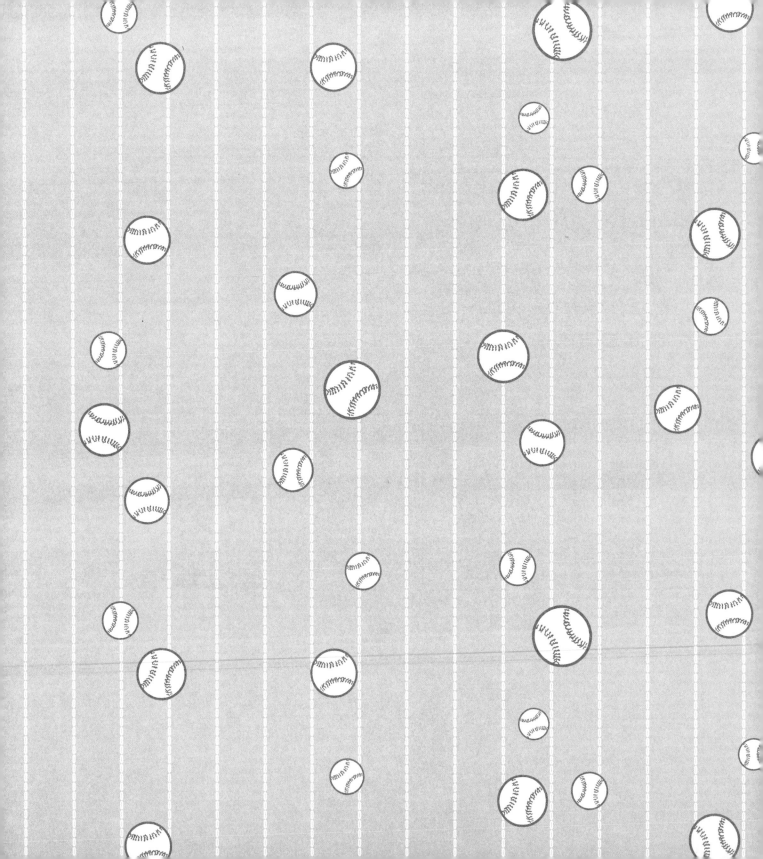

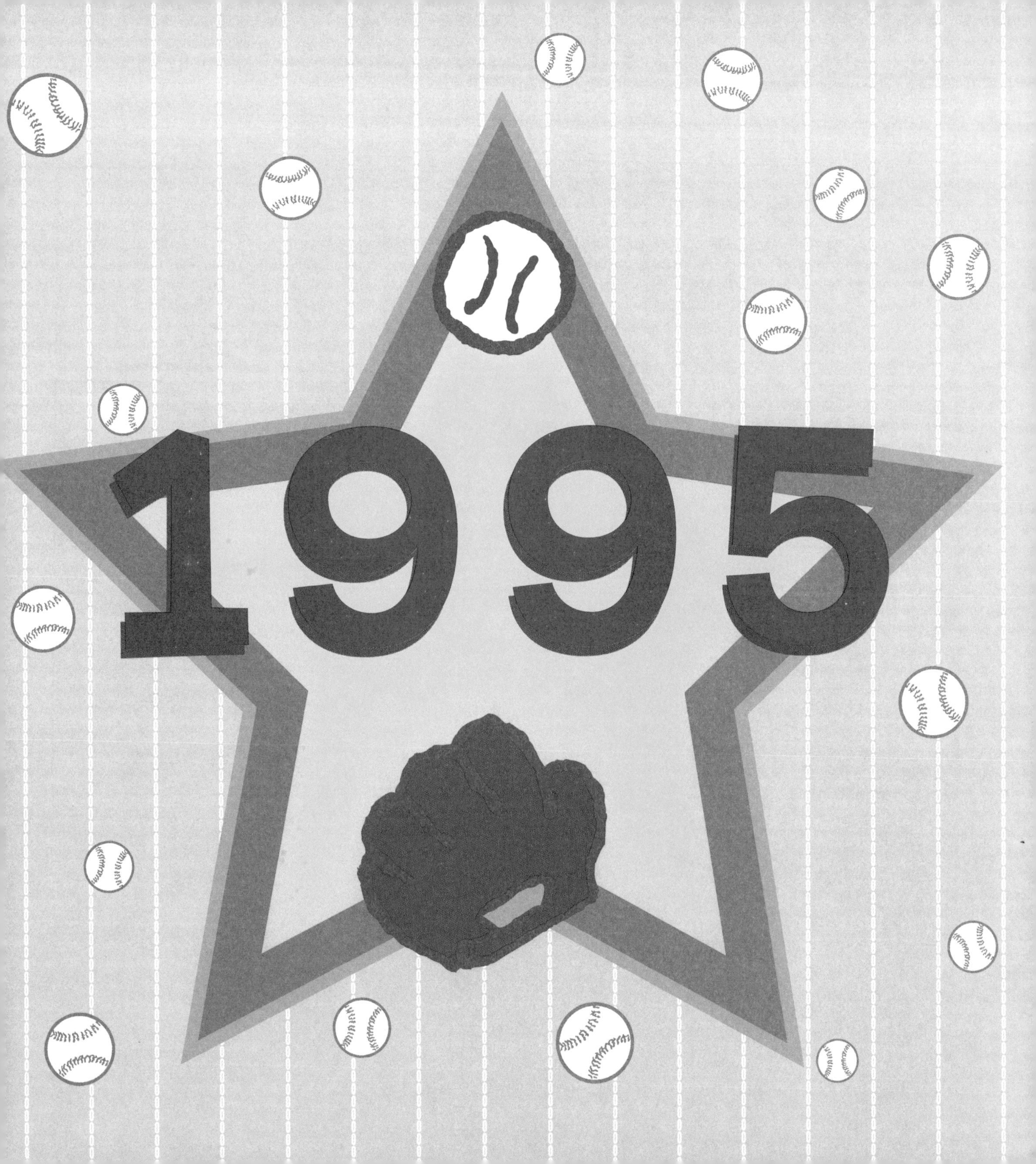
1995

PEANUTS
by Schulz
WHAT'S THIS?
IT'S CALLED "SARCASTIC REMARKS FOR MANAGERS"
BONK!
© 1995 United Feature Syndicate, Inc.
3-12
AH! HERE'S A GOOD ONE..
"MAYBE YOU CAN SUE THE BALL FOR HEAD HARASSMENT!"
HA HA HA HA HA HA!
HERE'S ANOTHER GOOD ONE..
EVERYBODY HATES OUTFIELDERS
SCHULZ

SO LET'S ALL KEEP CONCENTRATING..
IT'S JUST A MATTER OF KEEPING OUR MINDS ON THE GAME..
WE CAN'T LET OUR MINDS WANDER..
© 1995 United Feature Syndicate, Inc.
5/17
SOME PANCAKES WOULD TASTE GOOD RIGHT NOW..
SCHULZ

ARE YOU ASLEEP, OR ARE YOU RESTING YOUR EYES?
5-20
I WAS ASLEEP, BUT NOW I'M RESTING MY EYES
TELL YOUR EYES TO GET BACK IN THE GAME!
© 1995 United Feature Syndicate, Inc.
EYES ARE UP ALL DAY..THEY NEED LOTS OF REST..
SCHULZ

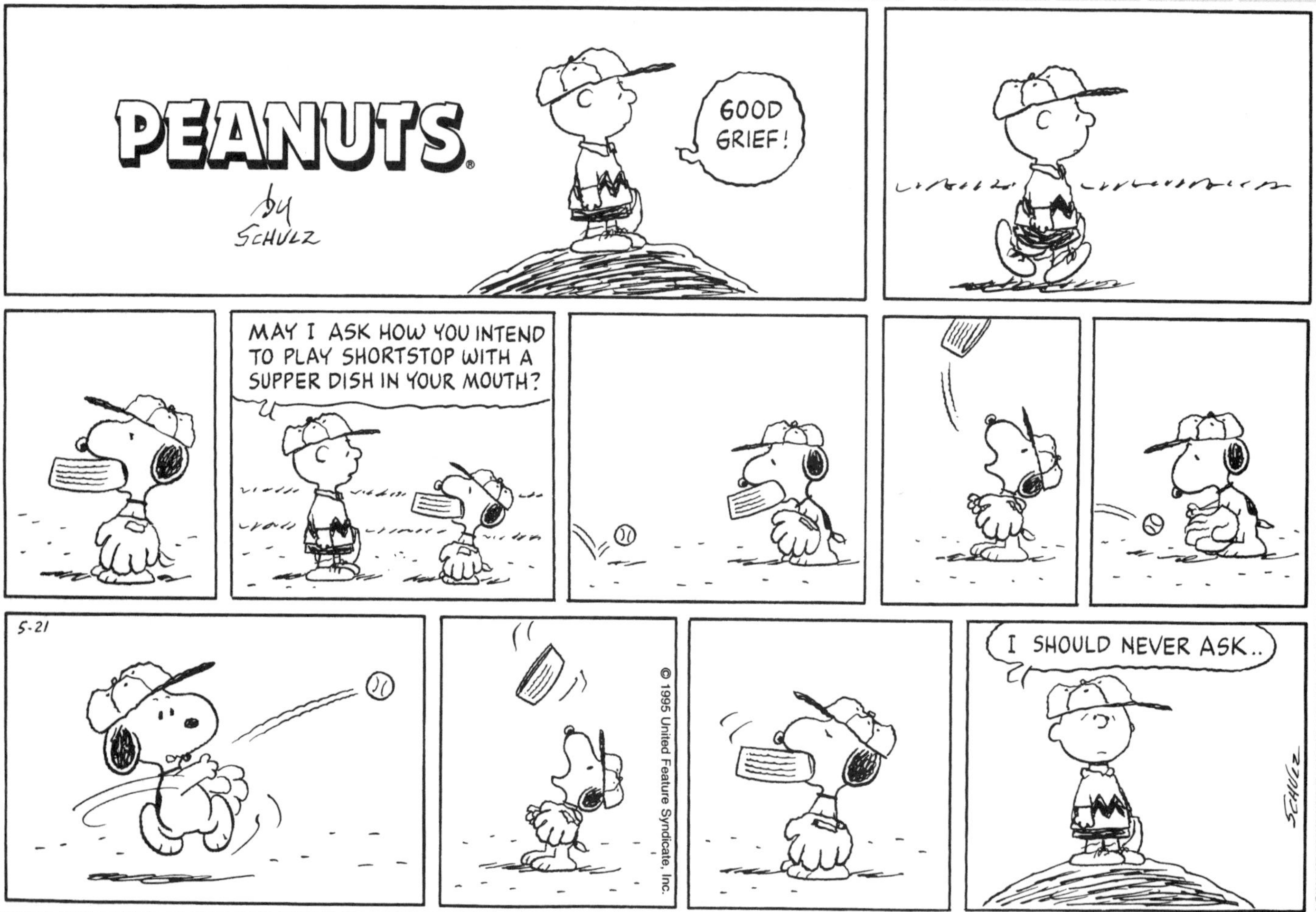
PEANUTS
by SCHULZ
GOOD GRIEF!
MAY I ASK HOW YOU INTEND TO PLAY SHORTSTOP WITH A SUPPER DISH IN YOUR MOUTH?
5-21
© 1995 United Feature Syndicate, Inc.
I SHOULD NEVER ASK..
SCHULZ

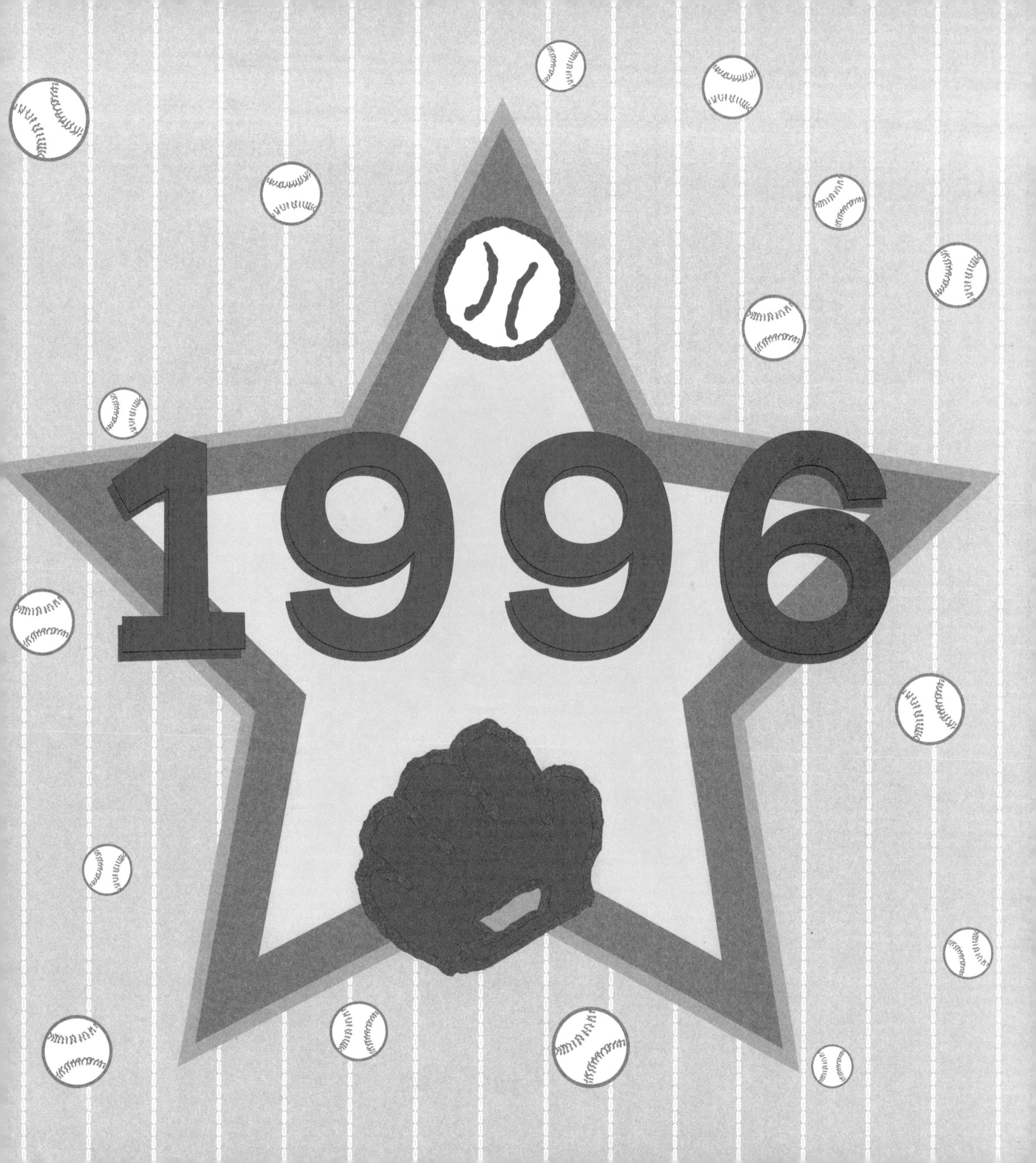
1996

I'M GOING HOME, MANAGER.. IF ANYONE HITS A BALL TO RIGHT FIELD, LET ME KNOW..
HERE'S MY PHONE NUMBER, OUR FAX NUMBER AND OUR E-MAIL ADDRESS..
4-27
© 1996 United Feature Syndicate, Inc.
OUTFIELDERS SEEM TO BE MUCH MORE CONSIDERATE THAN THEY USED TO BE..
SCHULZ

MY ARM HURTS.. I'M NOT SURE I CAN PITCH TODAY..
I THINK THROWING ALL THOSE CURVEBALLS PUT TOO MUCH STRAIN ON MY ELBOW..
7-9
© 1996 United Feature Syndicate, Inc.
SCHULZ
THOSE WERE CURVEBALLS ?

CHARLIE BROWN SAYS HIS ELBOW HURTS SO MUCH HE MAY NEVER BE ABLE TO PITCH AGAIN..

OH, WELL, HE WASN'T MUCH OF A PITCHER ANYWAY..

7-15

© 1996 United Feature Syndicate, Inc.

HOW'S YOUR ELBOW, CHARLIE BROWN?

WELL, THEY PUT SOME ICE ON IT SO IT FEELS BETTER..

7-16

POW!

DO YOU THINK YOU'LL NEED SOME MORE ICE?

LIKE MAYBE A GLACIER?

© 1996 United Feature Syndicate, Inc.

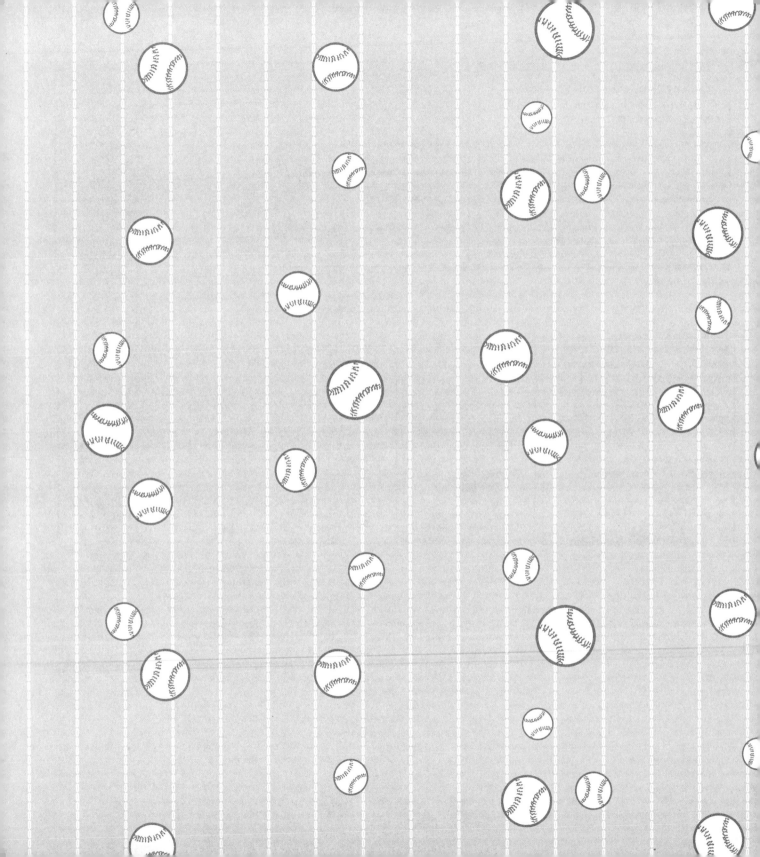

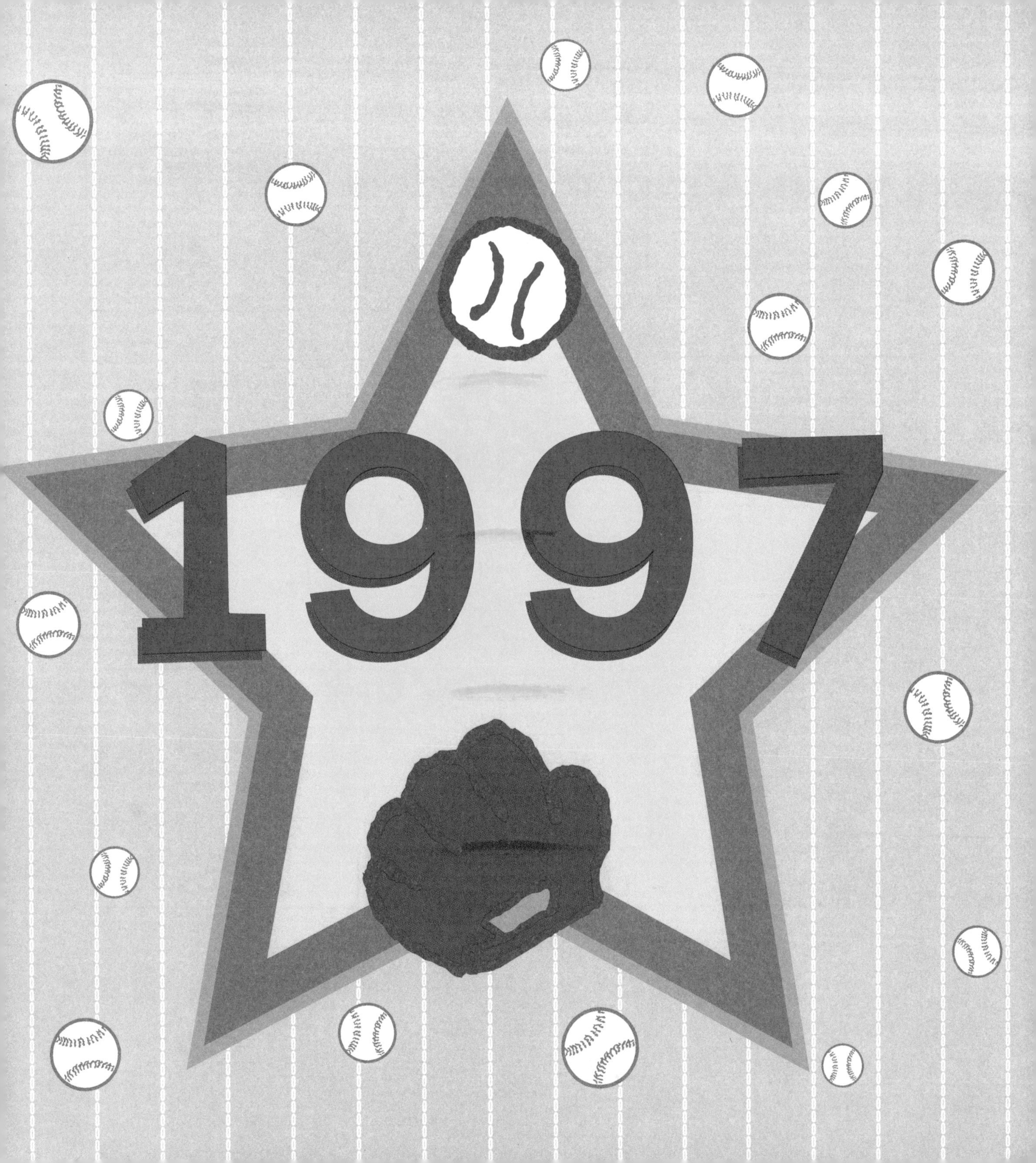
1997

"PIGPEN," I DON'T UNDERSTAND YOU..
THIS IS THE FIRST INNING OF OUR FIRST GAME, AND YOU'RE ALREADY COVERED WITH DIRT..
THIS ISN'T ALL FROM TODAY.. SOME OF IT'S LEFT OVER FROM LAST YEAR..
www.unitedmedia.com
© 1997 United Feature Syndicate, Inc.

DO ME A FAVOR..GO ASK "PIGPEN" WHY HE DOESN'T WEAR A BASEBALL CAP..
THE MANAGER WANTS TO KNOW WHY YOU DON'T WEAR A CAP..
HE SAID HE DOESN'T WANT TO MUSS UP HIS HAIR..
www.unitedmedia.com
© 1997 United Feature Syndicate, Inc.

"PIGPEN," WHY CAN'T YOU LOOK NEAT LIKE THE OTHER PLAYERS?
LAST YEAR I BATTED .712
NEATNESS DOESN'T BAT .712 !
www.unitedmedia.com
© 1997 United Feature Syndicate, Inc.

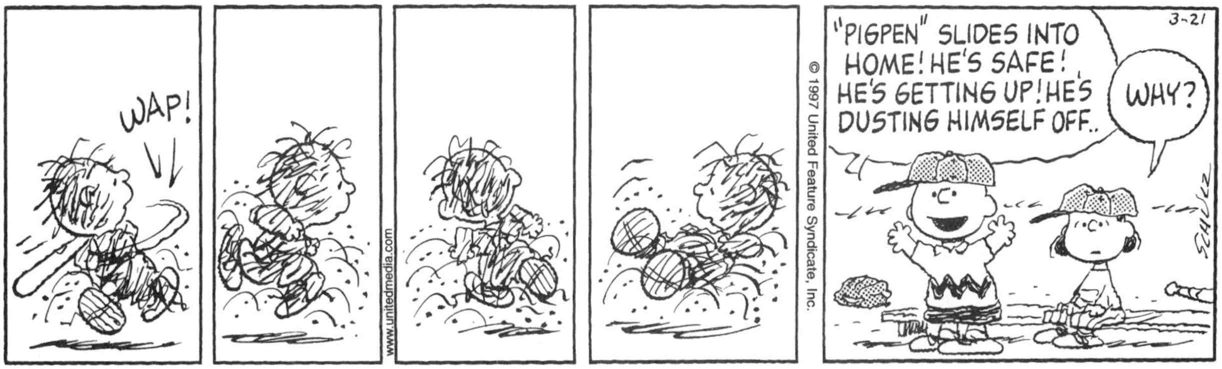
WAP!
"PIGPEN" SLIDES INTO HOME! HE'S SAFE! HE'S GETTING UP! HE'S DUSTING HIMSELF OFF..
WHY?
www.unitedmedia.com
© 1997 United Feature Syndicate, Inc.
3-21
SCHULZ

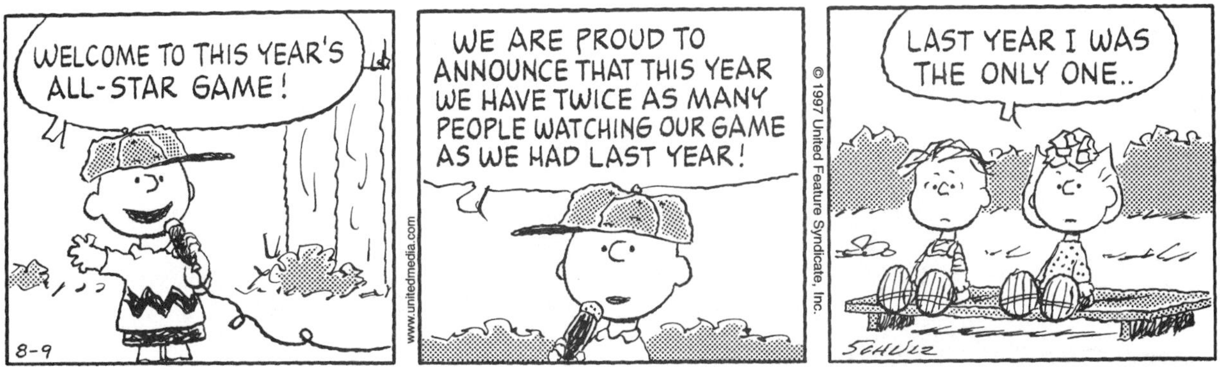
WELCOME TO THIS YEAR'S ALL-STAR GAME!
8-9
WE ARE PROUD TO ANNOUNCE THAT THIS YEAR WE HAVE TWICE AS MANY PEOPLE WATCHING OUR GAME AS WE HAD LAST YEAR!
www.unitedmedia.com
© 1997 United Feature Syndicate, Inc.
LAST YEAR I WAS THE ONLY ONE..
SCHULZ

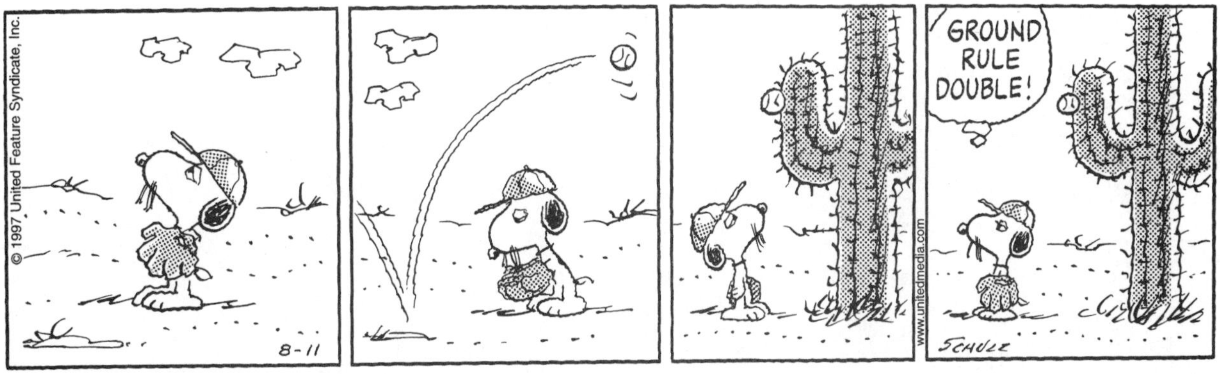
© 1997 United Feature Syndicate, Inc.
8-11
www.unitedmedia.com
GROUND RULE DOUBLE!
SCHULZ

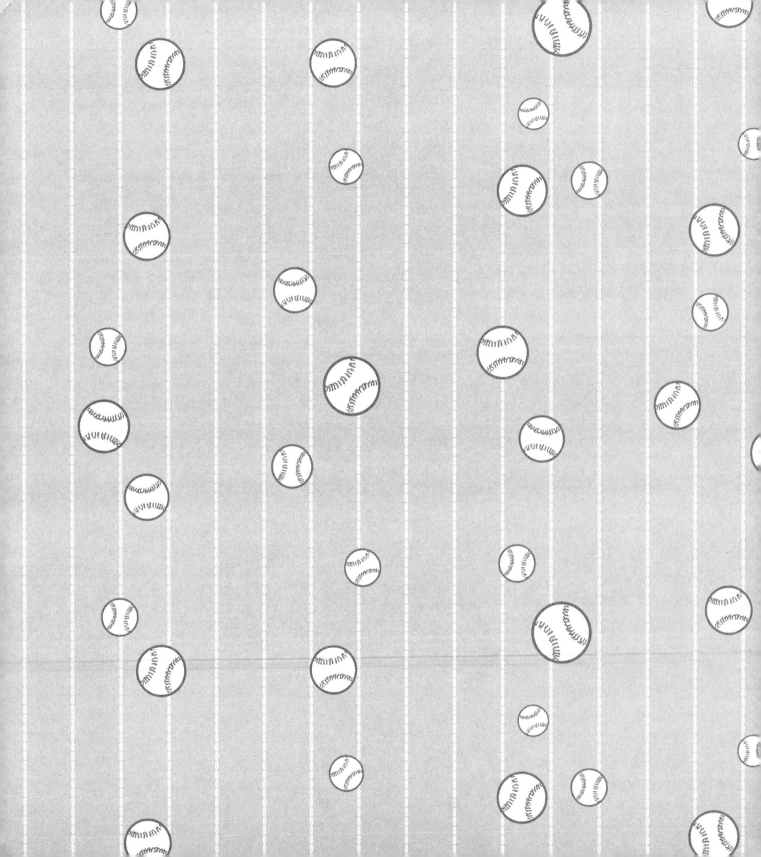

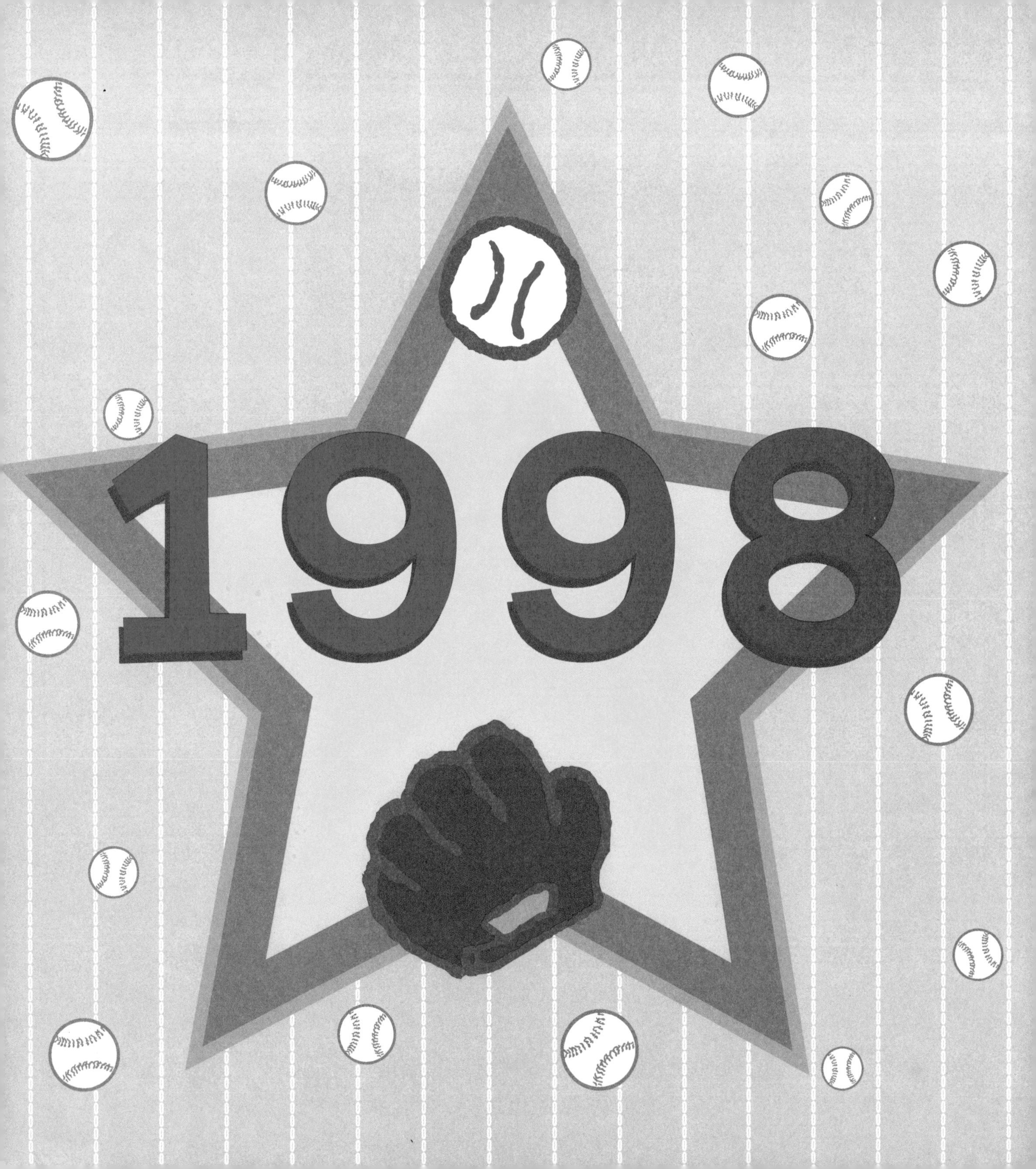
1998

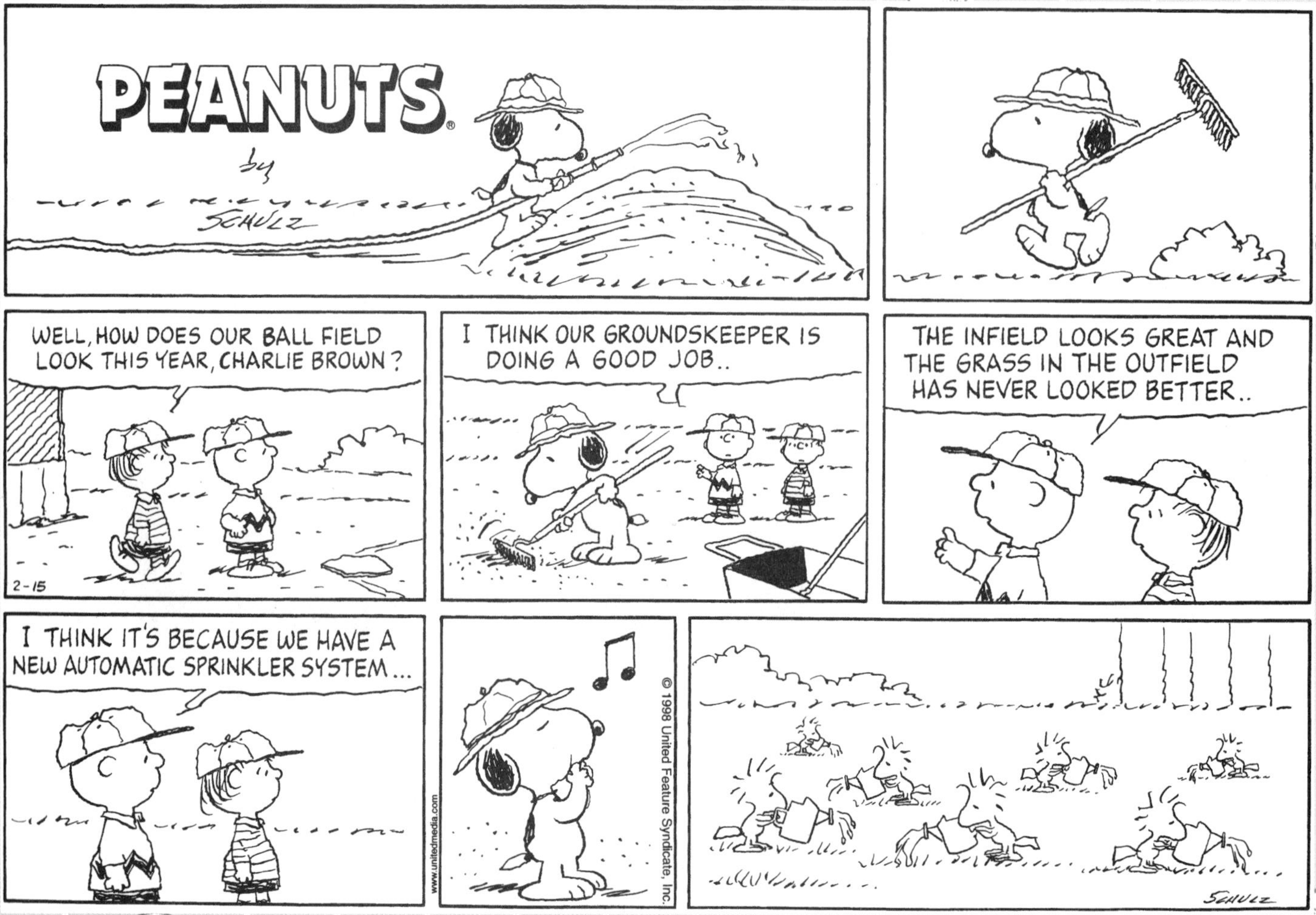
PEANUTS
by SCHULZ
WELL, HOW DOES OUR BALL FIELD LOOK THIS YEAR, CHARLIE BROWN ?
2-15
I THINK OUR GROUNDSKEEPER IS DOING A GOOD JOB..
THE INFIELD LOOKS GREAT AND THE GRASS IN THE OUTFIELD HAS NEVER LOOKED BETTER..
I THINK IT'S BECAUSE WE HAVE A NEW AUTOMATIC SPRINKLER SYSTEM...
© 1998 United Feature Syndicate, Inc.
www.unitedmedia.com
SCHULZ

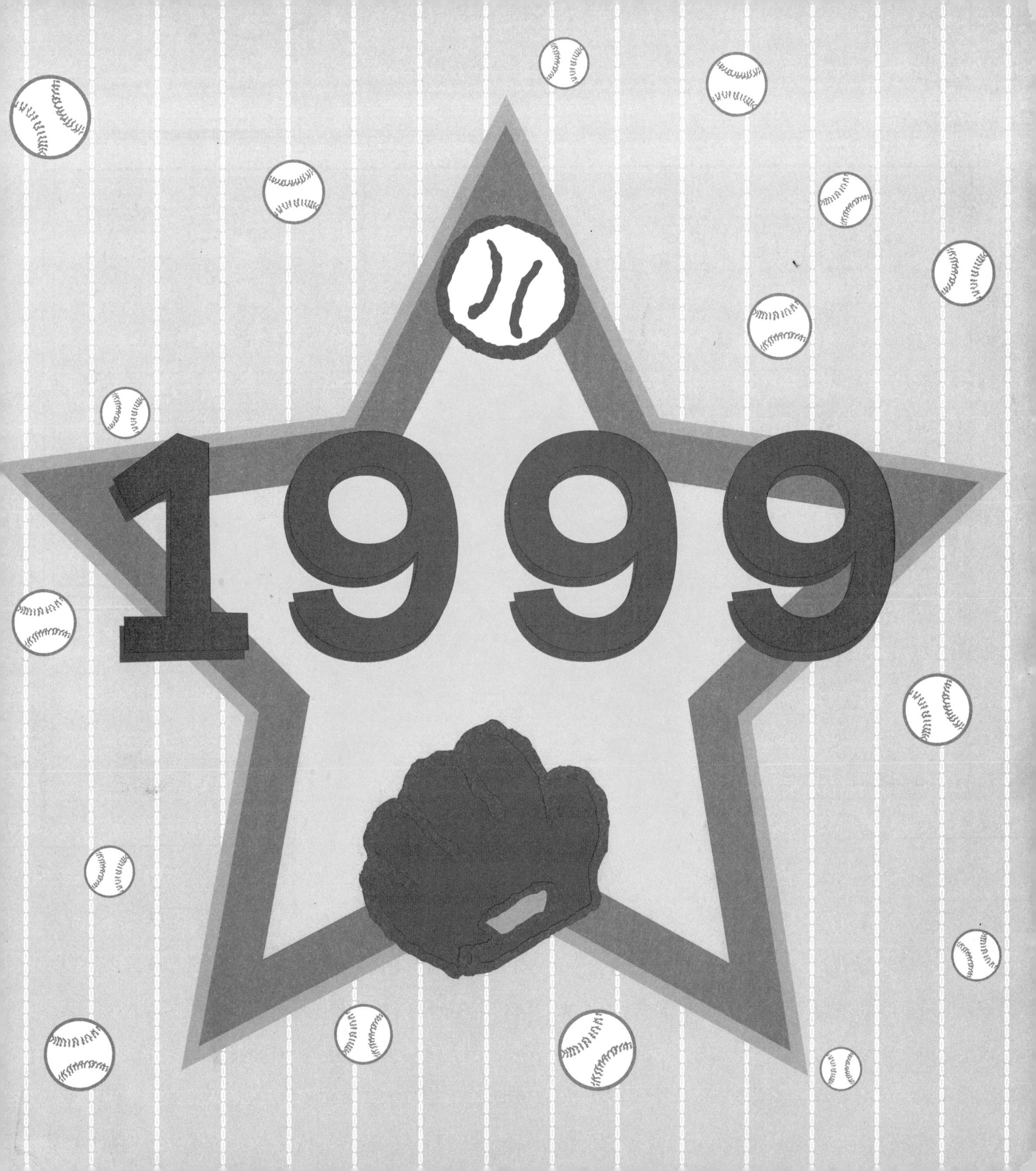
1999

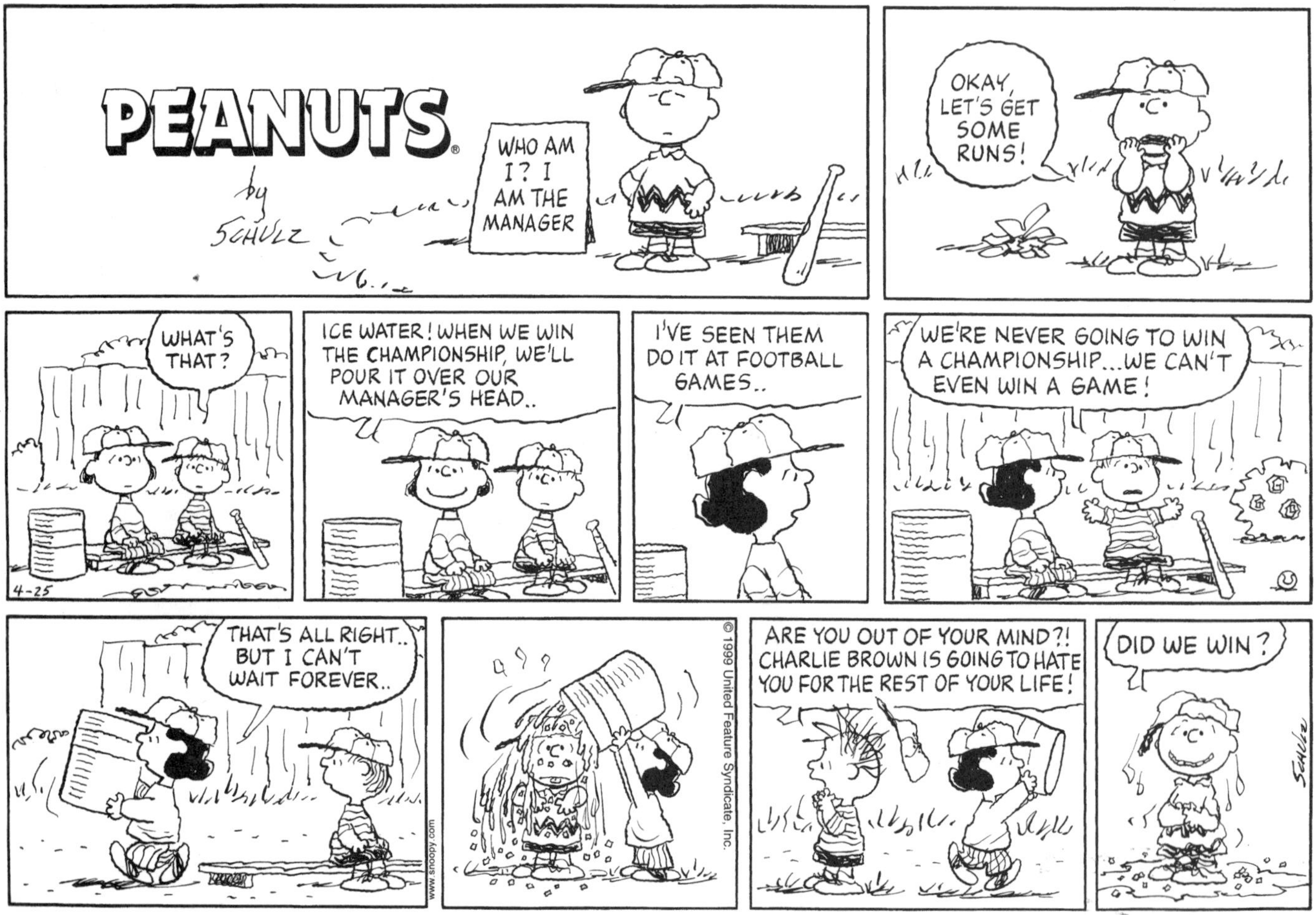
PEANUTS
by SCHULZ
WHO AM I? I AM THE MANAGER
OKAY, LET'S GET SOME RUNS!
WHAT'S THAT?
4-25
ICE WATER! WHEN WE WIN THE CHAMPIONSHIP, WE'LL POUR IT OVER OUR MANAGER'S HEAD..
I'VE SEEN THEM DO IT AT FOOTBALL GAMES..
WE'RE NEVER GOING TO WIN A CHAMPIONSHIP...WE CAN'T EVEN WIN A GAME!
THAT'S ALL RIGHT.. BUT I CAN'T WAIT FOREVER..
www.snoopy.com
© 1999 United Feature Syndicate, Inc.
ARE YOU OUT OF YOUR MIND?! CHARLIE BROWN IS GOING TO HATE YOU FOR THE REST OF YOUR LIFE!
DID WE WIN?
SCHULZ